Creative Conflict in African American Thought
Frederick Douglass, Alexander Crummell, Booker T. Washington, W. E. B. Du Bois, and Marcus Garvey

Building upon his previous work, Professor Moses has revised and brought together in this book essays that focus on the complexity of, and contradictions in, the thought of five major African American intellectuals: Frederick Douglass, Alexander Crummell, Booker T. Washington, W. E. B. Du Bois, and Marcus M. Garvey. In doing so, he challenges both popular and scholarly conceptions of them as villains or heroes. In analyzing the intellectual struggles and contradictions of these five dominant personalities with regard to individual morality and collective reform, Professor Moses shows how they contributed to strategies for black improvement and puts them within the context of other currents in American and, more broadly, Western thought, including Jeffersonian and Jacksonian democracy, Social Darwinism, and progressivism.

Wilson Jeremiah Moses is Ferree Professor of History at Pennsylvania State University. He holds degrees from Wayne State University and Brown University. He has taught at the University of Iowa, Southern Methodist University, Brown University, Boston University, the Free University of Berlin, and the University of Vienna. He has been a lecturer or panelist on more than one hundred occasions in the United States, England, Europe, and Africa. He is the author of *The Golden Age of Black Nationalism* (1978), *Black Messiahs and Uncle Toms* (1982), *Alexander Crummell* (1989), *The Wings of Ethiopia* (1990), *Afrotopia* (1998), and numerous articles, essays, and reviews. He has edited *Destiny and Race: Sermons and Addresses of Alexander Crummell* (1992), *Classical Black Nationalism from the American Revolution to Marcus Garvey* (1996), and *Liberian Dreams: Back-to-Africa Narratives from the 1950s* (1998). He has received fellowships from the National Endowment for the Humanities, the Andrew Mellon Foundation, the Ford Foundation, the American Council of Learned Societies, and the American Philosophical Society.

Creative Conflict in African American Thought

Frederick Douglass, Alexander Crummell, Booker T. Washington, W. E. B. Du Bois, and Marcus Garvey

WILSON JEREMIAH MOSES
Pennsylvania State University

CAMBRIDGE
UNIVERSITY PRESS

PUBLISHED BY THE PRESS SYNDICATE OF THE UNIVERSITY OF CAMBRIDGE
The Pitt Building, Trumpington Street, Cambridge, United Kingdom

CAMBRIDGE UNIVERSITY PRESS
The Edinburgh Building, Cambridge CB2 2RU, UK
40 West 20th Street, New York, NY 10011-4211, USA
477 Williamstown Road, Port Melbourne, VIC 3207, Australia
Ruiz de Alarcón 13, 28014 Madrid, Spain
Dock House, The Waterfront, Cape Town 8001, South Africa

http://www.cambridge.org

First published 2004

Printed in the United States of America

Typeface Sabon 10/13 pt.   *System* LATEX 2$_\varepsilon$ [TB]

A catalog record for this book is available from the British Library.

Library of Congress Cataloging in Publication Data
Moses, Wilson Jeremiah, 1942–
Creative conflict in African American thought : Frederick Douglass, Alexander Crummell,
Booker T. Washington, W. E. B. Du Bois, and Marcus Garvey / Wilson Jeremiah Moses.
    p. cm.
Includes bibliographical references and index.
ISBN 0-521-82826-0 – ISBN 0-521-53537-9 (pbk.)
1. African Americans – Intellectual life – 19th century.   2. African Americans – Intellectual
life – 20th century.   3. Conflict management – United States – Philosophy.   4. Douglass,
Frederick, 1818–1895 – Political and social views.   5. Crummell, Alexander, 1819–1898 –
Political and social views.   6. Washington, Booker T., 1856–1915 – Political and social
views.   7. Du Bois, W. E. B. (William Edward Burghardt), 1868–1963 – Political and social
views.   8. Garvey, Marcus, 1887–1940 – Political and social views.   9. African American
intellectuals – Biography.   10. African American political activists – Biography.   I. Title.
E185.M87   2004
305.896′073′00922–dc22   2003058434

ISBN 0 521 82826 0 hardback
ISBN 0 521 53537 9 paperback

An inestimable portion of the thought, labor, and passion that generated this work was provided by my wife, Maureen. We dedicate this book to our two sons, William and Jeremiah.

Contents

Acknowledgments

Two chapters on Frederick Douglass have been previously published. They have undergone some revision here to accentuate the relation of their central themes to the present volume. "Where Honor Is Due: Frederick Douglass as Typical Black Man" was originally published in *Prospects*, the American Studies Annual, published at Columbia University by Cambridge University Press. "Writing Freely? Frederick Douglass and the Constraints of Racialized Writing" appeared in Eric J. Sundquist, ed., *Frederick Douglass: New Literary and Critical Essays*, also published by Cambridge. "Frederick Douglass: Superstar and Public Intellectual," while original in form and content, incorporates a number of paragraphs originally published in a state-of-the-art paper in *Resources for American Literary Study*. These paragraphs have been drastically altered, documentation has been markedly enhanced, and footnotes have been added. "The Conservation of Races and the American Negro Academy: Nationalism, Materialism, and Hero Worship" was first published in *Massachusetts Review*. I wish to thank the original publishers for permission to bring them together in this volume. Special thanks are due to Jennifer Carey for her patient editorial assistance and to Lewis Bateman, without whose kindness this project could never have been brought to completion.

Preface

Struggle, Challenge, and History

In the puerile slang of the present age, "struggle" seems to mean no more than floundering or flailing. When a sportscaster refers to a football team as "struggling," it is equivalent to describing them as culpably deficient. To an earlier generation struggle was a necessary ingredient of progress and the mark of moral virtue. In Theodore Roosevelt's Darwinian conception of the "Strenuous Life" any individual who was not struggling was contemptibly weak – unfit for survival. The five thinkers addressed in these pages celebrated their own conception of "the strenuous life," for they believed moral fitness to be inseparable from constant moral struggle.

The words "challenged" and "history" likewise underwent bizarre transformations in the late twentieth century. To describe someone as "challenged" became tantamount to declaring that they were retarded or deficient. In teenage slang, the clause "he's history" implied that someone had been destroyed or rendered irrelevant. But in the romantic idiom of the late nineteenth century, "struggle" implied *Sturm und Drang* – storm and stress – the characteristic and necessary drive of the "world-historical figure" to meet the challenges of a heroic destiny. The hero of Goethe's *Faust* knows that he is damned if he even momentarily relaxes from struggle, or apprehends a happiness so great that he wishes the moment to endure forever; the Hegelian or Emersonian hero recognizes no higher praise than the description "He's history!"

The presupposition of this book is that all active thinking runs unavoidably into contradiction; that original thought is generated by the tragic and heroic struggle to reconcile conflict; that mythologies represent the spontaneous struggle of the human mind to encompass opposing ideas within a single thought-image. Any bright adolescent can discover contradictions within another person's thinking. It is the task of the historian to discover the processes by which thinkers seek to reconcile or, as some would say, to rationalize their own contradictions. This work is tacitly, or expressly, concerned throughout with identifying such attempts at reconciliation. Obviously, within this context, "contradiction" is not a term of opprobrium; in fact the term "contradiction" need not imply any value judgment at all – except the value judgment implicit in my acknowledgment that the thinking of a given author contains sufficient tension or friction to generate life-giving struggle and to awaken my interest.[1]

To deny the joyful necessity of struggling with contradiction is foolish and potentially wicked. This book addresses varieties of contradiction represented in, but by no means peculiar to, African American thought. It focuses on two varieties of contradiction – the inevitable conflicts between proponents of opposing ideas and the equally inescapable contradictions that exist within the minds of individual thinkers. I am not primarily concerned with "pragmatic contradictions," inconsistencies between theory and practice, but rather with the collision of ideas. How, for example, does Alexander Crummell reconcile his reverence for the English language with his commitment to the development of a Liberian culture and sense of national pride? How does he reconcile his belief that black people need to develop a spirit of individualism with his belief that they must develop a tradition of collective consciousness? How does Marcus Garvey reconcile his racialized pacifism with his conception of God as a War Lord?

The struggle over ideological contradictions offers a vitalizing challenge for an individual or a group to strengthen intellectual muscle. The methodology of challenge and response, called *disputatio* among medieval scholars, was a traditional means of seeking truth through the use of contradictions, as were rabbinical traditions of dialogue and debate.[2] Contradiction is, in fact, vital in many philosophical systems including those

---

[1] I sit on my deck and detect a motion at the corner of my eye; I turn my head and see a squirrel playing in the leaves; I have not made a value judgment as to the importance of the squirrel or its activities; I have simply made a reflexive response. So too, when I respond to contradictions in the thought of a given author or thinker, I am not making any necessary or immediate value judgment, but simply responding to evidences of sentient life.

[2] Joseph Piper, *Guide to Thomas Aquinas* (New York: Pantheon, 1962), pp. 72–82. Needless to say the rabbinical tradition of Talmudic discourse and the West African tradition of palaver instance the universality of disputation as a method for the investigation of truth.

of West Africa, where the tradition of "palaver" exists to the present day. The thinking of African American intellectuals, who were born in the nineteenth century, was necessarily contradictory, for contradiction is a universal aspect of the human condition. As I have said elsewhere, black American thought has inevitably mingled the particulars of black nationalism (and Pan-Africanism) with the more, *and* less, cosmopolitan processes of emulating Eurocentric civilization. It has simultaneously blended ethnocentric boosterism with conscious and unconscious striving toward economic and social integration in America. Its cultural mythology has betrayed the contradictions of United States nationalism, in which African Americans have identified simultaneously with the Children of Israel in Egyptian bondage and with the Afrocentric mythology of pharaonic Egypt.[3]

The persistence of such contradictions among any class of thinkers represents a particularistic manifestation of universal human experience. I think it is self-evident that all ethnochauvinistic doctrines are inescapably caught up in the contradiction of asserting both the singularity and the universality of their group's peculiar experiences. All human societies insist that their joys and sorrows are unique, but they usually invoke an abstract humanistic ethos of fairness, calling on the entire world to sympathize with them in their aspirations, and, with rare exceptions, they appeal to the universal justice of their claims on "inalienable rights."[4]

Our mental and emotional lives manifest many other varieties of conflict, and these may sometimes appear incongruous even to ourselves. *First*, we all experience internal conflicts because every person's attitudes and dispositions vary unsystematically according to time and circumstance; *second*, we experience conflicts between our own thoughts and those of other persons with whom we supposedly identify; *third*, but of lesser interest to this discussion, we experience pragmatic contradictions between our professed beliefs and our actual behavior. This book focuses on

---

[3] The ambivalence on whether to identify with the biblical Hebrews or with the Egyptians who held them in bondage is readily observable in the first African American newspaper, the New York–based *Freedom's Journal*, April 6, 1827, where the editors appeal to both myths. See also Wilson J. Moses, *Afrotopia*, pp. 39–95, and note especially pp. 45 and 85.

[4] The American Declaration of Independence claimed "a decent respect for the opinions of mankind" and appealed even to the higher authority of natural rights. Frederick Douglass alluded to this point in his famous speech of July 5, 1852, "The Meaning of July Fourth to the Negro," printed in Philip Foner, ed., *Life and Writings of Frederick Douglass*, Vol. 4 (New York: International, 1950), pp. 181–205.

controversial and contradictory elements in the thought of several exceptional individuals, whose contradictions embody the "constant anxieties" and "agonized strain" that Alexander Crummell viewed as essential to the condition and destinies of "men and angels."[5]

The complicated individuals who are subjects of this study were selected on the basis of their self-evident contradictions. These have either been minimized by their gushing admirers, or pounced upon by their enemies among past and present African American intellectuals. Frederick Douglass, for example, has sometimes been lionized as the "Heroic Slave" who fearlessly voiced the aspirations of the freedom struggle, but at other times has been viewed as an unconscious white supremacist who attacked racial pride and betrayed his true ideology by marrying a white woman.[6] Some have heroized Alexander Crummell as a "father of Pan-Africanism," but others see him as an apologist for European cultural hegemony. Some have venerated Du Bois as the major black intellectual of the twentieth century – an untouchable, irreproachable saint, but others regard him as an embarrassment, an elitist snob, who from pure spite joined the Communist Party and apologized for the butchery of Joseph Stalin. Some have seen Booker T. Washington as the "builder of a civilization," urging his people to develop skills, accumulate capital, and develop self-respect, but others see him as an accommodationist to segregation and a buffoonish teller of "darky stories" to condescending whites. Some view Marcus Garvey as a tragic hero who projected a dream of international black economic power. Others see him as the Quixotic promoter of a back-to-Africa scheme, an incompetent businessman, a megalomaniac, a diversionist, or even an embezzler.

---

[5] Alexander Crummell, "The Solution of Problems: The Duty and Destiny of Man," in Wilson J. Moses, ed., *Destiny and Race: Selected Writings of Alexander Crummell, 1840–1898* (Amherst: University of Massachusetts Press, 1992), pp. 31–44. I assume each of my subjects to be a unique individual, but sharing with others certain broadly comparable emotional experiences, which are the basis of human sympathy and of all appeals to morality. Thus, I believe the experience of each individual to be emblematic of a common human condition, regardless of such specific determinants as gender or ethnicity. Hazel Carby emphatically rejects this position in *Race Men: The Body and Soul of Race, Nation, and Masculinity* (Cambridge, MA: Harvard University Press, 1998).

[6] See Allison Davis's chapter entitled "Douglass, the Lion," in his *Leadership, Love and Aggression* (New York: Harcourt Brace Jovanovich, 1983). Negative reactions to Douglass' marriage to Helen Pitts are discussed elsewhere in this volume. Also see Thomas Dixon's venomous reaction to Douglass' second marriage in "Booker T. Washington and the Negro," *The Saturday Evening Post* (August 19, 1905), 1–3. Present-day African American negativism is more subtle; see Mary Helen Washington, *Invented Lives: Narratives of Black Women, 1860–1960* (Garden City: Anchor Press, 1987), p. 8.

I suspect that some readers will be relieved to see that many of their heroes and heroines are excluded from this study. Heroic proportions imply statuesque dimensions – ample surfaces for Brobdingnagian blemishes. Each of the five figures I have selected may be described in the words once applied to Du Bois: "Remarkable man; ambiguous legacy."[7] So it must be with every great intellectual, statesman, artist, or religious leader throughout history. "World-historical figures" are always caught up in "internal and incurable contradictions."

The greatest philosophical problems are unsolvable – as unanswerable as the questions of Job, and history is a "dismal science," fundamentally incompatible with America's compulsory cheeriness. My approach, alas, implies a tragic conception of history, indigestible to the American mind, whether liberal, conservative, or Marxist. The American "civil religion" is based on an upward and onward teleology in which the Kingdom of God can be realized in our lifetimes through the honest application of will and reason. Popular history has no place for tragic challenges, irreconcilable struggles, or incurable contradictions.[8]

Great societies may eliminate hunger, mitigate disease, and exalt the arts and sciences, but they will never abolish meanness, extinguish superstition, or defeat ignorance. Reality is not a series of dialectical oppositions and voluntary choices. It is a process of simultaneous struggles – incoherent, multifaceted, and permanently irreconcilable. Therefore, this work is not intended – in either the formal or the vernacular sense – as an exercise in "dialectics," a term I have avoided as much as possible. It is based on Alexander Crummell's idea that struggle is an unavoidable aspect of the human condition, and happy is the person who has the luxury of enjoying the challenge. Crummell anticipated Theodore Roosevelt's idea that the strenuous life must be a permanent feature of worthwhile human existence, and both reiterated an ancient wisdom.

The theme of contradiction in this work derives not from "books I read in college," but from the content of the materials produced by the

---

[7] Irving Howe's mixed emotions are revealed in the title of his article, "Remarkable Man, Ambiguous Legacy," *Harpers* (March 1968).

[8] Hegel's concept of the world-historical figure resembles Carlye's or Emerson's representative man. Engels finds an "internal and incurable contradiction" in Hegel's system because it rests simultaneously on dialectical relativism and idealistic absolutism (*Anti-Dühring*, Introduction: I. General). Engels also admits that Hegel has presented a problem that is insolvable, "*eine Aufgabe die keine einzelner je wird lösen konnen.*" If Engels is correct, and he seems to be, then Hegel, presumably a world-historical figure, illustrates the presumption of my work, that contradictions must surface within the intellectual productions of great minds.

five authors whose work I have treated. I do not deny having struggled to understand Hegel, Marx, Engels, and Nietzsche, sometimes in the original German, but Ralph Waldo Emerson and William Blake have been stronger influences. From early childhood, I learned – as many children do – that there are oxymoronic contradictions in the thinking and behavior of perfectly intelligent and rational people. Thus, I experienced no startling revelation when I encountered Richard Hofstadter's technique in *The American Political Tradition*, which highlights contradictions in thinkers and traditions but seeks to understand how these contradictions have been reconciled, or at least rationalized.

Seeking to understand how historical figures have attempted to reconcile contradiction does not make one a "consensus historian." Hofstadter asserted "that conflict and consensus require each other and are bound up in a kind of dialectic of their own." More cuttingly, he observed that "the important ground on which consensus as a general theory of American history should be quarreled with is not its supposed political implications, but its intrinsic limitations as history." Hofstadter insisted "that the idea of consensus is not intrinsically linked to ideological conservatism." It has been observed that Louis Hartz, the exemplary consensus historian, represented a liberal, not a conservative, tradition, and the Marxist historian Eric Foner suggests that Hartz presented American history in a critical, rather than an aggrandizing, mode.[9]

As have the subjects of this study, I use African American history as a means of discussing larger aspects of the human condition. Especially in the chapters on Garvey, I have been tacitly concerned with a fundamental paradox in Western thought, the problem of destiny, in both its Calvinistic and its Marxist forms. If social forces exist, whether created by God, or by material conditions, or by human thought, then what is the relationship of these social forces to the individual human will? Orthodox Christianity addresses the question by asserting that although nothing can occur unless God wills it, men and women paradoxically manage, nonetheless, to violate his will – hence, their pervasive depravity and deservedly frequent damnation. Benjamin Franklin confronted the question when as a young man he putatively rejected the puritan-rationalist form of

---

[9] Richard Hofstadter, *The American Political Tradition* (New York: Vintage, 1948), and Hofstadter, *The Progressive Historians, Turner, Beard, Parrington* (New York: Vintage, 1970), pp. 451, 452, 463. The historian, Eric Foner, overcomes his own Marxist values to praise Hartz's liberal consensus interpretation of American intellectual tradition as "brilliant and sardonic." See Foner, "American Freedom in a Global Age," *American Historical Review* (February 2001), pp. 1–16.

predestination, only to replace it with an eighteenth-century mechanistic form of determinism.[10]

Marx denied, unconvincingly, that his economic history was deterministic, but he made the following equivocal and evasive statement: "Men make their own history, but they do not make it just as they please; they do not make it under circumstances chosen by themselves, but under circumstances directly encountered, given and transmitted from the past."[11] He thus places himself in company with St. Paul, John Milton, and other Christian mystics who want to preserve determinism while trading liberally in free will. The boundaries of my freedom to interpret the works of my five subjects were determined long ago by the authors themselves. Their works, like those of all major thinkers, are thoroughly permeated by challenging contradictions, without which they would be unspeakably dreary and not worth reading.

A splendid example of the contradictions in African American thought is the previously mentioned Exodus myth. As I have said elsewhere, the myth of Moses and Pharaoh exemplifies the universal poetic function of mythology to reconcile the irreconcilable, or – as one preacher expressed it – to "screw up the inscrutable." In an earlier work, *Afrotopia* (1998), I observed that the Exodus myth exposes the conflicting identities of African American people, manifest in the desire to be Ramses II and Moses at the same time. The first issues of *Freedom's Journal*, published in 1827, asserted Afrocentric pride in the heritage of ancient Egypt, while simultaneously telling Pharaoh to let my people go.[12] The idea that mythology reconciles

---

[10] See Franklin's *Dissertation on Liberty and Necessity* . . . , written in 1725, and his restatement of the problem in "Letter to Theophilus," 1741, which should be compared to the ambiguous and unconvincing reconstruction of his religious prilgimage in the *Autobiography*, Part Two.

[11] Karl Marx makes this statement in the first chapter, second paragraph of *The Eighteenth Brumaire of Louis Bonaparte* (Hamburg, 1869), available in plentiful editions. It represents his struggle with a seemingly irrepressible paradox in Western thought, seen in John Milton's theological attempt to reconcile determinism with free will, and Thomas Jefferson's implicitly deterministic frontier theory. Friedrich Engels in Chapter 3 of the *Anti-Dühring* (1878) argues that socioeconomic forces, historically the determinants of human behavior, can someday be bent to the human will.

[12] I speak of myth as the attempt to reconcile contradictions in the preface to *Black Messiahs and Uncle Toms*. I wish I could take sole credit for this insight. Unfortunately, I must confess that Plato discusses the concept by way of the two manifestations of Aphrodite in the *Symposium*. Renaissance humanism also exploited the contradictory manifestations of Aphrodite, according to Jean Seznec, *The Survival of the Pagan Gods* (New York: Bollingen Foundation, 1953); also see Edgar Wind, *Pagan Mysteries of the Renaissance* (New Haven, CT: Yale University Press, 1958). My discussion of the Mosaic myth in *Afrotopia: The Roots of African American Popular History* (New York: Cambridge University Press, 1998),

contradictions was central to my book *Black Messiahs and Uncle Toms* (1982). I made the obvious point that Malcolm X and Martin Luther King, Jr., symbolized *both* resistance to, *and* accommodation to, American racism.

My interpretive frameworks are dictated – I repeat because I have learned that there is safety in repetition – by the five authors, who are my subjects, and not by artificial applications of unquestionably fascinating, but long-dead, Hebrew prophets, Greek philosophers, or German historians. William Blake and Ralph Waldo Emerson have influenced me more than any of them, but again, not to the same extent as the five authors themselves. Nonetheless, I confess to the influences of Biblical fatalism, Mediterranean classicism, and Germanic romanticism – as have my subjects, whether verbally or in practice. I acknowledge, as they have, the mutability of reality, the unreliability of appearances, and the inevitability of contradiction.

pp. 47–53, is more complicted than Benjamin Mays' passing allusion in *The Negro's God* (New York: Chapman and Grimes, 1938), p. 9, or Gayraud S. Wilmore's *Black Religion and Black Radicalism* (Garden City, NY: Doubleday, 1972), which do not discuss African Americans' strong identity with Pharaoh. Miles Mark Fisher's treatment in *Negro Slave Songs in the United States* (Ithaca, NY: Cornell University Press, 1953) is more satisfying, but still neglects any Egyptocentric interest. Eddie S. Glaude's *Exodus: Religion, Race and Nation in Early Nineteenth-Century Black America* (Chicago: University of Chicago Press, 2000) is a well-researched, well-written, and imaginative discussion of the Exodus theme, but despite the author's solid treatment of *Freedom's Journal,* the contradictions between mosaic and pharaonic mythology are not addressed.

I

Introduction

Reality and Contradiction

A Foolish consistency is the hobgoblin of little minds.

Emerson

"CONSTANT ANXIETIES" AND THE JOY OF STRUGGLE

To be engaged in the eternal struggle of the human mind – to contemplate
the tensions and ambiguities of a perpetually mysterious universe – was
Alexander Crummell's definition of heaven. The necessity and the pleasure
of mental exertion must eternally engage both the living and the dead,
he asserted in his address, "The Solution of Problems: The Duty and
Destiny of Man." "Grappling with indeterminate questions is one of the
inevitabilities of life"; and it was even more than that. "This fashion of
our life" presages eternity, he asserted. It "fills us with perplexities and
breeds constant anxieties, but these are the heritage of all God's spiritual
creatures, above and below; for both angels and men are created for the
unending, the everlasting ventures and anxieties of their spirits in the deep
things of God." The poet, Paul Laurence Dunbar, showed little knowledge
of the man when in his elegy, "Alexander Crummell: Dead," he thought to
tempt the old battler with an invitation to eternal rest. Crummell's concept
of heaven was incompatible with the poet's ideas of relaxation or repose.
Indeed, Crummell defined poetry as the "ofttimes agonized strain of the
heart of man to pierce the mystery of being, and to solve the inscrutable
problems of existence."[1]

[1] Alexander Crummell, "The Solution of Problems: The Duty and Destiny of Man" The
Annual Sermon of the Commencement of Wilberforce University, June 16, 1895. Reprinted
from *A.M.E. Church Review,* April 1898.

When Crummell expressed these ideas at a Wilberforce University commencement in 1895, W. E. B. Du Bois was present, and on his way to formulating a similarly rigorous conception of "our spiritual strivings." Du Bois well knew the truth of Crummell's doctrine of "everlasting anxieties and agonized strain." More than once he quoted lines from Goethe's *Faust*, "*Entbehren sollst du; sollst Entbehren!*," which he translated as "Thou shalt forego; shalt do without!" And, as a nineteenth-century American Negro, Du Bois certainly understood the bitter tone in which Goethe had intended Faust to speak them. But as a sensitive reader of poetry, Du Bois – a Faustian character in his own right – did not overlook the ironic twist at the climax of Goethe's drama, that "doing without" can imply something higher than mere frustration. He came to utilize Goethe's phrase as a reminder of the fundamental paradox that self-fulfillment comes from self-denial. The inescapable theme running through classical stoicism, Christian mysticism, and Faustian Romanticism is that the pathway to salvation is uphill and rocky.

POWERLESS MORALITY AND BLACK POWER

Reality is made up of contradictions. The clash of ideologies and personalities, symbolized by the confrontation between Alexander Crummell and Frederick Douglass at Harper's Ferry on May 30, 1885, is mentioned more than once in these pages. This clash was important as an instance of the irreconcilable collision between the primacy of morality and the primacy of power – sometimes unnecessarily in conflict. The conflicts between Crummell and Douglass, or between Du Bois and Garvey, for example, highlight something other than mere differences in strategy. They indicate basic differences in how their authors viewed racial reform. Douglass' rhetoric was based on an appeal to the moral traditions of European Christian civilization and the assumption that social reform was primarily a moral issue. Intensely aware of America's conviction of moral superiority, he sought to manipulate the rhetoric of American perfectionism to promote racial equality. Crummell was certainly no less Christian than Douglass and no less Eurocentric, but viewed reform as primarily a matter of institution building. Believing that moral suasion was no substitute for political and economic pressure, Crummell said, "What this race needs in this country is power."[2]

---

[2] Alexander Crummell, "The Social Principle Among a People," in Alexander Crummell, *The Greatness of Christ and Other Sermons* (New York: Whittaker, 1882), pp. 294–311.

"The collision of immoral power with powerless morality" identified by Martin Luther King, Jr. as "the major crisis of our times" was actually present during Reconstruction.[3] The moral exhortations of Frederick Douglass were becoming ineffective in Crummell's view that the real needs of black people must be met by internal institutional development. The debate was taken up in the twentieth century when Du Bois implied that Booker T. Washington had abandoned the moral crusade. He accused Washington of "failure to realize and impress the point" that the striving of black folk must be "aroused and encouraged by the initiative of the richer and wiser environing group."[4] Implicitly, Washington had forgotten the power of the old abolitionist moral rhetoric. Washington was never so naive as to ignore the uses of moral preachments, but his social gospel assumed that Christian morality was impossible in the absence of economic progress.

Ambivalent attitudes toward the relationship between moral and economic determinism were present in most black thinkers. The Civil War and the Emancipation that followed it were the culmination of a great moral struggle, in which black folk could not claim that they had seized their own freedom by unilateral force. White moralism had been crucial, but the question now was whether moral appeals would sufficiently spur on white progressives to complete the work of liberation; if not, then the task demanded the development of independent black power. There was an additional problem – the quest for power meant flirting with the corrupting influences of power. Abolitionism existed on the high ground of universal morality and immutable truths; Reconstruction demanded attention to the mundane requirements of industry and agriculture. Despite the steady failure of Reconstruction, Douglass could not abandon the once-successful abolitionist strategy of appeals to reason, morality, and justice. At times, he seemed to repress his own obvious suspicions that power may be incurably irrational, and that justice and morality are often defined by little more than the will of the strongest.

Alexander Crummell, his Christian optimism buttressed by clerical training in "moral science," certainly viewed the triumph of abolitionism as a proof of moral suasion as a historical force, but his Christian perfectionism was linked to the social gospel of economic and industrial reform. Frederick Douglass, while vastly more secular than Crummell, seemed to

---

[3] Martin Luther King, Jr., *Where Do We Go From Here* (Boston: Beacon, 1968), p. 37. Although, King never behaved as if he thought morality could be separated from power.
[4] *Souls of Black Folk*, p. 58.

believe that truth and justice had irresistible metaphysical power in the providential course of history.[5] The metaphysical presumption of the inevitability of moral progress was a current in the thinking of Washington, Du Bois, and Marcus Garvey. Booker T. Washington's progressivism was rooted, not only in economic utilitarianism, but in a faith that his program would receive the support of progressive whites. Du Bois, even in his later writings, constantly alluded to ideals of the social gospel, although increasingly supplementing its rhetoric with the Marxist dogma of inevitable progress. Garvey, too, believed in moral progress, and his ideas combined Christian teleology and Christian perfectionism with a Darwinian conception of racial competition.

The Civil War and Emancipation had convinced many black leaders that the world was progressing morally. Ironically, the power of abolitionist moral preachments had resulted in a great military struggle, in which freedom had been proclaimed by fiat and imposed at gunpoint. None would have challenged Theodore Roosevelt's belief that the exploits of Christian abolitionist soldiers in the war had represented a struggle for the survival of the moral fittest. Moral power had been enforced by the might of the United States Army. During the Civil War, Crummell made the startling proclamation that nothing civilizes a man so effectively as putting a gun in his hands.[6] There was something oxymoronic and contradictory about the concept of moral force, especially when the force involved was patently militaristic.

Other contradictions emerged. Crummell, like Douglass, believed that African Americans could not progress as a whole unless individuals developed personal responsibility for individual accomplishment, but Crummell believed that individual brilliance had little social meaning unless the race as a whole could demonstrate its collective genius for contributing to civilization. "Character," for Crummell, was "the great thing," but the collective "social principle" of "Civilization" was "the primal need of the race."[7]

---

[5] See Douglass' essay inspired by the trial of Galileo, "It Moves, or the Philosophy of Reform: Address . . . 1883," in *Douglass Papers*, Vol. 5, pp. 124–45.

[6] Crummell referred to the arming of African militias in Liberia, but the intended audience was American, where free blacks were agitating for admission to the Union Army. *African Repository* (September 1861), p. 277.

[7] Alexander Crummell, "The Social Principle Among a People" and "Character, the Great Thing," in Bragg, *Afro-American Group of the Episcopal Church*. "Civilization: The Primal Need of the Race," in *American Negro Academy Occasional Papers*. For increased depth, witness Crummell's move toward reconciliation of the contradiction in his address at the Atlanta Exposition of 1895, "Civilization as a Collateral and Indispensable

FREDERICK DOUGLASS: THE INDIVIDUALIST AS RACE MAN

The uneasy relationship between the individual ego and the racial self is symbolized by the preachments of Frederick Douglass, especially after Emancipation. So often did he emphasize individual accomplishment that he was sometimes accused of lacking race pride, and he did not deny the assertion.[8] "I have seen myself charged with a lack of race pride. I am not ashamed of that charge. I have no vindication to offer." Nonetheless, he went on to make reference to his "fifty years of uncompromising devotion to the cause of the colored man." And here was the contradiction to which I point in the present volume. Douglass' claim to fame was as a "representative man," who had experienced not only the ontological condition of blackness, but the social status of a slave, in an environment that made the words "Negro" and "slave" practically synonymous. The constant invocation of his former slave status was a gambit enabling him to engage in the identity politics that were his bread and butter.

Douglass was not alone in wrestling with this contradiction – however original and unique were his means of addressing it. In less personalized form, the contradiction between individualism and social identity loomed in the best-known essays of Ralph Waldo Emerson and George Bancroft. Both men addressed the paradox noted by Carlyle and Hegel that the greatest indivduals were really only representative men. The material forces of history produced not only a mind-spirit, but a world-historical figure who was its expression, an inconvenient problem for the Emersonian notion of self-reliance and Bancroft's ideas about rugged individualism. Marx and Engels attempted to reconcile the contradiction that was implicit in George Bancroft and Ralph W. Emerson and later addressed by Theodore Dreiser in the Nietzschean figure of Frank Cowperwood. If the most dynamic leaders are, willy or nilly, driven by their environments, then Emerson, Bancroft, Marx, and Dreiser are caught up in the same paradox of determinism and free will that bedeviled the Puritans.

If philosophies are nothing more than the products of historical forces, then I have wrongly faulted Frederick Douglass for not conceiving a

Instrumentality in Planting the Christian Church in Africa," in J. W. E. Bowen, ed., *Africa and the American Negro, Held under the Auspices of the Stewart Missionary Foundation of Gammon Theological Seminary in Connection with the Cotton States and International Exposition, December 13–15, 1895* (Atlanta: Gammon Theological Seminary, 1896).

[8] The editors of *The Frederick Douglass Papers*, Vol. 5, p. 404, cite letters by J. Willis Menard and Edward P. McCabe "which accuse Douglass of lacking race pride." *Washington Bee*, April 20, May 4, 1889.

program for Reconstruction. Alternatively, his refusal to preconceive a project for racial advancement was, perhaps, his strongest point. Perhaps he was correct in his presumption that a certain laissez-faire was the only adequate response to the questions of the hour. Perhaps his philosophy of "Free the slaves and leave them alone," was the wisest thing that the federal government might have done. But his position was not always so simply articulated. He was not above asking Charles Sumner to find his son a sinecure in the Freedman's Bureau, big government in its most extreme form, and the Bureau was hardly an exemplar of laissez-faire policy.[9] On the other hand he denied any interest in accepting the headship of the Bureau, if it were offered to him. Whether his refusal derived from a lack of confidence in the Johnson administration or from some philosophical objection to its big government functions is unclear.

From the perspective of his severest critics – today, as in the past – Douglass' one great fault was his second marriage to a woman of his father's race, as he once put it. Such critics conveniently develop amnesia during African American history month, when his leonine visage gazes down from countless bulletin boards in American elementary schools. Douglass is the heroic icon, the man who refused to be a slave, who resisted the slave breaker Covey, who escaped to the North and took up the cause of abolition in thundering tones, like the awful rush of ocean waters, to paraphrase his own imagery. He was better than most of us, possessing physical courage as remarkable as his extraordinary intellect. Unable and disinclined to find faults in Douglass' character, we are reluctant to find fault with his reasoning. In our refusal to address the contradictions that Douglass attempted to reconcile, we fail to appreciate formidable powers of reasoning that he brought to his heroic internal struggles.

Douglass was elegantly inconsistent on the entire question of black identity politics, which he supported or opposed as the spirit moved him. He voiced the demands of a race, while denying the value of racial consciousness. He constantly reminded white Americans of slavery, while insisting that black Americans should cease to make racial demands. Douglass vacillated between an assimilationist "melting pot" conception of American history and preachments of a multiethnic ideal. Toward the end of his life he seemed to recognize the changing landscape of American race relations and tried to reconcile the reality of multiculturalism with his idea of African American cultural assimilation. For Douglass, the ultimate goal of American democracy had always been in progress toward the

---

[9] Douglass to Sumner, April 29, 1865, in Foner, ed., *Douglass*, Vol. 4, p. 165.

egalitarian values of the Declaration of Independence. Jefferson's egalitarian presumptions contained the moral force of the United States's "undeveloped destiny." The use of the term "destiny" is significant, for it implies confidence in a progressive future. He repeated the term two sentences later, when he referred to the Declaration as "the ringbolt to the chain of your nation's destiny."[10]

ALEXANDER CRUMMELL: THE ANGLOPHILE AS AFROCENTRIST

Not all African Americans were committed, as was Frederick Douglass, to the unrealized ideals of Jeffersonian individualism. Certainly not Alexander Crummell, who placed himself in a Hamiltonian tradition consistent with the main currents of African American thought. The young Du Bois adopted certain elements of Hamiltonian thought, which were consistent with his later Marxist interpretation of African American history. Few African Americans have seen the usefulness of exploiting a Hamiltonian theory of American life. Crummell was a notable exception but his popularity is as dead as that of Alexander Hamilton. Like Hamilton, Crummell has become something of an embarrassment to egalitarian Americans and has been pushed to the margins of history or buried in the footnotes of scholarly treatises.

Viewed from the shallow perspective of twentieth-century liberalism, Crummell became a practically unmitigated villain. He did not pretend to be democratic, nor was he a multiculturalist. His brand of feminism is outmoded, although he was progressive on women's issues, and his ideas conform to the Victorian perfectionism of Anna Julia Cooper, Mary Church Terrell, and Margaret Murray Washington. His feminism was, therefore, on the trajectory that leads to twenty-first-century gender liberalism. On other issues, however, he does not remind us of present-day liberals. For example, he urged a moratorium on recriminations over slavery, and placed the burden of black uplift almost entirely on African Americans. In his belief in the doctrine of Anglo-Saxon cultural supremacy he was absolutely consistent.

But Crummell also contradicted himself, for his speeches and sermons frequently recalled as passionately as did Douglass' the sufferings of the race under slavery. He never specifically denied the legitimacy of claims for reparations from a white nation that owed debts to its formerly enslaved population, but such demands were fleeting and abstract. Crummell's

[10] Foner, *Douglass*, Vol. 2, p. 185.

appeals to the white conscience were usually framed with reference to the Christian's duty to bring good out of evil, to work for the saving of souls, and to improve material civilization in accord with the divine plan. Over a period of sixty years, whether in Africa or in America, the essential feature of Crummell's program was always self-help.

Crummell's black nationalist Eurocentrism has frequently roused the indignation of those who are sentimental about black popular culture. Afrocentrists are indignant that Crummell promoted establishing the English language in West Africa. And yet for obvious reasons, these same persons publish in English and with American university presses. They do not publish in Hausa with a Nigerian publisher, although Hausa is the African language with the largest number of native speakers. Crummell's promotion of the English language is conceptually naive, but no more naive than the approaches of some of his twentieth-century critics. The language of a pan-national movement must be capable both of transcending and undermining regional nationalisms. "Languages of state" must be able to effectively communicate across tribal boundaries and must do so without playing tribal favoritism. Better a language that we all hate equally than a language that some of us view as the speech of a favored caste or class.[11]

Crummell was always a churchman and a man of letters; he was by turns missionary, businessman, educator, Liberian nationalist, and African explorer. By intellectual temperament he was consistently the irascible public moralist, cultural elitist, and dark ironist. Crummell was presumed to have been of "unadulterated" black ancestry, a matter of some importance to his contemporaries, but ultimately conjectural, as such matters usually are. Denied admission to Yale University and the Episcopal Seminary in New York on racial grounds, he eventually passed examinations and took an "ordinary" degree from the University of Cambridge in England. Well versed in political theory (classical and modern), he embarked, in 1853, on a missionary career in the Republic of Liberia, where he devoted much of his life over the next twenty years to the cause of African nationalism. Then, in 1871, a violent coup led by a faction identified with mulatto dominance forced him to flee the country. He

[11] For example, see Tunde Adeleke, *UnAfrican Americans: Nineteenth Century Black Nationalists and the Civilizing Mission* (Lexington: University Press of Kentucky, 1998), pp. 70–91. Crummell, "The English Language in Liberia," in *Africa and America* (New York: Scribner, 1862). Senegal and Congo are French speaking. Angola and Mozambique are Portuguese speaking. Arabic is the only non-Western language with immediate potential as an African print language, but its adoption would carry strong political implications, as would adoption of any other non-African language.

returned to the United States and settled in Washington, D.C., where he established St. Luke's, an African American congregation of the Protestant Episcopal Church.[12]

Crummell identified strongly with the Federalist tradition and particularly admired "that great political prophet, Alexander Hamilton."[13] In our own era, the Federalists have only rarely and sporadically been the recipients of any praise, either from the left or from the right. There have been some interesting exceptions. Students of American history have learned well the truism that Hamilton was antidemocratic – and they are correct, for even more readily than James Madison, he feared the tyranny of the majority. On the other hand, Hamilton's abolitionist credentials are vastly more authentic than those of the more "radical" Thomas Paine. But Crummell never alluded to Hamilton's abolitionism, and he may not even have been aware of it. It was Hamilton's commitment to law and order that Crummell found agreeable, for nineteenth-century black Americans had unpleasant experiences with the democratic impulses of Jacksonian mobs.[14]

Crummell's black nationalist thought overlapped that of Edward Wilmot Blyden, his colleague at Liberia College and, like Crummell, a staunch Pan-Africanist.[15] Crummell believed, as did Blyden, that African Americans must be converted to monotheism, but unlike Blyden he did

---

[12] William Wells Brown, *The Black Man, His Antecedents, His Genius, and His Achievements* (New York: Thomas Hamilton, 1863), pp. 165–69. William J. Simmons, *Men of Mark: Eminent, Progressive, and Rising* (Cleveland: Geo. M. Rewell & Co., 1887), p. 530–35. Wilson J. Moses, *Alexander Crummell: A Study in Civilization and Discontent* (New York: Oxford University Press, 1989).

[13] Details on this and other aspects of Crummell's life and works may be accessed through index and footnote references in W. J. Moses, *Alexander Crummell.*

[14] Stephen F. Knott, *Alexander Hamilton and the Persistence of Myth* (Lawrence, KS: University Press of Kansas, 2002) appraises Hamilton's reputation in American history, and has a solid bibliography. Richard Brookhiser favorably contrasts Hamilton with Jefferson in *Alexander Hamilton* (New York: Free Press, 1999). Forrest McDonald, *Alexander Hamilton* (New York: Norton, 1982) is essential.

[15] Thomas W. Livingston, *Education and Race: A Biography of Edward Wilmot Blyden* (San Francisco, CA: Glendessary Press, 1975); V. Y. Mudimbe, *The Invention of Africa: Gnosis, Philosophy, and the Order of Knowledge* (Bloomington: Indiana University Press, 1988); Hollis Lynch, ed., *Black Spokesman: Selected Published Writings of Edward Wilmot Blyden,* (New York: Humanities Press, 1971); Edith Holden, *Blyden of Liberia* (New York: Vantage Press, 1967): Hollis R. Lynch, *Edward Wilmot Blyden: Pan-Negro Patriot, 1832–1912* (London: Oxford University Press, 1964); Hollis R. Lynch, ed., *Selected Letters of Edward Wilmot Blyden* (New York: KTO Press, 1978). For antihistoricism at its worst, see Tunde Adeleke, *UnAfrican Americans* (Lexington: University Press of Kentucky, 1998) from Crummell's published essays, meretriciously filtered through Anthony Appiah, who revealed no interest in Crummell prior to his article in *Massachusetts Review* (Autumn 1990), where he (interestingly) identified my *Alexander Crummell* (New York: Oxford, 1989) as an unpublished manuscript.

not advocate a half-way covenant with Islam as an intermediate stage. Crummell was impatient, especially in his later years, with the opinion that slavery had aided in the process of conversion. A letter of 1853 and a speech of 1882 both reveal that Crummell passionately denied that slavery had any Christianizing or civilizing influence on the masses of Africans or African Americans.[16]

Crummell's philosophy resembles the Roman Catholic doctrine that salvation comes from beating the self into submission. The religion of the black masses was frequently characterized by him and his contemporaries as an Africanized Calvinism in which salvation was usually associated with an emotional conversion experience. Crummell believed that virtue came from the rational, not the emotional, side of human nature. It has been suggested that his predilections, like those of many Episcopalians, were "high church." Interesting as is the issue of high church sympathy at least once imputed to him, it is more important to note that his doctrinal base was unequivocally "strict church," that is to say he placed much stress on the "law of Moses" and implicitly on a "doctrine of works." His thoughts on the subject were succinctly expressed in his sermon "The Episcopal Church in Liberia."[17]

There was no room in Crummell's missionary theory for antinomianism – the idea that faith without works could save the soul; no room for the idea that enthusiastic spirit possession is a step along the pathway to a higher realization of Christian truth; no room for Islam as the opening wedge for Christianity; no room for Jesuitism or for any other incomplete or imperfect form of monotheism. Such forms of religion were all distractions. Rational Victorian Protestantism was the only way. He held swooning and visions in extreme contempt and believed that the church must be of this world. The Gospel enjoined obligations to feed the hungry and clothe the naked; it could not be separated from the political economy of the material world, rigorously constructed by the social engineers of a muscular Christian army.

Blyden and Crummell, along with E. J. Roye, the Liberian president assassinated in the coup of 1871, specifically advocated intermarriage with the native peoples as a fundamental component of nation building. They sought to involve the native peoples in government-financed public

---

[16] Blyden, *Christianity, Islam and the Negro Race* (1887; reprint University of Edinburgh Press, 1967), p. 24. For Crummell's dissent see *Africa and America: Addresses and Discourses* (Springfield, MS: Willey, 1891), p. 319. Also see Moses, *Crummell*, index entries to Blyden, Islam, religion under slavery.

[17] Crummell, "The Episcopal Church in Liberia." Microfilm edition of his papers: Schomburg Collection.

works projects designed to bring the various indigenous ethnicities and immigrant groups together to form one amorphous nationality. The elite, led by Joseph Jenkins Roberts and A. F. Russell, secretly desired to displace the indigenous peoples of Liberia and set up a settler state after the American, Canadian, and Australian models.

Few things are so simple in the history of ideas as the position that Anthony Appiah attributes to Crummell. He is factually incorrect in saying that Crummell and his peers lacked a reverence for indigenous African life and customs. There is abundant evidence in the Crummell Papers at the Schomburg Collection, and in the Episcopal magazine *Spirit of Missions*, that Crummell was sometimes downright sentimental in his descriptions of African peoples. As for his contemporaries, including Blyden and Reverend Samuel Williams, their opinions were well known and readily available in published documents. It would be understandable if Appiah had simply overlooked evidence, but something more disturbing is at work here. The problem is not a mere methodological lapse, but a fundamental arrogance. Appiah studied very little Crummell before writing about him.

BOOKER T. WASHINGTON: THE IDEALIST AS MATERIALIST

Booker T. Washington is remembered as the incarnation of realism, materialism, and practicality. Du Bois was the first to make the observation, on which all subsequent interpretations have apparently been based, that Washington's philosophy resembled the pragmatic dogmas of the industrial-commercial North and its major apologists – Andrew Carnegie, John D. Rockefeller, William Graham Sumner, and other representatives of triumphant capitalism. Du Bois is the source of August Meier's observation that Washington saw the solution to the race problem in applications of the gospel of wealth and the attainment of material prosperity.[18] Louis Harlan follows in this tradition when he views Washington as a pragmatist, with "various personalities to fit his various roles." Furthermore, Harlan sees contradictions between Washington's public preachments and his "secret machinations." Harlan supposes that he did not need to reconcile contradictions because "being secret, they did not pragmatically require justification."[19]

---

[18] August Meier, *Negro Thought in America, 1880–1915: Racial Ideologies in the Age of Booker T. Washington* (Ann Arbor: University of Michigan Press, 1966), p. 100.
[19] Louis Harlan, ed., *The Booker T. Washington Papers* (Urbana: University of Illinois Press, 1972), Vol. 2, pp. 118 and 119.

The continuities between Washington's thought and his behavior are perhaps adequately treated according to Harlan's formula, but the contradictions within his thought are not so easily dismissed. The Tuskegeean constantly portrayed himself as a hard-headed materialist, and preached the doctrine that an improvement of material conditions must precede any elevation of the moral and intellectual status of black Americans. People given to vigorous religious exercises on empty bellies were likely to steal chickens on the way home from church. But Washington contradicted himself when he expressed the belief that religion could reshape the material behavior of the black masses. Thus, not only did he ridicule the traditional Africanized Calvinism of the black church, he sought to replace it with a theology of his own making. If the preacher could encourage his flock to worship rationally, and to think of religion as a means of inculcating industrial values, then black Americans could more readily become a race of tradesmen and entrepreneurs. Religion, rightly taught, would plant the seeds of the Protestant ethic that was necessary to material progress.

Booker T. Washington's theory of the Protestant ethic was not derived from Max Weber's, but independently invented and manufactured from whole cloth, as American as the cotton belt from which it sprang. His theory of history was as flawed as that of Weber, but it was not thoughtless, nor was it abstract. It was derived from his own ample experience, and was applicable to the people for whom it was intended. The difficulty was that he had not solved the problem of the relationship between ideology and behavior. There were, however, additional factors contributing to the rise of Western capitalism that neither Washington nor Weber had considered. The rise of a bourgeoisie might have more to do with consumption than with conservation.

Even as Washington told his woeful stories of sharecropper families mortgaging their meager resources to acquire pianos and other store-bought luxuries, black peasants in the South and menials in the North were increasing their wants by poring over the illustrations in Sears and Roebuck catalogues. It was Thorstein Veblen, not Max Weber, who provided an explanation for their behavior. It was conspicuous consumption, not self-denial, that drove the capitalist impulse. Washington lamented the fact that tenant farmers under the crop lien system were spending beyond their means, but the American dream of *infinite consumption* was not confined to the black peasantry. There was nothing singularly prodigal in the behavior of sharecropper-consumers. They were simply expressing the traditional consumerism that had led to the rise of European capitalism and presaged the values of twentieth-century America. The freedom to pursue happiness through consumption was inseparable from the obligation to mortgage labor for material possessions.

Washington's invention of the Protestant ethic preceded Weber's and differed from it in that it was not an explanation of history, but an attempt to control it. Washington was fighting a losing battle, because capitalism has always been based on "conspicuous consumption," not the "Protestant ethic," as Benjamin Franklin, Weber's supposed model, had long ago observed. The representative Negro, described by Washington in an 1896 speech as "Our New Citizen," was, ironically, the harbinger of things to come. The urban blacks, disparaged by Washington for living beyond their means, and the rural blacks, who purchased showy luxuries, were ideal Americans, eminently predestined to consume. Although they were functionally incapacitated from accumulating wealth, and lacked incentives to do so, their lack of capital did not deprive them of opportunities to spend money.

W. E. B. DU BOIS: PRAGMATIST, ABSOLUTIST, DEMOCRAT, AUTHORITARIAN

In a recent incisive probing of the thought of Du Bois, Ross Posnock attacks the "familiar" interpretation of Du Bois as "the fastidious Hegelian idealist" (119). From this, one might easily assume that the most important issue in Du Bois scholarship is a controversy between those who consider him a disciple of William James and those who would make him a Hegelian. To his credit, Posnock recognizes that Du Bois is not the unimaginative disciple of either. But Posnock's work is infected with a "pragmatic" contradiction, since, despite protestations to the contrary, he cannot resist frequently reverting to the theme of Du Bois's Jamesean pragmatism. To argue that Du Bois was a pragmatist is not difficult because "pragmatism" has been so variously defined that it is a simple matter to find elements of "pragmatism" in almost every American historical figure, from Thomas Jefferson to Hillary Clinton.[20]

---

[20] Ross Posnock, *Color and Culture: Black Writers and the Making of the Modern Intellectual* (Cambridge, MA: Harvard University Press, 1998). Posnock is impressively authoritative, and his close reading of the secondary literature gives evidence of scholarly integrity. With respect to primary sources, fresh insights abound as when he observes that Alexander Crummell's "metaphor of cosmopolitan thievery [made in 1877] is set against the historical fact that without plundering black talent, American popular art especially music and dance would be radically impoverished" (pp. 19–20). The deceptively intricate twist here

Several scholars, including Cornel West and Richard Cullen Rath, have insisted that Du Bois's thought was permanently and profoundly influenced by the "pragmatism" of William James.[21] Fair enough, but it is equally influenced by a moral absolutism that is congruent with – although certainly not derived from – the "unbending righteousness" that Du Bois seemingly admired in Alexander Crummell.[22] The pacifistic and pragmatic James may, indeed, have influenced Du Bois to the extent that these scholars claim, but it requires mental gymnastics to reconcile Jamesean relativism with "Hegelian" idealism and Marxist absolutism. It requires intellectual contortionism to reconcile James's (or Du Bois's) professed pacifism with Du Bois's later defense of Stalinist militarism. Du Bois once boasted, in the heat of pacifism, that he preferred to have others kill the chickens he ate; quite so, and he was also willing to allow Stalin to break a few eggs.[23]

George Hutchinson's suggestion that Du Bois influenced James's thinking is a tenable, but tantalizingly unprobed statement. Du Bois drew theory and praxis, in Jamesean or Deweyan fashion, when he spent summers teaching in rural Tennessee. The young idealist's ideas on the duty of "service" and the obligation of educated youth to work among the toiling masses antedated, by many years, James's ideas stated in "The Moral Equivalent of War." James's conversations with Du Bois may have influenced his celebrated essay, which suggested an obligatory service corps for bourgeois youth. One wonders how James would have reacted to Chairman Mao's practice of shipping students with "capitalist road" leanings off to work in factory and field.[24]

is Posnock's ability to reinvigorate a commonplace observation about black music and dance by attaching it to the much-neglected statement by Crummell, usually reductively characterized as a Eurocentrist. Graduate students in history, literature, and philosophy will find these chapters shrewdly discerning, but they should begin the study of Du Bois with an extended reading of his own works.

[21] Cornel West, *The American Evasion of Philosophy: A Genealogy of Pragmatism* (Madison: The University of Wisconsin Press, 1989), pp. 138–50. Richard Cullen Rath, "Echo and Narcissus: The Afrocentric Pragmatism of W. E. B. Du Bois," *The Journal of American History* (September 1997), 461–95.

[22] "Unbending righteousness" is Du Bois's own phraseology in his chapter, "Of Alexander Crummell," in *The Souls of Black Folk*.

[23] See the *National Guardian*, March 16, 1953, for Du Bois's obituary on Joseph Stalin. Describing him as "simple, calm, and courageous," Du Bois smooothes over the assassination of Trotsky, justifies the mass murder of the Kulaks, "rural bloodsuckers," views the deal with Hitler as morally equivalent to Chamberlain's prior compromise – not a bad comparison – and glorifies the attempt to dominate Greece.

[24] George Hutchinson, *The Harlem Renaissance in Black and White* (Cambridge, MA: Harvard University Press, 1995), pp. 36–38.

Herbert Aptheker, the noted communist historian, whom Du Bois selected as his literary executor, once publicly volunteered the statement that Du Bois was never a good Marxist.[25] There were more than two souls in Du Bois, and a complicated lacework of contradictions, existing between his pragmatism and his idealism, romanticism and realism, pacifism and Stalinism, Bohemianism and Prussianism, to name but a few. Although we know that Du Bois's life and works are filled with permanent irreconcilables, both ideological and "pragmatic," we also note that trait in most thinkers of any consequence. It is an adolescent exercise to identify the inconsistencies in Thomas Jefferson or Ralph Waldo Emerson, but more intellectually demanding and satisfying to understand the processes whereby they attempted to reconcile their contradictions.

Scholars have long commented on these contradictions, and I have pointed out the intriguing attempts Du Bois made to reconcile Afrocentrism with Marxism. Du Bois attempted, as did Alexander Crummell, to incorporate Victorian morality into his appraisal of West African village life. While Crummell made use of Christian doctrine in his prescriptions for the civilizing of Africa, Du Bois wrote his prescription after a Marxist formula. Du Bois, despite claims to the contrary, was as committed to Europeanization as Crummell was. Du Bois, like Booker T. Washington, became increasingly "Afrocentric" after 1900, and indeed seems to have been the first person to use that word. He was influenced early by Edward Wilmot Blyden, Leo Frobenius, Carter G. Woodson, and Franz Boas in his treatment of Africa. His path to Afrocentrism was complicated by his simultaneous commitments to pragmatic relativism and ideological absolutism.

MARCUS MOZIAH GARVEY: THE REALIST AS ROMANTIC

Marcus Garvey and Alexander Crummell are the two figures in these pages who claimed to have completely unadulterated black ancestry. Garvey embodied one of the striking contradictions found in Du Bois; he was both a realist and a romantic. As a man who claimed to seek practical solutions, he originally sought to pattern himself after Booker T. Washington, but without completely abandoning the Washington model, he soon showed himself to be a dramatic, flamboyant figure. He brought with him some of the classic contradictions associated with his Jamaican background, not

---

[25] At an NEH seminar at the University of Iowa in the summer of 1971, Aptheker stated that Du Bois was never a true Marxist, "because he was an idealist."

only the brashness associated with the Jamaican temperament, but also the elitist mannerisms of the colonial upper class. His elementary education was very solid, superior by twenty-first century standards, although it ended at around the eighth grade. He knew how to read a newspaper and use a library. He had learned the printer's trade, and since his writing and speech were polished and grammatically correct, he soon demonstrated a talent for journalism.

Garvey soon developed an interest in politics, traveling throughout the Caribbean and Central America, where he learned to speak Spanish and became involved in the labor movement. He traveled in England and in Europe and, while overseas, read Booker T. Washington's *Up From Slavery*. Then, as he later wrote, his doom of being a race leader dawned on him, as he posed to himself the question, "Where is the black man's Government? Where is his King and his Kingdom? Where is his ambassador, his army, his navy, his men of big affairs? I could not find them, and then I declared, I will help to make them."

Unlike the leaders of the National Association for the Advancement of Colored People (NAACP), Garvey did not mount a crusade against the segregation laws that he discovered on arriving in the United States. Realistically, he accepted the doctrine of "separate but equal," much to the dismay of black leaders like W. E. B. Du Bois. In a later stage of his career, he went so far as to meet with leaders of the Ku Klux Klan, whom he praised as hearty supporters of a race-pride ideal that any self-respecting and God-fearing person must endorse. Following the logic of racial separatism to its absurd conclusion, he eventually proclaimed that black Americans should create a black empire in "the land of our Fathers."

Garvey took advantage of the military enthusiasms of black Americans, who had experienced victories on two fronts during the war and had witnessed the spectacular march of returning black troops through Harlem.[26] He began to muster an army and dressed his soldiers in gaudy uniforms. His own imperial outfit was reminiscent of the uniforms worn by European archdukes. J. A. Rogers attributes to Garvey the now famous and often-quoted line, "We were the first fascists," by which Garvey certainly did not mean to express any particular liking for the man who had humiliated Ethiopia. His point was simply that he was more original and more creative than the Italian dictator. He never admitted that the idea of "extreme nationalism," which had not worked for Mussolini, whose

---

[26] Du Bois's famous catalogue of victories achieved by black Americans during World War I appeared in *Crisis*. The venerable Reverend Francis J. Grimké and the considerably younger socialist, Hubert Harrison, were the best-known critics of his accommodating opinions.

resources were superior to his own, certainly was not destined to work for him.[27] Even Du Bois, who considered him a theatrical megalomaniac, was not persuaded that his scheme was a complete swindle. Garvey began to purchase ships with the monies eagerly contributed by true believers, but these proved barely seaworthy. Garvey's talents were in the field of journalism, where he was a dazzling success, but he knew nothing about the establishment of an Afro-Atlantic shipping empire.

Garvey's contradictions were of epic proportions, as was everything else about him. He regarded himself a man of the people, and this self-appraisal was certainly valid, for he did indeed represent a broad cross-section of black Americans, including immigrant and native-born, rich and poor, educated and illiterate, capitalist and socialist. Nonetheless, he admitted that his aspirations were not egalitarian, and did not deny that one of them was to set up an African elite. He was a proletarian who affected the pomp and braggadocio of European monarchies. He was an advocate of "Africa for the Africans" who sought to establish a new form of colonialism in Africa. He was an opponent of Liberian mismanagement who sought to cooperate with the government of Liberia. He was an advocate of black liberation willing to endorse the posturings of white supremacists. As his economic fortunes sank, Garvey's contradictions imploded. His ideology, originally justified in realistic Bookerite terms, had evolved into the splendid, romantic fantasy that resulted in his unfair conviction for using the mails to defraud.

My reason for organizing this book around the theme of conflict is not to castigate these figures but to offer pragmatic confirmation of my belief that their thoughts should be taken seriously. Some readers will appreciate this position; others will not. I certainly believe that the only way to understand figures like Crummell, or Du Bois, is to spend a few years immersing oneself in their works. Most of their writings should be read several times and digested over a period of years. It is necessary to spend some time at the microfilm reader in order to approach these two, because publication of their complete works will require much work that has not yet been undertaken. The works of Douglass, Garvey, and Washington are more accessible than those of the former two because good editions of their papers have been published in well-edited volumes, although some work with microfilm may be necessary with these authors as well.[28]

---

[27] Joel Augustus Rogers, *World's Great Men of Color* (1947; New York: Collier, 1972), Vol. 2, p. 420.

[28] *The Frederick Douglass Papers: Series One: Speeches, Debates, and Interviews*. Vols. 1 and 2. John Blassingame, Jr., ed. (New Haven, CT: Yale University Press, 1979). *The Life and*

A disturbing tendency in some recent historical scholarship is the practice of reading superficially in one or two of an author's works, only to place them inside some sort of fashionable framework based on contemporary theoretical fads and to call this scholarship. A superior approach is to study authors thoroughly for several years – long enough to achieve a grasp of the ideas that were important to them in their own times, and to seek an understanding of them in terms of the things that interested them. This involves, in addition to the approach of "close reading," some effort to understand the material context – political, economic, sociological – within which the authors wrote. The best literary and intellectual historians have never questioned this idea. It is the fundamental doctrine of their craft.

This book is based on the assumption that African American thinkers should be judged by the same criteria as anyone else – their ability to identify the problematic, to recognize paradox, to anticipate counter-arguments, and to focus on contradiction. Only insofar as African American thought can be subjected to the same level of analysis as the thought of "mainstream" authors, can it be taken seriously, especially by African Americans. There is nothing wrong with writing history for children and young adults, and such efforts should never be discontinued. But there is a present necessity to develop a body of scholarship based on complicated historical memory, and a strict analysis of African American prose writing. Our continuing struggle to master a body of works, and to develop critical scholarship around them, will be the most effective means of earning the respect of younger African Americans for these thinkers, and proving our own regard for the depth and complexity of African American thought.[29]

Writings of Frederick Douglass. Five volumes. Philip S. Foner, ed. (New York, International Publishers, 1950–1975). Blassingame's edition was incomplete at the time of the editor's tragic and untimely death. Foner's edition, although selective and sparsely indexed, includes many documents not included in the published volumes of the Blassingame project.

[29] One evening in the autumn of 1970, a distinguished American historian in a seminar on reform in America that commenced with a discussion of Edward Bellamy's science fiction novel, *Looking Backward* (1888), announced that in late-nineteenth-century America "nobody gave a damn what the niggers were thinking!" I was aware of Ignatius Donnelly's science fiction novel *Dr. Hewitt* (1891), about a refined and educated white man suddenly transformed into an African American. I might have reminded the professor of the parallels between Bellamy and Donnelly, who complemented his literary successes with a successful career as a reform politician. Donnelly was unexplainably absent from this seminar on nineteenth-century reform, but although honesty urged me to disputation, prudence counselled otherwise.

FREDERICK DOUGLASS:
THE INDIVIDUALIST AS RACE MAN

2

Frederick Douglass

Superstar and Public Intellectual

Stunningly handsome at sixty years of age, with his burnished silver mane, his eyes large, piercing, and commanding, yet warm and sensitive – that is the portrait of Frederick Douglass reproduced in classic sepia tones on my study wall. Most African Americans can happily identify with that sterling bearded sage. With his ideas, however, we identify more abstractly, and Douglass' enduring popularity, in my view, derives almost entirely from the enduring forcefulness of his character and the courage of his freedom struggle. I do not know if we have a definite understanding of his political vision. We view his resounding moral indictments as the last word on American slavery, but slavery cannot be discussed completely in moral terms. Morality never prevented its existence, nor was it abolished entirely for moral reasons. And Douglass' moral reasoning, unassailable though it was, did not provide answers to the problems of what to do after the destruction of slavery.

Douglass' animal magnetism and strong character – not to mention his powerful intellect and astounding physical courage – usually gave him psychological advantages in dealings with challengers. But he had a tendency to be carried away in the sweep of his own rhetoric, and brilliant though he was, Douglass did not stand head and shoulders above every other African American contemporary. Some thought his ego obnoxiously overblown, and noticed in him a penchant for making generalizations on the African American condition that were little more than solipsistic projections of his own atypical career. His perpetual self-magnification led to prickly relations with Henry Highland Garnet and occasional friction with Alexander Crummell. John Mercer Langston found him difficult to work with as the two traveled together on the antislavery circuit. There were no questions regarding Douglass' moral or physical courage, and his intellectual endowments could not be overlooked, but neither could his enormous egotism.[1]

But criticisms were covert and rare, for Douglass with superior mastery caught the imagination of his times, and he did, in fact, achieve an unchallenged position as the voice of black America enjoyed by no black leader before or since. In retrospect, we endorse the man without analyzing his ideas. Thus, we appraise the "African civilization movement," for example, as if Douglass' were the only voice of any reasonableness or authority. We may agree with his position on the feasibility of African emigration and still be disturbed by the fact that his ideas on the subject are usually privileged to the exclusion of Martin Delany's in most American history courses.[2] We tend to overlook the shock and disapproval that many black people, especially women, expressed at his second marriage to Helen Pitts. We ignore Booker T. Washington's opinion that the marriage "caused something like a revulsion of feeling throughout the entire country."[3]

Douglass' present-day status reflects the genius with which he created the Frederick Douglass industry, which, like a runaway locomotive, went barreling through the twentieth century on its own steam, surviving the man who had been its inventor, fireman, and engineer.[4] It is not surprising

---

[1] John Mercer Langston, *From the Virginia Plantation to the National Capital, or The First and Only Negro Representative from the Old Dominion* (Hartford, CT: American Publishing Company, 1894). William and Aimee Lee Cheek, *John Mercer Langston and the Fight for Black Freedom, 1829–65* (Urbana: University of Illinois Press, 1989); see the index.

[2] A praiseworthy exception to the predominant neglect of Delany is in David A. Hollinger and Charles Capper, *The American Intellectual Tradition*, 4th edition (New York: Oxford University Press, 2001), pp. 481–96, although his emigrationism is downplayed. Alexander Crummell, despite his Cambridge education, catholicity of interests, and amount of publication, is not included.

[3] Booker T. Washington, *Frederick Douglass*, p. 306.

[4] There is no comprehensive, annotated bibliography of the writings of Frederick Douglass. The most extensive collection of Douglass materials is *The Papers of Frederick Douglass* in the Library of Congress, available on fifty-two microfilm reels. These are accompanied by a printed guide, *Frederick Douglass, A Register and Index of His Papers in the Library of Congress* (Washington, DC: Library of Congress, 1976). I am aware of no comprehensive catalogue of his published and unpublished works, or of a standard guide to the archival collections containing Douglass' manuscripts. *The Frederick Douglass Papers* editorial project, begun in the early 1970s under the editorship of the late John W. Blassingame, has assembled a large number of Douglass' writings, a portion of which have been published by Yale University Press. The introductions to these volumes provide a useful guide to archival collections and variant texts. William McFeely mentions several important archives in the "Acknowledgements" section of his *Frederick Douglass* (New York: Norton, 1991).

then that studies of Frederick Douglass usually teeter embarrassingly on the brink of hero worship, and there is a tendency even among serious scholars to accept his testimony on every event in antebellum history as the final and most authoritative word.

He constructed several versions of his autobiography over the course of his career. The *Narrative of the Life of Frederick Douglass* (1845) is the earliest and briefest version, and its simple title distinguishes it in no way from other examples of the slave-narrative genre. The second version *My Bondage and My Freedom* (1855) was subtly but substantially different, especially in that the author was more specific about details that were circumspectly omitted in the original. The panoramic scope of the third version is more than apparent in its self-confident title, *The Life and Times of Frederick Douglass*, first appearing in 1882. A substantially amended edition of *Life and Times* was published in 1892. This was reprinted with other narratives, as Frederick Douglass, *Autobiographies*, in a single volume by the Library of America (1994).[5]

The 1845 *Narrative*'s belated attainment of canonical status in American letters is symbolized by its inclusion in recent editions of the *Norton Anthology of American Literature*, where it is introduced with the interesting assertion that Douglass' life "has become the heroic paradigm for all oppressed people." William Andrews, in his fine preface to *My Bondage and My Freedom*, supports this variety of thinking with a quotation from Douglass' black abolitionist contemporary James M'Cune Smith viz. Douglass was a "representative American man."[6] On the other hand assumptions regarding the universality of black male paradigms have met

---

[5] The Library of America, a series created with the support of the National Endowment for the Humanities and the Ford foundation, is "dedicated to preserving the works of America's greatest writers in handsome enduring volumes, featuring authoritative texts." Douglass' *Autobiographies*, under the editorship of Henry Louis Gates, Jr., contains extensive notes, a chronology of superb quality, and a "Note on the Texts." The index can be frustrating, as are the indexes to most Library of America publications. Gates conscientiously acknowledges his debts to the primary research of William L. Andrews, John W. Blassingame, David W. Blight, William S. McFeely, and Dickson J. Preston, but somehow overlooks Waldo Martin's excellent, *The Mind of Frederick Douglass*. He also duly mentions the pioneering biography by Benjamin Quarles, *Frederick Douglass* (Washington, DC: Associated Publishers, 1948), and Philip S. Foner's *The Life and Writings of Frederick Douglass* (New York: International, 1952–1968), which remain indispensable after a half century. There are problems establishing a definitive catalogue of Douglass' autobiographical works, such as defining the difference between an "edition" and a "printing." The German translation by Ottilie Assing is of more than passing interest due to the controversial nature of her supposedly romantic relationship with the author.

[6] Andrews, ed., *Bondage*, p. xxiii.

resistance from feminist critics.[7] And Douglass certainly does not represent more ethnocentric authors like Martin Delany or Alexander Crummell. I have no fundamental hostility to viewing Douglass as "representative," but here and in a later chapter of this volume, I do insist that one ought to raise the question of what exactly we mean by "Representative Black Man."

William McFeely has identified what he diplomatically calls an "unidentical" quality in the autobiographies, and is necessarily skeptical regarding Douglass' matter-of-fact statement in the *Narrative* of 1845, "My father was a white man." In *My Bondage and My Freedom*, as McFeely notes, this was modified considerably to "My father was a white man or nearly white. It was sometimes whispered that my master was my father." In *The Life and Times of Frederick Douglass*, Douglass says, "Of my father I know nothing." Douglass shifts from an assertion that his father was a white man, possibly his master, to the speculation that his father was perhaps white or nearly white, to the admission that he knows nothing of his father. McFeely notes that no one has solved the question of whom Douglass referred to when he repeated the "whisper" that his father was his master, for Douglass referred to several persons as his master, including Aaron Anthony, Thomas Auld, and Edward Lloyd, any of whom might conceivably have been Douglass' father.[8]

It is a wise child that knows its own father, but mothers can also be mysterious, and thus are we impressed by Douglass' matter-of-fact statement, "I never saw my mother to know her as such, more than four or five times in my life." The short discussion of his maternity is certainly no less disturbing than that of his paternity, and it has evoked more than one angle of commentary. In his introduction to *My Bondage and My Freedom* James M'Cune Smith focused on Douglass' maternal lineage, as his purpose was to address the "intellectual puzzle" of whether Douglass' literary accomplishments were tenable as evidence of African American mental capability, given the fact that detractors of the race were inclined

---

[7] Mary Helen Washington, acknowledging the influences of Valerie Smith and Hazel Carby, makes valid observations on the limitations of Douglass' masculinist paradigms in *Invented Lives: Narratives of Black Women* (Garden City, NY: Doubleday, 1987), p. 8.

[8] William McFeely, *Frederick Douglass*, pp. 7, 8, 12, 14. Henry Louis Gates is uncharacteristically credulous in his treatment of the paternity question. His repetition of Douglass' claim that Aaron Anthony was "rumored among slaves" to be Douglass' father skirts the issue raised by McFeely. Even the assumption that Douglass' father was a white man is "inferential from such inconclusive evidence as a contrast of the 'deep black' complexion of the mother with the brown hue of her son," as Benjamin Quarles notes in *Frederick Douglass*, p. 2.

to attribute Douglass' abilities to his white paternity.[9] Smith thus directed the reader to passages in the autobiography that celebrated the character and intelligence of Douglass' grandmother, Betsy Bailey, and his mother, Harriet Bailey. The grandmother's skill as a netmaker, her knowledge of agriculture, and the mother's ability to read, despite obvious obstacles, were proof of their mental endowments. Smith took this as evidence "that for his energy, perseverance, eloquence, invective, sagacity, and wide sympathy, he is indebted to his negro blood."

A second point of interest to M'Cune Smith was Douglass' claim regarding his mother's appearance:

There is in 'Prichard's Natural History of Man,' the head of a figure – on page 157 – the features of which so resemble those of my mother, that I often recur to it with something of the feeling which I suppose others experience when looking upon the pictures of dear departed ones.[10]

The figure is a drawing of a pharaoh, Ramses the Great, and literary historian Jenny Franchot has astutely questioned Douglass' "selection" of a male figure to "impersonate" his mother. This symbolizes to Franchot "the impediment of the masculine in any recovery of the feminine."[11] A very good point, and it is not invalidated by the fact that the drawing in Prichard turns out to be soft, sensual, and almost androgynous. It must, in any event, be granted that Douglass' representation of his maternity is every bit as complicated and problematic as that of his paternity.

There are other problems in the autobiographies, for example, Douglass' relation of his youthful resistance to Covey, the slave breaker. Douglass' great physical courage is so well attested to by contemporaries that there is no reason to question his truthfulness. He demonstrated an almost reckless courage in clashes with proslavery mobs and seemingly went out of his way to provoke the hostility of Bowery pedestrians. Nonetheless, the events of the struggle with Covey admit of more than one interpretation, and on this Douglass was the first to publish thoughtful reflections on Covey's failure to punish Douglass' insubordination. His explanation was that Covey feared bringing him to the authorities for a

---

[9] James M'Cune Smith's introduction to *My Bondage and My Freedom* (1855) refers to Douglass' description of his mother on p. 52, where Douglass directs the reader to Prichard, *Natural History of Man*, p. 157. Jenny Franchot, "The Punishment of Esther," in Eric Sundquist, ed., *Frederick Douglass: New Literary and Historical Essays* (New York: Cambridge University Press, 1990).

[10] James M'Cune Smith, Introduction to Frederick Douglass, *My Bondage and My Freedom* (Rochester, NY, 1855).

[11] Douglass, *My Bondage and My Freedom*, Library of America ed., p. 136.

public whipping because "he was probably ashamed to have it known and confessed that he had been mastered by a boy of sixteen."[12]

The reasoning does not hold water. Slavery could not have lasted a day if the authority of slave breakers had to rest on their physical ability to wrestle every slave. Nor could it have existed if the slave breaker's code had forced them to accept a slave's challenge to "a fair fight." Covey certainly had means of bringing Douglass to submission without physically dominating him. He might have used a pistol, for example. If Covey was such a terrible man, why did the other slaves risk his wrath by refusing to assist him in administering the beating? It is more likely that Douglass' family connections were the cause of Covey's strangely restrained behavior. Elsewhere, Douglass tells us of Austin Gore, who murdered Bill Denby for a simple act of disobedience. By his own admission, Covey, brutal though he was, did not represent the slave breaker at his worst.[13]

It is understandable that some of his biographers like Shirley Graham and Lerone Bennett have been determined to present Douglass as a flawless hero, presumably for the edification of young people.[14] These authors have their counterparts in the "cult of the Founders," whose main concern has been with the illumination of upwardly spiraling saints painted on the ceiling of the national cathedral. The hagiographic tradition arrays its subjects in white robes and golden slippers, and speaks of realism as "airing dirty linen." The presumed need to create "positive images" means divesting historical subjects and their ideas of flavor and seasoning. Ambiguity, ambivalence, or interpretive problems are characteristically viewed as dangerous luxuries.

And such a view is especially ironic in the case of Douglass, who was a man of more than one mind – torn between his avowed commitment to universal human uplift and his more pragmatic loyalty to a racial movement. His ambivalence removed him from that group of his contemporaries who were in the process of developing a bourgeois ethnocentric conception of African American life and history. Major thinkers often display this trait of ambivalence, and their greatness often derives from their ability to recognize intellectual problems and emotional difficulties which lesser minds have the luxury of ignoring. The greatest honor we can

---

[12] Douglass, *My Bondage and My Freedom*, Library of America ed., p. 287.
[13] Earlier in the narrative, Douglass provides a typology of overseers, then describes Covey's brutality, pp. 122–24.
[14] Lerone Bennett, *Pioneers in Protest* (New York: Penguin, 1969); Shirley Graham, *There Was a Slave: The Heroic Story of Frederick Douglass* (New York: Messner, 1947).

bestow on Frederick Douglass and other black thinkers is to demonstrate that we take them seriously enough to see how they have struggled with the problems of human understanding and attempted to reconcile life's contradictions.

Even those who do not object to hero worship may suspect that Douglass' career is based as much on his abilities as a showman as his integrity as a social philosopher. Candidates for sainthood are often figures who are readily adaptable to competing or even contradictory political agenda. In historical memory, as in life, Douglass has been an exceedingly malleable icon. Ironically, although he professed to believe racial pride "ridiculous" he has come to be venerated among the most important saints in the Afrocentric pantheon. He remains very useful for public celebrations of ethnicity; political hacks love to quote him; schoolchildren still recall with enthusiasm his 1852 Fourth of July oration.

"What to the Slave is the Fourth of July?" he demanded on that occasion, denouncing the national celebration as a sham, "mere bombast, fraud, deception, impiety, and hypocrisy...." In another set of often-quoted lines from his address on West India Emancipation delivered in 1857, he said, "Power concedes nothing without a demand. It never did and it never will.... Negroes will be hunted at the North, and held and flogged at the South so long as they submit to those devilish outrages." This is the fiery orator whose words are conjured up by itinerant actors for the edification of our children in annual black history month pageants, in church basements, and in high schools across America. We have all heard the grunted assents and emphatic amens from the slick-haired deacons and ladies in floral-print dresses.[15]

What splendid words! One easily forgets that they were spoken by the same Douglass who had earlier attempted to silence Henry Highland Garnet's celebrated "Address to the Slaves." This inflammatory oration, delivered at the Convention of Colored Citizens at Buffalo, New York, in 1843, was widely reprinted in black studies anthologies during the late 1960s. It called on the slaves to "Let your motto be RESISTANCE! RESISTANCE! RESISTANCE! and remember that you are three millions." According to the minutes, the convention was at first "literally infused with tears," and Garnet concluded "amidst great applause." But Frederick Douglass then arose and turned his inimitable skills to suppressing publication of Garnet's speech. Douglass maintained that publication of the

---

[15] Frederick Douglass, "What to the Slave is the Fourth of July," in *Douglass Papers*, Vol. 2, pp. 359–93.

address would lead to an insurrection, and that "He wanted emancipation in a better way, as he expected to have it."[16]

Why his opposition to Garnet's *Address*? Douglass' hatred of slavery is beyond question, so why did he bend his energies to turning the convention against Garnet? He opposed wholesale slave insurrection, fair enough, but Garnet's blowing off steam certainly was not likely to cause an insurrection, and publication of the *Address* presented no danger to the convention movement as became evident when Garnet later published it privately. My suspicion is that ego had much to do with Douglass' opposition. He wanted to assert himself at the convention, and to make certain no one would forget his presence there. Throughout his life, Douglass frequently took issue with other speakers, even when they articulated positions that were at least rhetorically justifiable. He was a genius at semantical distortions, placing words in the mouths of others and then skillfully destroying arguments that his opponents had never made, bullying them into submission with a stentorian power, a talent for mimicry, and a personality as grandly unyielding as a stag in rut.

Douglass' oratory was like "the awful rush of ocean waters," to use one of his famous metaphors, but the forcefulness with which he expressed his opinions sometimes overpowered the fact that he had not really got things right.[17] One suspects that Douglass was frequently more interested in exercising his theatrical skills than in responding to a valid point. In extemporaneous debate, even before hostile audiences, he almost always carried the day.[18] But even the most steadfast of heroes may suffer moments of depression. Douglass was emotionally devastated when fire destroyed his home in Rochester, New York, in 1872, costing him $4,000 and many irreplaceable documents. He seemed to have suffered from depression as a result.

Not all his undertakings resulted in success. The Freedman's Bank failed in the aftermath of the 1873 panic, and Douglass was accused of irresponsibly selling his stock shortly after he assumed the bank's presidency. The accusations pained him, for he hardly benefited from the instability of the times. In fact, his continuing attempts to combine self-interest with

---

[16] *Minutes of the National Convention of Colored Citizens: Held at Buffalo* (New York: Piercy & Reed, Printers, 1843), p. 13. Reprinted in Howard H. Bell, ed., *Proceedings of the National Negro Conventions, 1830–1864* (New York: Arno Press, 1969).

[17] "The Significance of Emancipation in the West Indies: An Address Delivered in Canandaigua, New York, on 3 August 1857," in *Douglass Papers*, Blassingame, ed., Vol. 3, p. 204.

[18] For example, see the aging Douglass' response to hecklers at the World's Columbian Exposition described in William McFeely, *Frederick Douglass*, p. 371.

public service cost him $10,000 when his newspaper, *The New National Era*, failed due to his inability to collect from subscribers during the depression of the 1870s. As United States minister to Haiti, he deluded himself into believing that he could simultaneously advance American and Haitian interests. Resultingly, his superiors in the State Department accused him of ineptitude while African Americans were embarrassed by this position. To his credit, he resigned, instead of trying to tell face-saving lies or persisting in what would have been a false position.

With the passage of time, however, Douglass' moments of defeat have been transmuted into gold by the alchemy of a brilliant personality and the fact that black Americans have always felt a desperate need for heroes. This need is not peculiar to black Americans, who are hardly exceptional in their desire to erect a heroic pantheon. Thus, there will always be a contingent among scholars who will seek to play down the controversial elements in Douglass' autobiographical writings. Historians and biographers have mixed responsibilities to their audiences; they must address problematic issues without seeming to point accusing fingers or to assault the characters of long-dead heroes.

Douglass' sexual relationships were as interesting to his contemporaries as they are to current readers. He was tall and muscular, and his magnetic virility played a role in his success, on the podium and elsewhere. He owed his escape from slavery to the black woman, Anna Murray, who became his first wife. He was a product of plantation culture, which is frequently viewed as a hotbed of Victorian eroticism. Unlike that of his female contemporary, Harriet Jacobs, Douglass' autobiography is almost silent respecting the sexual dynamics of his life in slavery.[19]

Scholars are increasingly interested in his friendships with women, such as that which developed between the aging Douglass and the young black journalist, Ida B. Wells, which was engagingly presented in William McFeely's biography. Wells was one of the few black women who seemed not to resent his second marriage at the age of sixty-six to Helen Pitts, a forty-six-year-old white woman. Anna Murray Douglass, who died in 1882, had been an intelligent manager of his household economics, but he had relied on others for intellectual companionship.

Biographers are often forced to supply missing details in the lives of the saints, and Douglass' best biographers have been required to provide considerable information that he did not choose to reveal. Benjamin

---

[19] Although he does depict the sexual oppression of women, as in describing the beating of Aunt Harriet, Douglass, *Narrative*, Library of America, p. 19.

Quarles's still indispensable biography, *Frederick Douglass* (1948), provided information on Douglass' interactions with white women, that is, the Griffiths sisters and Ottilie Assing, the German reformer. Quarles's mention of his encounter with Assing, and the possibility of a sexual dimension to the relationship, was long overlooked until Maria Diedrich's biography of Assing made it even more "politically incorrect" to ignore it. Quarles commented on the fact that Assing left Douglass a substantial inheritance after her suicide in 1884. Maria Diedrich suggests that Assing's suicide may have been in response to his having chosen Helen Pitts, a younger white woman, as his second wife. Our memories of Douglass are now being reconstructed in ways that make him more fashionable.[20]

He has become more fashionable, although perhaps in ways shaped by the prejudices of present-day scholars. Douglass' belated inclusion in the American literary intellectual tradition has led to his increased prominence in American studies courses. It has accordingly seemed necessary to some scholars to move him from the margins and to resituate him within the "mainstream" American tradition. William L. Andrews, in a preface to *My Bondage and My Freedom*, marks, with a few deft strokes, Douglass' ties to his "Romantic literary" contemporaries of the New England Renaissance, particularly Henry David Thoreau and Margaret Fuller.[21] Such comparisons are, no doubt, helpful and valid, and in my view, worthy of extended exploration. The inclusion of black individuals in broadened definitions of the "American Renaissance" should lead to an enrichment of our ideas of transcendentalism, Romanticism, and nineteenth-century feminism.

To place him in such contexts, however, points up our contradictory aims of portraying him *both* as a figure who "transcends" the cultural limitations of his intellectual environment *and*, at the same time, ironically, as a man representative of that environment. The former role has been questioned by authors like David Van Leer and Jenny Franchot, informed as they are by feminist sensibilities. They view Douglass' self-projection as "The Heroic Slave" as "masculinist." In this vein, Mary Helen Washington and Valerie Smith seemingly concur that the angle of vision in Douglass' *Narrative* is disturbingly biased and thus places it in the category of documents that "by mythologizing rugged individuality,

---

[20] Maria Diedrich, *Love Across Color Lines: Ottilie Assing and Frederick Douglass* (New York: Hill & Wang, 1991), pp. 366–69, 380–82.

[21] Frederick Douglass, *My Bondage and My Freedom*, William L. Andrews, ed. (1855; Urbana: University of Illinois Press, 1987).

physical strength, and geographical mobility . . . enshrine cultural defini-tions of masculinity."[22]

Henry Louis Gates is distressed by the fact that Douglass' elevation to "father of the African American literary tradition is central to the con-struction of an image of the black canon as both male engendered and male dominated."[23] These charges must be taken seriously in any evalu-ation of the cultural and historical factors that have shaped Douglass' literary reputation and have lead to his canonization and continuing dominance within the pantheon of African American heroes and hero-ines. Philip Foner, on the other hand, stressed his activism on behalf of women's rights. Thus, Douglass' position may be seen as representing or transcending traditional cultural restraints. Ironically, placing him within the traditions of feminism and transcendentalism allows us to place a black male author snugly within the existing canon, rather than rethink-ing the canonical categories due to the presence of a black male author.

Another gender-related matter is Douglass' distaste for James Buffum, which may have been a matter of homosexual tensions due to "an enormous degree of love, affection, that Douglass does not respect." That may be what McFeely meant to imply with his citation of a contem-porary commentator, who attributed Buffum's manner to a "feminine" element.[24] There may have been other reasons for Douglass' dislike, how-ever, as the officious and condescending Buffom controlled all traveling expenses during the tour, and it was the presumption of incompetence or distrust that inspired Douglass' dislike, rather than any homophobia that may have been implied. Douglass found interactions with most men diffi-cult as a result of his competitive instincts and territorial obsessions. His hostility to Buffom may have had less to do with the "feminine" qualities than with an unwillingness to tolerate control or supervision by another male.

Allison Davis contrasted Douglass' initial perception of William Lloyd Garrison as "the personification of his fantasy of a 'good father,' with whom he 'initially over-identified.'"[25] Douglass was not unique in this ex-perience, as Alexander Crummell and John Mercer Langston are known to have adopted white males as older brothers or spiritual fathers. Blacks were understandably attached to friendly whites of either sex, as bearers

[22] Mary Helen Washington, *Invented Lives*, p. 8.
[23] Henry Louis Gates, Jr., "From Wheatley to Douglass," in Sundquist, ed., *Frederick Douglass*, p. 47.
[24] McFeely, *Douglass*, p. 121.
[25] Allison Davis, *Leadership, Love and Aggression*, p. 58.

of Christianity, as exemplars of elite American English, as looking-glass selves. Their willingness to accept such friendships, and the acculturation that came with them, hardly indicated slavish personalities. Neither logic nor evidence offers any indication that identification with Africa or with mass cultural traits increased tendencies to militancy or self-respect. In fact, the abolitionist William Cooper Nell rhetorically linked militancy to the acceptance of Anglo-Saxon ideals of heroism, and referred to rebellious slaves as "black Anglo-Saxons" in the tradition of Robin Hood.[26]

Douglass depicts himself as moving primarily in a world of white men and women, whose standard American English and Christian moralism he consciously adopts. His autobiographies leave amazing gaps regarding interactions with other African American leaders, and even the best literary detectives, despite exhaustive investigation, have not filled these lacunae. William Wells Brown reports that Douglass was once interrupted by a heckler who asserted that Douglass' oratorical ability was due to his white ancestry. The tall and substantially built Samuel Ringgold Ward, a man of unquestionably pure ancestry, rose from the audience to acquit himself with oratorical splendor said to surpass that of Douglass. This is interesting coming from Brown, whose mulatto background, abolitionist activity, and record of publication render him comparable to Douglass in several respects.[27]

The life of Douglass is not separable from the complicated and contradictory patterns of deprivation and privilege experienced by mulatto and other privileged slaves. His life illustrates the point that there was little class stratification on plantations. Most farms had too few slaves to allow for a rigid distinction between house Negro and field Negro. Douglass' travels to the "big house farm," his attachment to more than one white family, his urban experiences, his literacy – wherever and whenever acquired – certainly did not fit even the most accurate statistical patterns. Still, there were privileged slaves, and by his own account, he was one of them. Years later, Andrew Johnson, meeting with a group of black

---

[26] William Cooper Nell, *The Colored Patriots of the American Revolution* (New York: Robert F. Wallcut, 1855).

[27] Brilliant investigative work on Douglass has been accomplished by R. J. M. Blackett, *Building an Antislavery Wall: Black Americans in the Atlantic Abolitionist Movement, 1830–1860* (Baton Rouge: Louisiana State University Press, 1983), pp. 79–117, and Dickson J. Preston, *Young Frederick Douglass: The Maryland Years* (Baltimore, MD: Johns Hopkins University Press, 1980). William Wells Brown describes Ward's performance in *The Black Man: His Antecedents, His Genius, and His Achievements* (New York: Thomas Hamilton, 1863), p. 285.

leaders, mentioned his own resentment of privileged persons among the slave population who looked down on poor whites. Douglass responded, "Not I!"[28]

Douglass' autobiographies represent the experiences of a remarkably clever and attractive child who appealed to white adults and often received special treatment because of his personal charm and good looks. He was special, privileged, and extremely lucky – a mulatto who received special treatment, presumably because of white family connections. Douglass sought to render the status of slavery as amorphous as possible and to blur the distinctions between his experience and that of his darker brethren. Furthermore, Douglass, like many of his peers, occupied an ambiguous status between that of house slave and field hand. Douglass acknowledged the fact that his complicated status within the broad sociological category of slavery affected the specific features of his early mental growth and his later career as a writer.

Color diversity among black Americans is a taboo given wide berth in American cultural studies. While it is generally true that the distinction between black and mulatto has never been so clearly defined in North America as putatively as in the Caribbean or in Brazil, there is undeniable truth in the observation of the late Benjamin Quarles that in the United States there are "color lines within the color line." Perhaps it is only a coincidence that the mulatto Frederick Douglass is better remembered and more frequently quoted than his black rival, Martin Delany. Color is, in fact, crucial to understanding, not only the differences between Douglass and Delany, but also some problems with others among his rivals.

Douglass found it convenient to exploit more than one social identity; resultingly, there are points of sensitivity in Douglass' rhetoric, such as an occasional tendency to distinguish between blacks and mulattos. In 1886 he wrote:

> It is only prejudice against the Negro which calls everyone, however nearly connected with the white race, and however remotely connected with the Negro race, a Negro. The motive is not a desire to elevate the Negro, but to humiliate and degrade those of mixed blood; not a desire to bring the Negro up, but to cast the mulatto and the quadroon down by forcing him below an arbitrary and hated color line.[29]

---

[28] Edward McPherson, *The Political History of the United States During Reconstruction* (Solomons & Chapman, 1875), pp. 53–54.

[29] Frederick Douglass, "Future of the Colored Race," *North American Review* (May 1886). Reprinted from Howard Brotz, ed., *Negro Social and Political Thought, 1850–1920* (New York: Basic, 1966), p. 310.

Douglass was not shy about relating the topic of his mulatto status to that of his second marriage to Helen Pitts, a white woman. He insisted that Helen resembled him more closely in physiognomy than Anna Murray, his first wife, and he justified his second marriage not only in terms of his individual right to select his own marriage partner, but also in terms of his mulatto identity. This is most interesting in view of Douglass' sarcastic assertions at certain crucial junctures that he was "only half a negro," or that mulattos, like himself, were not really Negroes.[30]

Douglass' was not committed to ethnic pride. He could make a pilgrimage to the Great Pyramid, mouth the shibboleths of Egyptocentrism, or transform his mother into a pharaoh. He could deliver a lecture associating black Americans with the pyramid builders, and assert the claims of the American Negro to a noble Nilotic past. These displays had less to do with black chauvinism than with asserting that African Americans were fit for American assimilation. Whether he advocated racial amalgamation is difficult to ascertain, as historian Waldo Martin has noted. He did imply a belief that amalgamation was practically inevitable in his 1886 essay, "The Future of the Colored Race," where he virtually repudiated any African identity.[31]

Douglass also had a disturbing tendency to use the image of blackness as a metaphor for evil. Such phrases as "hell black crime of slavery," "heathen darkness," his description of the Fugitive Slave Law as a "hell black enactment," and again as a "hell black law," seem to have elicited little commentary from students of language. Douglass once described slavery as a "dark and ugly hag," an unfortunate metaphor to be employed by a black leader who eventually married a white woman.[32]

Douglass' radically assimilationist sentiments were unthinkable to Douglass' ethnocentric contemporaries, Alexander Crummell, Edward Wilmot Blyden, or the much younger W. E. B. Du Bois, who called for "The Conservation of Races." William McFeely has praised Douglass for repudiating "reverse racism"; Howard Brotz and George Will have made similar observations.[33] It is difficult, however, to believe that those who praise Douglass' advocacy of a "color blind society" are willing to crusade for biological amalgamation as the final solution to American racial

---

[30] *Douglass Papers*, Vol. 2, p. 239; Douglass to O. Johnson, 1885, in Foner, *Douglass*, Vol. 4, p. 427.

[31] Waldo Martin, *The Mind of Frederick Douglass*, p. 304 n. 72.

[32] *Autobiographies*, p. 932; *Douglass Papers*, Vol. 2, pp. 269, 375, 421.

[33] McFeely, *Douglass*, p. 379. Brotz in "Preface to the Second Edition," *African-American Social and Political Thought* (New Brunswick, NJ: Transaction Publishers, 1992).

divisions. Thus, many questions remain as to how we receive the legacy of Frederick Douglass if we view him as our guide toward a future American egalitarian society.

Douglass provides an assimilationist interpretation of black militancy that cannot be summarily dismissed by the cultural pluralists. Black protest and militancy were interwoven with the boisterous tradition of American libertarianism, but also with the amalgamationist "melting pot" ideal. Black militancy is implicitly a variety of American militancy and manifests the forces of cultural and biological assimilation; it does not run against them.[34] Douglass was no prophet of Africanity, and did not see himself at war with Anglo-American values. On the contrary, he and his contemporaries (even black nationalists) emulated the military values of Anglo-Saxon masculinity, accepted bourgeois perfectionist Christianity, and manifested their relish for standards of civilization as they understood them to exist in American society.

Parallels between the life of an even more privileged mulatto, John Mercer Langston, and that of Douglass should not be overstated, nor should they be denied. Langston was the son of Captain Ralph Quarles, a Virginia planter and his concubine, Lucy Langston, and John Mercer was acknowledged in his father's will.[35] At the age of four the boy was turned over to William Gooch, a former slaveholder named guardian in the will, and raised as a member of the family. He was taught to read and write by Virginia Gooch, whom he loved "as a sister." Langston recalled the years spent with the Gooches as a beautiful idyll during which the young mulatto lived the life of a Southern aristocrat. The Gooches remained in Ohio until the boy was seven or eight, but when the family moved to Missouri, he had to be left behind, ironically due to a suit brought by his older brother, William, who feared for his safety if he were carried into a slave state.

Douglass, like Langston, described the nurture and support he received from special members of the master class. He first began to relish the society and manners of the white elite through his relationship with Daniel Lloyd. The following sentence, which appears only in *Life and Times* (492),

---

34 Thomas Dixon, Jr., attacked Tuskegee's program as dangerous and dishonest, claiming, correctly, that Washington's advocacy of cultural assimilation was inseparable from his tacit goal of complete "social equality," but incorrectly insinuating that Washington promoted interracial marriage. See Dixon, "Booker T. Washington and the Negro," *The Saturday Evening Post* (August 19, 1905), 1–3, for Dixon's remarks on Douglass.

35 John Mercer Langston, *From the Virginia Plantation to the National Capital, or The First and Only Negro Representative from the Old Dominion* (Hartford, CT: American Publishing Company, 1894). William and Aimee Lee Cheek, *John Mercer Langston*, pp. 9–29.

is of profound significance, as it advances Douglass' own theory of his rejection of the slave vernacular in early childhood and even before leaving the plantation.

I have often been asked, during the earlier part of my free life at the North, how I happened to have so little of the slave accent in my speech. The mystery is in some measure explained by my association with Daniel Lloyd, the youngest son of Col. Edward Lloyd. The law of compensation holds here as well as elsewhere. While this lad could not associate with ignorance without sharing its shade, he could not give his black playmates his company without giving them his superior intelligence as well.

Already beginning to value and to emulate the "superior intelligence" of the white elite, he inevitably encountered the resentment of the other slaves, especially "the cold-hearted Aunt Katy," who resented Douglass' exposure to the Lloyds and "dem Lloyd niggers." But Douglass recalled, as did Langston, receiving special kindness from white females. Douglass had fond recollections of Daniel Lloyd, who was possibly a half brother, and of Lucretia Auld, a white female, who was possibly a half sister. His fancied relationship to either of them must depend on whether he happened to be thinking of Colonel Lloyd or of Captain Anthony as his possible father.

Langston, unlike Douglass, was acknowledged by his father and remembered in his will. As his biographers have observed, Langston conveyed sentimental recollection of his adoptive white family, the Gooches, sitting "at the evening table, while the handsome colonel and the three young ladies of the family coaxingly plied him with questions and sweetmeats, to which he shyly responded." Douglass was not nearly so advantaged as Langston, but he received more than a few special breaks, and in his narratives he acknowledged emotional ties to his white relatives and his sense of loneliness at the death of Lucretia Anthony Auld.[36]

William Wells Brown, whose experiences more closely resemble those of Douglass, also manifests a mulatto identity. His autobiographical writings are of interest, especially his curiously overlooked *Three Years in Europe, or Places I Have Seen and People I Have Met*. The presence of a group of persons in nineteenth-century America who were highly conscious of their mixed-racial ancestry is incontestable, despite the passionate refusal of some academics and politicians to accept the historical and cultural importance of mulattos in American life.

[36] Cheek and Cheek, *John Mercer Langston*, p. 33. In Douglass, *My Bondage and My Freedom*, see references to Lucretia Auld.

Even for those who did not have the support of white kin, there were advantages to being a slave in Baltimore rather than in the deep South or the frontier territories. There were also advantages to being light skinned, good looking, and a favorite with the owners of the plantation. The *Norton Anthology* tells us that Douglass taught himself to read, but Douglass' narratives reveal a more complex story. Douglass himself reveals that he learned the alphabet and the ability to read a few simple words from his mistress in Baltimore, Sophia Auld. Perhaps the story of Douglass' literacy begins even earlier.

Historian Rayford Logan, in noting, with perhaps intentional abstractness, that "Douglass learned to speak well, to read and write early in life," seems to suggest that his acculturation was never entirely that of a plantation slave.[37] Douglass attributed the fact that his speech contained few traces of slave accent to his early association with Daniel Lloyd, the son of a wealthy planter, Colonel Edward Lloyd, whom Douglass sometimes implied may have been his own father. It is obvious that Douglass acquired his first inclinations toward literacy on the plantation. Douglass had heard that his mother was able to read.[38] His association with Daniel Lloyd certainly did not diminish his discontent with slave vernacular or slave illiteracy. His partial assimilation contributed to his discontent, demonstrating the truth that he was later to hear from Thomas Auld in the telling adage, "Give a nigger an inch, he will take an ell."

This leads to the debate as to whether "mass culture" or "high culture" more typically inculcated militancy, a perennial question in African American studies. In the *Narrative* Douglass reveals an appreciation for both. On the one hand he was grateful for the assistance of the African magician, Sandy, in resisting Covey; on the other, he recognized that his exposure to the Lloyds, his special relationship to Lucretia Anthony Auld, and his residency with the Aulds in Baltimore were influences that brought him into contact with a wider world of culture, and lead to his developing literacy and his expectations of eventual freedom. Douglass poignantly associated his rising expectations with a recollection of a plantation ditty.

I am going away to the Great House Farm!
O, yea! O, yea! O, yea!

It will be useful to bear in mind that Douglass' infrequent references to African American culture included insightful commentary on slave songs

---

[37] Logan's preface to the second edition of *Life and Times*, p. 54.
[38] Douglass, *Bondage and Freedom*, pp. 57–58, 155.

and a strikingly respectful discussion of magical practices. The discussion of magic occurs in his recollection of his frequently celebrated physical contest with Covey the slave breaker. Shortly before his decision to resist Covey's final attempt to whip him, Douglass paid a visit to an older slave in the neighborhood named Sandy who was described as "a genuine African [who] had inherited some of the so-called magical powers said to be possessed by the eastern nations."[39] Sandy advised Douglass to carry the root of a certain herb on his right side, and promised that "with this root about my person, no white man could whip me." Douglass, as is well known, employed Sandy's witchcraft with success, for he "saw in Sandy, with all his superstition, too deep an insight into human nature not to have some respect for his advice" (Douglass, *Autobiographies*, 280, 281). The foregoing observation, present in all Douglass' autobiographies, expresses more than tolerance; it shows an outright sympathy for Afrocentric folk practices, and it would seem to be an unusual example of nineteenth-century "multiculturalism."

Howard Brotz has argued that Douglass rejected multiculturalism, an observation that is not entirely false, despite its obvious "presentism."[40] The term "multiculturalism" was not current in the 1880s, and the discourse of twentieth-century "multiculturalism" should not be carelessly interjected into nineteenth-century debates. What Douglass specifically rejected was the withholding of literate culture from the black population. This is something quite different than a rejection of multiculturalism, and cannot be separated from the tendency of the times to confuse cultural difference with racial inferiority. Nor, viewed within context, can Douglass' beliefs be separated from the Lamarckian beliefs that dominated his oft-cited essay "The Claims of the Negro Ethnologically Considered." Douglass' later interest in evolutionary theory led to some revision of his raciology, serving at the same time to buttress his progressivist views. Both issues, deriving from the influences of Darwinism, should be of interest to scholars who seek to understand Douglass' evolving theory of human progress.

Scholars should be interested in investigating this issue within the context of Douglass' perennial hostility to superstition, especially as he believed it to occur in the religious traditions of the black masses. Sterling Stuckey, in *Slave Culture*, has noted this tendency among other

---

[39] Not necessarily Africa, since roots have magical significance in European civilization as well. *The Columbia Encyclopedia*, 5th ed., (Columbia University Press, 1975) gives magical properties of Mandrake Root. Also see Genesis 30:14–16.

[40] Presentist scholarship has attempted to enlist Douglass in the debate over multiculturalism. See Brotz in the preface to the second edition of *Negro Thought in America*.

black leaders, most notably in the African Methodist Bishop Daniel Alexander Payne. Kenneth Warren has observed that "Douglass's disapproval of black Protestant oratory is well-known." Douglass admitted to some alienation from the southern style of mass leadership. He was infected with the somewhat condescending spirit of what Kevin Gaines has called "uplift ideology" (3).[41]

In *The Life and Times*, Douglass gives evidence of this missionary spirit, saying "In my communication with colored people I have endeavored to deliver them from the power of superstition, bigotry, and priestcraft." Douglass' political rhetoric, like the several versions of his narrative, was inconsistent, a point that is well documented by Kenneth W. Warren. His attitudes toward the black masses are most confusing in that he seeks to derive his authenticity from identification with those masses, while at the same time stressing his alienation from the "great unwashed," whether in Rome, Cairo, or the American South.[42]

Henry Highland Garnet practically accused Douglass, who had been elevated to the status of deacon in the African Methodist Episcopal Church, of apostasy in 1849, describing him as "Being matchless in mimicry and unrivaled in buffoonery, he amuses scoffers and infidels by imitating their religious services." Fellow abolitionist, Sojourner Truth, once supposedly confronted him with the question, "Frederick, is God dead?"[43] This public embarrassment may have been the source of continuing resentment that later occasioned his deprecation of Truth's speaking style (*Life and Writings*, 507). Douglass was accused of heresy by Reverend Walter Henderson Brooks when, in 1882, he critiqued the biblical account of creation and asserted that it was man, not God, who brought about progressive change in the world (*Papers*, 2:284). Future scholars may wish to investigate the changes in Douglass' uses of the Bible in his autobiographies and other writings.

David Blight sees Douglass as a clever manipulator of religious rhetoric.[44] To this I would add the observation that Douglass displayed complex and ambivalent feelings about religion and was not above

[41] Kenneth Warren, "Images of Douglass," in Eric Sundquist, ed., *Frederick Douglass*, p. 259. Kevin Gaines, *Uplift Ideology*, p. 3. David Swift notes friction between Douglass and Henry Highland Garnet in *Black Prophets of Justice*, p. 255.

[42] *Life and Times of Frederick Douglass*, Library of America ed., p. 909.

[43] Bennett, *Pioneers*, p. 126, but Nell Painter questions whether the incident ever occurred in *Sojourner Truth: A Life, a Symbol* (New York: Norton, 1996), pp. 260–62.

[44] David Blight, *Frederick Douglass' Civil War* (Baton Rouge: Louisiana State University Press, 1989). Also see James Moorhead, *American Apocalypse: Yankee Protestants and the American Civil War, 1860–1869* (New Haven, CT: Yale University Press, 1978).

employing emotional Christian fundamentalism in his 1854 attack on
scientific racism. Douglass made the emotional appeal that ethnologists
must obviously be wrong in their demarcation of Africans as a subhuman
species because their theories were in conflict with the Bible. This employment of a fundamentalist rhetoric is particularly interesting in view of the
frequent apostasy and infidelity charges.

Harold Cruse speaks of the "internal dialectic" between black nationalist and integrationist ideologies. Howard Brotz contrasted the assimilationist tradition represented by Frederick Douglass with a nationalist or emigrationist tradition represented by Martin Delany, Alexander
Crummell, and Edward Wilmot Blyden, *inter alia*. In a youthful work,
many years ago, I accepted the nationalist/integrationist distinction but
offered two caveats. Integrationists, like Douglass, have frequently engaged in black nationalist rhetoric and black nationalists, like Crummell,
have stressed cultural assimilation even while advocating geopolitical and
institutional separatism.[45]

Although Douglass was never comfortable with black American chauvinism, he occasionally – and perhaps even to his own surprise – expressed himself in a rhetoric harmonious with that of black nationalism.
As an independent black newspaper publisher, he became a sometime
supporter of African American institutional separatism. He accommodated pragmatically to the idea of separate black trade schools, at a time
when alternative opportunities for black industrial training were practically nonexistent. On the eve of the Civil War, he flirted with the idea of
African American emigration to Haiti. He supported the black chauvinist
tradition, which identified pharaonic Egypt with the rest of Africa, and
claimed that the ancient Egyptians were racially identical to nineteenth-
century African Americans. On the other hand, he opposed the "Back to

[45] Harold Cruse, *The Crisis of the Negro Intellectual* (New York: William Morrow, 1967).
    The original edition of Howard Brotz, *Negro Social and Political Thought, 1850–1925*
    (New York: Basic Books, 1966) bears comparison to his *The Black Jews of Harlem* (New
    York: Schocken, 1964), which was a celebration of black separatism and self help and
    reflected his admiration for the "Black Jews," who segregated themselves from American
    Judaism and were lifting themselves independently by their own bootstraps. A new in-
    troduction written for *African-American Social and Political Thought* (New Brunswick, NJ:
    Transaction, 1992) rejected the black separatism celebrated in his earlier work, but at-
    tacked "affirmative action," thus failing to endorse the alternative to separatism, which
    is institutional and biological intermingling of black and white people into a religiously
    undifferentiated and ethnically amalgamated America. My work *The Golden Age of Black
    Nationalism*, published in 1978, reissued with a new preface by Oxford University Press
    (New York, 1988), argued that black nationalism need not reject cultural assimalation.

Africa Movement" of the 1850s, and he never accepted the idea that black Americans were a "peculiar people" with a separate and independent destiny, apart from other Americans. In fact, in his later years, Douglass denounced the ideas of racial pride and ethnic solidarity.

Douglass claimed that he once seriously considered emigrating from the United States, but reconsidered immediately on the fall of Fort Sumter. Frederick Douglass claimed that he was on the brink of an exploratory mission to the black republic of Haiti, long a focus of black nationalist and emigrationist plans. Sure enough, if one takes a look at a facsimile of *Douglass' Monthly* for May 1861, one will see a front-page article in which Douglass describes a planned trip to Haiti, followed by another article in which he postpones the expedition. One wonders if this is not a somewhat dramatic exploitation of a journalistic situation, albeit the newspaper had been carrying a series of articles on Haiti for several months.

Douglass was primarily concerned with the African American struggle for abolitionism, despite universalist concerns. Abolitionism was the only arena of public intellectualism from which blacks were not summarily barred. Like all abolitionists and black nationalists, however, he frequently employed a rhetorical strategy that aligned the struggle for black freedom with a universal humanism and the struggle for the rights of all oppressed peoples. Douglass was in a tradition of African American leaders, including W. E. B. Du Bois and Marcus Garvey, who saw parallels between the contest for Irish independence and the African American freedom struggle. Douglass' courageous attacks on British anti-Catholicism may be seen as a form of nineteenth-century "multiculturalism." His defense of the struggles of Irish Catholics are particularly impressive at a time when hostilities between African Americans and Irish Catholic immigrants were bitter and violent. Douglass also supported the struggles of the Hungarian people.[46]

Crummell was correct to criticize him for his continued reliance on antislavery rhetoric, which reflected a persistent and unhealthy nostalgia for the great days of the abolitionist movement. It was on the petard of slavery that Douglass had hoisted himself into the position of principal black spokesman, and in the aftermath of the Civil War, Douglass' rhetorical platform began to slip from beneath him. With the demise of slavery, he was unable to construct a public role that spoke adequately to the problems of Reconstruction. During the reign of terror following the collapse of Reconstruction, new social and economic problems of staggering scope

[46] *Papers*, Vol. 2, p. 292. *Life and Times*, Library of America ed., pp. 428, 682–83.

required leadership in a different mold – not the cringing accommodationism of Booker T. Washington, whom Crummell despised, but certainly a leadership with something more to offer than powerless moralizing.

The success of the abolition movement confirmed Douglass' sense of himself as an American, and in his theory of history, the Civil War became a second American revolution in which his occasional and halfhearted black separatist nationalism was converted to American "millennial nationalism." David Blight has said that "Douglass staked his own claim to citizenship in a nation reborn and reunified.... He entered the Civil War in 1861 with a tattered but unbroken faith in his version of a promised America, and he emerged from the fury in 1865 with a sense of nationhood." This is true enough, if we remember that the concepts of American nationalism and black nationalism were both in flux during the Civil War. In the past, Douglass had flirted with black nationalism and even considered emigration, but the Civil War had redefined the American nation and enabled his complete and final rejection of black nationalism. Douglass had come to believe in a continuity between the egalitarian promises of the Declaration of Independence and those of the Emancipation Proclamation. In his mind the Civil War was an apocalyptic struggle that had proved that continuity. It had advanced his optimistic faith in the metaphysics of progress and his belief in an evolving American nationality, destined to include "Colored Americans."[47]

The nineteenth-century United States was an English-speaking, white, Protestant empire – a fact that was not altered during the twentieth century. Douglass simply was not equipped to meet the challenge of ethnic politics, which were beginning to influence American ward politics. Neither Irish Catholics nor German Jews were inclined to publicly object to the fundamentally Anglo-Protestant ideals on which it was assumed American institutions and values were based. They were, however, beginning to create their own alternative institutions that would eventually provide them with the economic experience and political leverage that later allowed them to shift into an integrationist stance. And this was the fundamental failure of Douglass – his inability to understand the coming age of ethnic politics and political ward bosses.

---

[47] David Blight's *Frederick Douglass' Civil War*, like the work of the present author, is influenced by James Moorhead, *American Apocalypse*. Blight's discussion of Douglass' evolving sense of American nationality is particularly innovative. See pp. 101–121, 244. For Douglass and the metaphysic of progress check index entries in Wilson J. Moses, *Afrotopia*.

Through abolitionism black Americans were Americanized and came to see themselves as Americans 1) institutionally through participation in an integrated movement and 2) culturally through participation in the American liberal tradition. At the end of the Civil War, black Americans were no longer calling themselves Africans. For the moment, at least, they believed they were Americans. They felt confirmed in their citizenship and vindicated in their faith that America's religious values and political ideology were destined for ascendancy over the emotional baggage of white supremacy.

On the day that Rebel troops began their shelling of Fort Sumter, Frederick Douglass editorialized in his newspaper, "They have shot off the legs of all trimmers and compromisers." In fact, the rebellion also shot the legs off Frederick Douglass. Over the preceding dozen years, Douglass had hoisted himself into the position of principal black spokesman. No black leader has ever enjoyed such unrivaled status before or since. Yet with the coming of the Civil War – which he sat out just as Thomas Jefferson sat out the Revolutionary War – Douglass lost his rhetorical platform. With slavery dead, he was unable to construct a public role that spoke adequately to the problems of Reconstruction. Retrospectively, the historian Howard Brotz has come to view this rejection of social engineering as a mark of wisdom, but neither Alexander Crummell nor Booker T. Washington nor W. E. B. Du Bois was inclined to such a view.[48]

Even the most rigorous scholarly appraisals of Douglass sometimes border on hagiography. Motivated by a desire to provide young African Americans with historical models, some historians have skirted such issues as Douglass' hostility to black unity and his pragmatic demonstration of a belief in racial amalgamation. These positions are not of necessity blameworthy, and even if they were, they would not require a cover-up. Douglass' greatness does not depend solely on his status as an African American hero. Frederick Douglass requires no special pleading, and should receive none. According to all evidence Douglass was one of the brightest lights among nineteenth-century orators. His speeches and writings display a timeless brilliance, a universal statesmanship, and a forceful logic. His greatness is undeniable – and so was his major flaw, an egocentric interpretation of history that led him to confuse his individual progress with the experience of an entire people.

---

[48] In the "politically corrected" 1992 edition of *African-American Social and Political Thought*, Brotz, by opposing both affirmative action and black separatism, leaves black people few choices (see pp. x–xxvii).

Douglass was capable of formulating a less egocentric theory of human progress, as he demonstrated in a lecture on Galileo, "'It Moves,' or the Philosophy of Reform." Douglass was, in fact, a "progressive," in the broadest sense of that term. He spoke in the traditions of Condorcet's enlightenment perfectionism and Comte's "scientific" optimism.[49] His philosophy, like that of Darwin and Marx, assumed the superiority of Western European civilization, but Douglass gave Eurocentrism an egalitarian twist. His theory of uplift was based on the moral absolutism of the progressive-liberal, white, upper-middle-class culture that eventually flourished in the egalitarianism of Mary White Ovington, Mary McLeod Bethune, and Eleanor Roosevelt. Like most progressive/liberals, black or white, Douglass was a cultural absolutist. In the approaching twentieth century, neither liberals nor conservatives nor feminists nor Christian conservatives nor Marxists were destined to accept the idea of moral relativism.

Cultural relativism would have undermined Douglass' claims to moral authority and given credibility to the preachments of slaveholders who argued that theirs was a "peculiar" society whose "peculiar institution" reflected and supported the habits and customs peculiar to the African personality, whose natural condition was subordination to whites. Douglass insisted that there was only one culture, only one civilization, only one theory of progress, and only one set of natural laws and rights. All people were the same under the skin, and all had the same ultimate destiny in a world that must ultimately make no distinctions of ethnicity. He vacillated on this last point, but almost invariably, he argued in favor of cultural assimilation.[50]

"Free the slaves and leave them alone" had been his motto for many years, and he was now reluctant to offer a definitive prescription for American race and ethnic relations, or a definitive plan for cultural and economic change. The collapse of the Freedmen's Bureau demonstrated the unreliability of government as defender of political rights. The decision of the Supreme Court in the Slaughterhouse cases signalled that government regulation meant little more than reconstructing the Fourteenth Amendment as a support for the privileges of business. Douglass had never had much faith in "complexional institutions," and after the

---

[49] Kenneth Warren tantalizes us with his allusions to Douglass' "Progressive Rhetoric" (Sundquist, p. 253), and Waldo Martin calls our attention to Douglass' observations on "the history of progress". (Sundquist, p. 277).

[50] Although there were some contradictory multicultural statements. See my *Afrotopia* for a fuller discussion on pages 127–28.

sabotage of the Freedmen's Bureau and the betrayal of the Freedman's Bank, he settled into a doctrine of laissez-faire, in which greed was to be regulated only by the invisible hand of moral sentiments.[51] He became suspicious of planned and regulated economies in an era when government regulation was synonymous with the privileging of business to the disadvantage of agricultural and industrial workers.

Douglass' most problematic contradiction was that he wanted social engineering and yet he did not. His career following the Civil War was inextricably bound up with the necessary growth of governmental bureaucracies, and yet he was emotionally committed to a doctrine of "Free the slaves and leave them alone." He was ideologically compromised by the fundamental contradictions of Jacksonian democracy, a doctrine that combined bully preachments of majority rule and leveling egalitarianism with uncompromising white supremacy. Nonetheless, he maintained a bias against "complexional institutions."

Douglass was not blind to the fact that America was changing from an agrarian empire into a smokestack civilization of iron, coal, steel, and railroads. He knew that the 1880s were an era of telephones, high finance, and international electronic communications, but Douglass does not seem to have grasped the need for new strategies to meet the needs of the postslavery industrial commonwealth. The inertial momentum of his own remarkable progress led Douglass to retain his faith in the evolutionary potential of antiinstitutional democracy – despite the proven dangers of that tradition – and to rely on the seemingly inevitable movement of American history toward its manifestly progressive destiny, unassisted by the mechanics of social engineering.

---

[51] The failure of the Freedman's Bank was one of several economic debacles during the later decades of the nineteenth century, a period erroneously characterized as the triumph of laissez-faire. Vigorous activism by all three branches of government regulated the economy to the advantage of favored commercial and industrial interests, and Congress participated in financial conspiracies. Ironically, the Fourteenth Amendment increasingly ignored the formerly enslaved people, whose rights it was supposedly intended to guarantee, and created new rights for the corporations, defined by the Supreme Court as "individuals" to be protected by the due process clause. Walter L. Fleming, *The Freedmen's Savings Bank: A Chapter in the Economic History of the Negro Race* (Chapel Hill: University of North Carolina Press, 1927). Carl R. Osthaus, *Freedman, Philanthropy and Fraud: A History of the Freedman's Bank* (Urbana: University of Illinois Press, 1976).

3

Where Honor Is Due

Frederick Douglass as Representative Black Man

Frederick Douglass' status as the greatest African American abolitionist and orator of the nineteenth century seems unshakable. He was certainly the most accomplished master of self-projection. Appropriating
with stunning genius the Euro-American myth of the self-made man, he
guaranteed that the story of his struggle would be canonized, not only
within an African American tradition, but within the traditions of the
mainstream. He manipulated the rhetoric of Anglo-Saxon manhood as
skillfully as did any of his white contemporaries, including such master
manipulators as Abraham Lincoln, Ralph Waldo Emerson, and Phineas
T. Barnum. I mention Douglass along with these wily exemplars of American showmanship, not because I want to drag out embarrassing cliches
about making heroes more human, but in order to address the truly monumental nature of Douglass' accomplishments. Douglass, like Lincoln,
Emerson, and Barnum, was abundantly endowed with the spiderish craft
and foxlike cunning that are often marks of self-made men.

Douglass, like his bluff contemporary Walt Whitman, made his living
by the art of self-celebration, a skill that has always figured in the strategies
of American literary figures. He sang his song of himself through four
main versions of his autobiography, creating himself as a mythic figure
and racial icon. The result is that even scholars and historians who may
be relatively unfamiliar with other black American personalities of the
nineteenth century are acquainted with the major events of Douglass' life,
or at least with his version of them. He was born into slavery in 1818,
escaped to the North in 1838, and with amazing rapidity, by 1840, was
well on the way to establishing himself as the principal black abolitionist
in the United States. Among his other accomplishments, Douglass served

as a newspaper editor, Civil War recruiter, president of the Freedman's Bank, minister to Haiti, recorder of deeds, and marshall of the District of Columbia. In the final analysis, he was a man of great dignity, principle, and courage, but he was also a showman, and he made his living mainly by cultivating the myth of Frederick Douglass.

When he attempted to function as a businessman or politician, he sometimes waded in beyond his depth, and thus, he was embarrassed by the failure of the Freedman's Bank shortly after he assumed its presidency. His tenure as minister to Haiti was troubled from the beginning. As he made preparations to assume the post, he found that he could not get first class accommodations by railroad or steamboat going south. Special arrangements were made for him to travel on a U.S. naval vessel, the *Kearsarge*, which moved some to comment that not every black American found it possible to avoid the indignities of Jim Crow travel. Douglass was constantly pressured by the State Department and the American business community to deal with the Haitians in an imperious and insulting manner. This, to his credit, he would not do. Black people everywhere identified passionately with Haiti, the world's first sovereign black republic, and Douglass could not allow himself to be seen as a puppet for American racist expansionism. As part of his duties, he attempted to negotiate for a military base at Môle St. Nicholas, but his respect for Haitian sovereignty led to his being accused of incompetency by those whose interests he refused to slavishly serve. When his efforts were unsuccessful, whites rebuked him as an inept representative of American interests.

But even Douglass' setbacks were somehow transmuted into victories by the alchemy of a brilliant personality and the fact that black America has always had a desperate need for heroes. Nonetheless, it must be admitted that many aspects of Douglass' life and writings are controversial. No serious historian can ignore the problem of self-serving selectivity that lies behind the veil of homely modesty that he assumed in his autobiographical writings. The task of every biographer of Frederick Douglass has been to fill in some of the discreet omissions in Douglass' skillful work of self-promotion. Historians and literary scholars are increasingly aware of the craft with which Douglass manipulated audiences, and readers, and they have recently provided us with considerable information that Douglass did not see fit to reveal. Many of these matters were discussed in the first full-length biography of Douglass, published by Benjamin Quarles in 1948.[1] More recent biographers have built on Quarles's work, giving

---

[1] Benjamin Quarles, *Frederick Douglass* (Washington, DC: The Association for the Study of Negro Life and History, 1948).

us a portrait that is admirable and believable; nonetheless, in far too many instances, Douglass has been allowed to dictate the terms of his own biography.[2]

Because even the best biographies of Douglass have been appendices to his own brilliant autobiographical writings, the point is often forgotten that Douglass was not a gigantic abnormality in black American history, but in many ways a typical black American man of the class and region he represented. In typical American fashion, Douglass sought, in his writings, to demonstrate his individuality along with his individualism. The very self-reliance and independence that he stressed in his autobiographies represented conformity to the American type of the self-made man. Thus, Douglass was, to use Emerson's phrase, a representative man. Much of the present day biographical and literary treatment of Douglass makes him appear to be exceptional. For his own part, Douglass, at times, stressed the Emersonian dictum that the great man is often great because he is representative, not because he is exceptional. Self-reliance, for him, as for Emerson, often existed in the paradox of blending one's ego into larger "transcendental" forces, of believing that what is true of one's self is true of others. Douglass' concept of self-reliance, like Emerson's, was grounded in the principle of universality, rather than difference. Douglass was, as I hope to show presently, not only a representative man, but a representative *black* man.

And then, on the other hand, there were ways in which he was not representative. Douglass seemed, at times, to be less attuned to the cultural sentiments of black Americans and to their political struggles than were some other black men among his contemporaries. Among black power advocates, he is celebrated as a prophet of self-determination. They celebrate his founding of *The North Star,* an independent newspaper, and it is with relish that they recall his rallying cry, "We must be our own representatives!" But Douglass could change positions dramatically on black power related issues. He did, at times, champion black institutions, and then, on other occasions, he denounced them as self-segregating. Douglass' ideology was thoroughly inconsistent, usually opportunistic, and always self-serving. I suspect that if Douglass were alive today, he

---

[2] Dickson J. Preston was the first scholar to address the contradictions in the autobiography of Douglass. See Dickson J. Preston, *Frederick Douglass: The Maryland Years* (Baltimore, MD: Johns Hopkins University Press, 1980). Preston's work inspired the psychological analysis of Allison Davis in *Leadership, Love and Aggression* (New York: Harcourt Brace Jovanovich, 1983). Henry Louis Gates in *Figures in Black*, (Oxford, 1987) p. 114, said "Preston has given us in his major biography a more three dimensional, more human Frederick Douglass than has any other biographer." The statement was true at the time.

would be as uncontrollable as ever, and that his often shifting ideology would be now, as it was then, often unacceptable to liberals and conservatives alike.

Douglass represented a class of free black males who were literate in English, influenced by Christianity, and afflicted with a sometimes unconscious Anglophilism.[3] Mary Helen Washington and Valerie Smith remind us he was obsessed with attempts to emulate and compete with white males in terms of the values of assertive masculinity.[4] Nonetheless, the recent interpretation by William McFeely depicts Douglass in ways specifically adapted to liberal ideologies of the 1980s.[5] A case in point is Douglass' relationship to the women's movement. He did indeed commendably support women's suffrage, but this support was, at times, less than lukewarm. Douglass gave black male suffrage a much higher priority than white female suffrage, even when his feminist friends became exasperated with him. While on the one hand he got along well with white liberal females, and even married one of them, he was not afraid to confront them when he felt their interests to be in conflict with his as a black male.

Today there is endless discussion of Douglass' private life, and his friendships with women, both black and white, for we now know much more about his personal affairs than did his earlier biographers. Douglass had a commanding personality; he was strikingly handsome and stood over six feet tall; he was athletic and he possessed an intense sexual attractiveness. I believe that a great deal of what he accomplished was a result of his magnetic virility. As Mary Helen Washington has observed, he largely owed his escape from slavery to a black woman, Anna Murray, who became his first wife. One historian has speculated, probably accurately, that Anna was pregnant with their first child, Rosetta, before the couple left the South. It is impossible not to be curious about the early sexual development of Douglass, who later portrayed himself as a puritanical feminist, an image that was so useful to him in his dealing with his New England abolitionist contemporaries. Was it really possible for a heterosexual black male to grow up in a slave society without being affected by the earthy values of plantation sexuality? Douglass' autobiography is

---

[3] See the chapter "Political Nationalism and Cultural Assimilation" in Wilson J. Moses, *The Golden Age of Black Nationalism* (1978; reprinted New York: Oxford University Press, 1988), pp. 15–31.

[4] Mary Helen Washington quotes Valerie Smith in Mary Helen Washington, ed., *Invented Lives: Narratives of Black Women, 1860–1960* (Garden City, NY: Doubleday, 1987).

[5] William S. McFeely, *Frederick Douglass* (New York: Norton, 1991).

silent on such matters, unlike that of his eighteenth-century predecessor, Benjamin Franklin, who admits to sexual adventurism during youth.

In recent years, black feminists have become increasingly critical of Douglass' treatment of his first wife. Anna Douglass was a dutiful help-mate to her husband; she was a hard worker and a thrifty housewife. A portion of Douglass' financial success has been attributed to her able administration of his domestic finances, but she was not up to the management of a newspaper, and she apparently never learned to read. Further-more, it does not seem that she provided Douglass with much in the way of intellectual companionship. For this, he often went outside his home. The women were usually white, and his friendship in later years with the young journalist Ida B. Wells is the best-known intellectual friendship he is known to have developed with a black woman. It is interesting to note, in this regard, that Wells frequently separated herself ideologically from other black women leaders. That uncompromising militancy that earned her the hostility of the leadership of the National Association of Colored Women apparently endeared her to Douglass, while isolating her from the likes of Mary Church Terrell and Margaret Murray Washington. Ida B. Wells was, significantly, one of the few black women who did *not* resent his second marriage at the age of sixty-six (after Anna's death) to Helen Pitts, a forty-six-year-old white woman.

Douglass' ambivalent feelings toward Sojourner Truth are mentioned in the previous chapter along with the untraceable legend that she once caused him public annoyance by responding to his declamations with the question, "Frederick, is God dead?" This was a matter of some embarrass-ment, since Douglass was more than once plagued by charges of irreligios-ity. Sojourner Truth, on the other hand, was closely associated with the strident religiosity of the day, and was much more closely related to pro-letarian evangelical Christianity than was the transcendental Douglass, with his increasing pretensions to gentility. Late in life, Douglass dealt with Truth rather ungenerously when he compared her speaking style to the ungainly dialect of a minstrel show, implying that her language was "grotesque" and only quoted in order to belittle and degrade black people generally.

Douglass' relationships with white women generated controversy as early as 1849, when he paraded down Broadway in New York with the two Englishwomen Julia and Eliza Griffiths – one on each arm. Julia even-tually moved in with the Douglass family to assist with the operation of *The North Star*, and within a year, she had brought it from the brink of ruin to a sound financial footing. Rumor was rife in the abolitionist community that the relationship between Douglass and Miss Griffiths had led to difficulties in the Douglass household. Apparently the relationship was purely a matter of business and political sympathy. Douglass' relationship with Ottillie Assing, a German reformer, is still the subject of speculation and some historians are convinced that the friendship had a sexual dimension. It has, however, long been known that Assing left Douglass a substantial inheritance after her suicide in 1884. Diedrich and McFeely suggest that the suicide was a result of hearing the news of Douglass' second marriage to Helen Pitts.

Douglass' relationships with white women were not without troubles of another sort. In 1865, he was angered by what Waldo Martin has called the "blatant racism" of Elizabeth Cady Stanton.[6] Stanton was incensed by the denial of women's voting rights, and protested that this denial placed white women on a level "classed with idiots, lunatics, and Negroes." This statement, and others that were even more offensive, would seem to indicate that Stanton saw black people as inferior to white women. Douglass took exception to being classed with idiots and lunatics, but the friendship apparently endured, and Stanton was a well-wisher at the time of Douglass' second marriage.

It is not difficult to understand why Douglass played up to white feminists after the demise of the abolitionist movement, for in them he found a receptive audience for his writings and speeches. Within this view, his marriage to a white feminist was not only an affair of the heart, but a significant political move. Black men and women were not well-positioned to help him maintain public visibility once the abolitionist movement had run its course; the women's rights movement, headed by white women, still offered him a forum. Another way of seeing it was that in his first marriage he made an alliance with a free black woman who could assist him in his flight to freedom. In his second marriage, he cemented ties with his new audience, which was largely composed of white feminists.

In an 1884 letter to Elizabeth Cady Stanton, Douglass argued the naturalness of his marriage to a white woman, saying that his closest personal friends for the preceding forty years had been white.[7] It was true enough that many of his friends had been white women, with whom he interacted in the abolitionist and women's movements. It was equally true that many

---

[6] Waldo Martin, *The Mind of Frederick Douglass* (Chapel Hill: University of North Carolina Press, 1984), p. 158.

[7] Frederick Douglass to Elizabeth Cady Stanton, May 30, 1884, in Philip S. Foner, ed., *The Life and Writings of Frederick Douglass*, 4 volumes (New York: International, 1950–1955), 4:410.

of his strongest supporters and most intimate associates had been black during those forty years. Had Douglass forgotten that his marriage to Helen Pitts had been performed in a black church, the Fifteenth Street Presbyterian, and the ceremony performed by the Reverend Francis J. Grimké, like himself a mulatto with privileged ties to his white family? Like Douglass, Grimké was the offspring of a wealthy white planter and a slave mother. Archibald Grimké, Frank's brother, had married a white woman in 1879.

Like other black male leaders of his generation, including the Grimké brothers, William Wells Brown, and John Mercer Langston, Douglass had a complex set of feelings regarding his identity as the son of a white man. There have been interesting speculations, of late, as to whether Douglass actually knew and loved his white father.[8] In one version of his autobiography, Douglass reports the rumor that his master was his father. In another version, he does not repeat the rumor, but instead describes the boyhood memory of his master leading him about by the hand, and treating him affectionately and calling him "his little Indian boy." The late Allison Davis, a distinguished black American psychologist at the University of Chicago, opined that Douglass did, in fact, know his white father, and that he spent his entire life attempting to win the love of his rejecting parent. Davis also made much of what he saw as a father-son relationship between Douglass and his white patron, William Lloyd Garrison.[9]

There can be no doubt that Douglass had great respect for Garrison, the contentious and courageous white abolitionist, who strongly influenced his ideology in the early years after his escape from slavery. As a Garrisonian, Douglass often shared the platform with Charles Lennox Remond, who until that time had been the foremost of Garrison's black supporters. But Douglass soon supplanted Remond as the premier black antislavery lecturer. Then, over the next several years, Douglass went through the painful process of separating himself from the Garrisonian position. Perhaps as a result of contact with Samuel Ringgold Ward, who rejected some of Garrison's positions, Douglass eventually began to challenge Garrison himself. In a move that occasioned much bitterness, he moved out on his own to become a newspaper editor and to champion

[8] Allison Davis, *Leadership, Love and Aggression* (New York: Harcourt Brace Jovanovich, 1983), pp. 18–19.

[9] Davis, *Leadership, Love and Aggression*, p. 58. But interestingly, Davis sees Garrison as having confused and complex feelings toward Douglass, who, Davis suggests, played dual roles as both dominant and subordinate male figures in Garrison's unconscious thinking, p. 69.

the view that the Constitution was not a proslavery compact, but a living document that could be effectively used in the crusade against slavery.

Douglass' complaints against the white abolitionists had a foundation on a personal level as well. On his first trip to England in 1845, Douglass was forced to travel with the officious and condescending James Buffum, a white American, who doled out Douglass' traveling expenses. One contemporary observed in Buffum "an enormous degree of love, affection," which he attributed to a "feminine" element in Buffum's manner "that Douglass does not respect."[10] But what truly enraged Douglass, we can be certain, was the idea that he could not be trusted to handle his own financial affairs. Douglass was also offended by the insistence of some white abolitionists that he deliver his speeches in plantation dialect. Plantation dialect was not Douglass' preferred style of discourse. He was proud of his standard English and he had acquired it before leaving the South, since he had spent some of his time on the plantation in the "big house." Furthermore, he was committed to expanding the content of his lectures to include not only his personal reminiscences, but his developing philosophy of human rights. In the second edition of his autobiography, he expressed his resentment of those white abolitionists who wanted him to confine himself to descriptions of his personal victimization.

But Douglass' break with Garrison arose from philosophical issues as well as personality conflicts. In large part, his changing attitude had to do with the influences of other black men, often occurring in conventions of black men. In his autobiography, he does, in fact, speak of the importance of these conventions. Douglass admits to bonding with black men before his escape from slavery, and describes these friendships with vivid detail. He shares with us the affectionate recollection of studying the Bible with Father Lawson, the pious preacher. He recalls, with gratitude, how Sandy Jenkins assisted him after his beating by Covey and how he gave him the magic root that helped him finally to resist him. And in his autobiography, he credits the influences of other black men with whom he interacted after his escape from slavery.

In a chapter of his autobiography of 1892 entitled "Honor To Whom Honor," Douglass acknowledged several black men who were rivals, and who clearly possessed intellects and rhetorical skills of their own. Douglass, to his credit, did pay tribute to Samuel Ringgold Ward, whom he acknowledged as the greatest black orator of the day. Ward probably had a hand in persuading Douglass away from the sterile and narrow

---

[10] Quoted in McFeely, *Frederick Douglass*, p. 121.

Garrisonian interpretation of the Constitution, since it was during a debate with Ward that Douglass was forced to analyze the logic of the Garrisonian position. Ward presented him with the position, putatively held by the majority of black people, that the Constitution could bear interpretation as an antislavery document.[11]

William Wells Brown, another black abolitionist, reports an interesting story concerning Douglass and Ward. Douglass was once interrupted on the podium by a heckler who asserted that Douglass' oratorical ability was due to his white ancestry. It happened that Ward, a tall and robust man of unadulterated African ancestry, was in the audience and rose to acquit himself in such a manner as to impress some in the audience that he was certainly on a par with Douglass.

Douglass' relationship with Martin Delany was also significant. When in 1848, over the objections of Garrison, Douglass founded his newspaper, *The North Star*, it was with Delany as coeditor. But Douglass soon fell out with Delany over a number of issues; most important among these was the issue of black pride. "I thank God for making me a man simply," said Douglass, "but Delany always thanks him for making him a '*black* man.'"[12] Douglass considered Delany a racial chauvinist and an extremist. Delany did, in fact, show a great interest in Africa and in the prospects of founding a national homeland for the black race, a position that Douglass could not endorse. He once said that, if he were inclined to go to Africa, he would unhesitatingly enroll under Delany's leadership, but Douglass had no interest either in going or in supporting the movement. Delany's position implied that American slavery would not be abolished until a powerful and independent black republic was founded in Africa, and thus placed much effort on achieving that end. Douglass relied on more immediate and direct means to abolitionism, based on moral persuasion and political agitation within the United States.

Douglass, of course, was proven correct when the Civil War eventually led to universal emancipation and black citizenship, but the war also delivered a serious personal affront to his ego. We know that Douglass and Delany each had meetings with Abraham Lincoln, seeking to obtain commissions in the United States Army during the Civil War.[13] To Douglass'

---

[11] Robert C. Dick, *Black Protest: Issues and Tactics* (Westport, CT: Greenwood Press, 1974), p. 62, also see Foner, *Life and Writings*, Vol. 2, pp. 51–54

[12] Frederick Douglass quoted in William J. Simmons, *Men of Mark* (Cleveland: George M. Rewell & Co., 1887), p. 1007.

[13] For Douglass' meeting with the president, see David Bryan Davis's review of William McFeely, *Frederick Douglass*, "The White World of Frederick Douglass," *The New York*

eternal chagrin, Delany was commissioned a major while Douglass was passed over. Delany's commission came through in early 1865, too late to make much of a difference; nonetheless, Douglass was involuntarily relegated to the brooding role of a black Achilles.

Douglass had several run-ins with Garnet, including his aforementioned refusal to endorse Henry Highland Garnet's call for a slave insurrection at the Convention of 1843. The matter receives scant attention in heroic treatments of Douglass' life. Garnet, who, like Delany, favored some aspects of African emigration, was a formidable opponent, and Douglass took his attacks seriously enough during the 1850s to respond to them in *Frederick Douglass Monthly*.

Douglass' hostility to the black congressman John Mercer Langston is one of the more intriguing puzzles in the lives of the two men. Their backgrounds as favored slaves of mixed background were similar, but similarity of background does not necessarily provide a basis for political friendships. In 1850, when Douglass was thirty-three and Langston was twenty-one, the two traveled together on an eastern speaking tour. But by 1853, Langston was accusing Douglass of using his newspaper primarily as a means of self-promotion. The journal reported the most trivial of events in the East. He wrote, "Men of the West cannot be noticed. . . . the *North Star*, edited by Frederick Douglass, is not the organ of the colored people."[14] A not altogether friendly rivalry persisted for many years. Langston advised against making Douglass president of the Freedman's Bank, recognizing correctly that the presidency would prove "difficult, trying and disappointing."[15] Douglass' embarrassment might have been avoided were it not for the egotism that Langston had long noted in him.

We seldom hear of Douglass' sometimes uneasy relationship with Alexander Crummell (1819–1898), the American-born and educated son

---

Review of Books (May 16, 1991), pp. 12–15. Delany told his biographer of a meeting with Abraham Lincoln. See Frank A. Rollin, *Life and Public Services of Martin R. Delany* (Boston: Lee and Shepherd, 1868). Victor Ullman, in support of Delany's claim that he obtained an interview, cites a note to Secretary of War Stanton in Lincoln's handwriting, but Ullman's idiosyncratic avoidance of footnotes makes the claim difficult to trace, and in any case the note simply reads: "Do not fail to have an interview with this most extraordinary and intelligent black man. A. Lincoln." See Victor Ullman, *Martin R. Delany: The Beginnings of Black Nationalism* (Boston: Beacon Press, 1971), p. 294.

14 William Cheek and Aimee Lee Cheek, *John Mercer Langston and the Fight for Black Freedom, 1829–65* (Urbana: University of Illinois Press, 1989), pp. 154, 159.

15 Philip S. Foner, ed., *The Life and Writings of Frederick Douglass*, 5 volumes (New York: International Publishers, 1950–1975), Vol. 4, p. 87.

of a West African captive and prominent spokesman of the back-to-Africa movement. Douglass had accused Crummell of abandonment during the 1850s at a time when he himself was being accused of dereliction by the nationalist emigrationists. Crummell, after several years' residence in England attending Cambridge University and lecturing for the abolitionist cause, had migrated to Liberia, West Africa, and dedicated himself to the building of a black republic. In 1855, Douglass called on him in the name of black unity to renounce the "agreeable duty" that anyone could perform, and return to the United States to perform the "disagreeable duty" of abolitionist struggle.[16] This spirit of accusation was consistent in the writings of Douglass when addressing Crummell, Garnet, Delany, and other black nationalists. Douglass maintained his confrontational stance long after the constitutional abolition of slavery and the decline of nationalist versus abolitionist controversy. In 1885, he challenged the position Crummell took during a speech at Storer College where Crummell had argued that black American leaders must stop dwelling on slavery and focus their attention on "new ideas and new aims for a new era." Douglass vociferously objected, saying that we should forever hold slavery in mind. Douglass and Crummell also disagreed over the need for black social institutions. Douglass considered them harmful, while Crummell insisted that they would remain a necessity of life for many years to come.

Douglass is not entirely to blame for the silence of his biographers on his interactions with other black men. It is not entirely his fault that historians have gigantized his image until he has come to be seen as the only great black man of the nineteenth century. Douglass has become more "politically correct" than some of his rivals, who, like Crummell and Delany, were extreme nationalists, advocating black separatism and boasting of their supposedly unadulterated African ancestry. Douglass, with his apparent disavowal of racial pride, is more acceptable to mainstream academic historians.

But if Douglass can be contrasted with others who were "too black," he could accuse others of not being black enough. During his trip to Paris in 1886, his attacks on the memory of Alexander Dumas were ill-founded when he wrote to friends:

So we have nothing to thank Dumas for. Victor Hugo, the white man, could speak for us, but this brilliant colored man who could have let down sheets of fire upon the heads of tyrants and carried freedom to his enslaved people, had no word in

---

[16] Foner, ed., *The Life and Writings of Frederick Douglass*, Vol. 2, p. 361.

behalf [of] liberty or the enslaved. I have not yet seen his statue here in Paris. I shall go to see it as it is an acknowledgement of the genius of a colored man, but not because I honor the character of the man himself.[17]

Professor John Wright has shown that Dumas had spoken out against slavery in his novel *Georges, or the Planter of the Isle of France.*[18] But if Douglass felt entitled to criticize Dumas for not speaking out on the issue of black slavery, Douglass himself had been criticized for failing to support African nationalism. True enough, he showed an interest in the African background of black folk and what he saw as their "ethnological" tie to ancient Egypt, but this should not be interpreted as support for nineteenth-century black nationalism or the African civilization movement of the day.[19] Douglass was unlike Edward Wilmot Blyden, who saw in the Egyptian heritage the basis for the future greatness of an African state. Douglass' pilgrimage to Egypt in 1887 and his writings on the claims of the American Negro to a noble Nilotic past were clearly aimed at proving that black Americans were fit for biological assimilation in America.

Douglass noted, with bitter humor, that many persons who would have had no objection to his marrying a person darker than himself, and the color of his mother, were shocked by his marriage to a person lighter than himself, and the color of his father.[20] He wrote to Oliver Johnson, making the point that his second wife resembled him more closely in physiognomy than did his first.[21] In his 1886 essay, "The Future of the Colored Race," he said it was "only prejudice against the Negro which calls everyone, however nearly connected with the white race, and however remotely connected with the Negro race, a Negro. The motive is not a desire to elevate the Negro but to humiliate and degrade those of mixed blood; not

[17] Frederick Douglass to friends Haydon and Watson, November 19, 1886, Frederick Douglass ms., Fisk University Library. Reprinted in Foner, ed., *Life and Writings of Frederick Douglass*, Vol. 4, p. 446.

[18] The profound importance of Alexander Dumas's novel *Georges, or the Planter of the Isle of France* was brought to my attention by Professor John Wright during a luncheon conversation in Cambridge, Massachusetts. Professor Wright informed the author that he conducted a seminar on the subject of Dumas's racial consciousness at the W. E. B. Du Bois Institute of Harvard University during March 1991.

[19] Frederick Douglass, "African Civilization Society," *Douglass Monthly* (February 1859), 19–20, is a response to the challenge of Henry Highland Garnet to defend himself with respect to African interest.

[20] Frederick Douglass, *The Life and Times of Frederick Douglass* (New York: Collier, 1962). Reprint of the revised edition of 1892 with a new introduction by Rayford W. Logan, pp. 14–24. For Douglass' defense of his marriage, see p. 534.

[21] Frederick Douglass to Oliver Johnson, in Philip S. Foner, ed., *The Life and Writings of Frederick Douglass*, Vol. 4, p. 427.

a desire to bring the Negro up but to cast the mulatto and the quadroon down." Douglass, in short, denied that mulattos, like himself, were truly Negroes.

Intermarriage and racial blending have never been among the spiritual strivings of the majority of African Americans, and Douglass denied advocating amalgamation. Nonetheless he declared:

> My strongest conviction as to the future of the Negro therefore is that he will not be expatriated nor annihilated, nor will he remain a separate and distinct race from the people around him but that he will be absorbed, assimilated ... I cannot give my reasons of this conclusion and perhaps the reader may think that the wish is father to the thought. . . . I would not be understood as advocating intermarriage between the two races. I am not a propagandist, but a prophet.[22]

But if the wish was not, indeed, father to the thought, it is difficult to dismiss the proposition out of hand. Douglass' relationships with white women, the Griffiths sisters, Ottilie Assing, and finally, Helen Pitts, seem to indicate that his attitudes on intermarriage were somewhat more than abstract and theoretical. He was thus, in at least this one aspect of his behavior, not a representative man. And he was not a race man, for although he remained true to the goal of racial equality in America, he repudiated any special feelings of racial pride, saying:

> Our color is the gift of the Almighty. We should neither be proud of it nor ashamed of it. . . . I have seen myself charged with a lack of race pride. I am not ashamed of that charge. I have no apology or vindication to offer. If fifty years of uncompromising devotion to the cause of the colored man in this country does not vindicate me, I am content to live without vindication. . . . When a colored man is charged with a want of race pride, he may well ask, What race? for a large percentage of the colored race are related in some degree to more than one race. But the whole assumption of race pride is ridiculous.[23]

The historian William McFeely and the conservative columnist George Will have praised Frederick Douglass for his repudiation of reverse racism. Are we to assume then that Americans, black or white, have come to endorse Douglass' advocacy of a "color-blind society" based on the biological amalgamation and cultural absorption of African Americans? That

---

[22] For further discussion of Douglass' confusingly shifting racial/ethnic attitudes, see W. Moses, *Afrotopia* (New York: Cambridge University Press, 1998), pp. 127–29.

[23] Frederick Douglass, "The Nation's Problem," a speech delivered before the Bethel Literary and Historical Society in Washington, DC, April 16, 1889, was originally published as a pamphlet (Washington, DC, 1889). It is reprinted in Howard Brotz, ed., *Negro Social and Political Thought, 1850–1920: Representative Texts* (New York: Basic Books, 1966), pp. 316–17.

was the message of Frederick Douglass, but does this embody the spirit of black America? What does it mean to be a hero? What does it mean to have the shaggy-headed, leonine portrait of Frederick Douglass staring down at us from the bulletin boards of schoolrooms across America during Black History Month?

My answer to the first question is that black Americans have always rejected Douglass' vision of America, and that neither black nor white Americans are committed to the eradication of racial distinctions in American life. While the spirit of black folk in the United States is clearly democratic and egalitarian, it is also essentially one of racial self-determination and ethnic pride. Douglass believed that the concept of ethnic pride and black unity was a mistake. He felt that it was actually unsafe for black people to stand together as a separate entity. We should beware the danger of isolating ourselves. We should not attempt to be "a nation within a nation." Rightly or wrongly, the spirit of black folk runs counter to such talk. There may be some exceptions, but these are rare and remarkable. The essential separatism of the black American people is to be seen in its marriage patterns. Marriage outside the race is uncommon and will probably continue to be so for the foreseeable future. Douglass ultimately renounced not only marital separatism, but all forms of racial unity and ethnic pride. Douglass offered the example of his own social adjustment, not only as a statement of personal preference, but as a proposed solution to the race problem in America.

If Frederick Douglass represents the spirit of black folk, then, he certainly represents it in all of its complexities, ambivalences, and contradictions. Who is to say whether the genius of self-promotion that characterized Douglass was more attributable to African American exuberance or to a typically American showmanship and flim-flammery. Like many black leaders of the present day and many American leaders throughout our history, Douglass made an industry of himself. When compared to other black men of the nineteenth century, Douglass was in no way a giant among dwarfs, but certainly he managed to stamp his name on an era much more effectively than did Martin Delany or John Mercer Langston. And the great irony of Douglass' sainthood is that he openly violated some of the most sacred canons of African American political culture. At the peak of his power and influence, Douglass scoffed at the idea of black unity, opposed the idea of separate black institutions, and sometimes denied the need for any concept of racial pride. And yet, he continued to participate in black institutions, took pride in black accomplishments, and exploited his status as a black spokesman.

Since Douglass seems to have attained an unassailable position in the pantheon of heroes we dutifully trot out every year for Black History Month, it is appropriate for us to ask what we really mean when we speak of an African American hero. Academic politicians will never find it necessary to ask the question, of course; for them it will be adequate simply to say that black people need heroes. After all, doesn't everyone need heroes? Hero worshippers are seldom committed to accurate reporting of what great men and women have thought and said. Analytical reflection on their writings is neither desired nor tolerated. Hero worshippers are looking for paper dolls that they can call their own, pasteboard silhouettes who can be clothed in the ideological garb of passing fancies.

Perhaps much of the continuing popularity of Frederick Douglass may be attributed to the facility with which he can be adapted to the conveniences of any hour. Douglass' aphoristic pontifications may be conveniently invoked on almost every occasion in this age of the "sound bite," and his ideologically malleable pronouncements may be rationalized with Emersonian blandness, as we recall the facile observation that "Consistency is the hobgoblin of little minds." Douglass may be claimed by nationalists like Molefi K. Asante as a symbol of militant black messianism, or by George Will as a representative of some vaguely imagined, and yet to be glimpsed, color-blind society. Perhaps one reason for our continuing fascination with Douglass is the amorphous quality of his symbolism. He seems to encompass the continuing ambivalence of black men in America with respect to many issues, including separatism, integration, Afrocentrism, Eurocentrism, and male-female relationships. He is, perhaps, more representative than he suspected of those other nineteenth-century black men to whom he paid cursory and fleeting tribute in his autobiographical writings. And he may have been, as I suspect, more typical of black people than even his most compulsive admirers have grasped.

4

Writing Freely?

Frederick Douglass and the Constraints of Racialized Writing

"Luckily for the World, Dumas was born in France and not in America, where he would have been circumscribed and might have used his genius in the struggle for elementary liberty like his notable Negro contemporary, Frederick Douglass."[1] This observation by J.A. Rogers, the unassailable icon of Afro-Atlantic history, outlines the fundamental struggle of Douglass' literary career. His development as artist and intellectual was circumscribed by the time and place in which he was born. Almost everything he wrote was informed by the struggle against slavery, racial discrimination, and the indelible imprint they left on his life.

Douglass' major work was an autobiography, which was dominated by the themes of his personal struggle against slavery, humiliation, stereotyping, and sexual repression. He was apologetic about the autobiographical nature of his writing. "I write freely of myself, not from choice, but because I have, by my cause, been morally forced into thus writing," said Douglass in the fourth and final version of his autobiography.[2] Writing freely, and yet lacking choice; writing freely and yet feeling forced. These contradictions did not result from a careless formulation of ideas, but from the dilemma of Douglass' life and literary career.

Douglass' early development as a writer had been assisted but also hemmed in by white friends who had strong ideas about what roles black Americans ought to play in American literary and intellectual life as well

---

[1] Joel Augustus Rogers, *World's Great Men of Color* (New York: Collier, 1972), p. 117.

[2] Frederick Douglass, *Life and Times of Frederick Douglass, Written by Himself: His Early Life as a Slave, His Escape From Bondage, and His Complete History.* With a new introduction by Rayford W. Logan. Reprinted from the revised edition of 1892 (London: Collier Books, 1962), p. 511.

as in their own emancipation. Early in his lecturing career, Douglass found himself in conflict with well-meaning patrons who suggested that he confine himself to the narration of his experiences as a slave. "Give us the facts, we will take care of the philosophy," said John A. Collins, general agent of the Massachusetts Anti-Slavery Society. Some of them even suggested that he should cultivate the plantation dialect when speaking in public.[3] But Douglass soon got tired of restricting himself to the theatrical display of his stripes and the dramatic mimicking of his erstwhile masters and overseers. He wanted to express himself on a variety of subjects, including, but not restricted to, slavery and the race problem in the United States. In his early years, Douglass struggled against confining himself to the narrative tradition on the podium. In his later years he attempted, with partial success, to free himself from the literary confinement of the slave narrative.

A metaphor for the literary confinement of Douglass can be found in the adventure of Henry "Box" Brown, who escaped from slavery by allowing himself to be nailed inside a large wooden crate and shipped off to the free states.[4] Douglass found that he must confine himself within a literary box. The slave narrative was a means to freedom, but it also represented a tactical confinement and imposed what might be called a genre slavery, which deprived its author of literary and intellectual elbow room. "I was growing, and I needed room," he said when reflecting on his rupture with the Garrisonians.[5] Throughout his career, Douglass gave evidence that he thought of liberal expectations as confining. The role of "escaped slave" and the literary convention of the "slave narrative" provided him with exposure to a reading public and provided him with work that he loved. It gave him an opportunity to say things that he wanted to say, and that very much needed to be said. But while Douglass rejoiced in the opportunity to make these statements, he sometimes disliked the way in which he was expected to make them. Douglass came to resent having to restrict his public speaking career to the recitation of his narrative. He resented being asked to speak in the plantation vernacular. He resented the advice of his white liberal friends that there was no need for him to found his own press.[6]

---

[3] Douglass, *Life and Times*, p. 218.
[4] Henry Box Brown, *Narrative of Henry Box Brown* (Boston: Brown and Stearns, 1849).
[5] Douglass, *Life and Times*, pp. 217–18.
[6] Robert B. Stepto, "Narration, Authentication, and Authorial Control in Frederick Douglass' Narrative of 1845," in Dexter Fisher and Robert B. Stepto, eds., *Afro-American Literature: The Reconstruction of Instruction* (New York: The Modern Language

Although Douglass never completely abandoned the slave narrative formula in any version of his autobiography, it is clear that he increasingly struggled to escape its confines. The later versions of the autobiography asserted a much stronger sense of individuality than did the earliest. The very title, *Narrative of the Life of Frederick Douglass, An American Slave*, reveals the dominance of the slave narrative formulas by which the author was bound. It reveals something of the expectations of Douglass' audience and the sponsors against whom he increasingly rebelled. Originally, his autobiography had been a generically typical work of abolitionist propaganda, a slave narrative of pamphlet length. Forty-seven years later, however, the work had grown to become a weighty seven hundred page tome and a very different sort of autobiography. In the final version, Douglass asserted that he was addressing questions "which range over the whole field of science, learning and philosophy . . . some of which might be difficult even for a Humboldt, Cuvier or Darwin." He was clearly struggling, in his old age, to fashion a work that would go beyond the genre of a slave narrative, and this was indicated by the magisterial title he gave it, *The Life and Times of Frederick Douglass.*[7]

Douglass expended many words asserting that his authorial motives were altruistic, saying that he wrote so freely of himself in order to give voice to the aspirations of "a people long dumb," who had been "much misunderstood and deeply wronged," but had not been able to speak for themselves.[8] Albeit Douglass' reasons for writing derived from moral conviction, it seems likely that he had additional motivations, and that beneath the assumed modesty of his introduction to the 1892 edition, there was a thinly veiled self-concern.

I know and feel that it is something to have lived at all in this Republic during the latter part of this eventful century, but I know it is more to have had some small share in the great events which have distinguished it from the experience of all other centuries. No man liveth unto himself, or ought to live unto himself.

Association, 1978), discusses the presentation of the author by white abolitionists. Douglass' struggle to found his own press and the attendant bitterness is in *Life and Times*, p. 259.

7 I have made no attempt here either at analytic bibliography or at complete publication history of Douglass' autobiography. The earliest form of the autobiography was *Narrative of the Life of Frederick Douglass, an American Slave. Written by Himself* (Boston: American Anti-slavery Society, 1845). Douglass expanded the narrative and described his early experiences in the abolition movement in *My Bondage and My Freedom* (New York and Auburn: Miller, Orton & Mulligan, 1855). *Life and Times of Frederick Douglass* was originally published in 1882 and a revised edition appeared in 1892.

8 *Life and Times*, p. 511.

My life has conformed to this Bible saying, for, more than most men, I have been the thin edge of the wedge to open for my people a way in many directions and places never before occupied by them.[9]

His superficial act of self-effacement was skillfully transformed into a shrewd act of self-presentation. Beginning with the artful device of a humble apology, he rapidly progressed to presenting himself as the embodiment of an age, but doing so with seeming modesty and professed candor. Douglass admitted to a desire to "tell my story as favorably towards myself as it can be," professing at the same time that he would exercise, "a due regard to truth."[10] The reader must assume, as one would when reading any autobiography, that Douglass might have had good reasons for not always revealing the inner workings of his mind. Furthermore, it is clear that while altruistic moral compulsions undoubtedly contributed to his becoming a writer, Douglass' frankness was certainly controlled by the fact that words were his livelihood.

If writing freely means writing not only abundantly, but with absolute or impolitic candor, Douglass did not "write freely" of himself. Douglass' literary acts of self-presentation were skillfully engineered to produce desired effects on certain sets of white liberals. He thus made certain to display his proletarian credentials as a "voice of the negro," a representative and advocate of the ostensibly "voiceless" black American. On the other hand he aspired to the position of a world-historical figure, asserting that his credentials were "the singularity of my career, and . . . the peculiar relation I sustain to the history of my time and country."[11]

Douglass, like his contemporaries Ralph Waldo Emerson, Abraham Lincoln, and Phineas T. Barnum – all cunning manipulators of their public images – was both a product and a casualty of his own self-promotion. Like these others, he was so successful a creator of himself as a public symbol that he frustrated the attempts of succeeding generations to know the man behind the image. The ability to manufacture a public personality was Douglass' bread and butter, and while he did not become rich directly from sales of his autobiography, he did become wealthy as a result of the literary creation of his life. It was a creation of self for economic, as well as for moral and ideological, ends. Like Emerson, Lincoln, and Barnum, he interpreted his life as a moral precept, inviting his contemporaries to learn from his experiences and to weave them into the developing web of

[9] *Life and Times*, p. 514.
[10] *Life and Times*, p. 514.
[11] *Life and Times*, p. 514.

American values. His life symbolized the myth of American individualism, but it also symbolized the ideals of American communalism, altruism, and self-sacrifice. The successful man in America was expected to share the secret of his success and to enrich himself by doing so. Poor Richard, like Horatio Alger's Ragged Dick and the legendary Dick Whittington, were prototypes of the American success manual. Frederick Douglass' rags to riches success story was typically American in that it was told, not only for the benefit of the teller, but for the benefit of the listener. But Douglass became a stereotype, limited by the constraints of the myths to which he so successfully contributed. These were the conventions shared by the myth of rags to riches and the myth of the heroic slave.

One need not question Douglass' sincerity to make the observation that his life as a literary creation was a market commodity. Nor is it necessary to doubt his honesty in order to observe that he was much concerned with depicting himself in ways that would appeal to liberal Christian readers and valorize bourgeois social conventions. The same qualities that make for effective propaganda often lead to financial success; the message must be simply and passionately stated in order to catch the attention of a broad audience. The author may find it advisable to avoid ambivalence and ambiguity in propaganda writing, since the material must deal in absolutes if the author is successfully to catch up one's audience in the swell of one's moral convictions. In a slave narrative, the purpose of telling one's life story was "to make slavery odious and thus to hasten the day of emancipation."[12] The early versions of the autobiography were intended to indict slavery, and Douglass insisted that it was only for this reason that he had originally written his life story. The later versions of the narrative he justified in much the same terms, arguing that his people, though free, were still oppressed, and "as much in need of an advocate as before they were set free."[13] In all versions, however, the author insisted that his personality was of less importance than the moral message that the life was supposed to symbolize. When W. E. B. Du Bois characterized the 1940 edition of his own personal narrative as *The Autobiography of a Race Concept,* he revealed an important truth about black autobiographical writing. It often reduces the individual to an abstraction, and converts the author into a mere representation of racial oppression.[14]

---

[12] *Life and Times*, p. 511.

[13] *Life and Times*, p. 512.

[14] W. E. B. Du Bois, *Dusk of Dawn: An Essay Toward an Autobiography of a Race Concept,* with a tribute to Dr. Du Bois by Martin Luther King, Jr. (New York: Schocken, 1968).

Douglass, like Du Bois, realized that he had converted his life into an expression of a "race concept," but in Douglass' autobiographical writings, subordination of self-consciousness to race consciousness is far more complete than in Du Bois's. Douglass lacks the confessional, self-critical quality that is present in Du Bois. The black American writer Carl Senna, in contrasting the slave narrative genre with works such as *The Autobiography of Benjamin Franklin,* notes that Franklin's confessions of youthful sexual improprieties give a quality of personality and sincerity to the work, convincing us of the reality of its author. The spirit of self-questioning and revaluation, the repentance of past attitudes that exists in the autobiographies of Franklin and Du Bois, the admission of mistakes, and the readjustment of fundamental conceptions of life is not evident in Douglass' autobiography. The lack of the confessional in Douglass' autobiography, especially in the area of his sexual life and moral values, demonstrates the extent to which Yankee, liberal, feminized, abolitionist culture determined the shape of his literary mask. Unlike his rival, William Wells Brown, Douglass does not invite the reader to vicarious participation in his amoral adventures, nor does he, like Josiah Henson, share with the reader his midnight anguish over remembered sins.[15] The autobiographical writings of Douglass, like those of Booker T. Washington, unveil no instances of personal malfeasance, sexual or otherwise.[16] Nonetheless, one is well aware that slave communities, with their peculiar moral codes, provided ample opportunity for sexual adventure.

Douglass admits to having been a mischievous child and a headstrong youth, but, as I have intimated previously, the autobiographical writings are devoid of any hint of the sexual precocity that is usually attributed to black boys and men in the United States. We must, perhaps, be willing to entertain the possibility that Douglass remained virginal throughout twenty years of slavery, since none of the versions of the *Narrative of Frederick Douglass* make any mention of sexual awakening or interest.

[15] The sometimes cruel and often tricksterish qualities of William Wells Brown are discussed by William Andrews in *To Tell a Free Story: The First Century of Afro-American Autobiography* (Urbana, IL: University of Chicago Press, 1986), pp. 146–47. Josiah Henson, in his *The Life of Josiah Henson* (Boston: A.D. Phelps, 1849), tells of his undying sense of guilt at having once betrayed a group of fellow slaves.

[16] One may, of course, define Douglass' confessed theft of food as malfeasance, but the present author is inclined to accept Douglass' reasoning that it makes no sense to speak of a slave's "stealing" food from his master, since the slave produces the food and the food consumed merely goes to increase the value of the master's possession. See *Life and Times,* pp. 105–6.

Although certain aspects of the narrative are, as other scholars have observed, determined by the gender of their authors, almost to a stereotypical degree, all versions of Douglass' autobiography avoid mentioning the author's attitudes toward sexuality or romantic love.[17] Sexuality has an ethnic dimension, but we are left to speculate on the putatively characteristic elements of black male sexuality that have been purged from Douglass' public statement of experience in order to meet the tastes of its audience. Personal experience is subordinated to political ends. The narrative is a sort of prison house in which the narrator describes himself both as actor and object but always in terms of the social situation to which his identity is subordinated. Unlike the continental mulattos Dumas and Pushkin, who created alternative imaginative worlds that practically reeked with sex, Douglass, in order to meet the needs of racial propaganda, created a literary self-image in which his own sexuality was brought into conformity with Puritan demands.[18]

Douglass' unwillingness to discuss his sexuality derives partially from his own conception of the slave narrative genre, which he admittedly viewed as less concerned with the freeing of ego than with the embodiment of the struggle for certain democratic and egalitarian ideals. These ideals were supposedly universal, transcending even the Christian moralism from which the abolitionist movement had derived. The slave narrative is propaganda, and propaganda often reduces its subjects to stereotypes, depriving them of the opportunity to express their personal singularities, idiosyncrasies, and quirks. Black males who wrote slave narratives were fully aware that their audience was made up of evangelical Christians. The ultimate foundation of abolitionist morality was based in the idea that slavery was an assault on the nuclear family and the sacred place of woman within the home. Their audiences wanted to be told that slavery destroyed households and corrupted sexual morality; they were not prepared to hear black males question the very sexual values that abolitionism was crusading to protect.[19]

As Mary Helen Washington has observed, Harriet Jacobs, author of *Incidents in the Life of a Slave Girl*, felt compelled to discuss her sexual life, and indeed it is this aspect of her narrative that has attracted the greatest

[17] Mary Helen Washington, *Invented Lives* (New York: Doubleday, 1987), p. xxii, notes that black women, by contrast, were compelled to discuss their sexuality.

[18] Rogers, *World's Great Men of Color*, pp. 79–88, 109–22.

[19] James A. McPherson, *Battle Cry of Freedom: The Civil War Era* (New York: Oxford, 1988).

amount of attention from recent critics.[20] Black men avoided the topic of their own sexuality, and when they alluded to sexuality at all, it was to condemn the sexual abuse of black women. Both in the antebellum and in the postbellum slave narratives, female sexuality is a constant theme. On the other hand, it is remarkable how little we know about the sexual lives of black males under slavery. Jacobs's sexuality is the source of much of her torment, and much of the attention that has recently been given to her narrative focuses on her reaction to sexual oppression as a component of the American social order. Black masculine sexuality could be mentioned only in oblique terms, which is why the narrative of Douglass spoke more openly of the sexual oppression of black females than of the sexual humiliation of black males. Nonetheless, although Douglass revealed little of the cultural aspects of black male sexuality that derived from the plantation experience, he made numerous oblique references to sexual aspects of the struggle. Furthermore, his narrative became an assertion of traditional masculine values, as the aforementioned feminist critics have observed.[21]

Professor Washington is correct; black females were indeed compelled to discuss their sexuality. They were compelled to do so by an audience of prurient white feminists who forced black women into hypersexual roles, thereby closing them off from any access to the cherished Victorian middle-class value system, which they denounced but nonetheless valued and protected. This same audience conspired with white males to deprive black males of their sexuality. Douglass capitulated to the demands of white men and women who insisted that black males become superior to sexuality, and that they deprive themselves of plantation sexuality, while at the same time demanding that they maintain plantation language, ignorance, and dependence. Douglass' imitation of standard English was thus an act of defiance, although it implied a preference for his oppressors' manners over those of the black proletariat. Douglass' repression of the plantation-derived, black male sexual standard, when seen in relation to his friendships with white women, represents a rebellion against the sexual expectations placed on black men but, at the same time, an accommodation to Anglo-American sexual attitudes, including veneration of white women.

---

[20] Mary Helen Washington, *Invented Lives* (New York: Doubleday, 1987), pp. xxii–xxiii, also see Jean F. Yellin's introduction to Harriet A. Jacobs, *Incidents in the Life of a Slave Girl Written by Herself* (Cambridge, MA: Harvard University Press, 1987).

[21] Mary Helen Washington quotes Valerie Smith.

Not all black male narrators avoided the subject of masculine sexuality. The various narratives of William Wells Brown are not characterized by the altruism or the puritanism that we find in the narratives of Douglass.[22] Brown, who was the personification of the Afro-American trickster, boasted of his ability to sweet-talk the wife of a local Ku Klux Klan leader.[23] Like Douglass, he underwent his childhood and puberty on a plantation where he witnessed and experienced the daily humiliation of black males by white males and females. Brown describes an occurrence in his childhood when all the young male slaves on his plantation were called by the old mistress and ordered "to run, jump, wrestle, turn somersets, walk on our hands, and go through the various gymnastic exercises that the imagination of our brains could invent." All of these exercises were performed while wearing the one piece "unmentionable garment" that was the sole article of clothing for slave children. Brown and his comrades exerted themselves without stint, however, since they realized that the winner of the contest would be selected as a house servant and the companion of the young master of the house, who was in need of a playmate and guardian.

> Every one of us joined heartily in the contest, while old mistress sat on the piazza, watching our every movement – some fifteen of us, each dressed in his one garment, sometimes standing on our heads with feet in the air – still the lady looked on.[24]

Whether, or to what degree, this incident might have been degrading to a prepubescent slave boy, Brown later reflected, when recalling the incident as an adult, that some indignity was involved on the part of the watchful mistress, as well as on the part of the performers. In retrospect, the occurrence revealed to Brown his sexual vulnerability and the willing participation of white women in his sexual humiliation.

Douglass' avoidance of the subject of sexuality is perhaps no more prudish than that of other black writers among his contemporaries, but he does give us some clues as to why he cannot write freely about his sexual and romantic concerns. He describes his dawning awareness of sexual vulnerability by recalling his perceptions of the behavior of adult men and women, both black and white. He describes himself as a small boy, hiding in a closet while his lascivious old master stripped his Aunt

---

[22] See Andrews, *To Tell a Free Story*, p. 146.

[23] William J. Simmons tells the story in his *Men of Mark, Eminent, Progressive, and Rising* (Cleveland, OH: Geo. M. Rewell & Co., 1887), pp. 448–49.

[24] William Wells Brown, "Memoir of the Author," in his *The Black Man, His Antecedents, His Genius, and His Achievements* (Boston: R. F. Wallcut, 1863).

Hester to the waist and administered a beating because of his jealousy of a young black man on another plantation.[25] This experience introduced him to the ability of white masters not only to abuse black women, but to make use of their sexual *Herrenrecht* to humiliate and terrorize black men and boys. Black men became agents in the humiliation of black women, as Douglass recalled, telling of how one woman was locked up in a cabin with a black man until she became pregnant.[26] Black women, by their liaisons with white men, whether voluntary or involuntary, became instruments for the humiliation of black men.

In the first edition of the *Narrative,* Douglass recounted the rumor that his master, Captain Aaron Anthony, was also his father, and in *My Bondage and My Freedom* he supplemented this revelation with descriptions of a complex and ambivalent relationship with Anthony, who sometimes led him by the hand, "patting me on the head, speaking to me in soft caressing tones, and calling me his little Indian boy."[27] In the earlier version of the autobiography, Douglass had mentioned the rumor that his master was his father, but made no mention of the affectionate fatherly relationship. In the final version of the autobiography, *The Life and Times,* he alluded to a fatherly relationship, but did not repeat the rumor of his paternity.[28] A reading of the middle and later versions is necessary in order to see the contradictions and complexities of Douglass' familial relations. In the 1845 version he tells us, "I was seldom whipped by my old master, and suffered little from anything else than hunger and cold" (29). In the 1855 version he says he received "a regular whipping from my old master, such as any heedless and mischievous boy might get from his father" (129).

Allison Davis recalled the rumor that Anthony Auld was Douglass' father and speculated on the possibility that Douglass' early life was significantly removed from the typical slavery experience. He was particularly interested in the relationship between Douglass and Lucretia Auld, who would have been his half-sister, assuming that Captain Anthony was his

---

[25] *Narrative,* pp. 6–7.
[26] *Life and Times,* pp. 123–24.
[27] *Life and Times,* p. 45.
[28] Allison Davis has observed these discrepancies. Davis also suggests that Captain Anthony, Douglass' putative father, was guilty of incest, and that incest is one of the "outrages dark and nameless" mentioned in *Bondage and Freedom,* p. 79. See Allison Davis, *Leadership, Love and Aggression* (New York: Harcourt Brace Jovanovich, 1983), p. 22. He may have sexually exploited his slave Betsy, who was Douglass' grandmother. According to Douglass' surmise, he had also imposed sexual relationships on Betsy's daughters, Harriet and Hester, who were Douglass' mother and aunt (2, 6).

father. Davis argued convincingly, based on Douglass' own recollections, that Douglass enjoyed a status quite different from that of other slaves because Miss Lucretia pitied him and perhaps even loved him. In addition to her tender words and looks, she would sometimes bestow on him an extra ration of bread and butter, "solely out of the tender regard and friendship she had for me." Once after a scrap that he had gotten into with Ike, another slave boy, she had bound up a rather severe wound on his forehead, "with her own soft hand." On the occasion of his leaving the plantation to live in Baltimore, it was Miss Lucretia who prepared him for the journey. She instructed him to scrub himself clean and promised him a set of trousers, "which I should not put on unless I got all the dirt off me." Davis identifies an important element in Douglass' life when he argues that Douglass "enjoyed a special status apart from other slave boys."[29]

"Enjoyed" may be too strong a term, but, as Douglass says, the experience of being transferred to a relatively benevolent situation at the age of seven or eight years, and going to live in Baltimore with Thomas and Sophia Auld, provided him with special advantages beyond the experiences of rural slaves in the cotton belt. It should not be forgotten, however, that Douglass traveled with the blessings of members of his extended white family. Both at Captain Anthony's and at the big house of Colonel Lloyd, he experienced the solicitude and affection of young white adults. He learned to speak a form of English that reflected "little of the slave accent." This resulted from his having been the companion of Daniel Lloyd, whom he accompanied on hunting trips and who protected him from the bullying and coarser influences of other slaves.[30]

Thus, while this family did not openly acknowledge him, they certainly did not ignore him. Its female members were particularly solicitous for his welfare, perhaps even affectionate and indulgent. In the 1845 *Narrative*, Douglass describes the initial kindness of Sophia Auld as a new and strange experience, claiming that he had never before seen "a white face beaming with the most kindly emotions" (32). With the 1855 publication of *My Bondage and My Freedom*, Douglass revealed that such benevolence was not altogether novel. He had been indulged by Lucretia from early childhood, and even "Master Hugh" tended to overlook his transgressions of the slave code for the most part, allowing him to meet with Father

[29] Davis, *Leadership, Love and Aggression*, pp. 24–25.
[30] In *My Bondage and My Freedom*, the author devoted a subsection to "Jargon of the Plantation." This discussion is replaced in *Life and Times* by Douglass's explanation for his own lack of slave accent, p. 44.

Lawson to pray and read the scriptures. In later versions of the autobiography, having exerted his independence to some extent from the confines of the propagandistic slave narrative, he was able to express somewhat more of the complexity of his experience. He demonstrated that his life experience had not been the simple parable that he had presented in the first version of the *Narrative*.[31]

He was a clever and mettlesome lad, probably very "cute." One wonders if his white relatives would have been so quick to look after him if he had been dull or deformed. There was clearly a gender dynamic in Douglass' early attempts at literacy. He was taught to read by Sophia Auld, who was torn between her maternal affection for the attractive, precocious youngster and her connubial loyalty to a husband who forbade her instructing the young slave. But neither of the Aulds seemed inclined to completely break the boy's will. The family had already decreed that he was to be afforded special treatment, hence the decision to send him off the plantation and make him into a house servant, and, as he later observed, "A city slave is almost a free citizen in Baltimore."[32]

By the time he reached adolescence, Douglass' independent spirit and the unfortunate fact of his being removed from the household of Hugh Auld and falling under the power of Hugh's vindictive brother Thomas led to his removal from Baltimore, and assignment to the slave breaker Edward Covey. The often-recounted story of his fight with Covey celebrated an initiation into manhood – a nineteenth-century ritual of regeneration through violence. One does not doubt either the brutality of the conditions to which Douglass was subjected, or his version of how he triumphed over Covey by resisting his brutality, but one must, nonetheless, question the exact nature of Douglass' experience on Covey's farm. How, indeed, was it that Douglass was able to resist Covey successfully, even though all the members of Douglass' white family were now dead, and there was no one left to protect him? The answer is that although the work was exhausting and the beatings were severe, the ordeal imposed by "Master Hugh" was never intended to break Douglass completely. It was rather to teach a favored, privileged, urban slave his place in society and to reinforce his awareness of his vulnerability.

In each version of the *Narrative*, Douglass speaks of the many beatings visited on him by Covey, and tells us that as a result his "natural elasticity

---

[31] Hugh Auld threatened to punish Douglass for meeting with Father Lawson in *Life and Times*, p. 91, but although aware of the continued meetings "he never executed his threat" (94).

[32] *My Bondage and My Freedom*, p. 147.

was crushed," his "intellect languished," and the dark night of slavery closed in upon him and he was virtually "transformed into a brute."[33] Strangely, however, he illustrated this brutalization by recalling the high-spirited emotions with which he often apostrophized the ships of the Chesapeake Bay.

You are loosed from your moorings, and are free; I am fast in my chains and am a slave! You move merrily before the gentle gale, and I sadly before the bloody whip! You are freedom's swift-winged angels, that fly round the world; I am confined in bands of iron! O that I were free! O, that I were on one of your gallant decks and under your protecting wing! Alas! betwixt me and you, the turbid waters roll. Go on, go on. O that I could also go![34]

From what we know of Douglass, it is easy enough to envision his Byronic figure poised "upon the lofty banks of that noble bay," addressing the ships with flashing eyes and floating hair. This does not, however, sound as if his "elasticity was crushed," or as if his "intellect languished," and these are not the thoughts of a brute or an automaton. Douglass' knowledge of standard American English dated back to his experiences on the Lloyd plantation.[35] His fascination with purple prose had begun in Baltimore when he had practiced his reading skills on the *Columbian Orator*. In fact, it is easy to believe that the early exposure to literacy, combined with an innate literary talent, must have led the youth to a heightened realization, especially during this wrenchingly unfamiliar experience, that his tragic experiences held great potential for literary exploitation.

Douglass' later oratory and writing celebrated not only a struggle against the reactionaries of the slave power, but also a victory over the abolitionists who encouraged him to speak substandard English (slave vernacular) and discouraged him from starting his own newspapers. No version of the narrative dwells in detail on Douglass' philosophical objections to Garrisonian tactics. Perhaps he felt compelled to pull his punches when it came to public criticism of white liberals. The issues in the clash were not limited to Garrison's interpretations of the Constitution, nor did they have to do solely with the headstrong and irascible character of Garrison. They had to do with attitudes among white liberals on the roles that black Americans were expected to play in American intellectual movements.

---

[33] *Narrative*, p. 66; *Life and Times*, p. 124.
[34] *Narrative*, pp. 66–67; compare to *Life and Times*, pp. 125–26.
[35] The very interesting observations of Professor Gates on possibilities of access to a master's library.

Douglass symbolically established his personal independence by rejecting the name he had borne as a slave. He established his literary independence by rejecting the urging of certain white supporters that he revert to the black vernacular. Abandoning not only the slave language but his slave name, he took his new one from the world of letters – Sir Walter Scott's novel *The Lady of the Lake*. He showed no interest in becoming a plantation variety of Robert Burns, preferring to cultivate an American bourgeois English that was literary rather than vernacular, more comparable to that of Daniel Webster than to that of his erstwhile peers on the Maryland plantation. His high-flown style of oratory, like that of Webster, had vernacular roots in the traditions of American evangelicalism, and to such an extent was proletarian, but it was not derived from the speech habits of the slaves.

The opposition that Douglass encountered from Garrison, as he developed his skills with words, recapitulated the problems he had encountered in the Auld household while learning to read. Hugh Auld did not approve of the affectionate and familial relationship that grew up between Douglass and Mrs. Auld, who taught Douglass to read. Garrison did not approve of the literary friendship that grew up between Julia Griffiths and Douglass. Years later, in order to accomplish his goals as a writer and editor, he worked closely with the white English woman, even moving her into his family household for a time. Garrison responded with sexual innuendo, which Douglass felt it necessary to publicly refute. Although Douglass felt it necessary to deny that the presence of Miss Griffiths had led to conflict between himself and his wife, he demonstrated by one of his own editorials his awareness that the relationship, despite its chasteness, constituted a violation of sexual mores.

Douglass knowingly displayed aggressive and competitive masculine sexuality, and defined himself in terms of sexual confrontation with white males throughout his life. Whether or not he was actually seen emerging from a house of ill repute in Manchester – a charge which he not only denied but was prepared to challenge with a lawsuit – there was always a hint of sexual transgression in his public image. He enjoyed being intentionally provocative, both in the opinions he expressed and in his personal conduct. It was hardly innocence or ignorance that led him to the "glaring outrage upon *pure American* tastes" that he described in his newspaper, *The North Star*:

There had arrived in New York, a few days previous, two *English* Ladies, from London – friends of Frederick Douglass – and had taken apartments at the Franklin House, Broadway; and were not only called upon at that Hotel by Mr.

Douglass, but really allowed themselves to take his arm, and to walk many times up and down Broadway in broad day light, when the great thoroughfare was crowded with pure American ladies and gentlemen.[36]

Aside from these lines, Douglass never wrote freely of his relationship with Julia Griffiths, at least not in any version of the narrative. The relationship was of dynamic importance for him both emotionally and intellectually, for it symbolized a symbolic eruption from the box of sexual confinement. The relationship with the Griffiths sisters facilitated his escape from the confinement of the slave narrative. Founding *The North Star* with the assistance of Griffiths came to represent both literary and sexual liberation. The relationship with Julia Griffiths recapitulated the relationship with Sophia Auld and presaged Douglass' second marriage to Helen Pitts after the death of his first wife, Anna. Douglass' relationships with women were of fundamental importance in his struggle for freedom, not only his freedom from slavery, but his freedom from the constraints of the American liberalism represented by Garrison. If Anna Douglass' assistance was of fundamental usefulness in gaining his physical freedom, Julia Griffiths's was of equal usefulness in gaining his literary freedom.

Douglass' freedom of spirit and his attractiveness to women clearly had much to do with his development as abolitionist and man of letters. Douglass tells us little of his relationships with women, either black or white. He reveals almost nothing of his relationship to Anna Murray Douglass, tells us nothing of how he met her, reveals nothing of the forces that compelled her to throw in her lot with him, to risk her financial resources and her freedom for him, and to assist him in his escape. In fact, neither of his wives plays much of a part in his narratives.

Douglass' decision, at the age of sixty-six, to marry Helen Pitts, a forty-six-year-old white woman, illustrates the ways in which his personal values often brought him into conflict with the expectations of American liberalism.[37] The biography of Douglass, ghostwritten by S. Laing Williams for Booker T. Washington, stated that Douglass lost status in the black community after his second marriage, and Douglass wrote bitterly of the "false friends of both colors" who had loaded him with reproaches.[38] His response to his detractors was that they had never complained of his marriage to his former wife, "though the contrast of color was more decided

---

[36] *The North Star*, May 25, 1849.

[37] Waldo E. Martin, Jr., *The Mind of Frederick Douglass* (Chapel Hill: University of North Carolina Press, 1984), pp. 98–100.

[38] *Life and Times*, p. 534.

and pronounced than in the present instance."[39] In a letter to Elizabeth Cady Stanton, he maintained that his second marriage had been a purely personal matter:

I could never have been at peace with my own soul or held up my head among men had I allowed the fear of popular clamor to deter me from following my convictions as to this marriage. I should have gone to my grave a self-accused and a self-convicted moral coward. Much as I respect the good opinion of my fellow men, I do not wish it at expense of my own self-respect. Circumstances have during the last forty years thrown me much more into white society than in that of colored people. While true to the rights of the colored race my nearest personal friends owing to association and common sympathy and aims have been white people and as men choose wives from friends and associates, it is not strange that I have so chosen my wife and that she has chosen me.[40]

Douglass' second marriage was symbolic of his long-held view that black and white America must eventually amalgamate. It represented his refusal to be confined to roles, values, or modes of thought that predominated in a society where all thinking was racialized. He denied the existence of a significant black culture, arguing that the "religion and civilization of [the Negro] were in harmony with those of the people with whom he lives," and that permanent territorial or even ethnic separation of the races was an impossibility. Black Americans were not destined to remain a distinct class:

Ignorant, degraded, and repulsive as he [the Negro] was during his two hundred years of slavery, he was sufficiently attractive to make possible an intermediate race of a million, more or less. If this has taken place in the fact of those odious barriers, what is likely to occur when the colored man puts away his ignorance and degradation and becomes educated and prosperous? The tendency of the age is unification, not isolation; not to clans and classes, but to human brotherhood.[41]

Waldo Martin has suggested that Douglass' marriage to Helen Pitts was the cause of his increasing opposition to racial separatism during his later years.[42] This is certainly a reasonable position. I think it more likely, however, that a long-standing distaste for racial chauvinism was probably the source of his ability to develop the relationship with his second wife. Douglass, who had been an opponent of territorial separatism and back to Africa movements since mid-century, began to state an unequivocal

[39] Philip S. Foner, ed., *The Life and Writings of Frederick Douglass* (New York: International, 1950–55), Vol. 4, p. 427.

[40] Foner, ed., *Life and Writings*, Vol. 4, p. 410.

[41] Foner, ed., *Life and Writings*, Vol. 4, p. 412.

[42] Martin, *The Mind of Frederick Douglass*, p. 100.

position against all forms of racial exclusiveness or constraint. A literary career that had begun as a protest against slavery, segregation, and what he referred to as "caste" had evolved into a protest against all varieties of racial consciousness and voluntary separatism. In a 1891 interview with Irvine Garland Penn, Douglass demonstrated a continuing ambivalence on the role of the black press, and by implication, the idea of a racial literature.

> Q: In your judgement, what achievements have been the result of the work of the Afro-American editor?
>
> A: It has demonstrated, in a large measure, the mental and literary possibilities of the colored race.
>
> Q: Do you think the Press has the proper support on the part of the Afro-American? If not, to what do you contribute [sic] this cause?
>
> A: I do not think that the Press has been properly supported, and I find the cause in the fact that the reading public, among the colored people, as among all other people, will spend its money for what seems to them best and cheapest. Colored papers, from their antecedents and surroundings, cost more and give their readers less, than papers and publications by white men.
>
> Q: What future course do you think the Press might take in promoting good among our people?
>
> A: I think that the course to be pursued by the colored Press is to say less about race and claims to race recognition, and more about the principles of justice, liberty, and patriotism.[43]

Douglass' statement on "The Negro Press" did not offer a definitive opinion on black writing. In fact his statements contradicted themselves at several points. He disparaged the quality of black journalistic writing, and yet claimed that it demonstrated the literary "possibilities" of the black race. He felt that the black press should "say less about race and claims to race recognition," yet called on it to "say more of what we do for ourselves." Douglass' prescription for black writers reflected the contradictions that he had demonstrated by his own career as a writer. He had protested mightily against racialization while making his living as a racial spokesman, writing almost invariably on racial themes. A desire to depart from the strictures of race led to a total immersion in racial themes. One might attempt to deracialize one's writing, but this was impossible

---

[43] Submitted by I. Garland Penn, in Philip S. Foner, ed., *The Life and Writings of Frederick Douglass*, 5 volumes (New York: International Publishers, 1950–55, 1974), Vol. 4, p. 469.

while engaged in the fight for racial freedom. This dilemma was one that he could not satisfactorily resolve, and hence the garbled and contradicting nature of his statement.

CONCLUSION

Long after his escape from slavery, Douglass felt that he was prevented from writing or speaking freely. I refer not only to the obvious point of his reluctance in the first version of the narrative to disclose the details of his escape or the names of persons who had helped him. Equally significant was the fact that he felt the necessity of abandoning the characteristic language and behavior of black males that predominated both on the plantation and in urban, nineteenth-century America. It is a matter of some significance that Douglass made every effort to separate himself from the speech patterns typical of the slave community.

As he developed as a speaker, he departed from the simple recitation of the wrongs that he had experienced as a slave. By the end of his career, his most popular lecture was on the subject "Self Made Men," a standard speech, which, according to Waldo Martin, owed more to the American success myth than to the slave narrative tradition.[44] What was true of his oratory was true of his writing, and with each successive version of the narrative, he progressed farther from the slave narrative formula.

It was, of course, necessary that he depart from the slave narrative formula in his later speeches and writings, not only because he had wider and more varied experiences to report, but because, as an intellectual, he was growing and needed space. He was increasingly discontented with writing protest literature and found himself straining toward a vaguely conceived goal outside the realm of racial apologetics. Douglass achieved a measure of escape from the role assigned to him by the white abolitionists of the 1840s by founding his newspaper and taking control of his own literary destiny, but he never realized the goal of deracialized writing that he preached in the interview with I. Garland Penn.

Perhaps one of the reasons for the rambling and confused quality in Douglass' statement to Penn arose from his ambivalence at having made his life into an industry, his recognition that in order to market himself as a product, he had to confine himself within a package. He wanted to deracialize his life but found that he could not divest himself of the

[44] Waldo E. Martin, Jr., *The Mind of Frederick Douglass* (Chapel Hill: University of North Carolina Press, 1984), pp. 256–57.

racial issue. Not only was race his livelihood, the struggle against slavery had been his entrée into American letters. There was a contradiction here, for while he resented the idea that race should be perceived as his only reason for being, he never became fully comfortable with the demonic egocentrism of the nineteenth-century artistic temperament. Flashing eyes and floating hair notwithstanding, he betrayed an apologetic attitude toward writing freely about himself, and justified his doing so in terms of racial loyalty and altruism.

Here, another contradiction arose, for it became increasingly evident with the passage of years that Douglass resented being classified as a black man. He protested against the prejudice that referred to "a man of mixed blood" as a Negro. The source of this attitude, he stated, "is not a desire to elevate the Negro, but to humiliate and degrade those of mixed blood."[45] By 1889, he was openly speaking against "the cultivation of race pride," saying, "I see in it a positive evil." While he sympathized strongly with the struggles of the black masses, he viewed himself, inwardly, as a man between the races. "I have no more reason to be proud of one race than another," he said, and while he claimed to take pride in "any great achievement, mental or mechanical, of which a black man or woman was the author," he insisted that this was "not because I am a colored man, but because I am a man."[46] Although he advised a rising generation of black writers to abandon the concepts of race pride and racial unity, he never came even close to escaping the constraints of racialized writing. His struggle against the literary confinement imposed by his audiences, whether white and liberal or black and conservative, was only partially achieved by the expansion of his autobiography beyond the confines of the slave narrative. Douglass was able to achieve only a partial literary emancipation, and he was fated never to attain any public image beyond that of racial writer and spokesman.

[45] Douglass, "The Future of the Colored Race," *The North American Review* (May 1886), pp. 437–40, reprinted in Howard Brotz, *Negro Social and Political Thought, 1850–1925*, (New York: Basic Books, 1966), p. 310.
[46] Douglass, "The Nation's Problem," a speech delivered before the Bethel Literary and Historical Society in Washington, DC, April 16, 1889, published as a pamphlet (Washington, DC, 1889) reprinted in Brotz, *Negro Social and Political Thought*, p. 317.

ALEXANDER CRUMMELL:
THE ANGLOPHILE AS AFROCENTRIST

5

Alexander Crummell and Stoic African Elitism

Alexander Crummell was a man of many contradictions, but the most obvious of these was the apparent disharmony between his Anglophilism and his black nationalism. While this yoking together of presumable opposites made him peculiar, it did not make him unique. Crummell belonged to a trans-Atlantic class of educated Africans and African American intellectuals who realized that they could never be completely at home in any existing cultural setting. Distrusted by the African and Afro-American masses and rejected by English and Anglo-American elites, Crummell sought, as did other assimilated blacks in Africa and America, to create a universal African civilization movement. In his voluminous writings and orations, he persistently argued the need for authoritative institutions, intellectual elites, disciplined religion, and organized labor, and for the rule of law to curb the enthusiasms of unwashed mobs and the machinations of ambitious individuals.[1]

---

[1] See *Constitution of the African Civilization Society* (New Haven, CT, 1861). For a note on "African Movement," a term commonly employed in the nineteenth and early twentieth centuries before it was replaced by "Pan-Africanism," see Wilson J. Moses, *Afrotopia: Roots of African-American Popular History* (New York: Cambridge University Press, 1998), p. 258, n. 67. Crummell's social and political thought are the primary concerns of Wilson J. Moses, *Alexander Crummell: A Study in Civilization and Discontent* (New York: Oxford University Press, 1989). Some of Alexander Crummell's published and unpublished autobiographical writings were collected and published by the present author under the title *Destiny and Race: Selected Writings, 1840–1898 [of] Alexander Crummell* (Amherst: University of Massachusetts Press, 1992). The title, an editorial distortion of my original, is misleading, as Crummell never published any book entitled *Destiny and Race*. He did publish three books made up of selections from his numerous pamphlets, sermons, addresses, and periodical articles. There is no adequate bibliography of Crummell's published and

Crummell believed that the essential traits of the native African personality embodied the highest universal values. He was a "civilizationist" who hoped the virile barbarians of indigenous Africa, infused with an elitist and disciplined Christianity, were destined to rival, and perhaps exceed, the accomplishments of Victorian civilization. Throughout his writings, a positive image of the pristine African is recurrent, contrasted with a negative image of the debased American Negro. As a so-called "free African," born in New York in 1819, he had no direct exposure to plantation society, but he was convinced that Southern slave culture was a hopelessly debilitating artifact, contrived by the white race for the sole purpose of degrading the black. Nonetheless, he detected in the American Negro some remnants of African superiority, such as their aesthetic sensitivity and instinctive "good taste." His seemingly contradictory blending of political black nationalism, Victorian "civilizationism," and Anglocentric elitism renders his thought confusing, or even threatening, to many who encounter his writings for the first time. Strange though it may seem, Crummell's Anglophilism represented a typical adjustment of even the most militant Africans, West Indians, and African Americans to the nineteenth-century encounter with slavery, racism, and colonialism.[2]

The ideas of Alexander Crummell were also informed by his personal experiences, however, which were unusual even for a free African American in the urban North. He was closer to African culture than most of his peers; for example, unlike most African Americans, he knew the name of his tribe, the Temne people of what is now Sierra Leone. Among the Temne in the late eighteenth century, everyone experienced some effects of the slave trade – sometimes as predators, sometimes as victims. Among the victims was Alexander's father, Boston Crummell, captured as

---

unpublished writings, but a brief guide is available in my *Alexander Crummell*, referenced previously.

[2] Anthony Appiah has appropriately noted Crummell's contradictions, but his analysis is ahistorical. See Appiah, *In My Father's House: Africa in the Philosophy of Culture* (New York: Oxford, 1993), Chapter 1, especially pp. 20–21. For another ahistorical and self-righteous condemnation of Crummell, see George Hermon's review of *Destiny and Race* in *Nineteenth Century Prose* 21.2 (Fall 1994). Extremely lacking in nuance is Tunde Adeleke, *UnAfrican Americans: Nineteenth-Century Black Nationalists and the Civilizing Mission* (Lexington: University Press of Kentucky, 1998). Vastly more sophisticated is Okon Edet Uya, ed., *Black Brotherhood: Afro-Americans and Africa* (Lexington, MA: D.C. Heath, 1971). Other seminal works include George Shepperson, "Notes on Negro American Influences on the Emergence of African Nationalism," *Journal of African History* 1:2 (1960), pp. 299–312, and J. Ayodele Langley's *Pan-Africanism and Nationalism in West Africa*. Adeleke provides no response to these earlier works' complex and nuanced interpretations of trans-Atlantic influences and cross-fertilization.

a young teenager "while playing on the beach." The exact date of his arrival in America and the circumstances of his emancipation are unknown, but one day, probably in the early 1800s, he simply refused to serve his master any longer. It was not necessary for Boston to flee the city; he was able to take advantage of the changing legal situation in New York and to establish himself as an oysterman, which meant that he opened and served oysters from a succession of addresses in the infamous Five Points district.[3]

Despite tremendous obstacles, the older African managed to shape the character of his son and miraculously influenced his mental development. W. E. B. Du Bois referred to "the hard thick countenance of that bitter father," although he never met him.[4] While it would hardly be remarkable if Alexander had remembered Boston Crummell as a bitter man, the impression that is strongest in his sparse reminiscences reveals him as an inspired educator and a sophisticated observer – lively, passionate, and talkative.

> My father was born in the Kingdom of Timanee. He was stolen thence at about twelve or thirteen years. His burning love of home, his vivid remembrance of scenes and travels with his father into the interior, and his wide acquaintance with divers tribes and customs, constantly turned his thoughts backward to his native land. And thus it was by listening to his tales of African life, I became deeply interested in the land of our fathers; and early in my life resolved, at some future day, to go to Africa.[5]

Among the five men discussed in this volume, only Crummell describes such a student-teacher relationship with his father. Crummell alone, among major African American thinkers, is the bearer of a sophisticated African narrative encompassing three generations of well-informed, male ancestors. Obnoxiously proud of his free birth and unadulterated

---

[3] Boston Crummell, discussed in Wilson J. Moses, *Alexander Crummell: A Study in Civilization and Discontent* (New York: Oxford University Press, 1989), pp. 12–13, was listed as an "oysterman" in Longworth's annual *New York Directory*, serving oysters at several addresses from 1824 to 1834.

[4] W. E. B. Du Bois, "Of Alexander Crummell," in Du Bois, *The Souls of Black Folk* (Chicago: McClurg, 1903). Contacts between Alexander Crummell and Du Bois's grandfather, Alexander Du Bois, can be pursued in the indexes of W. J. Moses, *Alexander Crummell*, and in W. J. Moses, *Afrotopia*.

[5] These sentences refering to Crummell's father and grandfather are taken from an undated and untitled manuscript to which the compilers of the *Catalogue of Manuscripts* in the Schomburg Collection of the New York Public Library assigned the title, "Africa and Her People." This fragmentary document, in Crummell's hand, has the appearance of lecture notes. To my knowledge it has never been published except in Moses, ed., *Destiny and Race*, pp. 61–67.

ancestry, he lived in a household administered by a father who was not only an African, but a man who had "refused to serve his master any longer." Crummell's experiences were considerably removed from those of the fatherless Frederick Douglass. He was exposed to an enterprising and successful father, a man competent enough in business to provide his son with the financial support and the leisure necessary to begin an education. This father indoctrinated him with the exact opposite of the usual pejorative views of Africa.

Boston Crummell was a serious man, and he expected his associates in New York's free African community to be equally serious. The Crummells affiliated with the staid Episcopal church. Their solemn religiosity represented a persistent strand in American black nationalism – a tendency to resist the frenzied expressiveness of Negro American folk religion.[6] Speaking acquaintances of the Crummells were of a similar sort, including the abstemious Samuel Cornish and the enterprising John Russwurm, who established *Freedom's Journal*, North America's first black newspaper, in 1827 at the Crummell home.

The clownish or improvident type of Negro did not frequent this home, nor was there much welcome for the unbridled enthusiasm, unfounded euphoria, or irrational exuberance associated with black mass culture. The serious and austere environment of African elitism into which Alexander Crummell was initiated sheltered him from the folkways of the majority of his African American contemporaries and culturally isolated him from them. Because he was not brought up in the stereotypical African American religion and culture, he was never comfortable with the traits attributed to African Americans by Thomas Jefferson, such as their assumed distractibility by the "slightest amusements" and their "want of forethought," or as Vachel Lindsay put it, "their irrepressible high spirits." Unlike Frederick Douglass, who spent his childhood on the plantation and empathized with the laughter and sorrows of the ordinary field hand, little Alexander grew up surrounded by serious black men who brooked no silliness, but were obsessive, enterprising, and constantly talking politics. David Walker, the Boston correspondent of *Freedom's Journal*, was disdainful of silly, improvident, ignorant, and emotional Negroes, whose minstrel antics encouraged whites to think of them as an inferior

---

[6] Many years ago, I presented an extended argument that a predilection for elite Eurocentric culture does not negate – indeed, may even facilitate – militant expressions of political black nationalism. See Wilson J. Moses, *The Golden Age of Black Nationalism, 1850–1925* (Hamden: Archon, 1978; reprinted New York: Oxford, 1988). See especially Chapter 1, pp. 16–31. Years later these points were further developed in Moses, *Afrotopia*.

species. Lewis Woodson of Pittsburgh wrote contemptuously in *The Colored American* of clownish young men who fixed their attention on fashionable clothing and neglected intellectual, political, and economic development. Samuel Cornish overcompensated all too fastidiously for putative Negro vulgarity, with the result that white abolitionists ungenerously agreed that his home was "the abode of sanctimonious pride and pharisaical aristocracy."[7]

Alexander was a little African prince, imaginative, discriminating, and cultivated, but "rather too sensitive, somewhat punctilious."[8] His emotions were powerful and visionary. Inspired, at the age of twelve, by reports of Nat Turner's uprising, he fantasized traveling south to lead a slave revolt. Du Bois declares that the boy "loved, as he grew, neither the world nor the world's rough ways."[9] Perhaps Du Bois projected his own memories of childhood onto the portrait of another, or, just as likely, he revealed a special sympathetic knowledge of a kindred spirit. Crummell apparently never mastered that reputedly common device of African American adjustment, "laughing to keep from crying"; his tears were converted into icy anger. Always more "African" than most of his peers, and blessedly alienated from slave culture, he was never completely Americanized. The pride and sobriety of his paternal heritage endowed him with the austere "lesson of a classic background, the lesson of discipline, of style of technical control pushed to the limits of technical mastery." These words were not Crummell's; they were the words that Alain Locke employed a century after Crummell's birth to describe what Locke opined was the fundamental difference between the West African and the African American spirit. American Negro traits were, characteristically, "naiveté, sentimentalism, exuberance, and improvising spontaneity," but the African personality was "disciplined, sophisticated, laconic."[10]

[7] David Walker attributes "Our Wretchedness in Consequence of Ignorance" to this class in *Walker's Appeal in Four Articles, Together with a Preamble to the Colored Citizens of the World, but in Particular to those of the United States of America*, 3rd ed. (Boston, 1830; reprinted University Park: Pennsylvania State University Press, 2000). Lewis Woodson expressed his disgust in his letter by "Augustine" in *The Colored American*, February 1, 1839, reprinted in Sterling Stuckey, *The Ideological Origins of Black Nationalism* (Boston: Beacon, 1972), p. 145. See opinions on the Cornish home in *Letters of Theodore Dwight Weld, Angela Grimké Weld, and Sarah Grimké Weld, 1822–1844*, Gilbert Hobbes Barnes and Dwight L. Dumand, eds. (American Historical Association, NY: Appleton-Century-Crofts, 1933).

[8] "Punctilious" is the description offered by Crummell's rather free-wheeling, almost mercurial, mulatto contemporary, William Wells Brown, in *The Rising Son* (Boston: A. G. Brown, 1874), p. 455.

[9] Du Bois, *Souls of Black Folk*, p. 217.

[10] Alain Locke, ed., *The New Negro* (New York: Albert & Charles Boni, 1935), p. 254.

Such generalizations on the differences between the Americanized and the pristine West African may have been unscientific, but Locke's impressions were not entirely unfounded. Africans, on coming to the United States, have often expressed an icy contempt for African American vernacular culture, which they perceive as silly or vulgar. Crummell's descriptions of native West Africans constantly assigned to them the inborn traits of Spartan stoicism or Ethiopian regality. At the same time, he praised the African race for being eminently malleable. He believed in "the destined superiority of the Negro" because he believed that Africans shared with other great races – the Hebrews, Greeks, Romans, and English – a trait of imitativeness, which made them supremely capable of assimilating refined manners and useful customs. Since the civilized tribes of Europe were, in fact, cosmopolitan thieves, the fruits of Christian civilization were arguably the legacy of anyone clever enough to appropriate them. It is not surprising that a historian as astute as George Frederickson has noticed a contradiction within his theories, which straddled a universal "civilizationism" and an ethnocentric "romantic racialism."[11]

It requires no great skill to discover contradictions in the writing of any complicated thinker. The challenge is to understand how Crummell reconciled his belief in "Negro Superiority" with his reverence for English culture, or his Eurocentrism with his view of Greeks and Romans as "cosmopolitan thieves" scavenging the ancient Near East. It was a complex system in which he constructed his complicated world view. His notes on "Africa and Her People," never published during his lifetime, and other descriptions of African peoples published while he worked in Africa, provide the basis for understanding his contradictory views on Africa. When we place his abstract theoretical writings on Africa in juxtaposition to concrete descriptions, we view the theory in connection with complimentary and sometimes conflicting data. Basically, he was favorably impressed by much of what he saw in the cultures of African tribes, especially when he compared them to the degraded victims of American slavery. But the pristine virtues of African societies did not endow them with wealth or power approaching that of Victoria's empire. None of his theories can be deciphered without understanding Crummell's conviction that Christianity was the source of Britain's military might and economic power.

[11] Alexander Crummell's theory of cultural diffusion was outlined in *The Destined Superiority of the Negro, A Thanksgiving Discourse, 1877*. Reprinted in Moses, *Destiny and Race*. Frederickson in *Black Liberation* (Oxford, 1995) strangely confuses ethnochauvinistic "romantic racialism" with cosmopolitan "civilizationism," p. 69.

Thanks to early indoctrination by his father, Crummell's youthful imagination had never conceived Africa in Phillis Wheatley's famous terms, as "the land of darkness and Egyptian gloom." He tells us that his "imagination literally glowed with visions of its people, its scenery, and its native life," and he compared his images of Africa to "Arabian Nights Tales." His first impressions, on arriving in West Africa in 1853, at Goree, a desolate spot where the desert meets the Atlantic, were less romantic and more ambivalent. Stepping ashore, he encountered a group of "Jolloffs of the Senegambia region," men and women, "all wrapped in large striped clothes; their heads bent toward their knees and talking in deep guttural tones." Although unimpressed by the music of their language, he was clearly impressed by their physical appearances. Grand and stately, they were "the tallest human beings I had ever met with."

Their average height was about 6 feet 3 or 4, but with their remarkable slenderness, they appeared two or three inches taller. I was much struck with both the depth and the brilliancy of their complexions. Such utter blackness of color I had never seen in our race; not either the copper of the ashy blackness which is common to the Negro of America, but black like Satin; with a smoothness and thinness of skin so that you could easily see the blood mantling in their cheeks.[12]

Crummell's descriptions of the indigenous Africans' physiques were always overwhelmingly positive, although his impressions of African languages and religions were usually negative. He discovered mental alertness and vigorous economic activity everywhere. On arriving at Sierra Leone, he witnessed that the waters were "crowded with canoes and boats of the native fishermen, and crafts of various size were lying in the harbor." The people, he noted, were bustling and energetic, about the business of "loading and unloading their canoes." This accorded with his impression, repeatedly stated, that West African life and customs were dominated by a spirit of enterprise, that the whole continent was "a beehive."[13]

Crummell opposed restructuring viable African institutions, when they obviously functioned effectively and credited African people with military power and political organization. He wrote admiringly of the strong states of Dahomey and Ashante, "whose fundamental governmental basis

---

[12] Alexander Crummell, "Africa and Her Peoples," in *Destiny and Race*, p. 62. The original document, unpublished in Crummell's lifetime, is in the Schomburg Collection.

[13] Crummell's "A Defence of the Negro Race in America from the Assaults and Charges of Rev. J. L. Tucker, D.D., of Jackson, Mississippi," a paper read at the Church Congress of the Protestant Episcopal Church in 1882, was published in Crummell's third book, *Africa and America: Addresses and Discourses* (Springfield, MA: Willey and Co., 1891), p. 88.

it seems to me is not for the interests of civilization and Africa to revolutionize or to disturb." Such impressions render problematic the simplistically pejorative caricature of Crummell as promoter of settler-state colonialism.[14]

Settler-state colonialism refers to a policy, emphatically opposed by Crummell and his party, of removing or exterminating an indigenous population and replacing it with aliens. Liberia's True Whig Party, led by the nation's fifth president, E. J. Roye, along with Edward Wilmot Blyden and Crummell, fought the policies of ethnic cleansing and displacement of the indigenous peoples, which was promoted by a faction dominated by Monrovia's "mulatto" elite. Roye articulated the position that "The aborigines are our brethren, and should be entwined with our affections, and form as soon as possible an active part of our nationality. *In fact we cannot have a permanent and effective nationality without them.*" These attitudes were little appreciated by the settler-state colonialists, and Roye's reward for his policies was deposition, imprisonment, and probable assassination.

The attitudes of Crummell, Roye, and Blyden toward the mass population, whether native or immigrant, should never be confused, however, with democratic egalitarianism. The ideological stance of the spokesmen for Liberian nationalism was a whiggish, elitist, capitalistic, and statist republicanism. The government proposed to be centrally organized, authoritarian, planned, and thoroughly committed to the active promotion of banking, transportation, commerce, and industry. The exploitation of labor was fundamental to its precepts, and there was no distinction in their attitudes on the treatment of immigrant or indigenous labor. Thus, Crummell and Roye both envisioned internal developments carried on as government policy with the cooperation of indigenous leadership. Roads, canals, and railroads were to be constructed by native labor, contracted by agreements with local chiefs.[15]

---

[14] For Crummell's praise of the Dahomey and Ashante states, see his *The Future of Africa: Being Addresses and Sermons, etc., etc., Delivered in the Republic of Liberia* (New York: Charles Scribner, 1862), p. 250. For the simplistic/pejorative treatment of African American political theory vis-à-vis Africa, particularly that of Crummell, Martin Delany, and Henry McNeal Turner, see Tunde Adeleke, *UnAfrican Americans: Nineteenth-Century Black Nationalists and the Civilizing Mission* (Lexington: University Press of Kentucky, 1998).

[15] President Edward James Roye's program was articulated in his Inaugural Address, January 3, 1870, printed in Abayome Cassell, *Liberia: History of the First African Republic* (New York: Fountainhead Publishers, 1970), p. 270; Crummell proposes similar projects in *The Future of Africa*, p. 87.

Crummell frequently made allusions to the industrious habits of the native peoples, describing qualities – often regarded as lacking among the masses of American immigrants – that offered a promise for the development of Africa as a whiggish commercial republic:

Heathen though these people are, their system is a most orderly one – filled everywhere with industrious activities; the intercourse of people regulated by rigid law. The whole continent is a beehive. The markets are held regularly at important points. Caravans, laden with products, are constantly crossing the entire continent; and large, nay at times immense, multitudes are gathered together for sale and barter at their markets.[16]

But this nascent commercial culture must somehow be brought under the discipline of a national political economy, which would be no mean trick. Liberia in the mid-nineteenth century was the home of at least six or seven major language groups, comprising considerably more "indigenous" peoples depending on what is meant by indigenous. Neither ethnic groups nor their constituent individuals were immovably rooted in the soil. Furthermore, as Crummell noted, there were in Sierra Leone, the sister colony of Liberia, established by the British, large numbers of men and women from various "tribes," recaptured from intercepted slave vessels by the Royal Navy's coastal squadron. In his movements between the two countries, Crummell had contact with "people of not less than sixty different tribes." Venturing onto the uncertain terrain of nineteenth-century ethnography, he offered descriptions of peoples he had encountered from various subregions of West Africa, noting their tribal distinctions and "points of interest and superiority," including traits of "personal beauty, mercantile shrewdness . . . , [and] intellectual ability."[17]

Crummell's laudatory depictions were consistent with those of some other African American observers, notably Samuel Williams and Martin Delany, but his contemporaries included others who believed in the physical inferiority of tropical Africans. Frederick Douglass made disturbing comments on what he believed to be their physical inferiority, "gaunt, wiry, ape like appearance," which he attributed to the environment of the rain forest. Douglass believed, however, that when exposed to better climatic conditions, such as those in Egypt or North America, the Negro evolved naturally into a physically superior type.[18] Crummell claimed

[16] Alexander Crummell, "Africa and Her Peoples," in *Destiny and Race*, p. 62. "Defence of the Negro Race," in *Africa and America*, loc. cit.

[17] Alexander Crummell, "Africa and Her Peoples," in *Destiny and Race*, p. 64.

[18] Frederick Douglass, "Claims of the Negro Ethnologically Considered" (1854), has a complicated publishing history, described in John Blassingame, et al., *The Frederick Douglass*

that he had been taught in the geographies of his school days "the personal inferiority of the Negro." "He was [depicted as] a creature almost approaching the brute, in appearance, that he had a retracting forehead, flat nose, a long projecting heel." His travels in Africa convinced him that such descriptions were absolutely false.[19]

The debased Negro "in many places" in the United States was inferior to the pristine African, and Crummell allowed that he had witnessed in America the "at times repulsiveness of the race." However, he contrasted the gross "ashy blackness" of the American Negro with the glossy deeper blackness – delicately nuanced – of the Jolloffs as described previously. By contrast, he observed, "I was greatly surprised to find the native man in tribe after tribe an erect, finely proportioned, well-developed, symmetrical, and a noble being." There were, to be sure, differences in the characteristic physiognomies of the various tribes. "But so far as completeness and beauty of form is concerned, the native African is the equal of any and of every nation in Europe; can furnish as fine specimens of the manly [physique]."[20]

The native Africans were also superior in character to the American Negroes arriving "with rare and individual exceptions, ignorant, benighted, besotted, and filthy, both in the inner and the outer man." In contrast, he wrote that the native Africans were noted for their vigor, industry, and enterprise. The Kroomen were sailors of "prodigious size girth – breadth of shoulders." They displayed great strength, carelessly hefting a bushel of flour, displaying in the physical power of their movements the "spirit of free men." They neither practiced slavery nor participated in the slave trade. The Dahomean recaptives from an American naval vessel had the appearance of demigods, despite the fact of their warlike history and character, their cruel customs and purported cannibalism.

An appreciable number of the immigrants settling in West Africa were among this class of recaptives, all of whom were classed together as "Congoes" in the vernacular.[21] This group of people tended eventually to

---

Papers, Series I, Vol. 2, (New Haven, CT: Yale University Press, 1982), pp. 497–99. Numerous manipulations of Lamarck, Darwin, *inter alia* by African American intellectuals are traceable through the index to *Afrotopia*, and by Douglass especially on pp. 119–20.

[19] Crummell, "Africa and Her Peoples," in *Destiny and Race*, p. 64.

[20] Ibid., p. 65.

[21] Elliot Liebow writes, "The term 'Congo' is loosely applied to all Americo-Liberians by many tribal persons today." See Liebow, *Liberia: The Quest for Democracy* (Bloomington: Indiana University Press, 1987), p. 49. Liebow understates. I discovered that all Liberians descended from immigrants had come to be called Congoes. By 1979, Liberians of diverse backgrounds divided the population into the categories, "Congo," to signify the

unite with the darker Americo-Liberians, indigenous citizens, and race-conscious nationalists in the True Whig Party. By the time Crummell's friend E. J. Roye became president of Liberia in 1870, recaptives were participating in Liberian politics. Crummell had long been sympathetic to the recaptives and was happy to see them assimilating rapidly into the citizenry. He remarked in 1861:

Two years ago a large number of this class was recaptured in the slaver *Echo*. They are quiet, peaceable, industrious men. No vestiges of idolatry, such as fetishism, obeahism, or devil worship – have been observed among them, and they have embraced the Christian faith. They have now become citizens of the Republic. They have been enrolled among her soldiers, and they can perform their duties with as much precision as the others. There is nothing which does so much for civilizing a man as putting a gun into his hands.[22]

Special regard was bestowed on the Temne people, his father's people, who were known for their "great nobility of character, indomitable spirit," and were "unconquerable." The British had "subdued all others [but] never them." The Mandingoes were, however, "the most celebrated tribe in West Africa," tall and stately at six feet two, well proportioned, of noble character and intelligence. Unlike the mass of improvident American immigrants, they were known for their enterprise and famous for their caravans of trade. The women of the Vai (or Vey) people he described as remarkably beautiful. "Industrial activity in farming and manufacturing – e.g. weaving" was well-developed among them. The Vai were also known for their "mental activity and real genius, e.g. Invention of Alphabet and Literary spirit."

Industry and moral character were the most readily observable traits of indigenous West Africans. Their economies were well established, owing much to their inborn physical traits. Characteristically they were "strong, healthy, vigorous, long-lived." His sketchy notes recorded that they had "no deformed people" and among them "disease seldom found." On this base of almost miraculous congenital superiority, the native peoples had built an "industrious farm life," yielding "plenteousness of food" and "interior markets visited by 10,000 people." He praised "their mechanical

---

urbanized, literate elite, and "Country," those still practicing ethnic folkways and speaking native languages. Needless to say, the distinctions between the two categories were extremely nebulous and fortuitously assigned.

[22] *African Repository* (September 1861), p. 277. This mind-boggling statement about the civilizing effect of firearms is perhaps somewhat mitigated by the fact that Crummell made it during the first year of the American Civil War, probably to encourage the enlistment of African Americans for military service.

ingenuity, their Cotton cloths" and the "100,000 looms in Bombas town," and spoke of "Iron blacksmithing in Cavalla" and "Gold manufacturing in Freetown."

With respect to manners and customs, while the native peoples were admittedly pagans, and while their paganism led to "degradation of women, darkness of mind, [and] cruelty in war,"these were not their "normal characteristics." African societies were marked by "social purity of women," by honesty, and by hospitality to strangers. In 1871, Crummell published a report in an Episcopal missionary magazine, *Spirit of Missions,* describing in the most glowing terms a journey to the Dey and the Vai Countries, where he had been "sent for by the two chiefs or kings, to talk with them about schools and missions." The report contained his usual glowing tribute to native commerce and agriculture. It also contained repeated references to the "*intellectual* desire; for everywhere the demand was for schools and school-masters."

Crummell's writings reveal a contradiction between his friendliness toward certain "pagan" individuals and his abstract abhorrence of "pagan" customs. Crummell had a high regard for King Bomba of the Vai people, who was "very pleasing in his manners, and seems to live in great love and friendship with a large number of wives and a host of children." He spoke in most glowing terms of both the king and his people, and of their desire to have a Christian school in their region. His impressions of the Vai culture are jarringly inconsistent.

The Vey people are an industrious people, highly intelligent, polite and spirited. The women are beautiful, as well in face as in figure; and the king's wives treated me to great hospitality, providing me with everything pleasant and agreeable, preparing fire for me in my house and a warm bath at night. As I sat in the town in the mornings, and saw these women – mere children – dressing themselves with their hand mirrors (*i.e.* adorning their faces with clay paint), and heard their childish laughter and their glee, and observed their artless ways, I felt more keenly than ever before in my life the deep degradation of heathenism, and how that it is only by the evangelization of women we can ever break the chain of paganism in this land.[23]

Again, we see the fundamental contradiction in Crummell's attitude to Africa. On the one hand, he recognized virtue in the pristine societies; on the other, he believed that Protestant Christianity was necessary to African advancement. He witnessed a terrible threat on the horizon, to wit, the invasion of competing religious movments, to which the Vai and

---

[23] *Spirit of Missions,* Vol. 35, 1870, pp. 415–19.

other pristine Africans were vulnerable. There were dangers other than heathenism to which they might fall prey, namely "the approach of the Romanists . . . with large charities and profuse gifts of money." In addition, there were the missionary activities of the Muslims, whose corrupting influences were a serious, but less immediate threat.[24]

Edward Wilmot Blyden, in contrast to Crummell, was sympathetic to Islam, which he perceived as a civilizing influence. The scholarly and influential Blyden, a West Indian of Ibo descent, believed that the Muslims, as a "people of the book," with their fidelity to the God of Moses, offered to indigenous peoples a pathway of faith that might lead eventually to Christianity. Just as Ishmael had preceded Isaac, so it might be that Ishmael must precede Jesus in the evangelization of Africa.[25] In later years, Marxism would become a competing gospel along with Christianity and Islam for the minds of African redemptionists. Crummell, and eventually Garvey, favored Christianity, as did Blyden, although he was willing to accept an Islamic detour. W. E. B. Du Bois and George Padmore sympathized with the secular evangelical movement of Marxism, endorsed with varying degrees of enthusiasm by African nationalists in the twentieth century.

The Ibo Samuel Ajayi Crowther (1806–91), a Nigerian missionary and the first African bishop of the Anglican Church, whose *Experiences with Heathens and Mohemadens in West Africa* describes efforts to discourage indigenous religious practices within his jurisdiction, was the most noticeable of Crummell's African intellectual peers who vigorously promoted Christian conversion. Despite individual peculiarities, he represented a group of African thinkers whose constructions of African redemptionism were obviously similar to Crummell's. Crowther preached against polytheism, but the natives were well equipped with a sophisticated counterargument.

Their defense was that their gods were inferior deities commissioned by the great God to superintend inferior matters on earth. Having received the same from their forefathers, they insisted upon continuing their worship as they found it was good for them. . . . On the next Sunday morning I went to them according to promise; but they had made their plan how to receive me. On my entering the house, and saluting them according to custom, the women burst out in loud praises of Shango, and the drummers took to their drums, which they beat as loud as possible with

---

[24] Moses, *Crummell*, for Roman threat, p. 172, and Muslim danger, p. 184.
[25] "Blyden, Mohamedanism, and the Negro Race," *Fraser's Magazine* (November 1875), republished in Blyden, *Christianity, Islam and the Negro Race* (1887; reprinted Edinburgh: Edinburgh University Press, 1967), p. 24.

great rapidity and noise, so that my voice was completely drowned. At the same time others were boisterous in telling me that the gods against whom I spoke were the gods of my forefathers. . . . I had to return home completely defeated.[26]

Crowther, no less than Crummell, was alienated from his ancestral gods and dedicated to the promotion of Christian civilization. Although he took pride in his Temne origins, he was nonetheless estranged from the traditional religion of Temne, not to mention the slave-trading history, to which he made few, if any, allusions.[27] Crummell and Crowther both rejected Blyden's view that Islam could be an agent for civilizing Africa. Both men believed that Christianity and civilization were "collateral" agents in the uplift of Africa – although Crummell emphatically rejected the idea that Roman Catholicism could have positive effects. The later ideas of Du Bois and Lumumba that the ideology of atheistic socialism could be an agent for progress and uplift would have been incomprehensible to them. Crummell was emotionally incapable of entertaining such an idea.

Crummell's rejection of Islam as a civilizing influence paralleled that of James Quaker, who clashed even more noticably with Edward Wilmot Blyden over the issue of whether Islam could be a civilizing agent in Africa. Like Crummell, he entertained no cheerful picture regarding Islamic influences. Broadly distrustful of Blyden's ideology, Quaker was frightened by the West Indian's increasingly radical conception of "African personality," which he implicitly represented as anticolonial. He advised Blyden that "Israel is not to be delivered by killing the Egyptians. . . . Africa still stands in need of all the aid she can get from British philanthropists."[28] Quaker insisted not only on the need for British philanthropy, but also on what he perceived as a need for English education:

The native gentlemen feel that they want a good substantial English school under well qualified English and native masters, where their sons will enjoy all the advantages of a complete English education. . . . I am sure this is what the intelligent portion of the community wants. They understand nothing about an institution where 'race feeling,' and 'the national idiosyncrasies' etc. etc. will be developed or respected. . . . We want an English school to be established in Sierra Leone.[29]

---

[26] Samuel Ajayi Crowther, *Experiences with Heathens and Mohemadens in West Africa* (London: Society for the Propagation of Christian Knowledge, 1892); reprinted in Lalage Bown, ed., *Two Centuries of African English* (London: Heinemann, 1973), pp. 137–38.

[27] Kenneth G. Wylie, *The Political Kingdoms of the Temne: Temne Government in Sierra Leone, 1825–1910* (New York: Holmes and Meier, 1977), pp. 71–90.

[28] James Quaker to Henry Venn, October 28, 1872, in Robert W. July, *Origins of Modern African Thought* (New York: Praeger, 1967), p. 147.

[29] George Nicol to C. C. Fenn, August 14, 1873, C.M.S. CAI/0164, quoted in July, *Modern African Thought*, p. 148.

West Africans were, in general, no more and no less Eurocentric than Crummell or Blyden. George Nicol, who was married to one of Crowther's daughters, believed that Africa could not progress without European influence and guidance. Nicol, like Quaker, was suspicious of Blyden's constant talk of "African personality." He was, however, nationalistic enough to assert in 1854 that "... if Africa could be raised from its present degraded state of barbarism, superstition, and vice to any equal with the civilized world, recourse must be had to the native agencies. Africans must be the principal harbingers of peace." As late as 1885, Blyden did not come readily to this "Afrocentric" position, but remained strangely convinced that the principal agents of African uplift must be "the millions of Africans in the Western hemisphere." By the end of the century, Crummell had publicly expressed the opposing conviction of "the absolute need for an indigenous missionary agency."

It was within this context that Blyden and Crummell continued to recommend European protectorates in West Africa. In 1877, Crummell supported the extension of the Belgian empire into the Congo, with no foresight of the tragic consequences of King Leopold's "protective" influences. Blyden praised Leopold even after his authority was reinforced in 1884 at the Congress of Berlin, and even as late as 1895, when Belgian rule was becoming an international scandal. Neither Blyden nor Crummell had any premonition of the nightmares that would beset independent Africa a century later. Blyden and Crummell both looked to Europe as the source of civilizing ideas and as the provider of a peacekeeping function among various warring African ethnicities. By the early twentieth century, Booker T. Washington was denouncing the Belgian government's brutal exploitation of intertribal hostilities.[30]

Africanus Horton, a Sierra Leone "creole" who claimed Ibo descent through both parents, served with the British army as a military surgeon and tried to reconcile African nationalism with Anglocentric civilization. Horton agreed with Crowther that Christianity was an essential component of African redemption, but like Blyden, he encouraged the study of Arabic, along with French, German, and Hebrew. Closer to Blyden than to

---

[30] Further discussion of the opinions of Quaker and Nicol are in July, *Modern African Thought*, pp. 143–50. For Crummell's and Blyden's changing views, check index citations in Moses, *Golden Age*, and Moses, *Alexander Crummell*. On Booker T. Washington, see Louis R. Harlan, "Booker T. Washington and the White Man's Burden," *American Historical Review* 71.2 (January 1966), 441–67. Also on B. T. Washington, see Vernon J. Williams, *Rethinking Race: Franz Boas and his Contemporaries* (Lexington: University Press of Kentucky, 1996).

Crummell, Horton demonstrated a respect for the African languages and noted their diversity: "some ... are harsh and guttural ... others ... soft and mellowy." He advocated English education, if for no other reason than its commercial benefits.[31]

It is within this context that Crummell's aggressive promotion of the English language in Liberia is to be understood. In his predilection for English, he was not unique; the cultural assimilationist pattern prevailed among indigenous West African nationalists. They adopted the same position; they simply did not argue it as systematically. Benedict Anderson has noted that the relation of language to nineteenth-century nationalisms was a mass of incongruities and irrationalities. The desire to impose linguistic uniformity within invented national groups invariably led to uncomfortable compromises, as both local dialects and cosmopolitan languages were sacrificed – sometimes bloodily – to nationalistic sentiment or bureaucratic convenience.[32]

In an essay of 1860, "The English Language in Liberia," Crummell argued his Anglophonic preferences systematically, if unscientifically. His arguments were rational to the extent that he provided pragmatic reasons for adopting a language that was universally employed in the arts and sciences and already spoken throughout the world. But his aesthetic and linguistic judgments were ungrounded in any demonstrable knowledge of the African languages that he so recklessly condemned. He presented no empirical evidence, but simply accepted the judgments of a Dr. Leighton Wilson that African languages "are harsh, abrupt, energetic, indistinct in enunciation, meagre in point of words, abound with inarticulate nasal and guttural sounds, possess but few inflections and grammatical forms, and are withal exceedingly difficult of acquisition." Wilson's were the weakest arguments that Crummell might have enlisted. No language is lacking in the tortures of grammar, and English itself, despite its conspicuous lack of inflections, provides innumerable syntactical pitfalls. If Dr. Wilson found the Grebo language "exceedingly difficult" or if he had difficulty grasping the Mandingo syntax, such problems should, by his own

[31] James Africanus Beale Horton, *West African Countries and Peoples, British and Native* (London: W. J. Johnson, 1868), pp. 107, 193.

[32] Benedict Anderson, *Imagined Communities: Reflections on the Origin and Spread of Nationalism* (London: Verso, 1983), pp. 18, 67–83. Benedict Anderson's work on nationalism, *Imagined Communities*, raises issues concerning the intrinsic cultural validity of "print vernaculars" and "languages of state." Pan-Africanism from the 1780s through the nineteenth century shared such problems with contemporary Pan-Germanism. Appiah, despite his enthusiastic references to the "elegant" work of "Ben Anderson," appears oblivious to the sophisticated ironies with which the work is replete.

reasoning, have suggested to him, and to Crummell, some hint as to their subtleties.[33]

To his credit, Crummell did not ignore the political implications of adopting the language of conquest. He alluded to the "sorrowful history ... the bloody strife, the heartbreaking despair, agony, and death" that had rendered him an English speaker. But, he argued, most national languages, including the language of England, had been painfully acquired through "conquest and subjection." Crummell made the valid argument that English was a print language, which provided access to cosmopolitan ideology and to technical and scientific education. Unquestionably, it opened the doors to studies in chemistry, botany, and other branches of "Natural Philosophy." French and Arabic, of course, offered possibilities as unifying languages, but French was associated with Romanism, revolution, and moral instability, and Arabic with the spread of Islam; Crummell had no sympathy for either. Crummell did not stress the strongest argument for the acceptance of English as a national language – that English could be a language of unification among the various indigenous ethnic groups.

With Switzerland as the most obvious exception, few nation-states have thrived among groups of people who do not share a common language. In the nineteenth century, black nationalists might have pointed to the Ottoman or the Austro-Hungarian Empires as examples of instability. China's cultural disunity was one of the factors that had made it vulnerable in the face of European expansionism, and polyglot India had been dominated by the British. Crummell and his generation had ample case studies from which to learn the dangers of linguistic and cultural diversity, which characteristically weaken an empire or a nation. Since in Crummell's estimation force "that is authority" would be necessary for the imposition of any national language, it made more sense to make the case for the dialect of the English educated classes, rather than for some indigenous African dialect lacking a written form or a print tradition.

Crummell's language theory was strong on the pragmatic level, if embarrassingly clumsy on the cultural level. He sought to force Anglo conformity on West Africa as a means of forging political unity and rapidly introducing literacy. Pan-Germanists had Luther's bible and Goethe's verse as a starting point, but even in the case of Germany, linguistic unity involved force and cultural domination to impose the supremacy of High

---

[33] Leighton Wilson is quoted by Crummell in "The English Language in Liberia" (1861), republished in *The Future of Africa*, p. 19.

German over Tyrolean, Plattdeutsch, and Bavarian. This end was not achieved by democratic means.

Mandarin triumphed over Cantonese in the struggle for a dominant political language in China not because of any intrinsic superiority of Mandarin, but because of historical circumstances whose precise characteristics can be debated, but whose ultimate result cannot be denied. In India, English became at least one of the official languages and functions as a unifying means of communication precisely because it is not indigenous. A nonindigenous European language can be more unifying because it avoids the problem of valorizing any one indigenous speech and thereby exacerbating tribal jealousies. Crummell may well have realized that to the rural tribesman, English might be preferable as a national language, rather than the dialect of some hated ethnic rival. Ironically the greatest champion of African languages among the major Pan-Africanists of the nineteenth century was not an indigenous African but Edward Wilmot Blyden, a West Indian.

Crummell's views on indigenous Africans – a mass of contradictions and opinions – were tailored to his audiences so that on one occasion he would write of them in glowing terms, on another with darkest pessimism. Nonetheless, inconsistencies permeated all his thought and reflected personal ambivalence as well as a tendency to force facts into preconceived political molds. Crummell was highly motivated to portray Africans as having the essential capacities for "civilization" and eventual "self government." In later years, therefore, he compared Africans to the virile barbarians that Roman legions had encountered in Europe's primeval forests. The "native Negro" was a diamond in the rough: "The very words in which Cicero and Tacitus describe the homes and families of the German tribes can as truly be ascribed to the people of the West Coast of Africa....Every female is a virgin to the day of her marriage."[34]

These sentiments aside, Crummell did not advocate majority rule or democratic government for the masses of any people anywhere. He rejected Jeffersonian democracy, and not only because of its inherent and inextricable racism. It was obviously unworkable when applied to peoples who were illiterate, unworldly, economically undeveloped, and politically disorganized – and that included most people on the face of the earth. Crummell believed in civilization from the top down. He had little faith in democracy, which he revered as an ideal in the mind of God but found

[34] Crummell, "Defence of the Negro Race," p. 87.

dangerous when applied to superstitious, untutored peoples – such as the Irish of New York. He had experienced, after all, the evils of Jacksonian democracy during his youth when white racist mobs burned and looted his neighborhood. In Africa and in America, he had witnessed ample evidence of democracy's dangerous potential. He had barely survived West Africa's first coup, which occurred in 1871. A mob had dragged his friend, President E. J. Roye, from his jail cell and lynched him in public.[35] Crummell had departed Liberia with bullets almost literally whizzing around his head. On returning to America, he took up residence in Washington, with its reminders of Lincoln's assassination, and in 1881, he was shocked by the news of Garfield's. In each case, perhaps illogically, he blamed the assassinations on the spirit of a lawless democracy, a lack of reverence for constituted authority.

Crummell's authoritarian civilizationism forboded the dictatorial policies that would characterize African nationalisms in the twentieth century, most notably that of Kwame Nkrumah, who received the endorsement of New World Pan-Africanists like George Padmore and W. E. B. Du Bois, but was certainly not their puppet. Nkrumah was, of course, one of the less brutal dictators to arise in postcolonial Africa, if compared, for example, to Idi Amin. Nonetheless, he threw Anthony Appiah's father – whom Du Bois despised – into prison, but Appiah has been less critical of Nkrumah than of Pan-Africanism in general, and has remained silent for many years on the fact that Du Bois was one of Nkrumah's strongest supporters. He has chosen to exhume the ideological shortcomings of Alexander Crummell, ignoring the fact that in the nineteenth century, Christian redemptionism was favored by African nationalists no less than by New World Pan-Africanists. It is surprising that some scholars still resist that idea or even consider it remarkable.

Over the past half century, scholars have demonstrated the seminal nature and pervasiveness of Christianity in indigenous African nationalism. George Shepperson, Robert July, and St. Clair Drake have shown how "redemptionism" and the "civilizing mission" were crucial to Pan-Africanism in the nineteenth century and dominated the thinking of Africans, no less than American or West Indian blacks. More recently,

---

[35] Abayome Cassell, *Liberia: History of the First African Republic* (New York: Fountainhead Publishers, 1970), describes Roye's removal from office on pages 267–93. When I interviewed the aging Professor Cassell at his Monrovia residence in the spring of 1980, he reported that he had not been able to locate a grave, and that no one can say for certain how, or when, Roye died. For further discussion of Roye and his fate, see Moses, *Alexander Crummell*, pp. 189–94.

historian James T. Campbell has continued to caution against the setting up of crude dichotomies such as militant/accommodationist or nationalist/assimilationist. Nationalist ideologies have always incorporated external ideological components. The African movement's discourses of redemption and civilization were not perpetually linked to Christianity; the ideas eventually found expression in a Marxist rhetoric. After all, as Bertrand Russell once argued, Marxist ideology is structurally identical to the progressive paradigm of Christian messianism. It requires no particular genius to recognize that the Marxist Pan-Africanism of Du Bois, Nkrumah, and Lumumba in the twentieth century was intellectually contiguous with the Christian progressivism of Alexander Crummell in the nineteenth.[36]

---

[36] George Shepperson and Thomas Price, *Independent African: John Chilembwe and the Origins, Setting, and Significance of the Nyassaland Native Rising of 1915* (Edinburgh: Edinburgh University Press, 1958). James T. Campbell, *Songs of Zion* (Chapel Hill: University of North Carolina, 1998). Bertrand Russell, in his *History of Western Philosophy*, irreverently attributes messianic delusions to Marx, whose theory he describes as an "eschatology," that is, an inescapable course of predictable events. See Bertrand Russell, *A History of Western Philosophy* (New York: Simon and Schuster, 1945), pp. 363–64.

6

Alexander Crummell and Southern Reconstruction

On May 30, 1885, Alexander Crummell addressed the graduating class of Storer College at Harper's Ferry, West Virginia. Alexander Crummell – tall, black, regal, erudite, dramatic, but overshadowed by Frederick Douglass on this as on other occasions – so handsome, so romantic, so glamorous and eloquent was Douglass! The conflict between them – always respectful, but never to be denied – was one of images and personalities, as well as ideologies. On that occasion, as usual, Crummell voiced his perpetual suspicions regarding mass democracy, although, ironically, he had always worked more intimately with the grassroots than Douglass had done or cared to do. Although born free and provided a classical education by long-suffering and devoted parents, Crummell had devoted his youthful energies to poor, unlettered black congregations in several American cities and in African frontier settlements, although in his later years he worked, very testily and with much turmoil, among Washington's "aristocrats of color."[1]

---

[1] Crummell's pastoral duties and contemporary remarks on his appearance and bearing circa the time of this confrontation with Douglass are described in Wilson J. Moses, *Alexander Crummell*, pp. 222–23. August Meier has called Crummell the most prominent Negro intellectual of the nineteenth century in *Negro Thought in America, 1885–1915: Racial Ideologies in the Age of Booker T. Washington* (Ann Arbor: University of Michigan, 1963). Other contenders would be Frederick Douglass, Edward Wilmot Blyden, and James M'Cune Smith. For additional appraisals of African American intellectual life in the nineteenth century, see Richard Bardolph, *The Negro Vanguard* (New York: Knopf, 1959); Leonard I. Sweet, *Black Images of America, 1784–1870* (New York: Norton, 1976); Jane H. Pease and William H. Pease, *They Who Would Be Free: Blacks' Search for Freedom, 1830–1861* (New York: Atheneum, 1974); and William M. Banks, *Black Intellectuals: Race and Respectability in American Life* (New York: Norton, 1996).

Douglass was born a slave and had an instinctive "feel" for folklore and folkways that many anthropologists never master, but – although putatively a man of the people – he had moved beyond all that. He became a "public intellectual." He had a comfortable house in Anacostia. His best friends, and most faithful admirers, were middle-class white women. He had recently married one of them and was about to embark on a honeymoon in Europe. Douglass made it clear that he had no taste for toiling among the masses. This had long been noted by other black leaders whose careers, because they were preachers, kept them, of necessity, deeply involved in black communities. He was often accused of contempt for religion and especially black religion, as it found expression among the uneducated. Douglass shied away from political leadership, for although born in the South, he admitted to some alienation from the southern style of mass leadership. He lacked, so he said, "the peculiar oratory found to be most effective with the newly enfranchised class." He referred, presumably, to demagogic preaching, designed to elicit and manipulate irrational exuberance.[2]

"In my communications with colored people I have endeavored to deliver them from the power of superstition, bigotry, and priestcraft," he wrote in *Life and Times*. But he found the masses tied to outmoded fashions in evangelicalism, "strutting around in the old clothes of the masters," and spoke prematurely of "the rapid decline of an emotional, shouting, and thoughtless religion." As did Crummell, Daniel Alexander Payne, Booker T. Washington, and others, he associated traditional black religious traditions, such as the "ring shout" and other "Africanisms," with escapism and political backwardness. It would require a sociologist like W. E. B. Du Bois, sensitive to the new intellectual trend of cultural relativism, and familiar with the rhetoric of German *Volksgeist* ideologies, to develop even a rhetorical enthusiasm for the frenzy of backwoods religion.[3]

---

[2] See Henry Highland Garnet's criticism of Douglass in David Swift, *Black Prophets of Justice: Activist Clergy Before the Civil War* (Baton Rouge: Louisiana State University Press, 1989), p. 255. Kenneth Warren makes additional helpful observations in "Frederick Douglass's *Life and Times*: Progressive Rhetoric and the Problem of Constituency," in Eric J. Sundquist, ed., *Frederick Douglass: New Literary and Historical Essays* (New York: Cambridge, 1999), pp. 253–270.

[3] Douglass' words are in *Life and Times*, in Douglass, *Autobiographies*, Library of America Edition, pp. 835, 937. W. E. B. Du Bois's poetic rhapsody on "pythian madness" and "Frenzy and Shouting" is in DuBois, *Souls of Black Folk*, pp. 190–91. Orishatukeh Faduma is critical of religious enthusiasm, although, like Du Bois, he compares enthusiastic black religion to similar cultural expressions among the ancient Greeks, in "Defects of the Negro Church," in *American Negro Academy Occasional Papers*, No. 10 (Washington, DC: Published by the Academy, 1904).

Crummell's cultural attitudes were no more egalitarian than Douglass', but his work as clergyman necessitated a routine interaction with ordinary black folk. Poor whites elicited his profound distrust. As a black youth in Jacksonian America, he had personally experienced the violence of New York's Negro-hating proletariat. A gang of Fourth of July celebrants had destroyed a school he attended during his early teens. His contempt for the great unwashed did not derive from the elitism of his Eurocentric education, but from his American experience. His hostility to Jeffersonian democracy was no emotional reaction to Jefferson's racist diatribe in *Notes on the State of Virginia*. Neither was it a reaction to Jefferson's proslavery position. Nor was it Hamilton's active abolitionism. Crummell had more basic ideological reasons for agreeing with the Federalists.

Setting racial issues aside, Crummell simply could not accept Thomas Jefferson's dictum that "governments derive their just powers from the consent of the governed." He called the idea "crude" and "incomplete." American democracy in the Jeffersonian tradition was ill-considered and dangerous. "The theory of the Declaration is misleading," he said. Jefferson's dogma had "shut out a limitation which the pride and self assertion of degenerate humanity is always too reluctant to yield and too tardy to supply." The "great political prophet" Alexander Hamilton had predicted not a few of the "evils" of "licentious liberty," averred the preacher, "although he did not live to see them."[4]

Alexander Crummell's philosophy was a blend of the material and the ideal, of the concrete and the universal. The titles of his sermons revealed a predilection for universal themes, addressing the human condition in general, but his treatments of universal topics almost invariably returned to the issue of what Marcus Garvey would later call "Universal Negro Improvement." His treatments of racial themes such as abolitionism and Liberian nationalism reflect a cosmopolitan outlook resulting from broadness of experience and catholicity of reading habits. Sometimes he viewed racial uplift in terms of the application of universal ideals to specific problems. At times he was a materialist, working from the specifics of African American life toward reflections on such abstractions as culture, civilization, and the nature of authority. We may call

[4] Even the most superficial reading of *Notes on the State of Virginia* belies the nonsense that Jefferson opposed slavery. The logic of the *Notes* was that coexistence of free blacks and whites in the same republic is impossible because it would lead to mulaticization; that deportation of blacks is impractical because it would necessitate big government spending; that since deportation is impractical, blacks must remain in America as slaves in order to prevent mulaticization – Q.E.D.

Crummell an idealist only if it is possible to apply the term to a personality so frequently associated with mordant humor and so often committed to material or economic solutions to problems.

Those who knew Crummell best remarked on his "Platonic idealism," but he was also known for his sardonic humor and his predilection for sarcasm. His sermons presented a pessimistic view of human nature and a constant awareness of human depravity, and yet he was idealistic in the vernacular sense of the term, advancing lofty social ideals and optimistic convictions. He was also idealistic in the formal sense of the word, believing ideas to have greater reality and endurance than their experiential cognates. But while he believed in the power of ideas, he did not believe ideas could exist in the vacuum of immateriality. In this, he may be compared to the much oversimplified Ralph Waldo Emerson, who drew a rhetorical distinction between materialism and idealism, but never denied the obvious necessity of matter as the "home for mind."

Crummell's theory of social change recognized at least three issues: the importance of individual character, the need for collective racial institutions, and the pervasiveness of racial prejudice as an obstacle to the aspirations of both the individual and the group. He was, of course, sensitive to the residue of slavery's heritage on the manners and customs of the black population. He was just as aware of the problem of racist democracy or "tyranny of the majority." Since notions of democracy in America were traditionally intertwined with Jeffersonian and Jacksonian racism, he was hostile to those traditions. American democracy, in his view, meant provincialism, racial violence, and white supremacist doctrines. While he tacitly acknowledged an incidental presence of these evils in the history of the Federalist and Whig Parties, he viewed their Hamiltonian origins as the sources of Lincoln's Republican Party, which had destroyed the intrinsically evil, and fundamentally race-based, Jeffersonian democracy.

A new social order had arisen as the armies of Grant had crushed Jeffersonian democracy beyond hopes of resurrection, but black communities lacked the civilization, the cosmopolitanism, and the leadership that were, in Crummell's view, necessary to take advantage of the new order. African Americans had yet to master the collateral agencies of individual effort and collective discipline. Black individuals must develop the personal integrity on which group progress must ultimately be based. Hence, the emphasis that Crummell placed on the concept of personal "character." By no means did he minimize "the deadly trials and the formidable hindrances which are our heritage in this land." Nonetheless, he articulated "the strong conviction that our future success and triumph are to come from our own inward resources, from the force of the CHARACTER which we may attain through discipline."[5]

Douglass understood the importance of character and individual discipline all too well. His entire career and philosophy were the personification of moral and physical courage. Douglass viewed both racial prejudice and racial pride as the products of ignorance and moral weakness. Suspicious of black institutions, and sometimes speaking against them, he was not one of those figures vigorously asserting himself as a "race man." His impatience with the idea of racial pride was conspicuously clear on more than one occasion, as we have already witnessed. Although he was capable of occasionally exploiting a variety of racial romanticism, his detestation for the concept of race was frequently stated, and of Nietzschean proportions. With his slogan, "Free the slaves and leave them alone," he revealed himself a laissez-faire liberal. The solution to racial prejudice must be in the hearts and heads of individual men and women. Institutional reform, once slavery had been abolished, was not one of Douglass' obsessions.[6]

Throughout the decades that Crummell spent in England and Africa, Douglass constantly admonished him that his place was at home, in the United States, in the daily rhetorical contest against slavery. Crummell decided that he would rather take his family into the malarial environment of Liberia than return them to the poisonous conditions of the United States. Douglass and his faction among black leaders opposed not only the Liberia–based black nationalism of Crummell and Blyden, they were equally impatient with the efforts of Martin Delany and Henry Highland Garnet, who denounced Liberia, but considered other approaches to black independence including on Caribbean prospects.[7]

Only once did he actually go so far as to present any scheme resembling black nationalism. Earlier in 1862 his *Douglass' Monthly* editorials had advocated a policy of "Free the slaves and leave them alone," but in November of that year he proposed a plan to develop Florida as a black state, saying, "If the country were at peace and labor and capital were

---

[5] Moses, ed., *Destiny and Race*.

[6] The reader is invited to peruse my discussions of Douglass' racial attitudes in the present volume, and in *Afrotopia*, Chapter 4.

[7] The complicated vacillations of Martin Delany and others on migration, as well as Delany's variable opinions on Liberia, East Africa, and West Africa, are sketched in the introduction to Wilson J. Moses, *Classical Black Nationalism* (New York: New York University Press, 1996), and in the introduction to Wilson J. Moses, *Liberian Dreams* (University Park: Penn State Press, 1988). Lincoln's support of colonization, carried over from his Henry Clay Whig Party days, was half-hearted by 1862. For details, see indexes to Moses, ed., *Classical Black Nationalism*, and Moses, *Alexander Crummell*.

left to flow on in their natural channels," there would be no need for the federal government to adopt any special policy regarding freed persons. Perhaps he was only toying with this idea of colonization in Florida as a whimsical response to Lincoln's equally vague proposal for new world colonization. "Colonizing the freed men there," he wrote, "would cost nothing in comparison." Blacks could migrate to Florida from the North, where there were "colored men . . . with attainments high enough to govern a state." Freed slaves should be relocated there "with implements to till the soil and arms to protect themselves."[8]

Otherwise, however, Douglass gave very short shrift to such institutionally based programs for reconstruction. By sheer power of personality, he obfuscated Crummell's assertion that black economic organization and institutional development, rather than recycling abolitionist moralisms, should be the strategy of the hour. Crummell insisted that the struggle for racial equality in the United States demanded structural and behavioral remedies, to be applied by black groups within black communities. These remedies implied not only individual effort (which was indispensable) but institutional reform. Crummell, no less than Douglass, was an ardent preacher of the gospel of individual character, but he was also an unequivocal advocate of collective effort and what he called "the social principle." Individual effort and personal character must be supplemented by reforms within the church, the family, and the labor system. Moral protest, directed at white America, was admittedly crucial to the struggle, but moral preachments did not always seem to be an effective means of achieving black power.[9]

This point can hardly be overstressed because Crummell's theories were an assault on those qualities often assumed to constitute the essence of African American religiosity at what W. E. B. Du Bois called "the dawn of freedom." Innumerable scholars, including Du Bois, Sterling Stuckey, Eugene Genovese, and many others, have so thoroughly chronicled the enthusiastic qualities of black religion in the Reconstruction period that little more need be added here.[10] To the extent that African American religion centered on ceremonial spirit possession and the conversion experience,

---

[8] In 1860, Douglass claimed to have been on the verge of a trip to Haiti in order to investigate possibilities of resettlement until he heard the reverberations of thunder at Fort Sumter. See *Dougass Monthly* (May 1861). His thoughts on Florida are in *Douglass Monthly* (November 1862).

[9] Crummell's ideological confrontations with Douglass in the 1860s are traceable through the index of Moses, *Alexander Crummell*.

[10] Du Bois's *The Souls of Black Folk* is replete with religious themes. Also see Sterling Stuckey, *Slave Culture: Nationalist Theory and the Foundations of Black America* (New York: Oxford,

Crummell's ideas of religion certainly ran counter to main currents in the popular culture. His ideas on religious reform dictated the abandonment of enthusiastic traditions and the adoption of a gospel of works. The antinomian strain in his thinking was intertwined with his belief that religious reform was essential to the institutional restructuring of the manners and customs of the masses, an idea differing sharply from Douglass' doctrine of "free the slaves and leave them alone."

By 1885 it was clear, at least to Crummell, that laissez-faire was not working. Thus, the "leading thought" of the Harper's Ferry address was "the shifting of general thought from past servitude to duty and service in the present." In the address, he made some ancillary remarks to the effect that "we should escape 'limit and restraint' of both the word and the thought of slavery." The constant recollection of slavery was, in his words, "a degrading thing," and "the constant recalling of it to the mind serves, by the law of association, to degradation." The rest of the speech addressed the status of the family, the conditions of labor, and the necessity of character building, but at least one person in the audience refused to allow the matter of slavery to drop.

The idea met, as he later put it, with "emphatic and most earnest protest [from his] distinguished neighbor, the Hon. Frederick Douglass [who] was one of the audience." Douglass "took occasion, on the instant," Crummell recalled, "to urge his hearers to a constant recollection of the slavery of their race and of the wrongs it had brought upon them." No supplementary record of the incident has yet been retrieved, but Frederick Douglass had spoken, and Douglass was the black public intellectual of his day, the darling of white liberals, the idol of black church ladies, the expert on all things black. And Douglass seemed committed to the idea that moral preachments to white Americans provided the means for the advancement of African Americans.

Crummell agreed with Douglass on the need for moral argument; they shared opinions on many things. Both men agreed that it was important to protest the injustices of American society and both preached the necessity of cultivating personal accountability among black Americans. They shared a unilinear progressive conception of progress and civilization,

---

1987). Eugene Genovese, *Roll Jordan Roll: The World the Slaves Made* (New York: Vintage, 1974). Conversion experiences are well chronicled in the slave narrative collections of the Federal Writers Project and Fisk University, and works derived from those collections, for example, Clifton Johnson, *God Struck Me Dead: Religious Conversion Experiences and Autobiographies of American Slaves* (Philadelphia, PA: Pilgrim Press, 1969) and Paul D. Escott, *Slavery Remembered* (Chapel Hill: University of North Carolina Press, 1979).

believing, as did all literate and thinking black Americans, that American society – despite its obvious injustices – embodied the loftiest possible conception of civilization. All black leaders of the period agreed that black Americans should emulate the ideals of bourgeois democracy with its ethos of hard work, cleanliness, and competitive enterprise. It was clear that Anglo-American society represented the highest point of evolutionary progression on an ascending cultural scale.[11]

But there were irreconcilable differences between Douglass and Crummell, and the most significant of these related to economic and institutional reform. Crummell insisted on collective group action and the necessity of creating a recognizable black American culture or civilization; Douglass showed little interest in such devices. Crummell was a "race man," his program presupposed ethnic chauvinism and depended on emphasizing social discipline and institutional development within black communities. Douglass, unlike Crummell, was not technically a "race man," for he worked toward a completely amalgamated society. At times, he seemed to advocate the total eradication of race and ethnicity and the extirpation of all ethnocultural differences through biological mixing. His hostility to the traditionalism and institutional structure of organized religion was part and parcel of the extreme progressive liberalism that he embraced. Thus, he paid little homage to the idea of the black church as a reform institution.

Without denying the sharpness of Douglass' mind or the excellence of his morality, Crummell simply could not see how, when called on to address African American problems in post-Reconstruction America, Douglass had conceived any program at all. Crummell's sermons always acknowledged "the tragedy of white injustice," but did not dwell on it. As a Christian minister, he could hardly minimize moral issues; nonetheless, he had come to view the solution to problems in terms of the manipulation of power – both political and economic – and in a global arena. Preaching to black people would be inadequate so long as their religious traditions placed more emphasis on the conversion experience than the development of character, the acquisition of wealth, and the manipulation of power.

August Meier has noted that many of Crummell's later positions, after his return to the United States at age fifty-three, were adaptations of ideas developed during his Liberian nationalist phase. He believed,

---

[11] Wilson J. Moses, *The Golden Age of Black Nationalism, 1850–1925* (Archon, 1978; 2nd edition, Oxford University Press, 1988).

as did his contemporaries Martin Delany and Henry Highland Garnet, that the elevation of the black masses in the United States was inextricably intertwined with the development of Africa. He worked toward the encouragement of "Christianity, Commerce, and Civilization" in order to promote African economic nationalism as the basis of universal African advancement. His mid-career African redemptionism and later Pan-Africanism prefigured the later efforts of Du Bois's Pan-Africanism and Marcus Garvey's "universal Negro improvement."[12]

Without a doubt, Crummell viewed lynching, disfranchisement, and economic repression as fundamental issues of the day, and he never ceased to protest against such "outrages." American culture in 1885 was unremittingly racialized in every respect and its democratic-egalitarian preachments were violated with ruthless and relentless consistency. But protest against white injustice would never be sufficient to advance "the destined superiority of the Negro." "A system of severest training" was prerequisite before any people could make the transition from barbarism to civilization. In a segregated society, only educated black people could undertake the work of replacing barbarous superstitions and crazed imaginings with civilized ideals. Adapting his earlier Liberian nationalist thinking to the postbellum environment, Crummell viewed the creation of black institutions as the essential issue of Reconstruction.

Crummell frequently opposed the prevailing African American leadership stance of powerless moralizing. His position entailed a striking combination of Calvinistic realism and evangelical optimism, for while he recognized black powerlessness, he maintained a faith in the "destined superiority of the Negro." When speaking publicly he did not avoid addressing what he called "these dreadful wrongs and outrages" that black people faced during the late nineteenth century.[13] Nonetheless, he constantly advised self-help – both individually and collectively – for while sharply denouncing white injustice, he resisted the urge to focus entirely on black grievances. Driven to find a providential meaning in the distress of African Americans, he insisted that the finger of destiny pointed to independent institutions as the necessary means to African American advancement.

It was not difficult, therefore, for Crummell to perceive the central contradiction within Douglass' philosophy, which preached the abandonment

---

[12] August Meier, *Negro Thought in America, 1880–1915: Racial Ideologies in the Age of Booker T. Washington* (Ann Arbor: University of Michigan, 1963), pp. 42–43.
[13] "Discipline of Freedom," in *Destiny and Race*, pp. 245, 246.

of racial pride and racial institutions while he derived his livelihood from his position as a racial spokesman. At the Storer College Commencement of 1885, he was willing enough to engage in special pleading as the representative of an oppressed class, and yet Douglass obstinately refused to address the need for racial institutions as a means of achieving class remedies.

Crummell's theory of social change stressed adaptation to changing environments, and provided a moral and institutional formula for racial elevation. This arose from his religious conviction and his social philosophy that human advancement must be grounded in the social instincts of humanity. His ideas paralleled those of reform "social Darwinists" like Lester Ward, who saw social instincts as part of the evolutionary formula for human survival. Similar ideas, within a Christian framework, were not new and had been expressed by Henry More, the seventeenth-century Cambridge Platonist, who argued on theological grounds that mankind was a class of creatures that naturally possessed social instincts.[14] If both theology and science agreed that humans were social beings, it was necessary to speak of institutions as well as personal character in the reconstruction of black life.

Crummell's ideas were always complicated. On the one hand he believed in the systematic cultivation of individualism, which he saw as a prerequisite of "civilization." Thus, he specifically addressed the need for missionaries to encourage not only Christianity, but individualism among African peoples.[15] On the other hand, he saw the need for patriotism, national unity, and collective responsibility as indispensable agencies of happiness that were in accord with the instincts of human nature and the laws of human progress. The balance between the necessities of

[14] Crummell's relationship to seventeenth- and nineteenth-century Cambridge Platonism can be traced in the index of Moses, *Alexander Crummell*. For a further discussion of the varieties of social Darwinism, see Richard Hofstadter, *Social Darwinism in American Thought* (Philadelphia: University of Pennsylvania Press, 1944). William Whewell lectured on the Cambridge Platonists, especially celebrating the ideas of Henry More, while Crummell was at Cambridge. See William Whewell, *Lectures on the History of Moral Philosophy* (Cambridge: Deighton Bell, 1862), and index to Moses, *Crummell*.

[15] Crummell developed these ideas in "Civilization a Collateral and Indispensable Instrumentality in Planting the Church in Africa" and "The Absolute Need of an Indigenous Missionary Agency for Evangelization of Africa," reprinted in W. E. Bowen, ed., *Africa and the American Negro: Addresses and Proceedings of the Congress on Africa, Held Under the Auspices of the Stewart Missionary Foundation for Africa of Gannon Theological Seminary in Connection With the Cotton States and International Exposition, December 13–15, 1895* (Atlanta: Gannon Theological Seminary, 1896), p. 138. Both are republished in *Destiny and Race*.

collectivism and individualism in human affairs was a delicate one, exceedingly difficult to maintain except through perpetual stress and struggle.[16]

Furthermore, Crummell was an advocate of the strenuous life, long before Theodore Roosevelt coined the phrase. He believed that human happiness was to be found only in everlasting efforts at the solution to problems. His audiences demanded that he consistently denounce the evils of white injustice, which he did, willingly and with relish. Nonetheless, he insisted on expressing what he called his "deep conviction of the black man's weakness." Without denying the evils of white supremacy, he insisted that the condition of the colored people resulted ultimately from their own lack of power. "Our entire history as a Race, on this continent, has been a perpetual entailment of weakness," he wrote, quoting with fair enough accuracy, the words of Milton,

> To be weak is to be miserable!
> ... Our feeble forces, like a rope of sand! Like the leaves of the forest our poor people, in divers sections, were scattered abroad at the fierce breath of their enemies! In all this tempest of rage and murder, weakness was the general [condition].[17]

Milton's words, but Milton spoke them through the mask of Satan, so that we must ask whether Crummell based his reform theory on a "proverb of hell." Among those who remember him at all, Crummell is known for his prescription, "What this race needs in this country is power – the forces that may be felt." And power derived from a list of forces, both spiritual and material. He constantly preached the necessity of "character," but character was not only a source of wealth and power – it was a derivative.

Character building and institution building were interdependent and essential to racial advancement. Mere agitation would never solve problems that must be solved within the soul of the individual or the institutions of the race. It was not the responsibility of black people to go "among the Philistines and destroy their idols" of prejudice and racism. Our efforts must be combined "for industrial effort," "for social industrial ends," for the attainment of "wealth and power." In short, he linked the solution of problems to the *material* condition of blacks, rather than

---

[16] Alexander Crummell, "The Solution of Problems: The Duty and Destiny of Man." The Annual Sermon of the Commencement of Wilberforce University, June 16, 1895. Reprinted from *A.M.E. Church Review*, April 1898.

[17] "Discipline of Freedom." Crummell quoted from memory; the actual words are, "To be weak is miserable," John Milton, *Paradise Lost*, Book 1, Line 157.

the *moral* failings of whites. He rebuked the "folly" of "mere idealists," with their exclusively moralistic preachments, and pointed to material realities:

The needs of our race are, to a large extent, material. We are oppressed everywhere by terrible poverty, and menial occupation.... We complain, and rightly too, of our exclusion from the trades and business occupations of the country...[18]

He had been making such observations for at least the past ten years:

...thousands of mechanics would make a strike rather than work at the same bench, in the same yard with a black carpenter or brick maker!
...we shall be scattered like chaff before the wind before the organized labor of the land, the great power of capital, and the tremendous tide of emigration, unless, as a people, we fall back upon the might and mastery which come from the combination of forces and the principle of industrial co-operation.[19]

Characteristically sardonic, he noted that the condition of the emancipated population was even more economically vulnerable than it had been before the Civil War. Under slavery, all the powers of the black population were diabolically "marshaled to definite ends."

The Race was one great machine, every member in his place; working with severest regularity, and producing vast and valuable results. Within a range of both narrow and material interests, but alas, with a constant muzzling of our personal wills, the whole world saw the physical value of the Negro Race. Every man was made to stand in his own place; every man to do his own work; every man to yield a distinct and telling product! Out of this came labour; industrial order; servile systematized energy and activity; great increases of Negro population; vast crops of Corn, Rice, Tobacco, and Cotton; enormous revenues to individuals, and to the national treasury.[20]

None of the abolitionist clichés about southern inefficiency, later to be recycled by Booker T. Washington, appeared in Crummell's analysis of plantation industry. His words echoed the antebellum management rhetoric of what James Oakes has called "factories in the fields."[21]

---

[18] Crummell rebukes "mere idealists" in "The Social Principle Among a People," reprinted in *Destiny and Race*, p. 263. He specifies material needs in "Discipline of Freedom," *Destiny and Race*, p. 253.

[19] "The Social Principle Among a People," reprinted in *Destiny and Race*, pp. 260, 267.

[20] "Discipline of Freedom," *Destiny and Race*, p. 246.

[21] James Oakes, *The Ruling Race: A History of American Slaveholders* (1982; reprinted New York: Norton, 1998), pp. 153–91, describes the antebellum South rhetoric of industrial efficiency, which to this reader seems to pre-echo the callous prescriptions of Frederick Winslow Taylor and the more ironic and incisive descriptions of William Graham Sumner or Thorstein Veblen.

Slavery had been as industrially efficient and as socially functional as it was morally reprehensible. Although it was a "terrible system," and designed to benefit whites at the expense of blacks, it was nonetheless "a system." Emancipation had arrived with "unspeakable blessings ... of personal freedom; the right of will; the exercise of the acquisitive principle; suffrage; property-holding; schooling and education; aspiration; family rights; freedom of conscience and religion!" but freedom did not automatically bring with it the principles of social organization and institutional structure that were necessary to the exercise of power within the Hamiltonian leviathan of postbellum America.

The answer to problems in the new era implied the need for new principles of organizing labor and capital. Hard work alone could not solve the Negro's problems; the history of slavery had proven that fact. Thus Crummell constantly addressed audiences on "The Dignity of Labor."

The beasts of burden that toil in the fields and carry heavy loads, they understand what labor is. Void of reason though they be, they have nevertheless understanding. When trained they know their places before carts and vehicle; know how to fit themselves to severest tasks; come to know painstaking and endurance in their tasks and toil. But they don't know the full value of their labour; they don't know the skill where they might participate in the rich gains which their sweat and toil yield to their owners.[22]

The "skill and cunning" of the slaveholders had enabled them to reduce the black worker to the level of a brute. "Indeed," he observed, "it is generally the selfish instinct of Capital to regard the labouring man as fit for use; regardless of his comfort, his rights, and his well being, as a man, a citizen and an immortal being."

African Americans were a "new people" entrusted, he believed, with a new mission in the modern industrial world. "Everything in this work is new," he wrote, "and believe me, as severe as it is new." There was, he asserted, very little in the labor history of African Americans that would be useful in the new millennium. Aware that he was living in an "industrial age," Crummell looked to the industrial world for models of the industrial and scientific efficiency that he hoped to see black people acquire in the rising world order.

Thus, he was never among those Americans who were drawn toward Jefferson's "boisterous sea of liberty." He felt that the "furious storms and tempestuous waves" of democracy predicted by Hamilton must definitely

---

[22] All three essays are in Crummell, *Africa and America*. He makes the distinction between work and drudgery in *Africa and America*, p. 391.

be avoided. His rhetoric was even more alarmist than Hamilton's, when Crummell spoke as follows:

One more peril to the American system calls for notice, and that is the wild insanity and the increasing corruption of our political life. For our political life and action are not seldom hurricanes i.e. in their fierceness, burning blasts in their heat and intensity. So extravagant are the incitements of partisanship, that they leave but little room for thought and sober reason. The masses of men, carried away by the tempestuousness of overwrought passion, seem for the time to put sense and judgment out of sight.[23]

Crummell appreciated, far better than de Tocqueville, the meaning of "tyranny of the majority," and with rare insight that would never have appeared in the writings of James Madison or John C. Calhoun. Crummell had bitterly experienced the turbulence of democracy, not only in America, but in Africa – and by the end of the century he had witnessed the disruption of two societies, each of them claiming to be democracies, as they bathed their citizens in blood.

Crummell's intellectual roots and emotional ties were "Federalist," and I do mean Federalist, rather than "whiggish." For many years Crummell maintained a friendship with John Jay, grandson of the chief justice. Like Alexander Hamilton, Crummell was suspicious of democracy as an ideology and believed in the rule of law through a strong national government. His earlier experiences were in large part responsible for his authoritarian view of government and his well-grounded fear of mob psychology. He had received an excellent schooling in the meaning of "Jacksonian Democracy" as a youth in New York City, where antiabolition mobs frequently carried out reigns of terror. His hostility to mob rule was reinforced during his years in Liberia, where he witnessed the whimsical violence and fortuitous morality often associated with frontier societies.[24]

Crummell was profoundly shocked as he lived through the first instance of revolution against a democratically elected government in Africa. He was horrified in 1871 when his friend, Edward James Roye, the fifth president of Liberia, was forcibly driven from office and presumably

---

[23] "Address: The Negro as a Source of Conservative Power," in *Destiny and Race*, p. 239. Crummell entitled this document simply "Address." Internal reference to twenty-five years of freedom suggests a date around 1888. The Schomburg Catalogue lists it as "The Negro as an American Citizen Must Make a Contribution to its Life and Character," MS. C. 315 [cf. Hamilton in Federalist 9 first paragraph].

[24] Otey Scruggs, "Two Black Patriarchs: Frederick Douglass and Alexander Crummell," *Afro-Americans in New York Life and History* (January 1982), pp. 17–30.

assassinated. Crummell fled the country for fear of his own life soon thereafter and returned to the United States. Correctly or incorrectly, he abstracted a series of political lessons from his experiences in Africa and America. The New York riots, the Liberian coup, the assassinations of Lincoln and Garfield, and the rise of white supremacy in the South rendered him fundamentally unsympathetic to the American form of democracy.

It is a system calculated most directly to carry men beyond themselves, to taint the brains of thousands with incipient insanity, and to hurry them on to wild and irresponsible actions. We talk, in common parlance of the wildness of money speculations and of the madness of unlawful lottery schemes. But these ventures are actual soberness compared with the intense and extravagant incitements which come out of our political agitations. We have in our country settled organisms and established modes in politics, which, in their operations, seem designed as certainly they do to produce widespread upheavals.[25]

Some historians have suggested that there is an intrinsic relation between the American democratic tradition and American evangelical Protestantism among the sunburned and the sweaty. Crummell, indeed, saw the connection, and he was appalled by the American democratic tradition's structural and substantive similarities to camp-meeting revivalism.

Why the very caucuses of parties – and they are multitudinous – are flames. Our vast political assemblages, what are they but burning blasts? Our national conventions, but tempests? Our grand elections, what but tremendous tornadoes? And then when success has attended these almost frenzied partisan efforts, what can we call the uprising and the passionate pressure of the mighty army of anxious, greedy determined office seekers – what but blasting hurricanes?

American democracy was like holy-rollerism, like red-necked American Protestantism, and it had led to a perversion of democracy. The idea of democracy was not intrinsically evil; it had its existence in the mind of God; but any divinely inspired democracy must be fundamentally different than that which had evolved in the United States.

When I speak of Democracy I have no reference to that spurious, blustering, self sufficient spirit which derides God and authority on the one hand and crushes the weak and helpless with the other. The democratic spirit I am speaking of is that which upholds the doctrine of human rights ... This principle has its root in the Scriptures of God, and it has come forth in political society to stay! In the hands

---

[25] "The Assassination of President Garfield" (preached Sunday, July 10, 1882), in *The Greatness of Christ and Other Sermons* (New York: T. Whittaker, 1882), p. 319.

of man it has indeed suffered harm. It has been both distorted and exaggerated, and without doubt it needs to be chastised, regulated, and sanctified. But the democratic principle is in its essence of God. . . .

In this land the crucial test in the race-problem is the civil and political rights of the black man. The only question now remaining among us for the full triumph of Christian democracy is the equality of the Negro.

Crummell's hostility to the prevailing state of American democracy was tied not only to his racial grievances, but to his appraisal of American religion, which placed far too much stress on the "conversion experience" rather than moral rectitude. His dislike for and distrust of the enthusiastic religion of the African American masses – derived not, as some suppose, solely from a hostility to African cultural survivals. Antagonistic as he was to West African tribal paganism, he was even more hostile to American enthusiastic revivalism. Ironically, he believed that even the traditional ethnic religions of Africa were superior to the pseudo-Christian heathenism that had grown up under slavery. Crummell's opposition to black mass religion stemmed from his aversion to its essentially American – more than its African – character. It arose from his hostility to the antinomian evangelicals and "the extravagances and wildness of many of their religious practices." The masses of African Americans, he once said, "would have been more blessed and far superior, as pagans, in Africa than slaves on the plantations of the South."

Native Africans were, in his view, virile barbarians, wise in their ways, but naive in their understanding of the world-historical forces that had placed them under the heel of white domination. African Americans, stripped of their ancestral cultures, were even more naive than Africans, and presently too weak and too ignorant to offer more than a sporadic and ineffectual resistance to white domination. Simplistically viewed, from a purely moral standpoint, slavery and the doctrine of white supremacy were manifestations of human depravity. Nonetheless, slavery had another explanation – painful and unavoidable. It had occurred because those who were enslaved lacked the power to prevent it. If Africans in the sixteenth century had strategically controlled the highways of progress and civilization, they would never have been the victims of slavery. The cultural and social backwardness that had allowed for the debasement of slavery were manifested on the individual level.

Thus, for Crummell the crisis of reconstruction was more than a moral issue; it was a matter of reforming the family, addressing the issue of labor, and developing individual character.

Douglass had practically no commitment to racial-ethnic politics or to institutions for the purpose of creating a racial-ethnic power base. He viewed the struggle over slavery as a moral rather than an economic crisis. Douglass viewed slavery as the offspring of the slaveholders' moral cowardice. Unlike Crummell, Douglass did not analyze slavery as an industrial system. He never accepted in principle the idea that laws and institutions exist primarily as instruments for furthering economic interests. Douglass viewed the Declaration of Independence and the Constitution as *statements of moral philosophy* that had imperfectly achieved their aims due to the human weakness of the individuals who drafted them. Crummell viewed the Declaration and the Constitution as *statements of political economy* that had, with brutal efficiency, achieved their ultimate purpose – the creation of a magnificent civilization, but one that was historically tied to the subordination of the southern Negro.

In the final analysis, neither Crummell nor Douglass was able to formulate a plan for Reconstruction. Neither understood what Booker T. Washington was to understand with such ironic clarity, despite his tragic inability to implement it effectively. Washington understood that black leadership required not only the passion of a moralist, but the cunning of a ward boss.

Crummell's destiny was a rendezvous with obscurity – as was that of every black male leader of the nineteenth century, with the exception of Frederick Douglass. All the others, Martin Delany, Henry Highland Garnet, John Mercer Langston, and William Wells Brown, have disappeared from view. On Crummell's death in 1898, the colored newspapers duly published obituaries, but one of them, while noting Crummell's passing, dedicated its front page to a commemorative article on Frederick Douglass, who had died three years and seven months earlier.[26] Powerless in memory as he was in life, he is remembered today only by a few encyclopedists, "harmless drudges," who celebrate him as "the leading nineteenth century [American] Negro intellectual."[27]

Alexander Crummell reproved, in his own day, what Martin Luther King, Jr., later called "powerless morality," although he would have rejected the idea that morality could ever be powerless or lacking in historical force. He tried to stimulate an awareness of "the great power of capital," of "the combination of forces," and of "industrial cooperation."

[26] *Washington Bee*, September 17, 1898; *Colored American*, September 17, 1898.
[27] August Meier, although by no means a "harmless drudge," may be credited with describing Crummell as "the leading nineteenth century Negro intellectual" in *Negro Thought in America* (Ann Arbor: University of Michigan Press, 1963), p. 42.

He associated himself with the belief that the practical solution to the problems of Reconstruction must be found in the understanding of economic systems. Slavery, for all its moral wrongness, was a brutally operational principle of economic and social organization. Now that the evil of slavery had been destroyed, African Americans must develop from their own internal resources a new principle of social organization.[28]

"What this race needs in this country is power," he said, but without diminishing the importance of personal character. For if he believed that material social structures shaped human history, he believed just as strongly that morality and abstract ideals had the power to shape material historical developments. Was this contradictory? Of course it was! It was a central contradiction faced by others of his generation – by Emerson, for example, as George Frederickson has so perceptively disclosed.[29] Crummell was a philosophical idealist and was correctly identified as such by more than one of his contemporaries. Nonetheless, he contradicted himself pragmatically with his frequent articulations of materialistic formulae for success. He firmly believed that labor and economics were interdependently locked with moral systems. This amounted to an admission that history was not driven solely by ideas. He should be remembered for his most characteristic statements, stressing the need for social structure and institutional power to control the passions of the mob and the enthusiasms of the individual.

[28] Martin Luther King, Jr., *Where Do We Go From Here: Chaos or Community?* (Boston: Beacon, 1968), p. 37.
[29] George Frederickson, *The Inner Civil War: Northern Intellectuals and the Crisis of the Union* (New York: Harper & Row, 1965), p. 177.

7

Crummell, Hero Worship, Du Bois, and Presentism

Saunders Redding once observed that the passing of Frederick Douglass in the spring of 1895 marked the end of an era in African American political ideology and cleared the way for Booker T. Washington's assumption of the race's symbolic leadership.[1] Washington's Atlanta Exposition Address, delivered later that year, marked a departure from the crusading idealism of the abolitionist era in the direction of a materialistic and occasionally servile pragmatism. The manifesto was, nonetheless, initially hailed by the young W. E. B. Du Bois as "a phenomenal success" and "a word fitly spoken." Edward W. Blyden sent Washington his pontifical congratulations on his "wonderful address," calling him the new "Father of his country" and adding that "your work in some respects" was greater than his, for while George Washington freed one race from foreign domination, Booker T. Washington was destined "to free two races from false views of life." William J. Cansler, a black teacher in Knoxville, Tennessee, bestowed a more realistic distinction on Washington, declaring, "Upon you has fallen the mantle of the illustrious [Frederick] Douglas[s], to you we accord the title as leader, all intelligent and thinking colored men will follow."

The first stirrings of the American Negro Academy in 1896 betokened an implicit denial of both the symbolic leadership of Douglass and the

[1] J. Saunders Redding, *They Came in Chains* (New York: Lippincott, 1969), pp. 196–97. Lerone Bennett, *Before the Mayflower* (Baltimore: Penguin, 1966), pp. 227–29. Louis R. Harlan, *Booker T. Washington: The Making of a Black Leader* (New York: Oxford University Press, 1972), pp. 222–23, 226–27.

belief that his mantle should be passed on to Washington.[2] The idea of a national academy was first proposed to Alexander Crummell by William H. Crogman and Richard R. Wright in 1894, but Crummell is reported to have termed the idea "completely impracticable."[3] Why he should have expressed such a view is unclear, but perhaps he was correct, because the Academy never did manage to become the center of black American literary and intellectual activity. It is unlikely that Douglass would have hailed the founding of an American Negro Academy with enthusiasm. Douglass had often expressed opposition to institutional separatism, and Alexander Crummell possibly sensed that such a national organization would have lacked authority without Douglass' support. Within months of the death of Douglass, however, Crummell moved to implement the idea.

Although Booker T. Washington was invited to the organizational meeting of the American Negro Academy on March 5, 1897, it is probable that a number of those present were relieved that he begged off, pleading prior commitments. Francis Grimké, who already feared that the two were irreparably estranged, still hoped to act as a go-between, and thus encouraged John W. Cromwell to issue the invitation.[4] It may be that Washington felt he had nothing to gain from joining an organization in which he must meet with other black men as equals. Or perhaps he felt, as he would insist on a similar occasion some years later, that his presence "might restrict freedom of discussion, and might, also, tend to make the conference go in directions which it would not like to go." Neither Wright nor Crogman were present at the Academy's first meeting, despite their authorship of the idea, perhaps having become more fully aware of the political embarrassments involved. Crummell, who was becoming

[2] Responses to Washington's "Atlanta Exposition Address" are contained in *The Booker T. Washington Papers*, Louis R. Harlan, ed., Vol. 4 (Urbana: University of Illinois Press, 1975), statements of Du Bois, Blyden, and Cansler on pp. 26–27, 30–31.

[3] The problematic nature of Crummell's original reaction to the proposal of an American Negro Academy is discussed in Wilson J. Moses, *Alexander Crummell: A Study of Civilization and Discontent* (New York: Oxford University Press, 1990), pp. 75–78.

[4] For organization of the American Negro Academy, see Alfred A. Moss, Jr., *The American Negro Academy* (Baton Rouge: Louisiana State University Press, 1981), pp. 1–57. Also see Moses, *Alexander Crummell*, pp. 258–75. Both Moss and Moses base their studies of the Academy on documents in the possession of Dr. Adelaide Cromwell, especially the typescript verbatim account of Edward J. Beckham, stenographer, entitled "Organization of the Academy for the Promotion of Intellectual Enterprise Among American Negroes," and an untitled manuscript in the handwriting of John Wesley Cromwell that describes the early organizational meetings of December 18, 1896, through February 15, 1897, as well as the official organizational meeting of March 5, 1897.

increasingly open in his hostility to Washington, had nothing to lose. He had privately referred to Washington as a racial traitor while expressing public doubts as to his educational policies.[5] Washington had responded with a swift display of his increasing power, even gaining access to the Episcopal journals as instruments to undermine Crummell's base within his own denomination.

The speedy and unanimous election of Alexander Crummell to the presidency of the American Negro Academy must be seen within the context of a partisan struggle. If there was any doubt as to this, Crummell promptly removed it by politicizing his opening address, attacking Washington's ideology of economic determinism and industrial materialism. He decried those leaders who "were constantly dogmatizing theories of sense and matter . . . Blind men! For they fail to see that neither property, nor money, nor station, nor office" were capable of saving the race.[6] In his second address to the convention, Crummell attacked the intellectual pedestrianism of the "Gradgrinds," who said that "the Negro has no business in the higher walks of scholarship."[7]

That evening the Academy heard Du Bois's paper on "The Conservation of Races," which had been solicited by the organizational committee.[8] The paper, with its attacks on "the individualistic philosophy of the Declaration of Independence and the laissez-faire philosophy of Adam Smith," was more a disavowal of Douglass than of Washington. In fact there was little, if anything, in the speech that repudiated Washington, for while Crummell and Du Bois disavowed Washington's antiintellectualism, they endorsed his doctrine of self-help and even his accommodation to some forms of institutional segregation. It was more a public repudiation of Douglass' assimilationism than of Washington's accommodationism.

---

[5] Crummell to John W. Cromwell, October 5, 1897. Bruce Papers, Schomburg Collection. Gregory U. Rigsby, *Alexander Crummell: Pioneer in Nineteenth Century Pan-African Thought* (New York: Greenwood, 1987), pp. 166–67; Moses, *Alexander Crummell*, p. 261.

[6] John Oldfield in *Alexander Crummell and the Creation of an African-American Church in Liberia* (Queenstown, Ontario: Edwin Mellen, 1990), p. 123, asserts that Crummell's increasing dissatisfaction with the leadership of Booker T. Washington "eventually led to the organization of the American Negro Academy," indicating fundamental agreement with the present author in *Alexander Crummell: A Study of Civilization and Discontent* (New York: Oxford University Press, 1989), pp. 261–70.

[7] Crummell's reference to Dickens's Gradgrind is in his "The Attitude of the American Mind Toward the Negro Intellect," published in *The American Negro Academy Occasional Papers*, No. 3 (Washington, DC, 1898), p. 16.

[8] W. E. B. Du Bois, "The Conservation of Races," published as *The American Negro Academy Occasional Papers*, No. 2 (Washington, DC, 1897), p. 7. For the solicitation of the paper, see Moss, *The American Negro Academy*, p. 31.

It was a declaration that Du Bois intended to support the racial collectivism and separatism of Crummell, whose opposition to the assimilationism of Douglass was well known.[9] Speaking in support of Crummell's nomination to the presidency, Du Bois had said, "We, as Negroes, perhaps have too little reverence. One of the things we have all to learn is reverence for age, and for the performance of past duties. And I say right here, there could be no greater a reverence paid by us to worth than by recognizing such a man as Dr. Crummell."[10]

"Instinctively, I bowed before this man," Du Bois later said in his eulogy on Crummell, which most of us know from *The Souls of Black Folk*.[11] It is a beautiful and moving chapter, but those who seek a factual treatment of Crummell's life have often been misled by Du Bois's romanticizing and hero worship. Du Bois was born fatherless, but not out of wedlock, in 1868, and grew up in Great Barrington, Massachusetts.[12] His mother was an impoverished cripple, sometimes working as a domestic in a town where few secrets could be kept. The late Allison Davis, a distinguished black psychologist at the University of Chicago, discovered in Du Bois's autobiographical writings the fear that he might be an out-of-wedlock child, like his vanished half brother Adelbert.[13] He had been painfully rebuffed by his grandfather, Alexander Du Bois.[14]

---

[9] For differences of opinion between Douglass and Crummell, see Moses, *Alexander Crummell*, pp. 226–27, 289–92. A public confrontation between Douglass and Crummell at Storer College on May 30, 1885, is mentioned in Alexander Crummell, *Africa and America: Addresses and Discourses* (Springfield, MA: Wiley & Co., 1891), pp. iv–v.

[10] Beckham, "Organization of the Academy," p. 10.

[11] W. E. B. Du Bois's chapter on Alexander Crummell in *The Souls of Black Folk* (Chicago: McClurg, 1903), p. 216. The eulogy was originally delivered at Tuskegee in 1899. The historian Gregory U. Rigsby reports that William James, who was present on the occasion, was unaware that Crummell was actually a real person. See Gregory U. Rigsby, *Alexander Crummell: Pioneer in Nineteenth Century Pan-African Thought* (Westport, CT: Greenwood Press, 1987), p. 174.

[12] Herbert Aptheker, Du Bois's friend and erstwhile literary custodian, made mention of Du Bois's fear that he may have been illegitimate in a conversation with the present author in his New York office during January 1972. Allison Davis also speculates as to this fear in *Leadership, Love and Aggression* (New York: Harcourt Brace Jovanovich, 1983), p. 108. Professor David L. Lewis tells the present author that he has resolved the question by locating a copy of the marriage license.

[13] Davis, *Leadership, Love and Aggression*, pp. 108–12.

[14] *The Autobiography of W. E. B. Du Bois*, Herbert Aptheker, ed. (New York: International Publishers, 1968), p. 67, makes only passing reference to the connection between Alexander Crummell and Alexander Du Bois, who had been a vestryman in Crummell's New Haven congregation. Crummell had visited Yale lectures as an unregistered student. It is not certain when Du Bois became aware that Alexander Du Bois kept records of the meager collections for Crummell's preaching in New Haven, although Du Bois eventually

One need not accept the Freudian methodology underlying Davis's analysis to understand "the impact on [Du Bois's] personality of his father's desertion and his mother's disgrace, which forced him to depend largely upon charity during both childhood and adolescence." And it requires no inordinate stretches of the imagination to accept the arguments of Davis and Dickson Preston that the numerous contradictions in the several versions of Du Bois's autobiography represented fantasies that were the result of "internal conflicts."[15] Even without Davis's psychological analysis, it is easy to understand the impression that the venerable Crummell made on the younger man. Davis did not, in fact, mention in his treatment of Du Bois the possibility that Crummell was a paternal figure and a substitute for the father Du Bois had never known. Nonetheless, one cannot resist the possibilities of extending Davis's analysis to a reading of Du Bois's romantic first encounter with Crummell, standing "Tall, frail, and black, with simple dignity and an unmistakable air of good breeding." He tells us that "instinctively" he "bowed before this man, as one bows before the prophets of the world," or perhaps as a son in some patriarchal society might bow to receive his father's blessing and birthright.[16]

The thing that is most striking about Du Bois's characterization of Crummell is its vagueness and its dreamy, romantic quality. Du Bois did not know, or else chose to ignore, much about Crummell at the time he wrote the eulogy, and Crummell's ambition, irascibility, and sardonicism do not impinge on the author's imagination. The narrative is dominated by such words and phrases as "frail . . . soul in search of itself . . . grave shadow . . . haunting the streets . . . wingless and alone . . . beneath a dark despair. . . ." Du Bois portrayed Crummell as "a dark and pierced Jew," wandering the world on a weird pilgrimage, a battered victim of prejudice, a suffering servant and messianic saint. The portrayal must have occasioned many a wink and a nudge among Crummell's other acquaintances. Crummell was an entirely different breed of cat and the words that he once used to describe his bishop, speaking of his "pertinacity," might have been applied to himself. He spoke of the characteristics found "in the great Gregory, Innocent, Calvin; good men; earnest servants of God,

---

obtained these records. W. E. B. Du Bois Papers, "Account of Money Contributed for the Benefit of Mr. Alexander Crummell," manuscript in the microfilm edition, Reel 89, Frames 94–97. *The Autobiography of W. E. B. Du Bois* (New York: International, 1968), p. 67.

[15] Davis, *Leadership, Love and Aggression*, pp. 105–6.

[16] Du Bois, *Souls of Black Folk*, p. 216.

but who nevertheless like most men of the irascible temperament never spared the men who differed from them or who they disliked."[17]

Although politically assertive and possessed of a fighting spirit, Crummell was not a man of the people. His sometimes strident black nationalism was not complemented by any appreciation for the folkways of the black American masses. Crummell's elitist ideology was inseparable from his religious opinions. Indeed, he viewed slave culture as degraded and useless, consisting of nothing more than a systematic introduction into licentiousness and irresponsibility.[18] The unadulterated native African possessed a certain barbarian vigor and spirit of enterprise, which many black Americans had unfortunately lost. Crummell viewed the religion of the masses as dangerously escapist, based as it was on waves of revivalism that were purely emotional. It represented an obsession with spirit possession, a reliance on visions of Jesus, and a heretical "antinomianism," a belief that heaven could be attained purely by faith in Jesus's vicarious atonement.[19]

Crummell was fairly well known by the time he retired from his pastorship at St. Luke's Episcopal Church in 1894, but his intellectual attainments and international reputation did not overcome the hostility of his parishioners. He was accused of coldness, sarcasm, and contempt, and he was frequently away on speaking tours. When he preached at home he denounced drinking, adultery, grossness, and abominations from the pulpit. There was considerable rejoicing among some members of his congregation when he stepped down after twenty-two years. Of course, he left behind a small but influential core of supporters, including John W. Cromwell, the journalist-historian, and Anna Cooper, the author and scholar, who gave him an affectionate farewell, presenting him with "a purse of gold." The dissenters of St. Luke's Church breathed a sigh of relief, and began looking for a new pastor, who they hoped would give the fashionable parish less-contentious leadership.[20]

At age seventy-six, Crummell had more time on his hands than he could comfortably endure. He bravely claimed to be "up to my eyelids in work," but he was clearly searching for new fields of activity and more trouble to get into. He turned to working on his fourth book, having already

[17] Crummell to Denison, September 9, 1870, Domestic and Foreign Missionary Society Papers, Episcopal Archives of the Southwest, Austin, Texas.
[18] Crummell's theories on African and slave cultures are discussed at length in Moses, *Alexander Crummell*, pp. 93–94 and 278–79. *Africa and America*, pp. 91–97.
[19] Crummell on revivals in Moses, *Alexander Crummell*, pp. 193–94.
[20] Moses, *Alexander Crummell*, pp. 242–44.

published three before his retirement. He took up an active career of public speaking, giving two addresses at the famous Atlanta Exposition in the fall of 1895. Booker T. Washington was not the only black person to address the convention that fall. Other speakers included representatives of the national women's club movement and speakers for and against African colonization. After Atlanta, Crummell made a foray into the Midwest to address the graduating class at Wilberforce University, where the prickly young scholar William Edward Burghardt Du Bois was teaching Greek and Latin.

The subject of Crummell's address at Wilberforce was "The Solution of Problems: The Duty and Destiny of Man," and even if he had slept through the address, Du Bois would have known the sentiments Crummell expressed on that occasion. The speech was reprinted in the *A.M.E. Church Review*, the most important black periodical of its time, and reissued as a pamphlet, and Du Bois was totally in agreement with its rigorous puritan sentiments. Crummell spoke on the eternal necessity of work and struggle, and on the immorality of indolence, saying that "the grappling with indeterminate questions is one of the inevitabilities of life." He defined the eternal destiny of men and angels, heaven, in other words, as "the unending, the everlasting ventures and anxieties . . . in the deep things of God." He defined poetry as the "ofttimes agonized strain of the heart of man to pierce the mystery of being, and to solve the inscrutable problems of existence."[21]

Du Bois well knew the truth of this doctrine of constant anxieties and agonized strain. His motto at the time, taken from Goethe's *Faust*, was "*Entbehren sollst du; sollst Entbehren!*," which he translated as "Thou shalt forego; shalt do without!" As a sensitive reader of poetry, he knew from the context that Goethe had meant the words ironically, but their truth was evident to him, and beneath his hand they were transformed from a lament into a heroic challenge.[22]

Eighteen months after the Wilberforce address, Crummell met with Paul Laurence Dunbar, Walter B. Hayson, Kelly Miller, and John W. Cromwell in the latter's Washington, D.C., home to organize the American Negro Academy. Du Bois was selected as one of the original thirty-one

---

[21] Alexander Crummell, "The Solution of Problems: The Duty and Destiny of Man." The Annual Sermon of the Commencement of Wilberforce University, June 16, 1895. Reprinted from *A.M.E. Church Review*, April 1898.

[22] Cited in *The Souls of Black Folk*, p. 60, reprinted in *The Autobiography of W. E. B. Du Bois*, p. 212.

who were to be invited to join.[23] At its first official organizational meeting in 1897, the American Negro Academy was dedicated to principles similar to those that had guided the old African Civilization Society. It was "civilizationist" in that it stood for the uplift of the African derived peoples, wherever dispersed. It pre-echoed the rhetoric of Marcus Garvey's Universal Negro Improvement Association, which elevated two of the Academy's members to exalted status. Crummell's inaugural address was entitled "Civilization: The Primal Need of the Race." In it he called for an elite but self-sacrificing cadre of leaders "to guide both the opinions and habits of the crude masses." The kinship between this principle and Du Bois's Jesuitical ideal of a "Talented Tenth," as servants of the servants of God, was not accidental.[24]

Simply noting the filiopietism in Du Bois's relationship to Crummell is not sufficient to demonstrate the intellectual continuities between the two men. "The Conservation of Races" was a specific endorsement of Crummell's ideas and an attack on those of Douglass. Douglass had delivered a well-known address before Washington's Bethel Literary Society in 1889, in which he took a strong stand against black separatism. He had vigorously opposed not only the principles that were to be espoused in "The Conservation of Races," but, on occasion, the very idea of racial organizations such as the one he addressed on that occasion. The following statement left no doubt as to where Douglass stood on such matters.

The trouble is that when we assemble in great numbers anywhere we are apt to form communities by ourselves, and our occupation of any part of a town or city, apart from the people surrounding us, brings us into separate schools, separate churches, separate benevolent and literary societies, and the result is the adoption of a scale of manners, morals and customs peculiar to our condition and to our antecedents as an oppressed people. When we thus isolate ourselves we say to those around us: 'We have nothing in common with you,' and, very naturally, the reply of our neighbors is in the same tone and to the same effect; for when a people care for nobody, nobody will care for them. When we isolate ourselves we lose, in

---

[23] Moss, *American Negro Academy*, p. 27. A printed version of the constitution provided to the present author by Dr. Adelaide Cromwell from the papers of John Wesley Cromwell specifies that membership is to be limited at fifty, cf. Moss, pp. 24–25, who conveys the information that Crummell's original draft of the constitution planned to limit membership to forty.

[24] Alexander Crummell, "Civilization, The Primal Need of the Race," *American Negro Academy Occasional Papers*, No. 3 (Washington, DC: The American Negro Academy, 1898). W. E. B. Du Bois, "The Talented Tenth," in Booker T. Washington, et al., *The Negro Problem* (New York: James Pott Co., 1903), pp. 31–75.

a large measure, the common benefit of association with those whose advantages have been superior to ours. . . . A nation within a nation is an anomaly.[25]

Crummell's opposition to such a philosophy was well known, and he had made his position clear in an essay called "The Social Principle Among a People." He spoke against "the dogma which I have heard frequently from the lips of leaders, personal and dear, but mistaken, friends, that the colored people of this country should forget as soon as possible, that they are colored people." He reminded his audience, in case they needed to be reminded, that black people were denied travel accommodation, employment opportunities, and the right to vote. They might "Turn madman, and go into a lunatic asylum, and then, perchance," forget that they were black.

But not only is this dogma folly, it is disintegrating and socially destructive. For shut out, for instance, as I am and you are from the cultivated social life of the superior classes of this country, if I forget that I am a black man, if you ignore the fact of race, and we both ostrich-like, stick our heads in the sand, or stalk along high-headed oblivious of the actual distinctions which do exist in American society, what are you or I to do for our social nature? What will become of the measure of social life among ourselves which we now possess? Where are we to find our friends? Where find our circles for society and cheerful intercourse? . . . we are a nation set apart in this country.[26]

Thus, the terms of debate had been long established by the time Du Bois presented his paper, "The Conservation of Races," and awareness of this helps us to understand why Walter B. Hayson responded to it by saying that "the day for the work of Mr. Douglass has passed."[27] The choice of topics was inseparable from a pattern of discourse that had dominated black writing and oratory for the past fifty years, the principal

---

[25] Frederick Douglass, "The Nation's Problem," a speech delivered before the Bethel Literary Society in Washington, DC, December 16, 1889, was originally published as a pamphlet, (Washington, DC, 1889), reprinted in Brotz, *Negro Social and Political Thought*, p. 319. Like Ralph Waldo Emerson, Douglass was not intimidated by the hobgoblin of small minds. His opposition to racially congregating in great numbers and in separate communities is contradicted by his hostility to migration out of the South. See his "The Negro Exodus From the Gulf States, address before Convention of the American Social Science Association, Saratoga Springs, September 12, 1879," reprinted in Philip S. Foner, ed., *The Life and Writings of Frederick Douglass* (New York: International Publishers, 1955), pp. 324–42.

[26] Crummell, "The Social Principle Among a People," a Thanksgiving sermon delivered in Washington, DC, 1875, was reprinted in his *The Greatness of Christ and Other Sermons*, pp. 296, 297–98.

[27] Edward J. Beckham, "Organization of the Academy," p. 19.

disputants being Frederick Douglass and Alexander Crummell. Du Bois
was siding with Crummell against Douglass when he asserted that "there
can be no doubt first as to the widespread, nay, universal prevalence of
the race idea, the race spirit, the race ideal, and as to its efficiency as the
vastest and most ingenious invention for human progress."[28]

But racial awareness was not the only concern of this paper. Du Bois declared his support of the strict puritanical values that Crummell had long
preached, saying, "We believe that the first and greatest step toward the
settlement of the present friction between the races – commonly called the
Negro Problem – lies in the correction of the immorality, crime, and laziness among the Negroes themselves, which still remains as a heritage from
slavery. We believe that only earnest and long-continued efforts on our
own part can cure these social ills." Here, Du Bois was stating ideas that
dominated *The Philadelphia Negro,* which he was currently researching.[29]
It was a sociological work, true enough, and served as a model for sociological studies during the shaping years of the discipline, but its final
chapter, however, was the sermon of a strict churchman. With rhythms
of the pulpit he preached his prescription for progress and prosperity,
calling for "Work, continuous and intensive; work, although it be menial
and poorly rewarded; work though done in travail of soul and sweat of
brow, must be so impressed upon Negro children as the road to salvation,
that a child would feel it a greater disgrace to be idle than to do the hum-
blest labor." Although lengthy discussion ensued after a reading of "The
Conservation of Races," William H. Ferris, although taking exception to
certain ideas expressed in the address, affirmed the idea that "our books
and our schools should put before the people the real influence of sexual
immorality upon vitality."[30]

Finally, the issue of idealism versus materialism was in the mind of everyone in the assembly. Crummell's inaugural address was reminiscent of
the Cambridge Platonism that was revived by William Whewell, whose
lectures he had attended while at the university. With an anti-Lockean
rhetoric reminiscent of Whewell's, he attacked those men who "are constantly dogmatizing theories of sense and matter as the salvable hope of

[28] Du Bois, "Conservation of Races," p. 7.
[29] Sexual stereotyping and gender-role conservatism were present in Du Bois's early formulae for black advancement. His language when addressing "the conjugal relation" was,
at best, quaint, and would certainly be problematic in any document published today.
See *The Philadelphia Negro* (Philadelphia: University of Pennsylvania, 1899), pp. 66–72,
391.
[30] Ferris, quoted in Beckham, "Organization of the Academy," p. 20.

the race."[31] He had insisted that "neither property, nor money, nor station, nor office, nor lineage [were] vitalizing qualities in the changeless hopes of humanity." It was the ability to "grasp the grand conceptions of being" that would inspire a people to change their destinies. It was "the absorption of a people, of a nation, of a race, in large majestic and abiding things that lift[ed] them up to the skies." He read the history of Europe as the triumph of lofty ideals of Aristotle, Plato, and Euclid. "These were the great idealists; and as such, they were the great progenitors of all modern civilization, the majestic agents of God for the civil upbuilding of men and nations. For civilization is in its origins, ideal."[32]

Crummell's philosophical idealism was observed by contemporaries. In the opinion of T. G. Steward, who was present at the meeting on March 5, the conflict between Crummell and Washington originated in basic philosophical differences. Crummell was a Platonic idealist, while the practical Washington belonged, in Steward's view, to an Aristotelian tradition. "Washington says a man's life depends upon what he has," continued Stewart; "Crummell says life is but the manifestation of what a man is. Washington is practical and objective; Crummell is idealistic and subjective. Washington looks at the branches and deals with applications; Crummell studies the root and the trunk and deals with principles. Washington is a disciple of Aristotle; Crummell is a follower of Socrates and Plato." This was more than inflated rhetoric. The Academy ideology reflected Crummell's long-standing opposition to Jeffersonian egalitarianism and Lockean materialism. During his years at Cambridge, Crummell had been influenced by the lectures of William Whewell, who sought to revitalize the Cambridge Platonism of the nineteenth century. Du Bois was not a Cambridge Platonic idealist. He was, however, a Berlin-educated Hegel-influenced idealist, and a Hegelian strain is readily identifiable in his theory of history and the quasi-religious vignettes of *Darkwater*.[33]

There can be no doubt as to Crummell's belief that ideas were the forces that drove history and that it was the responsibility of educated

[31] Crummell, "Civilization," p. 4. See William Whewell, *Lectures on the History of Moral Philosophy* (Cambridge: Deighton Bell, 1862). Also see discussion of Whewell in Wilson J. Moses, *Alexander Crummell: A Study of Civilization and Discontent* (New York: Oxford University Press, 1990), pp. 75–78.

[32] Crummell, "Civilization," p. 5.

[33] Joel Williamson, "W.E.B. Du Bois as a Hegelian," in David G. Sansing, ed., *What Was Freedom's Price?* (Jackson: University Press of Mississippi, 1978), pp. 21–49, 116–18. Hegelian themes are apparent in Du Bois's poem "Hymn to the Peoples," in W. E. B. Du Bois, *Darkwater: Voices from Within the Veil* (New York: Harcourt Brace, 1920), pp. 275–76.

leadership to give ideas substance in everyday life. The educated classes
had a duty consisting of "lifting up this people of ours to the grand plane
of civilization ... to a height of noble thought, grand civility, a chaste and
elevating culture [and] refinement."[34] The ideas that were responsible for
the glory of civilization were present from all eternity in the mind of God,
and were given historical expression through the progress of civilization.
"The Conservation of Races" was a restatement of a mystical Christian
idea that Crummell had long preached, the idea that races were "the
organisms and ordinance of God." In Crummell's ideology, as in "The
Conservation of Races," we find the idea that each race represented an
expression of some divine ideal or plan for the advancement of civilization. There could be no doubt, as Du Bois put it, "as to the widespread
prevalence of the race idea, the race spirit, the race ideal."

In "The Conservation of Races" racialism is valorized through association with a mystical, teleological rhetoric, a pattern that is prominent in
Crummell's addresses, such as "The Race Problem in America" (1888).
Du Bois drew on both his Germanic training and on the black nationalist
tradition epitomized in the writings of Crummell and Edward Wilmot
Blyden to proclaim that each race was the manifestation of a spiritual
ideal, a sacred mystery that existed in the mind of God. Every race was
striving, "each in its own way, to develop for civilization its particular
message, its particular ideal." Whether from conviction or from purely
rhetorical motives, Du Bois gravitated to the rhetoric of Christian idealism and theological racialism when he insisted that each race, by fulfilling
"its particular message, its particular ideal, which would help to guide
the world nearer that perfection of human life for which we all long, that
'one far off Divine event.'"[35]

"The Conservation of Races" demonstrated the conflict between idealism and materialism in black leadership ideology. It was a practical
illustration of the "idealistic" belief that race problems could be greatly
ameliorated by intellectual activity. It represented a search for a post-
Reconstruction agenda, rejecting Douglass' assimilationism in favor of
Washington's program for institutional self-help. Although Du Bois disapproved of Washington's overly materialistic approach to education, he

---

[34] Crummell, "Civilization," p. 6.
[35] Crummell, "The Race Problem in America," in Crummell, *Africa and America* (Springfield,
   MA: Wiley, 1891), p. 46. For Edward Wilmot Blyden's theological racialism, see his "The
   Call of Providence to the Descendants of Africa in America," in *Liberia's Offering* (New
   York: John A. Gray, 1862). Du Bois's quotation is from Alfred Lord Tennyson's "In
   Memoriam."

emphatically supported Washington's view that the masses must be culturally refashioned and uplifted from their present "vice and immorality." And like Crummell, he believed that the burden of reform must be carried out by black people working through black institutions.

The problem of idealism, and the practicality of conserving races within the environmental reality of the United States, was taken up in the discussion that ensued. One extemporaneous commentator from the floor opined that while "in an academy the only ideas will be idealistic ideas," Du Bois's position was "too idealistic." He did not see how black people could live in the United States and still maintain the identity of the race. He did not believe that the ideal of racial integrity was destined to survive in the material environment. The "law of environment" and the fact that "mere race distinctions are of no consequence" seemed to indicate that "here on the American continent, where we have a conglomeration of the races of the world, it is a fact that we are erasing these distinctions."[36]

Kelly Miller defended Du Bois's position, urging that African Americans should resist assimilation and work out "within ourselves the idea of race . . . the idea that we should surpass every other race." William S. Scarborough, the classical scholar, sided with the previous speaker, however, opining that he could not "conceive of two races, equal in education, equal in every particular, living side by side, without intermingling." Crummell expressed the opinion that the examples of England, France, and Austria provided evidence to the contrary. Francis J. Grimké insisted that the identity of the Negro race would endure forever, regardless of intermingling or amalgamation. Like Du Bois, he was a man of obviously mixed ancestry, and like Du Bois, he seemed to view race as an abstraction, rather than as a set of biological traits. Crummell then closed the discussion with a lengthy and rambling monologue in which he proclaimed that race, like the family, had been established by God, and that it was "God's order and God's law that races shall be continued."[37]

Crummell was obviously pleased with what Du Bois had said on the usefulness of the concept of race and called the paper "essentially good." Some weeks later, on hearing a rumor that T. Thomas Fortune and Richard T. Greener had charged the Academy with hostility to mulattos and that Crummell was determined to keep them out, Crummell angrily denied the charge. Du Bois was a mulatto, and furthermore, as Crummell pointed

---

[36] The speaker is not clearly identified in Beckham, "Organization of the Academy," p. 20.

[37] All discussion of Du Bois's paper is in Beckham, "Organization of the Academy," pp. 21–24.

out, his paper had been an excellent defense of the principles of racial conservation.[38] One is tempted to speculate that perhaps Du Bois, well aware of Crummell's suspicion of mulattos, felt it necessary to assert his racial loyalty with particular forcefulness. "The Conservation of Races" may have been an attempt to win Crummell's respect and affection, and that end it achieved. Du Bois's German idealism was perfectly consistent with Crummell's Cambridge idealism. It is unlikely, however, that Du Bois tailored his ideas to the occasion, for his commitment to Hegelian racial mysticism did not cease with the death of Crummell.[39]

Some scholars have seen an implicit attack on the accommodationist philosophy of Booker T. Washington in the founding of the American Negro Academy.[40] True, the Academy was more committed than was Tuskegee to theoretical defenses of black equality, but the methods of the Academy were more consistent with Washington's self-help doctrine than with Douglass' protest ideology. "The Conservation of Races," Du Bois's address on the Academy's first day of meetings, is a manifesto for ethnic separatism and racial exceptionalism, and a call for enlightened despotism over African American culture. Du Bois presented the document while under the influence of Alexander Crummell, as a "study-in-honor" of the senior black nationalist, and as a declaration of solidarity with the man he had adopted as a father. The address celebrated ideas with which Crummell had long been associated: the firm belief in collective identity, the preachment of self-help, the unabashed advocacy of racialism. Thus, despite Crummell's loathing for the rapidly consolidating Tuskegee machine, the speech manifested principles that were decidedly those of Washington. Du Bois was to give spirited defenses of racial separatism throughout his career, notably in *Dusk of Dawn* (1940) where he surprised those who did not know him well by proclaiming that Washington's emphasis on separate institutional development had always been a valid idea. During his later career, he did not pledge himself to assimilationism, but seemed to recognize a similarity between his own ideas and the Stalinist agenda of multinationality within an American union. The Du Bois who

---

[38] See Moss, *The American Negro Academy*, pp. 54–57, for further discussion.

[39] For Du Bois's racial mysticism, see Vincent Harding, "A Black Messianic Visionary," in Rayford W. Logan, ed., *W. E. B. Du Bois: A Profile* (New York: Hill and Wang, 1971).

[40] August Meier, *Negro Thought in America: Racial Ideologies in the Age of Booker T. Washington* (Ann Arbor: University of Michigan Press, 1963), p. 267, detects in the rhetoric of ANA founders the idea that "Negroes...were too impressed by material things." See Oldfield, *Alexander Crummell*, pp. 122–23; Moss, *American Negro Academy*, pp. 22–23; and Moses, *Alexander Crummell*, pp. 261–69.

preached collectivism in "The Conservation of Races" was the same man who was later to apologize for Stalin.[41]

"The Conservation of Races" represented Du Bois's and the Academy's tacit acceptance of the pronouncement of Walter B. Hayson that "the day for the work of Mr. Douglass has passed." It took exception to "the liberal principles of the Declaration of Independence." It asserted in the face of all evidence to the contrary that race was "the vastest and most ingenious invention for human progress." Anthony Appiah, following in the tradition of Douglass, has correctly challenged this assumption. "The Conservation of Races" is an exceedingly troublesome document, revealing its author's rejection of the liberalism represented by Frederick Douglass. Furthermore, it reveals what Allison Davis calls the "Tamburlanian ambitions" of Du Bois and demonstrates its author's affinity to the tsarlike traits of the man whose approval it was intended to win.

Du Bois and the Academy repudiated Washington's materialism, but not his self-help approach to solving "the Negro problem" by the imposition of Victorian moral standards. Marxists, feminists, and Afrocentrists have thus, understandably, been uncomfortable with the document. It is a *vade mecum* of attitudes that were common among black Americans a century ago, but completely inconsistent with the liberal academic agenda of the late twentieth century. It is an elitist document, a far cry from the recent approaches to a black American agenda that have privileged the folk culture and popular culture of the masses.[42] The new social history is unsympathetic to the high-culture biases of a document proclaiming that "an alarmingly large percentage of our men and women are sexually impure." Women's studies specialists do not forget that the American

---

[41] W. E. B. Du Bois, *Dusk of Dawn: An Essay Toward An Autobiography of A Race Concept* (New York: Harcourt, Brace, and World, 1940), pp. 173–220. For Bismarck, see *The Autobiography of W. E. B. Du Bois*, p. 126, but Du Bois here gives evidence of false memory. His actual words on Bismarck were critical and amazingly prescient. For Stalinism, see *The Autobiography*, pp. 27, 40, and "Dr. Du Bois on Stalin: 'He Knew the Common Man . . . Followed his Fate,'" *The National Guardian*, March 16, 1953. Reprinted in Julius Lester, *The Seventh Son: The Thought and Writings of W. E. B. Du Bois* (New York: Vintage, 1971), pp. 617–19. Davis, *Leadership, Love and Aggression*, pp. 105–6, speaks of Du Bois's "Tamburlanian ambitions."

[42] Du Bois, nonetheless, shows remarkable sensitivity to black mass culture in some chapters of *The Souls of Black Folk* (Chicago: McClurg, 1903). See especially Chapters 4, 7, and 14. For more recent treatments of slave culture, see John Blassingame, *The Slave Community* (New York: Oxford University Press, 1972); Lawrence Levine, *Black Culture and Black Consciousness* (New York: Oxford University Press, 1977); and Sterling Stuckey, *Slave Culture: Nationalist Theory and the Foundations of Black America* (New York: Oxford University Press, 1987).

Negro Academy did not admit women, and academic feminists find it difficult to ignore the "Victorian" gender bias that becomes evident when Du Bois speaks of uniting "to guard the purity of black women and to reduce that vast army of black prostitutes that is today marching to hell." Afrocentrists, too, are disturbed by the document despite its call for race solidarity, organization, and unity. While sympathetic to the idea that African Americans have a special mission and that they should "maintain their race identity," Afrocentrists are put off by the essay's implicit hostility to proletarian culture and its employment of such terms as "immorality, crime, and laziness among the Negroes."[43]

While the ideological biases of academic conservatives are far more pernicious than those of leftists, academic liberals, like academic conservatives, often do an injustice to the history of black leadership with "presentist" interpretations of their writings. Academic conservatism often ignores, undervalues, or stereotypes black writers and the ideas they express, but it is not only conservatives who favor ideological righteousness over historical accuracy. In discussing "The Conservation of Races," we often ignore the fact that Du Bois's program, like those of other thinkers of one hundred years ago, focused on a set of social goals that many writers at the end of the twentieth century considered foolish, embarrassing, or downright evil. It has therefore become necessary for some readers to reconstruct "The Conservation of Races" as healthy ethnic boosterism, ignoring those of its elements that are offensive to present-day tastes.

The "Age of Booker T. Washington" has been the focus of endless moralizing and the center of numerous ahistorical debates. Admittedly it is difficult to approach the period in terms of its actors' avowed concerns. We resist the knowledge that Du Bois, Crummell, Frances E. W. Harper, and numerous other black men and women were just as obsessed as Washington was with puritanism as a panacea for the cultural reform of the black masses. Booker T. Washington cannot be reduced, as Crummell once implied, to "a white man's nigger."[44] He was, rather, as Du Bois observed, an ideological materialist who "intuitively grasped the spirit of the age that was dominating the north, and so thoroughly did he learn the speech and thought of triumphant commercialism, and the ideals of material prosperity, that the picture of a lone black boy poring over a French grammar amid the weeds and dirt of a neglected home seemed to

---

[43] "Conservation of Races," pp. 14–15.
[44] Moses, *Alexander Crummell*, p. 292. Crummell to John W. Cromwell, October 5, 1897. Bruce Papers, Schomburg Collection.

him the acme of absurdities."[45] Washington's pronouncement represented pragmatism and a rejection of idealism, however, not a disparagement of intellectual effort. Washington simply did not wish to expend energies on the sort of intellectual effort that occupied the Academy.[46]

Professor Kwame Anthony Appiah has faulted Du Bois for buying into theories of race that are today considered scientifically invalid.[47] Du Bois was, indeed, writing in accord with the dominant social theories of his own time. Most likely he was attempting to appropriate the rhetoric of what Thomas F. Gossett has called "Teutonic racism."[48] His goal of creating a racial messianism was understandable enough, but such an enterprise clearly had little power to influence the thinking of American racists. The treatment that black folk received in public accommodations was not likely to be affected by Du Bois's attempts at transforming Teutonic myths into black Aryanism. A lynch mob was not likely to be influenced by the abstract arguments of "The Conservation of Races." Du Bois must certainly have realized this.

What then was his purpose if it was not to influence white racialists? Most probably it was to establish his credentials as a race man in a gathering made up of race men and presided over by the venerable Alexander Crummell. It was to repudiate the "individualistic . . . laissez-faire philosophy" of Frederick Douglass and to manifest support for the collectivist race aims that Crummell had expressed in his oratory earlier that day. "The Conservation of Races" tacitly supported Washington's ideology of racial collectivism and self-help, while rejecting his antiintellectualism. It was, as Vincent Harding and numerous other scholars have long observed, a black nationalist manifesto.[49] The document clearly placed the young

[45] Du Bois, *Souls of Black Folk*, p. 42.

[46] Booker T. Washington, "The Fruits of Industrial Training," in his *The Negro in Business* (Boston and Chicago: Hertel, Jenkens, & Co., 1907), Chapter 30.

[47] Anthony Appiah, "The Uncompleted Argument: Du Bois and the Illusion of Race," in Henry Louis Gates, Jr., ed., *"Race," Writing and Difference* (Chicago: University of Chicago Press, 1986), pp. 21–37. Houston A. Baker, Jr., "Caliban's Triple Play," in Gates, op. cit., pp. 381–95. Also see Kwame Anthony Appiah's resumption of the argument in "The Conservation of 'Race,'" *Black American Literature Forum* 23. (Spring 1989), pp. 1–16.

[48] Thomas F. Gossett, *Race: The History of an Idea in America* (Dallas: Southern Methodist University Press, 1963). See especially Chapter 5, "The Teutonic Origins Theory."

[49] Vincent Harding, "W.E.B. Du Bois and the Black Messianic Vision," *Freedomways* 9.1 (1st Quarter 1969), 44–58. Howard Brotz, *Negro Social and Political Thought, 1850–1920* (New York: Basic Books, 1964), pp. 19–24. Harold Cruse does not focus on "The Conservation of Races" in *The Crisis of the Negro Intellectual* (New York: Morrow, 1967), but he stresses Du Bois's nationalist leanings in *Dusk of Dawn*, pp. 230–34. August Meier, Elliott M. Rudwick, and John R. Bracey discuss "The Conservation of Races" as a black

Du Bois well outside the tradition of American liberalism. It foreshadowed his lifelong penchant for racialistic collectivist dogmas and presaged the Stalinist authoritarianism that would dominate the final years of his intellectual life.[50] Nothing could be more incorrect than to view this young authoritarian mystic as an heir to the liberalism of Thomas Jefferson or the pragmatism of William James.[51] But, as we shall see in the following chapter, his indebtedness to Alexander Hamilton and to Vladimir Lenin was real and constant.

To read "The Conservation of Races" as a "conservative" document does not imply acceptance of its antiquated, racial superstitions. It should lead to questioning the Jeffersonian liberal orthodoxies as Du Bois did, although little of the essay's doctrines seems applicable to the problems confronting black intellectuals at the present time. If we find Du Bois and other nineteenth-century authors worth reading, then we ought to have confidence in their ability to teach us something. I do not assume that we can always hear their voices clearly across the abyss of time. Past generations were not constituted of fools incapable of expressing their thoughts, and we ought to have the humility to listen to them, even when what they are saying exists outside the parameters of doctrines presently vying for dominance in the academy. We shall probably never attain the noble goal of complete historical objectivity. But only to the extent that we can cherish this goal shall we enjoy the benefits of judging the present in terms of the past, an end which is at least as legitimate as judging the past in terms of the present.

nationalist document in *Black Nationalism in America* (Indianapolis: Bobbs Merrill, 1970), p. 246.

[50] Harold Isaacs discusses Du Bois as romantic racialist in *The New World of Negro Americans* (New York: Viking, 1964), pp. 195–230.

[51] For views considerably at variance with my own, see John Hope Franklin, *Race and History: Selected Essays, 1938–1988* (Baton Rouge: Louisiana State University Press, 1990), pp. 301–2, and Cornel West, *The American Evasion of Philosophy* (Madison: University of Wisconsin Press, 1989).

BOOKER TALIAFERO WASHINGTON:
THE IDEALIST AS MATERIALIST

8

Booker T. Washington and the Meanings of Progress

What oldest star the fame can save
Of races perishing to pave
The planet with a floor of lime?
Dust is their pyramid and mole:
Who saw what ferns and palms were pressed
Under the tumbling mountain's breast,
In the safe herbal of the coal...
But when the quarried means were piled,
All is waste and worthless, till
Arrives the wise selecting will,
And, out of slime and chaos, Wit
Draws the threads of fair and fit.
Then temples rose, and towns, and marts,
The shop of toil, the hall of arts;
Then flew the sail across the seas
To feed the North from tropic trees;
The storm-wind wove, the torrent span,
Where they were bid, the rivers ran;
New slaves fulfilled the poet's dream,
Galvanic wire, strong-shouldered steam. . . .

Ralph Waldo Emerson, in the above lines, outlined a seemingly conventional version of the meaning of "Progress," based on Charles Lyell's historical geology, and dynamic applications of other sciences, on economic and industrial frontiers. The underlying metaphysic of the poem was one of constant change, represented by exploration, invention, and cycles of boom and bust. Overwhelmingly pervasive attitudes of commercial exuberance and industrial euphoria prepared Emerson and his contemporaries to think of progresss and change as normal conditions of the universe. Emerson was born during the presidency of Thomas Jefferson, whose contrasting metaphysic defined progress very differently, as movement toward a more perfect understanding of self-evident and stable truths – the unalterable laws of nature and nature's God. The instability or extinction of species, Emerson's "races perishing to pave the planet with a floor of lime," seemed disorderly to Jefferson, and as disturbing as the questionable phenomenon of meteors falling from the heavens. But Emerson perceived a dynamically unstable universe in which it was impossible to step into the same river twice and where life was "a choice between soft and turbulent dreams." [1]

In that same decade, a year before Charles Darwin published his theory of natural selection, Herbert Spencer published his essay, "Progress: Its Law and Cause," and laid out the principles that came to be known – anachronistically – as "Social Darwinism." For Spencer, if not for Darwin, evolution was teleological, and competition was the mainspring of "progress." It was he, and not Darwin, who invented the phrase "survival of the fittest, "which Darwin later said meant "more or less the same thing" as "natural selection." But where Darwin viewed competition as only one of the elements that drove progress, Spencer gave it primacy. To Spencer, any restraints on competition, the driving force of evolutionary progress, would lead to biological degeneration of the human species. The principle of laissez-faire was essential to the progress of the human species, and moral altruism was misguided.

Spencer had misappropriated Adam Smith's principle of laissez-faire although he had no use for any benevolent invisible hand in his system of cutthroat biological competition. Marx and Engels rejected Spencer's version of laissez-faire morality, but shared his teleological bent and progressive metaphysic. No less than Spencer, Marx admired *Origin of Species*, which he felt "serves me as a basis in natural science for the class struggle in history." Engels's publication *Anteil der Arbeit in der Menschwerden des Affen* attacked Spencer's bloodthirsty individualism, but accepted, as did Spencer, such Adam Smith concepts as division of

---

[1] Emerson's poem, "Wealth," was prefixed to the essay "Wealth" in *The Conduct of Life* (1860), not to be confused with the essay "Wealth" in *English Traits* (1856). Since its date is indeterminate, the question of whether the poem represents direct influences of Darwinian or Spencerian ideas, or Emerson's analogous musings, remains open. See Ralph H. Orth, A. L. Von Frank, L. Allhardt, and D. W. Hill, eds., *The Poetry Notebooks of Ralph Waldo Emerson* (Columbia: University of Missouri Press, 1986), pp. 951–62, for approximate date of composition as around 1859.

labor, which, to Engels, implied socialization of the industrial process. Engels's peculiar spin on evolution was that labor implied cooperation that stimulated social progress and the humanization of apelike creatures.[2]

Emerson was hardly dependent on Spencer, Darwin, or Marx to teach him theories of evolution. Archeozoic extinctions, recorded in stone, were one source of his poetic imagery. Adam Smith's views on commerce were another, but the principal source of Emerson's progressive theory was the direct experience of witnessing American economic and industrial change. His conception of change arose from witnessing the constant innovations of industrial capitalism. James Watt's teakettle, Gridley Brant's locomotive, and Samuel Morse's telegraph were elements of his poetic imagination. Only six years after Jefferson's demise, Emerson took a ride on the railroad, which inspired him to the following observations:

... Matter is phenomenal whilst men & trees & barns whiz by you as fast as the leaves of a dictionary. As our teakettle hissed along through a field of mayflowers, we could judge of the sensations of a swallow who skims by trees & bushes with about the same speed. The very permanence of matter seems compromised & oaks, fields, hills, hitherto esteemed symbols of stability do absolutely dance by you.[3]

Mutability was at the core of Emerson's observations; his progressive ideology was based on the conscious assertion that change is inevitable, teleological, and upwardly spiraling. Emerson asserted, in fact, that industrial progress led to moral progress. Herbert Spencer was wrong if he meant to assert that the laws of universal progress trumped the laws of universal morality. Commercial and technical progress were the agents that advanced morality. Progressivism discovers self-evident progress in the realm of social studies, once, significantly, referred to as natural history and the forgotten discipline of "moral science." In fact, the very idea that morality was progressive and could be studied as science was one of the assumptions of progressivism. Industrial capitalism could fulfill the dreams of moral philosphers and poets when it harnessed electricity and steam and, thus, eliminated the need for human slavery. The triumph of capitalism over feudalism was a necessary stage, in the thought of Marx and

---

[2] I translate the title as "Participation in Labor: The Process Whereby Apes Become Human," or more vividly, "The Role of Labor in Humanizing Apes." The noun *Anteil* has connotations of sympathy and/or cooperation.

[3] There is apparently no consensus on Emerson's place in the history of Western thought. One may stress his Jeffersonian "pragmatism" and utilitarian relativism, or his ties to "idealism" and moral absolutism that are seen in his abolitionist sentiments. For his musings on time, space, and the railroad, see Emerson, *Journal*, 1834.

Engels, toward the development of higher forms of social and economic organization. Darwinism, they recognized, was not inextricably coupled to the interests of the ruling classes.[4]

Social Darwinism was a "malleable theory," as Mia Bay has observed, and not always perceived as racist. Frederick Douglass knew this, as I have observed elsewhere, and discovered that the ideas of Darwin and even Spencer could easily be appropriated and evolutionism could be repositioned for the crusade against racism. Black Americans and continental Africans were heartened by Darwinism because it attacked the old nineteenth-century idea of "polygenesis," or multiple origins, with its argument that whites and blacks were separate species that had evolved separately. Polygenesis undermined the Christian precept that "God made of one blood all nations." Not surprisingly, some black intellectuals greeted even the French racialist Gobineau positively, for, as a devout Catholic, he believed that all human beings shared a common ancestry, and that miscegenation could sometimes produce superior nations.[5] Lamarckism and Darwinism contributed to Frederick Douglass' belief that moral progress was as inevitable as the progress from ape to man. In his worldview, the advance of science was the driving factor behind human progress – moral as well as material. He was happy enough to enlist evolutionism as a scientific buttress to a metaphysic of progress that was basic to his entire

---

[4] Much has been written on the words "progress" and "progressivism," and their sociopolitical implications. In 1908, Georges Sorel argued in *The Illusions of Progress*, from a Marxist perspective, that progress, as commonly understood in Western thought, was little more than a justification for bourgeois oppression. Marxism itself might be termed a bourgeois ideology of progress, an irony that was fully appreciated by Bertrand Russell in his *History of Western Philosophy* (1945; New York: Simon & Schuster, 1965), pp. 363–64. For other critiques of Marxist teleology, see Karl Popper in his *The Poverty of Historicism* (1957; London: Routledge, 1989) and Jacques Barzun in *Darwin, Marx and Wagner* (1941; Garden City, NY: Anchor, 1958). Other twentieth-century authors offering analyses of the progressive myth are Charles and Mary Beard, *The Rise of American Civilization New Edition, Two Volumes in One, Revised and Enlarged* (New York: Macmillan, 1930), Vol. 1, pp. 444–45, Vol. 2, pp. 828–31. J. B. Bury, *The Idea of Progress* (New York: Macmillan, 1932); Sidney Pollard, *The Idea of Progress* (1968; New York: Pelican, 1971); Bernard James, *The Death of Progress* (New York: Knopf, 1973); Bronislaw Baczko, *Lumière de l'Utopie* (Éditions Payot, 1978); Judith Greenberg, trans., *Utopian Lights: The Evolution of the Social Idea of Progress* (New York: Paragon House, 1989); Christopher Lasch, *The True and Only Heaven: Progress and its Critics* (New York: Norton, 1991). Robert Nisbet seeks to redeem the concept from its detractors in *History of the Idea of Progress* (New York: Basic Books, 1980); cf., C. Owen Paepke, *The Evolution of Progress: The End of Economic Growth and the Beginning of Human Transformation* (New York: Random House, 1993).

[5] Reactions to Gobineau are discussed in Moses, *Afrotopia;* see index. Also see George Wells Parker, *Children of the Sun* (Hamitic League of the World, 1918), p. 23.

philosophy.[6] Du Bois embraced its metaphysical underpinnings, if not its ideological forms. Garvey and his associates were soon to discover revolutionary potential in the reformation of Social Darwinist arguments.[7] Human beings have demonstrated boundless creativity in transmogrifying the most unlikely theories to their personal ideological agenda.

Industrial progress has a complicated and counterintuitive relationship to the concept of biological evolution; the developments are coeval and the ideologies derived from them are mutually derivative. Biological evolutionism developed simultaneously with the industrial revolution in a civilization where technological improvement was universally observable. The material environment was dominated from 1810 to 1860 by a revolution in markets, transportation, communications, agriculture, and machinery. It was a world dominated by the undeniability of industrial progress and set the metaphysical foundations for a belief in biological progress as well. Reciprocally, biological theories obviously encouraged industrialism, and so-called "social Darwinism" was an attempt to apply the metaphysics of biological competition to industrial societies.[8]

By the late nineteenth century, "progressivism" was emerging as a political movement that, like "liberalism," subsumed contradictory ideas. Both were reform ideologies, rooted in the social gospel's mission to improve the living conditions of the lower classes. The philanthropical social Darwinist and admirer of Spencer, Andrew Carnegie, may be called a progressive because he sought, spasmodically, to make the world better. The liberal socialist Jane Addams, with her commitment to mitigating the harshness of the industrial process, was also a progressive. Some attempts

---

[6] Moses, *Afrotopia*, p. 268, n. 70; Frederick Douglass, *Papers*, Vol. 5, p. 124.

[7] Mia Bay in *The White Image in the Black Mind* (New York: Oxford, 2000), p. 190. Isaiah Berlin and others have reflected on connections between Darwin and Marx. For a thoughtful interpretation of this scholarship, see Francis Wheen, *Karl Marx: A Life* (New York: Norton, 1999), pp. 363–69. Hofstadter, *Social Darwinism*, pp. 115–17. The editors of the *Frederick Douglass Papers*, Vol. 4, p. 129, presuppose but do not demonstrate a Darwinian connection to Douglass. A Lamarckian tendency is attributed to Douglass in Moses, *Afrotopia*, pp. 111–12, 119–29.

[8] Richard Hofstadter recognizes the impact of biology on industrial thought, but not the converse, in his brilliant *Social Darwinism in American Thought* (Philadelphia: University of Pennsylvania Press, 1944); Chapter 3 and the index include references to industrialism. Also see Gertrude Himmelfarb, *Darwin and Darwinism in American Social Thought* (New York: Oxford, 1991); Carl N. Degler, *In Search of Human Nature* (New York: Oxford, 1991); and Pat Shipman, *The Evolution of Racism: Human Differences and the Use and Abuse of Science* (New York: Simon & Schuster, 1994). Vernon Williams provides a bibliography and discussion of some of the literature in *Rethinking Race: Franz Boas and his Contemporaries* (Lexington: University Press of Kentucky, 1996).

to improve society were based in private philanthropy, others were rooted in various proposals for nonviolent socialism. The ideological content of progressivism is contradictory and indefinite. This contradictory quality was evident in the overlap between ideas of Herbert Spencer and William Graham Sumner.[9]

Sumner endorsed, as did Spencer, the laissez-faire ideology, and he disparaged, as did Spencer, "the absurd movement to make the world over," but the resemblance ended there. Sumner, at one time rector of the Church of the Redeemer in Morristown, New Jersey, applied "survival of the fittest" to the machine processes of "industrial organization." He came to view collectivism and complexity of social organization as features of progressive evolution. Industrial warfare, Sumner argued, was an unstoppable force, and he acclaimed the victories of powerful businessmen and industrialists, who provided a public service by eating up their weaker competitors. Sumner opposed government regulation of business and insisted that the capitalist must live by the same laissez-faire ethics of evolution that Spencer applied to widows and orphans. The law of survival was "root hog or die," and if that law was merciless to the weak, it should be just as merciless to the strong. Laissez-faire did not perpetuate competition, but destroyed it. Thorstein Veblen also observed that the "heroic role of the captain of industry" was to eliminate the small fry who gummed up the workings of the industrial process by their own inefficient existence.[10]

Social Darwinism was reconcilable with industrial democracy and Christian socialism, as Richard T. Ely, a devout Christian, expressed in his "Social Aspects of Christianity." As did Sumner, he recognized the inevitability of "industrial organization," but tempered social progressivism with the idea that naturally evolving monopolies could be altruistically administered for the general good. Ely was a Christian socialist Darwinist,

---

[9] The temporal boundaries of "the progressive era" are indefinite, sometimes extending broadly from the 1880s to the 1920s, sometimes restricted to the presidential campaigns and the contradictory progressive ideologies of Theodore Roosevelt and Woodrow Wilson during the years 1912 to 1918. For problems of definition, see Leon Fink, ed., *Major Problems in the Gilded Age and the Progressive Era* (Lexington, MA: D. C. Heath, 1993).

[10] William Graham Sumner, "The Absurd Attempt to Make the World Over," *Forum* (March 1894), and "The Concentration of Wealth: Its Economic Justification," *Independent* (April–June 1902), both reprinted in Robert C. Bannister, ed., *On Liberty, Society and Politics: The Essential Essays of William Graham Sumner* (Indianapolis, IN: Liberty Fund, 1992). Sumner's laissez-faire attitudes are celebrated by Robert C. Bannister in his introduction to op. cit., but Sumner's celebration of collectivism and his applications of "social relativism" are less appreciated by the conservative fan club responsible for his current beatification.

as were the black social gospellers Richard R. Wright, Reverdy C. Ransom, and George Washington Woodby. Josiah Strong represented a different variety of social gospel based on a Spencerian conception of white supremacy, which he expressed in the Christian imperialism of his book, *Our World.*[11]

Numerous scholars have noted that the fundamentally irrational basis of Spencerism could not sustain itself as science. Spencer viewed evolution as another word for progress, and relied on a theological metaphor, a pseudo-God whose cruel, providential teleology dictated an ethnocentric but absolute good. By the 1880s, professional anthropologists had begun to attack popular social Darwinism, or as Carl Degler calls it, "social Spencerism." John Wesley Powell attacked Spencerism, observing in 1888 that "man does not compete with his fellow man for existence, for he emancipates himself from the brutal struggle by the invention of institutions." Lester Ward attacked social Spencerism on both ethical and scientific grounds, noting in 1884 that "The laissez-faire doctrine is a gospel of inaction, the scientific creed is struck with sterility, the policy of resigning all into the hands of Nature is surrender."[12]

In 1893, Thomas Henry Huxley, who was more intellectually independent than is suggested by his reputation as "Darwin's bulldog," questioned the Spencerian concept of "survival of the fittest" due to its "unfortunate ambiguity." Huxley pointed out that an organism well suited for one environment might be ill suited for another, and he disassociated himself from the idea that nature was teleological or that species devised strategies for survival. A more sophisticated and cosmopolitan intellectual than Darwin or Spencer, Huxley ridiculed the cutthroat "ethics of evolution" that grew out of Spencer's theories. Spencer insisted that civilization was based on the "serviceable qualities" of "social organization" and that cooperative instincts had undeniable survival value, while Huxley's concept of evolution was relativistic, not synonymous with progress. He did not see evolution as driven solely by competition but by adaptation to constantly changing environments.[13]

---

[11] Richard T. Ely, *Social Aspects of Christianity* (New York, 1889); Josiah Strong, *Our Country* (New York: Baker & Taylor, 1885); *Our World: The New World Life* (Garden City, NY: Doubleday, Page & Co., 1913); Philip S. Foner, ed., *Black Socialist Preacher: The Teachings of Reverend George Washington Woodby and his Disciple, Reverend G. W. Slater* (San Francisco: Synthesis, 1983); Gayraud S. Wilmore, *Black Religion and Black Radicalism: An Examination of the Black Experience in Religion* (Garden City, NY: Anchor Books, 1973).

[12] Carl Degler, *In Search of Human Nature*, p. 13.

[13] Huxley and Wallace, like Darwin, made extensive voyages collecting biological data. Huxley's studies of primate anatomy were seminal and Wallace independently drafted a paper on natural selection before 1858. At Huxley's prompting, Darwin "scooped"

Booker T. Washington was a social Darwinist in more than one sense. As did Engels, he viewed cooperative labor as humanizing, and, as did Huxley, he saw adaptation, rather than competition, as the means to survival of the fittest. Although he recognized, of course, that black labor was in competition with white labor – particularly the labor of immigrant Europeans – he hoped that African Americans, by timely adjustment to the industrial-technological environment and their prior assimilation of Anglo-Protestantism, might steal a march on white ethnics. There was some reason to hope that with the assistance of such Tuskegee sponsors as John D. Rockefeller and J. P. Morgan, a program of industrial adaptation might be successful. If tougher methods were the order of the day, then Andrew Carnegie, a noted supporter of Spencer, as well as Tuskegee, had cynical reasons for encouraging African Americans in their competition with racist labor unions.

By 1901, the year of Booker T. Washington's celebrated dinner with Theodore Roosevelt at the White House, the numerous expressions of social Darwinism were intermingled with the varieties of industrial "progressivism." American progressivism was no less a justification for Anglo-American supremacy than it was a doctrine of social reform. Washington, as a black progressive, had the tricky task of adjusting Anglocentrism and social Darwinism to his reform agenda. His program necessarily emphasized the historic ties of American Negroes to Protestantism and the English language. He sought to harness the momentum of industrial evolutionary progress, by firmly securing a place for African Americans within the machine processes of industrial capitalism. The primitive agrarian notions of Thomas Jefferson had done nothing for black Americans, but the triumph of a mighty industrial capitalism had freed the slaves, made them citizens, and now portended their children's progress.

Theodore Roosevelt was a "social Darwinist" and a "progressive" who symbolized both Anglo supremacy and racial egalitarianism. An emotional man whose genius was seldom inhibited by excessive rationality, Roosevelt interpreted American history as a teleology of moral progress, in which the Civil War figured as a Darwinian struggle between freedom and slavery. Roosevelt's progressivism was in the Whig/Federalist tradition of Alexander Hamilton, Henry Clay, and Abraham Lincoln, which had opposed the plantation economy and advocated aggressive

Wallace with the publication of *The Origin of Species* in 1859. See *In Darwin's Shadow: The Life and Science of Alfred Russel Wallace: A Biological Study on the Psychology of History* (New York: Oxford University Press, 2002).

governmental support of business and industrial interests. Eventually, Roosevelt embraced the collectivism of Sumner and Ely, which assumed that industrial collectivism and consolidation must be the inevitable result of evolutionary progress. He supported Booker T. Washington's view that African Americans' fitness for survival presupposed their adjustment to the industrial process. Industrial capitalism should pragmatically cast down its bucket amidst the legions of African Americans, who as English-speaking Protestants could efficiently be accommodated within the industrial machine, the concatenation of industries that constituted the American leviathan. That is to say, black or white mattered very little in the machine process, since workers of equal skill would be standardized via interchangeable parts.[14]

Roosevelt believed that competition provided a bracing stimulus that should enhance the individual's fitness, rather than expedite his extinction. Washington entertained similar ideas, and thus attempted to construe evolutionary theory as a challenge, rather than a threat. Viewed from the perspective of his dealings with Washington, Roosevelt embodied the contradictory ideas of social Darwinism and social equality. His ideas, like those of Richard T. Ely and Thorstein Veblen, could easily accommodate the likes of Booker T. Washington, who argued for making African Americans useful within the new industrial economy, where it was hoped that racial sentiments would prove to be less potent than economic interests.

Washington believed, as did sympathetic progressive liberals, that what was good for business might be good for American race relations. His progressive ideology presupposed that human society was evolving morally just as it evolved scientifically and industrially. As the American South evolved economically from Jeffersonian agrarianism to Hamiltonian commerce and industrialism, African American civil and economic rights would accordingly evolve to a higher plane. He thus encouraged his followers to seize the time and move apace with the evolutionary progress of the United States. At the same time he proclaimed that African Americans should be encouraged to preserve a set of distinctive group characteristics within a biracial society. He assumed, not unreasonably, that by accepting the triumphant rhetoric of business and grafting it onto the postbellum

[14] By the campaign of 1912 Woodrow Wilson's anticonsolidationist progressivism could be contrasted with Roosevelt's advocation of natural monopolies under government regulation. In foreign policy both men revealed missionary ethnocentrism, and Wilson's League of Nations, while less overtly militaristic, was no less Eurocentric than Rooseveltian imperialism.

industrial commonwealth, African Americans would catch the wave of the future and leave behind the stagnant culture of slavery and peonage.

Washington was not a simple man, although he strategically presented his personal narrative as an uncomplicated teleology of conventional American optimism. He was fully aware that Americans grumble over complications, choke on contradictions, and hiss at irony, and he did not wish to confuse his restless audience. Therefore, he portrayed himself as a man whose homely pleasures were to inspect his pigs, feed his chickens, and play marbles with his children. On the lower frequencies, however, he raised a number of sophisticated questions and presented a number of intriguing problems. Washington was not lacking as a thinker, and his philosophy amounted to more than a simple optimism. He was aware of the contradictions and the implicit ironies in the oxymoronic position of separate-but-equal assimilationism, but he wasted little time explaining, to those who were sometimes deliberately obtuse, the obvious fact that militancy could accomplish nothing in the Alabama of 1900.

Washington's reluctance to draft extended philosophical statements did not stem from a shallow philistinism, but from a belief that overt intellectualism could be dangerous. He used words with meticulous care, in order not to frighten or distract potential allies. His reticence was comparable to that of George Washington or Dwight D. Eisenhower – the gravity of his situation and the magnitude of the issues make such comparisons entirely appropriate. Like Washington at Trenton, he was stealthy and deceptive, and like Eisenhower during the Little Rock crisis, he was capable of a statesmanship that was obscured by his own reputation for pussyfooting conservatism. It was not disappointing to him that his more abstract or incisive statements were frequently forgotten, overlooked, or reduced to inanities, for that was what he intended.

Ruthless and cunning, he was a fox – stealthy, covert, and self-obscuring – in the presence of white power, but a lion, brooking no opposition, in his dealings with blacks who challenged his authority.[15] He sought to establish himself as the supreme "ward boss" of black America. His ideas encompassed something more far-reaching than a mere theory of education. The aptly named Tuskegee Machine functioned, in some

---

[15] Washington's manipulations are thoroughly discusssed in August Meier, *Negro Thought in America, 1880–1915: Racial Ideologies in the Age of Booker T. Washington* (Ann Arbor: University of Michigan, 1963); Emma L. Thornbrough, ed., *Booker T. Washington* (Englewood Cliffs, NJ: Prentice Hall, 1969); Louis Harlan, *Booker T. Washington: The Making of a Black Leader, 1856–1901* (New York: Oxford University Press, 1972); and *Booker T. Washington: The Wizard of Tuskegee* (New York: Oxford University Press, 1983).

respects, as a Tammany Hall or a Chicago ward, and its functions were similar. Like the machine politics of the faraway urban metropolises, it embodied a motley mixture of progressive and reactionary impulses. It was a means of distributing patronage to its supporters, but it also provided laboring people with patronage and indirect power. Tuskegee was, at once, a center of corrupt bargaining and a seat of enlightened despotism.

Washington recognized the exploitability of his brief enslavement during childhood, and the title of his *Up From Slavery* made the most of it, although there was little of the slavery experience he could remember. The time he spent in the salt mines and coal mines of Malden, West Virginia, was unpleasant, but fortunately not extended. Washington received his puritan indoctrination at an impressionable age, and there were enduring effects on his practical religiosity and utilitarian ethic, his constant emphasis on work, cleanliness, and thrift. He came under those influences at around ten years of age – according to his own self-conscious narrative – on going to work for Viola Ruffner. She was a Yankee woman, he recounted, who "had a reputation all through the vicinity for being very strict with her servants [who] wanted all things done promptly [and] wanted absolute honesty and frankness." The experience with Viola Ruffner prepared him for his encounter with Mary F. Mackie, the head teacher at Hampton, who later became "one of his strongest and most helpful friends." What these women taught him, and the lesson he seems to have valued most strongly, was the New England Protestant ethic, which lay at the basis of Washington's later economic/industrial theory.

His first exposure to the false progress of the black middle class, with their conspicuous consumption, crass materialism, and petty snobbishness, came during several months at the Wayland Seminary in Washington, D.C. The experience contributed to his lifelong hostility toward the black bourgeoisie. He wished that "by some power of magic" he might "remove the great bulk of these people into the country districts and plant them upon the soil." Washington returned to Malden, where he taught school for two years. He then returned to Hampton, where he gained two additional years of teaching experience. In 1881, he was offered a position in Alabama, where he founded the Tuskegee Normal and Industrial Institute.

Patient as a spider, Washington began to construct a network of power and influence, and to maneuver himself into the position of spokesman for black America. Then, on September 18, 1895, seven months after the death of Frederick Douglass, he capitalized on an opportunity to address the Atlanta and Cotton States Exposition. With stunning brilliance, Washington used the occasion to exploit the white South's legend of the contented slave, which he transformed into a myth of black loyalty during the Civil War. He advised white-controlled business and industry to entrust its destiny to the loyal black population, saying, "Cast down your bucket . . . among the eight millions of Negroes whose habits you know, whose fidelity and love you have tested in days when to have proved treacherous meant the ruin of your firesides." He also exploited the South's xenophobia with respect to European emigrants, promising a loyalty "that no foreigner can approach," and casting suspicion on those "of foreign birth and strange tongue and habits." Washington also called on black Americans to cast down their buckets "in agriculture, mechanics, in commerce, in domestic service, and in the professions."

His goal was never to consign black Americans to menial occupations, but rather to develop a stratified society in which the masses would be prosperous farmers and handworkers, led by a managerial elite of college-trained technocrats. He was a missionary to the children of slavery, preaching the "Gospel of Wealth," the "Protestant Ethic," and family values. Tuskegee established extension programs among the agrarian masses, instructing them in such useful skills as crop rotation, animal husbandry, personal hygiene, and the management of household finances. Washington was contemptuous of education that was not oriented toward the creation of material wealth and believed that persons of marginal ability who "wasted" their time studying Greek and Latin were assuring their own economic failure. Tuskegee, nonetheless, had a solid liberal arts curriculum, and students were provided the basic elements of cultural literacy, economics, history, and the arts of communication. The better graduates were encouraged to undertake advanced studies at such leading northern universities as Harvard and Cornell.

The nature of his interaction with the white rural South forced Washington to make compromises that Alexander Crummell considered abominable. His tough-minded practicality was masked by a subservient public image that was incompatible with the personality of Crummell. Frederick Douglass also rejected subservience, and thus retained his practical unassailability, although he failed to provide a strategy suited to the needs of the reconstruction era. True enough, Douglass continued to speak out against lynching and other outrages against black men and women, but his message was almost entirely moral. The problem was that white America had ceased to listen, and America was a little tired of having wasted so much energy concentrating on the problems of African Americans.

Douglass, although conceived and socialized in the South, quickly learned to manipulate northern imagery and symbolism, particularly the myth of Benjamin Franklin's self-made man. Like Franklin, he possessed superior genius as a writer and was a master of irony and acerbic social commentary. Like Franklin, he was physically strong and attractive to women. He was endowed with an almost magical understanding of human nature, which enabled him to land on his feet catlike and to amass a respectable fortune. In this he also resembled Ralph Waldo Emerson, and possessed the northeasterner's skill at combining romanticism with realism and materialism with idealism. Douglass, like Franklin and Emerson, was nimble enough to become rich while simultaneously preaching pragmatism and moral absolutism.

Booker T. Washington likewise "intuitively grasped the spirit of the age that was dominating the North." And like Douglass, he learned to manipulate the myths and virtues of "Franklinism," with his American penchant for pragmatic moralizing. Washington preached that slavery had been impractical as well as evil; it had been as economically inefficient as it was morally wrong. He opined that the slave system "in large measure, took the spirit of self-reliance and self-help out of the white people."[16] His appraisal of slavery was contradictory, for on one page of the compilation *Black Belt Diamonds*, he would claim that "If in the providence of God the Negro got any good out of slavery, he got the habit of work."[17] But on the same page, he presented the contradictory opinion that as a result of slavery it was necessary to "teach the Negro that labor is not degrading."[18] Washington was consistent, however, in his encouragement of the Franklinian values of work and thrift, and the Emersonian virtue of self-reliance.

Like Alexander Crummell, Booker T. Washington viewed human nature and social progress as essentially collective and communal. Crummell's progressivism was fundamentally elitist, and in this respect, the programs of Washington and Du Bois were similar to his, for all were

---

[16] Booker T. Washington, *Up From Slavery*, in Louis Harlan, et al., *The Booker T. Washington Papers*, Vol. 1 (Urbana: University of Illinois Press, 1975), pp. 223–24.

[17] *Black Belt Diamonds: Gems from the Speeches, Addresses, and Talks to Students of Booker T. Washington*, selected and arranged by Victoria Earle Matthews, introduction by T. Thomas Fortune (New York: Fortune and Scott, 1898), p. 10.

[18] *Black Belt Diamonds*, p. 10, but he maintains that the freed people were not ashamed to work in *Up From Slavery, Booker T. Washington Papers*, Vol. 1, p. 224.

based on the idea of cultivating a leadership elite. The difference was that Washington's elite would consist of technocrats, scientific farmers, businessmen, and enterprising women. The American Negro Academy's elite would stress leadership in the literary, the artistic, and the higher realms of the natural sciences; where the practical Washington would encourage a mathematically gifted youth to become an engineer, an architect, or a surveyor, Crummell might encourage that same youth to investigate the theories of abstract mathematics, astronomy, and physics.

The progressivism of W. E. B. Du Bois, like that of Richard T. Ely, advocated public administration of natural monopolies and government regulation of banking and commerce. His progressivism amounted to an attack on the shibboleths of the free enterprise system, Jeffersonian democracy, Lockean liberalism, and laissez-fairism of Adam Smith. Like Crummell, an uncloseted Hamiltonian, Du Bois followed in the Federalist/Whig tradition, seeking to align himself with the progressivism of Theodore Roosevelt and Herbert Croly. It was, by his own admission, the refusal of Roosevelt to work with him that led him to endorse the alternative progressivism of Woodrow Wilson in 1912. This was odd, because Wilson's Jeffersonianism, while nominally democratic, specifically rejected the concept of government regulation of natural monopolies that Du Bois had advocated in his essay "Socialist of the Path."[19]

Washington had no reason to oppose Roosevelt-style progressivism, but the exigencies of operating an industrial college with limited public funding made him, of necessity, a fund-raiser, and mandated a policy of courting the friendship of wealthy philanthropists. Thus, the progressivism of Andrew Carnegie had more to offer him than that of Theodore Roosevelt, especially after Roosevelt left office. As for the socialistic progressives, there was no reason to believe they would ever be in a position to support programs at Tuskegee or anywhere else. Washington thus simultaneously tied his program to the alternative tradition of Lockean liberalism, consistent with a directly self-interested interpretation of Christian doctrine, in which self-love inspires the Christian to practical Christianity. His preachments reflected what Robert Bellah has called the doctrine of "Salvation of Success in America."

Washington certainly never claimed that God and Mammon were in league, although Crummell and Du Bois accused him of doing so. He did, however, unabashedly seek to exploit the traditional puritan belief that there was no dividing line between the practical and the religious. He

[19] Du Bois, "Socialist of the Path," *Horizon* (February 1907), 7–8.

realized, as Max Weber would later realize, that American values were an elaboration on Franklin's secularization of the Protestant ethic. Although he was at least once referred to as the Benjamin Franklin of his race, allusions to the Franklin myth in Booker T. Washington's own writing are uniformly indirect.[20] Like Franklin, he took a practical view of education, opposing the study of Greek and Latin, for example, but advocating, as Franklin had, "the promotion of useful knowledge."

Booker T. Washington's approach to reform is often described as "pragmatic," a term that is as confusing as "progressive." The concepts pragmatism and progressivism frequently overlap and there are few figures in American intellectual history who meet the definition of progressive better than William James and John Dewey, founders of the concept of pragmatism. In colloquial speech, pragmatism usually refers to the American penchant for informality and practicality. Pragmatism may be used in a pejorative sense, as a "dignified alternative to unprincipled or timeserving."[21] Some scholars will allow that Washington was "a pragmatist in the colloquial sense," in recognition of his "accommodations" to southern "realities." If there are cognates between Washington's thinking and that of John Dewey or William James, these are dismissed as casual or unsophisticated. Parallels between Washington's missionary ideals and the social gospel of James seem to have impressed few, if any, biographers.[22]

Washington was not a follower of James, nor would his importance be enhanced if he had been. Whether or not any such ideological influence existed, Washington had nothing to gain by claiming it. The appearance of pragmatism in Washington was spontaneous and should not seem incongruous, if pragmatism is, as some scholars seem to think, a peculiar product of the American environment. Washington's theories, whether

[20] Reference to Franklin in *The Journal of Florence Ledyard Cross Kitchelt,* April 3, 1901, *Booker T. Washington Papers,* Vol. 6, p. 84. W. Fitzhugh Brundage insightfully compares and contrasts Washington's and Franklin's autobiographies in his edition of *Up From Slavery* (Boston: Bedford, 2003), pp. 19–20.

[21] James and Dewey acknowledged Charles Peirce as the inventor of "pragmatism," a term for which there is no universally acceptable definition. Raymond Williams notes the term's pejorative use in *Keywords: A Vocabulary of Culture and Society* (New York: Oxford, 1976).

[22] Louis Harlan advises against seeking correlatives in the educational philosophies of Washington and Dewey in *Booker T. Washington: The Wizard,* pp. 144, 151. Bertrand Russell praises James's philosophy and personality in *A History of Western Philosophy* (New York: Simon and Schuster, 1945), pp. 811–19. In "The Moral Equivalent of War" (1910), James called for an army of dedicated youth to engage in manual labor and for an entire society to wage war on social problems, an idea similar to the Tuskegee philosophy. The essay ended on a note of cultural relativism as he compared Theodore Roosevelt's myrmidons to cannibals of the Congo.

in education or in politics, seem consistent with the supposedly distinctive American characteristic of shaping ideology around practice. He was seemingly stimulated by the "fluidity of American life" and "antipathy to control" that Frederick Jackson Turner saw as distinctively American. Pragmatism, as an American ideology, does not spring full-blown from the head of Peirce, James, or Dewey. Its genealogy can be traced through the "policy" of Benjamin Franklin, the opportunism of Thomas Jefferson, and the circumspection of Abraham Lincoln. Washington adopted Lincoln as a hero and patron saint, claiming to have read "nearly every book and magazine article that has ever been written about Abraham Lincoln." Washington also cites Lincoln's "Speeches and Addresses," politically safe, maybe, but neither shallow nor uncomplicated. Lincoln's speeches are, in fact, models of frontier "pragmatism."[23]

The common interpretation of Washington that isolates him from the realm of intellectualism grows out of *The Souls of Black Folk,* where Du Bois says, "It is as though Nature must needs make men narrow in order to give them force." The truth was that Du Bois, in order to make Washington into a forceful symbol, found it useful to make him narrow. Du Bois was perfectly aware of how thoroughly Washington grasped the formula for American success, which was a blend of progressive Christianity and the gospel of triumphant commercialism. In fact, Washington's writings anticipated many of the ideas formalized in Max Weber's *The Protestant Ethic and the Spirit of Capitalism.* Although Du Bois presumably appreciated the purely formalistic sociology of Weber's "Protestant ethic," he dismissed the instrumentalist or pragmatic approach of Washington's social engineering as shallow and narrow.[24]

Booker T. Washington's utilitarian educational theory, which grew spontaneously out of his own experience, may be called progressive. Although it resembled the educational philosophy of John Dewey in some practical aspects and was developed around the same time, there is no evidence of any relationship to Dewey's formal theories of pragmatism or instrumentalism. In *My Larger Education,* Washington told a charming story of how his theory worked, describing himself playing by a woodland stream with his pupils, where they constructed a three-dimensional commercial map, with rivers, harbors, and "great ships carrying their cargoes of merchandise from one part of the world to another." One contrasts

---

[23] Washington makes his claim in *Up From Slavery, Booker T. Washington Papers,* 1:355; Lincoln was referred to as Booker T. Washington's patron saint, Vol. 6, p. 365; Lincoln heroized by Booker T. Washington, Vol. 10, pp. 26–27, 33–39; Vol. 12, p. 188.

[24] W. E. B. Du Bois, *The Souls of Black Folk* (Chicago: McClurg, 1903), p. 43.

this with Du Bois's traveling into the communities of rural Tennessee, where he sometimes persuaded sharecroppers to educate their children by spontaneously paraphrasing Cicero.[25]

The challenge of W. E. B. Du Bois to Washington's leadership was never so much an attack on his theory of education, as on the public perception of it. Influenced by his German training and the Volksgeist tradition of the Brothers Grimm, Du Bois celebrated the homely roots of black American peasant culture in ways that the pragmatic Washington considered dreamy and romantic. Where Washington sought to stamp out the enthusiastic, orgiastic religion of the folk and disparaged window-shopping, Du Bois defended the harmless leisurely pursuits of the peasantry. He found Washington too materialistic, and felt his cold-water theories not only denied human nature, but bordered on the philistinism that characterized a period of standardization, efficiency, and the machine process. Du Bois was fascinated by the frenzy and shouting and the African survivals that he saw and heard in the *schwarze Volksgeist*.

Washington expressed his impatience with such frenzy and also with the "sentimental Christianity which banks everything in the future and nothing in the present," calling it "the curse of our race."[26] While it was clear that Washington followed the tradition of self-interested utilitarian religion, it was not at all clear whether his utilitarianism was ultimately idealistic or materialistic. Was religion the prime mover behind industrious habits and enlightened self-interest, or were industrious habits the material foundation of true religion? At times, Washington's philosophy seemed to be materialistic. "It is not easy to make a good Christian of a hungry man," he once said. "I mean that just in proportion as the race gets a proper industrial foundation – gets habits of industry, thrifty, economy, land homes, profitable work, in the same proportion will its moral and religious life be improved."

Washington's undisguised contempt for the mindless euphoria of plantation religion that had grown up under slavery was an attitude he shared with Alexander Crummell and Daniel Alexander Payne. All of them believed that enthusiastic religion with its colorful "ring shouts" and ceremonial spirit possession was an obstacle to materialistic Christianity and the commercial values that were necessary components of modern civilization. Thus, like Crummell and Payne, Washington opposed the exclusive otherworldliness and irrational exuberance of plantation religion.

---

[25] Booker T. Washington, *My Larger Education*, pp. 134–36; Du Bois on "Pro Archia Poeta" in *The Souls of Black Folk*, p. 65.
[26] *Black Belt Diamonds*, p. 35.

Ecstatic exercises awakened many corporal appetites and could easily degenerate into a midnight hunger for stolen chickens.[27] There was no place in Washington's black social gospel for the sentimentalization of religious "frenzy" that appeared in the writings of American Negro Academicians like W. E. B. Du Bois and Orishatukeh Faduma. Religion for Washington, as for Crummell, must be adapted to "life in this world," and this meant the ethics of work and wealth.[28]

Long before he published *Up From Slavery,* Washington made this clear in an oblique but unmistakable caricature of Alexander Crummell as a miseducated colored minister

preparing his Sunday sermon just as a New England minister prepares his sermon. But this colored minister was in a broken down, leaky, rented log cabin, with weeds in the yard, surrounded by evidences of poverty, filth, want, and the want of thrift. This minister had spent some time in school studying theology. How much better it would have been to have had this minister taught the dignity of labor, theoretical and practical farming in connection with his theology, so that he could have added to his meager salary, and set an example to his people in the matter of living in a decent house, and correct farming.[29]

It was almost certain that Washington stole the anecdotal formula for this story from Crummell, because Crummell had employed the formula in his well-publicized testimony delivered in 1880 before the United States Congress.[30]

I went in 1872, in the city of New York, into the kitchen of the Union League Club, and there I saw a young man with a copy of Euripedes and Tacitus, in the originals, sitting there with his apron upon him awaiting his turn, as a servant, to stand as a waiter behind the table. I have seen young men who have graduated from college as lawyers and doctors, who have been forced at last to gain a livelihood as servants.

Washington may have encountered the story in *The People's Advocate,* an African American newspaper published in Washington, D.C., or in some other newspaper report. In any case, he used the formula many times in subsequent years, notably in *Up From Slavery,* where to the astonishment and dismay of Du Bois, he disparaged a young man's attempt to decipher a Latin grammar.[31] Washington's obsession with the practical, noted Du Bois, cemented him to the Gospel of Wealth and divorced him from

[27] Christianity impossible on an empty stomach, *Black Belt Diamonds*, p. 32.
[28] *Black Belt Diamonds*, p. 35.
[29] Moses, *Alexander Crummell*, p. 266. *Booker T. Washington Papers*, Vol. 5, p. 367.
[30] Moses, *Alexander Crummell*, pp. 233–34.
[31] Du Bois, *Souls of Black Folk*, p. 43.

the otherworldly tradition of St Francis. One doubts that Washington would have been bothered by the point. Roman Catholic hagiography, antinomianism, and superstition annoyed him as much in Italian Catholics as they did in his own people, which he made clear in a chapter of his book *The Man Farthest Down*.[32]

A practical, muscular, cold-water Christianity was supposedly ingrained in Booker T. Washington's mind from those early days of hearing the utilitarian slave songs. From the beginning, he apparently saw religion as having to have sociopolitical utility. To his tremendous advantage, he encountered in early youth those influences that led him to conceive of religion in terms of struggle and duty rather than comfortable and fatalistic contentment. He was apparently never tempted to view religion in terms of an ecstatic conversion experience – at least nothing of the sort is mentioned in *Up From Slavery*. He does not seem obsessed with the personality of Jesus, but addresses his prayers, so he tells us, to a God who providentially blesses peoples and individuals with a series of trials along the road to a material salvation in a material world.

Washington's sleight of hand in relating the story of his struggles blends the seemingly contradictory themes of self-interest and self-sacrifice with a facileness that would have done Bernard Mandeville proud. He skillfully manipulated one of the most interesting conundrums of American Christianity, which clearly is not confined either to America or to Bookerite ideology. American Christianity would seem, on one level, to reinforce the traditions of republican virtue and civic humanism that have received so much attention from Douglass Adair, Gordon Wood, J. G. A. Pocock, and others. Within this interpretation of American Christianity, Washington memorialized General Samuel C. Armstrong as a "type of that Christlike body of men and women who went into the Negro schools at the close of the war by the hundreds to assist in lifting up my race." Armstrong's Christianity is the civil religion of disinterested republican humanism, a reinvigorated communitarianism in the Reconstruction South, on which the emancipated masses must depend after the Hamiltonian leviathan of federal government had withdrawn.

If there was any fundamental weakness in Washington's theory, it was in the area where he took greatest pride – his understanding of human relations. Everything was based on the idea that black Americans could win a place in American life by making themselves economically indispensable,

---

[32] Booker T. Washington with Robert E. Park, *The Man Farthest Down* (New York: Doubleday, Page, & Company, 1912), pp. 116–91.

as they had been during slavery, but on a higher and more intelligent level, better suited to the industrial age. J. Max Barber and Ida B. Wells were less optimistic and were convinced that the very admirable values that Tuskegee represented would ultimately make black people more threatening. There was, in fact, a certain *Kristalnacht* quality to some of the race riots of the early twentieth century, such as Atlanta and Tulsa, where neighborhoods of the striving black middle class were selected as targets by white mobs.

These were serious concerns, but I see no evidence that anyone had an answer for them. Whatever the weaknesses of the Protestant ethic as a formula for black success, Washington's approach to it was not naive. He attempted to reconcile the problem of idealism and materialism, laying equal emphasis on both. Whatever failures one witnesses in his program, they may not be attributed to naiveté; they were a response to an American tradition that had traditionally undermined the material status of African Americans, and that had behaved irrationally with regard to the moral and ideological undergirding of the industrial culture that it sought so inconsistently to inculcate.

Urban industrial culture introduced African Americans to a set of problems that had existed in antebellum America, as black and Irish American immigrants competed for a place at the bottom of the economic ladder. Black Americans were engaged in changing "from a caste to a minority," as historian Vernon Williams has described the incomplete process. It was necessary at one level to perceive African Americans as a permanently separate race, but necessary, at another level, to insist that they were just one more American ethnic group. Frederick Douglass' statements on American multiethnicity were admirably liberal, but Washington sought to exploit ethnic stereotypes in order to minimize the importance of race. "Compared to Italian and Irish labor," he wrote, "the Negro is far more teachable and trustworthy."[33] Washington attempted to exploit Anglo-supremacist xenophobia of the sort expressed more vitriolically by Thomas Bailey Aldrich:

> Wide open and unguarded stand our gates,
> And through them presses a wild motley throng –
> Men from the Volga and the Tartar steppes,
> Featureless figures of the Hoang-Ho,
> Malayan, Scythian, Teuton, Kelt and Slav,
> Flying the Old world's poverty and scorn;
> These bringing with them unknown gods and rites,

---

[33] *Black Belt Diamonds*, p. 44.

Those, tiger passions, here to stretch their claws.
In street and alley what strange tongues are loud,
Accents of menace alien to our air,
Voices that once the tower of Babel knew!
O Liberty, white Goddess! is it well
To leave the gates unguarded?

The "white Goddess" had nothing to dread from the faithful homely Negro, a fact attested to by Joel Chandler Harris, who portrayed his Uncle Remus at the end of the Civil War sharpening an ax to protect "ole missus" from the Yankee invaders. Frederick Douglass alluded to what he called "the Negro's clean record during war time." Washington claimed that "the slave who was selected to sleep in the big house during the absence of the males was considered to have the place of honor [and] any one attempting to harm 'young Mistress' or 'old Mistress' during the night would have had to cross the dead body of the slave." This was the source of allusions in his Atlanta address to hearth and fireside, the universal symbols of wifehood, motherhood, and woman as a treasure. That Negroes were indisputably trustworthy in such circumstances was the proof of their innate conservatism. They were, said Washington, "the most patient, law abiding, and unresentful people that the world has seen."[34]

Washington, like Crummell, was opportunistic in attempting to exploit xenophobic fears of Anglo-American elites concerning the dangers imported by white immigrants.

... the question has arisen in my own mind, and I know it has disturbed the minds of others – where, under God, may this nation look for corrective influences, to stay the progress of the great social and political evils which are arising in the land? Whence shall come the conservative power of this nation? ... Not from the crazed Bohemian, with his criminal propensities and his animal instincts! Not from the German, with his godless speculations and his wild theories! Not from the superstitious Italian, ignorant of the simplest alphabet of freedom, and paralyzed, in every faculty by the stupidness of priestcraft! Not from the angry Irishman, with his 'blind hysterics' and his 'school boy heat!' Not even from the more sober Anglo-Saxon; who is always preaching submission to oppressed people; yet himself ever shrieking 'Liberty or death!' at a disagreeable tax, or an imaginary encroachment.

---

[34] Foner, ed., *Douglass* Vol. 4, p. 498. The Atlanta allusion transforming the Negro male into the "Guardian of the Hearth" involved a sophisticated manipulation of traditional imagery. Freud typically discovers a phallic association in the tradition that makes women guardian of the hearth – namely the fear that a male might extinguish the fire by urinating on it. *Civilization and its Discontents* (1930; reprinted New York: Norton, 1961), p. 37. Booker T. Washington reversed the cliché by attributing eudæmonistic-tutelary functions to black males.

But the great paradox was that Washington, like Crummell, wanted to argue that black people could simultaneously influence the society, while at the same time remaining socially distinct from it. He was forced to acknowledge that his public statements were sometimes framed in ways that allowed for misinterpretation of his goals, thus giving comfort to those who resisted black attempts to assert their civil rights. When the New England feminist and liberal Ednah Dow Cheney wrote to ask him for clarification concerning his position on social equality, Washington explained:

> . . . I find by experience that the southern people often refrain from giving colored people many opportunities that they would otherwise give them because of an unreasonable fear that the colored people will take advantage of opportunity given them to intrude themselves into the social society of the south. I thought it best to try to set at rest any such fear. Now of course I understand that there are a great many things in the south which southern white people class as social intercourse that is not really so. If anybody understood me as meaning that riding in the same railroad car or sitting in the same room at a railroad station is social intercourse they certainly got a wrong idea of my position.[35]

In a convincing essay written in 1908, Kelly Miller found that it was impossible to separate black leaders into neat categories of radicals and conservatives, observing that Washington critics, even at that date, were "opposing the Washington of long ago rather than the Washington of to-day."[36] From the 1940s to the 1950s, black intellectuals like Rayford Logan, Saunders Redding, and Kenneth Clarke often oversimplified Washington's program and were openly hostile to his memory. Later investigations by the historians Louis Harlan, August Meier, and Emma Lou Thornbrough did much to reveal his often frustrated attempts to counteract the reactionary tendencies of his era. The portrait of "the Wizard of Tuskegee" became more subtle, nuanced, and detailed in the scholarship of the 1960s and assisted a generation of students in becoming familiar with Washington's behind-the-scenes activism.[37]

Attempts to "rehabilitate" Washington, have, nonetheless, sometimes led to extravagant excesses. Because of his emphaisis on self-help he has

---

[35] Booker T. Washington to Ednah Dow Littlefield Cheney, Oct. 15, 1895, in Harlan, et al., *The Booker T. Washington Papers*, Vol. 4 (Urbana: University of Illinois Press, 1975), pp. 56–57.

[36] Kelly Miller, *Race Adjustment*, 1908, republished as *Radicals and Conservatives* (New York: Schocken, 1968), p. 39.

[37] I am much indebted to insights of August Meier, *Negro Thought in America: Racial Ideologies in the Age of Booker T. Washington* (Ann Arbor: University of Michigan Press, 1963).

occasionally been too broadly interpreted as an incipient black nationalist. This has led to exaggerations of his influence on or connections with
Marcus Garvey.[38] In 1915, Garvey wrote to Washington expressing a desire to visit him with the purpose of studying methods of industrial education. Washington responded with a graciously noncommittal letter of
welcome, but by the time Garvey arrived, the Sage of Tuskegee had died.
As it developed, the Universal Negro Improvement Association (UNIA)
program had strong appeal to many of that class of black folk who sub-
scribed to Tuskegee principles as a means to achieving bourgeois status.

By the end of the twentieth century, middle-class black youth were
aggressively pursuing the Tuskegee educational philosophy – often in integrated colleges and universities.[39] They favored the practical admon-
ishments of Booker T. Washington to learn hotel management and master engineering, while Du Bois's beckoned to the "gilded halls" where
they might "sit with Shakespeare" or "summon Aristotle." Militantly
"Afrocentric" students positively scorned the invitation, expressing their
admiration for Carter G. Woodson's sermons on *The Miseducation of the
Negro*, which argued aggressively for Booker T. Washington's educational
principles and questioned those of Du Bois. Today, young people who have
never heard of Tuskegee pay tacit homage to its precepts by treating the
university as a trade school. As in ages past, only a few are committed to
the pursuit of the abstract arts and sciences as advocated by Crummell,
Du Bois, and the American Negro Academy.

Washington's intellect was neither shallow nor narrow, facts attested
to by his well-maintained ties to the Talented Tenth, as August Meier
has noted. Tuskegee policy toward Africa provides ample evidence of his
breadth and vision. Through his partnership with Robert E. Park, the
Tuskegeean became involved in the exposure of brutalities in the Belgian
Congo. Washington's denunciation of British colonial misrule, his col-
laboration with prominent Pan-Africanists, and his gradual acceptance
of the Afrocentric approach to history are finally being recognized in
scholarship.[40] Louis Harlan has written on Washington's African interest
and has mentioned connections between Booker T. Washington and

---

[38] Harold Cruse once called for a reappraisal of Booker T. Washington within the context
of black nationalism. For exaggeration, see Raymond L. Hall, *Black Separatism in the
United States* (Hanover, NH: University Press of New England, 1978), p. 242.

[39] Judith Stein has emphasized the theme of bourgeois consciousness and participation in
the Garvey movement. See *The World of Marcus Garvey* (Baton Rouge: Louisiana State
University Press, 1986).

[40] For Washington and Africa, see Vernon Williams, *Rethinking Race: Franz Boas and His
Contemporaries* (Lexington: University Press of Kentucky, 1996), pp. 54–72, and Louis

the Gold Coast editor J. E. Casely Hayford, who sided with Booker T. Washington in the controversy with Du Bois. The following protest against the methods of British colonialism in Africa was issued from Tuskegee in 1896.

> On the very day, perhaps at the very hour that the British troops were mowing down these Africans simply because they tried to defend their homes, their wives and their children, hundreds of prayers were being offered up in as many English churches that God might convert the heathen in Africa and bring them to our way of thinking and acting. What mockery!
>
> Have not these Matabele warriors as much right to lay claim to the streets of London, as the English have to claim the native land of these Africans? What England has done every Christian (?) nation in Europe has done.[41]

Such a statement does not jibe with the interpretation of Washington as an unprincipled time server or an artfully self-effacing confidence man.

Washington was typical of American liberals from Emerson to Theodore Roosevelt, who spoke up for the oppressed, but always in terms that smoothed over the conflicts between capital and labor interests. Like most progressives, he courted the good will of established elites and recognized that he was one of them. As a member of the arriviste class, as were Andrew Carnegie and W. E. B. Du Bois, he promoted traditional Euro-American aristocratic culture. Like them, he believed and preached the progressive gospel – that scientific and industrial progress led inevitably to moral progress, and he believed that the nation must almost inevitably evolve toward an increasingly comprehensive and egalitarian democracy. Thus, Washington, like most progressive liberals, was committed to promoting fundamental changes in American race relations, but like most conservatives, he believed that these changes must occur naturally within the framework of evolving corporate capitalism in the new commonwealth of triumphant Hamiltonianism.

Washington once related an anecdote about Ralph Waldo Emerson, who was observed gazing out a window and was asked, "What are you looking for, Mr. Emerson?" The answer was, "I am trying to find Ralph Waldo Emerson."[42] Like Emerson, Booker T. Washington was placid, but deep and deceptively complex in terms not only of personality, but of ideology as well. Finding his center is every bit as difficult as trying to pin down Emerson, and for similar reasons. Like Emerson, Engels, and Marx,

---

R. Harlan, "Booker T. Washington and the White Man's Burden," *American Historical Review* 71. 2 (January 1966), 441–67.

[41] *Booker T. Washington Papers*, Vol. 4, pp. 251–53.

[42] *Booker T. Washington Papers*, Vol. 3, p. 154.

he foundered on the difficulties of the materialism/idealism dichotomy. Booker T. Washington was a materialist who believed that industrial evolution would determine the position of the Negro in American life. But he was also an idealist who believed that exhorting the workers to a new ethic would be an essential step toward the improvement of material conditions.

9

Protestant Ethic versus Conspicuous Consumption

FRANKLIN, WEBER, VEBLEN, AND BOOKER T. WASHINGTON

Booker T. Washington's *Up From Slavery* has been appropriately compared to the *Autobiography of Benjamin Franklin*. His *Black Belt Diamonds* (1898), a compilation of speeches, addresses, and advice to students, may be compared to Franklin's *The Way to Wealth*. Max Weber drew on Franklin's collection of maxims as the basis for his theory in *The Protestant Ethic and the Spirit of Capitalism* (1905). Washington might have served him just as well, or perhaps even better. Weber propounded a descriptive theory in which religion was a counterintuitive, indirect, and almost subliminal stimulus to habits of capital accumulation. Washington anticipated Weber in drawing a connection between wealth and Christian stoicism, but he was closer to Franklin in that he "instrumentalized" his version of the Protestant ethic – a conscious and pragmatic plan of action.[1]

---

[1] E. Franklin Frazier, *Negro in the United States* (New York: Macmillan, 1949), p. 504, makes the comparison, but disparages its literary or intellectual merit. Louis Harlan makes the comparison in his *Booker T. Washington, Vol. 1, The Making of A Black Leader, 1856–1901* (New York: Oxford University Press, 1972), p. 249. Max Weber's "essay," *Die Protestantische Ethik und der Geist des Kapitalismus*, was originally published in 1904–5. I have used the 1930 translation *The Protestant Ethic and the Spirit of Capitalism* of Talcott Parsons, published in a second edition with an introduction by R. H. Tawney (New York: Scribners, 1958). Franklin's "The Way to Wealth," also known as "Father Abraham's Speech," has a complicated publishing history. Weber identifies his Franklin sources in footnote 5 on page 192 as follows: "from *Necessary Hints to Those That Would be Rich*, Written, 1736, Works, Sparks edition, II, p. 80, [and] *Advice to a Young Tradesman* (written 1748, Sparks edition, II, pp. 87 ff.)."

Tuskegee Chapel sermons offered a program for economic reform.[2] With this in mind, Washington's ridicule of the enthusiastic religion of the Black Belt becomes something more than a set of "darky stories." He opposed the religion of the masses because it was not useful to his program of supply-side economics, not because of its Africanness.[3] Tuskegee sent forth cold-water puritans to obliterate the "ring shout" and other retentions of "slave culture" among the black masses and replace them with the gospel of industrial capitalism. While he practiced "the speech and thought of triumphant commercialism," he inserted caustic observations on the improvident consumerism of the black peasantry. Thus, he anticipated not only what Weber defined as an ethic of capital accumulation and investment, but also Thorstein Veblen's attack on "conspicuous consumption" in *Theory of the Leisure Class.*

Max Weber's argument in *The Protestant Ethic* is complicated enough to be frequently misrepresented. His avowed purpose was to offer a non-racialist explanation of the rise of Western Europe to economic and industrial superiority over the rest of the world. Not only did he reject racial explanations, but also purely materialistic causation. He hypothesized that the rise of Protestantism was the factor that explained the economic dominance of Western Europe. The Protestant ethic disparaged consumption and encouraged saving because puritans were motivated to accumulate wealth, but not to spend money. Good Calvinist "roundheads" would hardly impress their "civil suited" neighbors by appearing "trickt and frounc't" in cavalier buttons and bows. Nor could they decorate their churches with expensive paintings and stained glass. They could do nothing with their wealth but plough it back into the field where reinvestment led to the further accumulation of capital.[4]

---

[2] Booker T. Washington, *Character Building: Being Addresses Delivered on Sunday Evenings to the Students of Tuskegee Institute by Booker T. Washington* (New York: Doubleday, Page & Co., 1902).

[3] Booker T. Washington, *Black Belt Diamonds: Gems from the Speeches, Addresses, and Talks to Students of Booker T. Washington,* selected and arranged by Victoria Earle Matthews, introduction by T. Thomas Fortune (New York: Fortune and Scott, 1898). Negative references to black popular religion are abundant throughout the 115 pages of this compilation. Vernon Williams devotes a chapter to Washington's incrementally developed respect for the history and culture of Africa in *Rethinking Race: Franz Boas and his Contemporaries* (Lexington: University Press of Kentucky, 1996), pp. 54–72. Also see Louis Harlan, "Booker T. Washington and the White Man's Burden," *American Historical Review* 71.2 (January 1966), 441–67.

[4] Max Weber, *The Protestant Ethic*, p. 172. "When the limitation of consumption is combined with the release of acquisitive activity, the inevitable practical result is obvious: accumulation of capital through ascetic compulsion to save."

Critics of Weber often observe that the American puritans preached doctrines and established laws that were hostile to capitalism, but Weber did not present the puritans as exemplars of a commercial spirit.[5] He claimed that "the spirit of capitalism" was not an expression of the Calvinist ethos but an outgrowth from it. Thus, although Benjamin Franklin was not a Protestant, but in Weber's words, a "colorless deist," he could be said to have developed a typically capitalist spirit as a result of his puritan indoctrination in childhood. Essentially Weber defined capitalism in terms of presumably representative quotations from *The Way to Wealth*. These he cited as evidence of its author's ostensible belief in "the earning of more and more money" as an end in itself. Although Weber denied implying that Franklin's ethic was completely covered by these selected quotations, he blatantly ignored the fact that Franklin, after amassing a comfortable fortune by the age of forty-two, retired from business and focused his attention thereafter on civic affairs and scientific pursuits.

Franklin attacked conspicuous consumption, true enough, but his reasons owed less to puritan sentiments than to materialist logic. As did Adam Smith – conspicuously missing from Weber's interpretation – Franklin viewed the "Riches of a Country" in terms of "the quantity of Labour its Inhabitants are able to purchase, and not by the Quantity of Silver or Gold they possess." He viewed money primarily as a "Medium of Exchange, because by its Means Labour is exchanged for Labour, or one Commodity for another." Franklin advocated a policy that was intended to support the price of labor for "Artificers and laboring Men," thereby "making the balance of our Trade more equal than it now is." Franklin noted a scarcity of money due to the British government's mercantilist policies of hoarding precious metals in the national treasury. American merchants and traders, lacking hard money and discouraged from printing paper money, were often forced to pay their employees with commodities – largely imported. Carpenters, bakers, and shoemakers in colonial America were often compelled to accept as "Goods in Pay" luxury items that were being dumped in the colonies. The circulation of paper money, although mildly inflationary, would have the effect of encouraging thrift and savings at the household level. The existing policy of paying workers in goods

---

[5] R. H. Tawney offers many thoughtful reflections and respectful caveats on Weber's hypothesis in *Religion and the Rise of Capitalism: A Historical Study* (New York: Harcourt, Brace and World, 1926). Especially interesting are pp. 212–27 and 316–17. John A. Garraty, without referring directly to Weber, aggressively attacks Weber's thesis in his excellent textbook, *The American Nation*, 10th edition, Vol. 1 (New York: Longman, 2000), pp. 60–61.

encouraged "Pride and prodigality" because "Working Men and their Families are thereby induced to be more profuse and extravagant in fine Apparel and the Like."[6]

Franklin's statement contained the basic elements of Booker T. Washington's later economic preachments: the same hostility to extravagance and the resentment of systemic practices that had the effect of forcing ordinary workers to accept payment in overvalued luxury items. Franklin admitted that he benefited from the expression of these opinions, which helped him to increase his credit, to enlarge his savings, and to win more than one contract for the printing of paper money. He "went on swimmingly," as he put it, advocating savings accumulation for one class in society, and a policy of inflation, ostensibly for the benefit of that same class. He claimed to have the interests of the common people at heart, and recalled many years later that his pamphlet "was well received by the common People in general; but the Rich Men dislik'd it; it increased and strengthened the Clamour for more Money."[7] America had not yet developed the consumer economy in which the "rich men" would support inflation in order to bolster "consumer confidence."

Thorstein Veblen introduced the term "conspicuous consumption" in *Theory of the Leisure Class*, to explain a society based on industrial capitalism. He anchored his ideas in evolutionary anthropology, and did not interpret industrial capitalism in terms of American exceptionalism, or as the product of any singularly Western trait such as Calvinism. He viewed the acquisitive nature of capitalism as arising from primeval anthropoid psychology. Therefore, it was irreconcilable with Weber's "Protestant ethic," for where Weber defined the spirit of capitalism as saving for the sake of saving, Veblen associated it with spending for the sake of spending. In *The Theory of Business Enterprise* Veblen described an opposition between the productive, efficient "instinct of workmanship" and the exploitative, inefficient "instinct of sportsmanship." The word "exploit" had depth of meaning for Veblen; it denoted swashbuckling activities that conferred masculine status. Predatory exploits such as hunting, warfare, and athletics were the source of honor among primitive tribes, and

---

[6] "The Necessity of a Paper Currency," Franklin, *Writings*, p. 122, argued that a limited money supply encouraged employers to pay artisans with British and foreign goods, whereas an increased money supply would keep wealth inside the country. Like the Populists of another day, he believed that increasing the money supply would increase the price of labor. Franklin defended the 1729 essay in *Autobiography* (1771); see *Writings* (New York: Library of America, 1987), pp. 1368–69. It is seldom observed that the youthful Franklin entertained William Petty's labor theory of value, pp. 127–29.

[7] Franklin, *Autobiography*; in *Writings* (New York: Library of America, 1987), pp. 1368–69.

exploits on the football field at Harvard, on a hunting trip out West, or at the Battle of San Juan Hill were the source of status in modern times.[8]

The "atavistic," exploitative instinct of sportsmanship was identical to the warlike traits that William James attributed to the personality of Theodore Roosevelt. Productive labor in tribal societies was always relegated to women and slaves. As a result, labor in any society must be indistinct from drudgery and conferred neither dignity nor status. Modern plutocrats, like their forebears in primitive tribes, derived status from consuming the products of the work of others. Labor was demeaning, while leisure conferred honor, and consumption was a manly virtue. By analogy, the sporting and competitive qualities of business conferred higher status than the workmanly and productive qualities of industry. Veblen characterized the spirit of capitalism as an expansive consumerism – clearly incompatible with Weber's Protestant ethos of self-denial.[9]

Wealthy men might even amplify their status through "vicarious consumption," as their wives, servants, and children were dragooned into the process of consumption while remaining otherwise idle, thus assisting in the display of wealth. The plutocratic household stood at the apex of the leisure class and conspicuously displayed the surfeit of leisure at their disposal. Veblen noted that they might even assign to servants the task of vicarious consumption of leisure. It is conceivable that on great plantations there might be sufficient division of labor to accommodate a liveried slave whose only duty might be to hold the master's stirrup or to wave a fan over the mistress. But most slaves never encountered such conditions, and at James Burroughs's farm, where Booker T. Washington was born, there was no unbreachable distinction between field hands and house servants. A slave boy might, as Booker did, work the fields mornings and wait table in the evenings.[10]

In *Up From Slavery*, Washington referred on one page to "the school of slavery," but on the next, he did not remember the plantation as a

---

[8] Thorstein Veblen, *Theory of the Leisure Class* (1899; reprinted New York: Mentor, 1953), pp. 30–33. Thorstein Veblen, *The Theory of Business Enterprise* (1904; reprinted New York: Mentor, n.d.), pp. 16–36.

[9] Veblen, *Theory of the Leisure Class*, pp. 41–60. Franklin's founding of the Junto and subsequent membership in London dining clubs, 1757–62 and 1764–75, were examples of "conspicuous consumption of leisure" that would have added a layer of complexity to Veblen's observations and would splendidly confirm the thesis of cultural historian Josef Piper in *Leisure, the Basis of Culture* (New York: Mentor, 1963), which observes that "leisure in Greek is *skole*, and in Latin *scola*, the English, school," p. 20.

[10] Harlan, *Booker T. Washington*, Vol. 1, p. 15. *Up From Slavery* in Harlan, ed., *Booker T. Washington Papers*, Vol. 1, p. 217.

particularly effective school in the work ethic. He averred that due to the association of work with the status of slavery, none of the masters' children ever learned to do simple housework or to master trades. And, as we have noted in an earlier chapter, he claimed that work was, for the same reason, considered degrading by many of the slaves. But his statements were inconsistent on this score. In *Black Belt Diamonds,* he asserted that "If in the providence of God the Negro got anything good out of slavery, he got the habit of work." Further down the page, he justified the Tuskegee mission by saying, "We teach the Negro that labor is not degrading."[11]

Washington was equally confusing on the subject of black religion, insisting on one page that slavery had Christianized black folk, lamenting on another that it had failed to do so. In some instances he described black religion as too otherworldly; in another he claimed to have detected a pragmatic note in plantation hymns. He recalled the spirituals as having a radically realistic function, revealing a practical desire for "freedom of the body in this world."[12] Presumably Washington learned from his childhood experience that religion could be enlisted to pragmatic ends. In any case, he had little patience with religion as a quaint expression of peasant culture, insisting that it must become a practical instrument for the advancement of material interests.

Such attitudes were manufactured independently of Weber and Veblen and seem to have paid neither of them any more homage than they paid to one another. He claimed to have learned his philosophy from his own experience, and he had begun to promote doctrines of industry, thrift, and reinvestment before the ideas of either sociologist were published. In any case, *Up From Slavery* and *Black Belt Diamonds* offered something other than Weber's descriptive sociology. Their approach to the ethos of saving and capital accumulation was not intended as mere descriptive sociology but as "instrumentalism," a theory of social change. His utilitarian approach to Protestant virtue anticipated traits that Weber later attributed to Franklin, but Washington, like Franklin, was more critical of commercialism than some critics allowed.[13]

Du Bois claimed that Booker T. Washington had so thoroughly absorbed the spirit of "triumphant commercialism" that Socrates or St. Francis of Assisi would have been appalled. One might ask Du Bois

---

[11] *Black Belt Diamonds*, pp. 10, 29.
[12] *Up From Slavery* in *Booker T. Washington Papers*, Vol. 1, p. 224.
[13] "Instrumentalism" is defined by Morton White, *Social Thought in America: The Revolt Against Formalism*, 2nd ed., (1949; Boston: Beacon, 1957), p. 7, as "Dewey's doctrine which holds that ideas are plans of action."

what the saints and martyrs would have thought of the schoolboy who ceased to envy the other boys their "store hats" when his mother made him a cap from two pieces of homespun jeans, lovingly stitched together. Washington later expressed pride that she had "strength of character enough not to be led into the temptation" of conspicuous consumption. He noted that several of the boys who had begun their careers with "store hats" had ended up in the penitentiary or unable to afford any sort of hat. Later, while studying briefly in Washington, D.C., Booker T. Washington had the opportunity to witness the flow of cash through the black community as "young men who were not earning more than four dollars a week spend two dollars or more for a buggy on Sunday to ride up and down Pennsylvania Avenue, in order that they might try to convince the world that they were worth thousands."[14]

Booker T. Washington was well prepared by his mother for his first encounter with New England Protestantism in the person of Viola Ruffner, who employed him as a house boy and reinforced his growing awareness that the virtues of honesty, industry, thrift, and abstinence were marketable commodities. The lessons proved indispensable in the missionary environment of Hampton Normal Institute, where Mary F. Mackie and Samuel Chapman Armstrong reinforced his training in Yankee virtues. This indoctrination led, he tells us, to negative impressions of Washington, D.C., where students strove to compete in the arena of conspicuous consumption, then sank to the depths of "unemployment and poverty." The Protestant ethic was not an abstract sociological theory, but a practical strategy to transplant New England Protestantism along with its political and economic blessings to the black belt.

Booker T. Washington's Protestant ethic was not a dogma, but a pragmatic intuition derived from his own experiences by the age of fifteen, and subsequently confirmed, that religion was an instrument for economic uplift. There was narrowness in this view. Washington had absorbed an incurable bias against conspicuous waste that made him incapable of appreciating the irrationally exuberant consumerism of modern industrial capitalism. The ethos of conspicuous waste, and competitive consumption, must be vigorously assaulted, he believed, whether in the cabins of southern peasants or among the fatuous black bourgeoisie of Washington, D.C.

---

[14] *Up From Slavery* in *Booker T. Washington Papers*, Vol. 1, p. 261. E. Franklin Frazier, who was one of Washington's most hostile detractors, later published *Black Bourgeoisie* (1957), which was practically an extended footnote to Booker T. Washington's castigation of the black petite bourgeoisie. In a similar vein, see Carter G. Woodson, *The Miseducation of the Negro* (Washington, DC: Associated Publishers, 1933).

Bookerism perceived consumerism as a peculiarly Negro weakness; Weber's independently developed theory viewed it as peculiarly, although not singularly, American; Veblen appreciated that modern acquisitiveness was an expression of primal human instincts that were universally manifest.

Washington recognized, as Martin Delany had before the Civil War, the moral and economic effects of a system in which white capitalists marketed industrial products and a black petty bourgeoisie consumed them. Crummell had linked material showiness to extravagance in education, an obsession with "aesthetical culture; an inordinate desire for the ornamental and elegant in education to the neglect of the solid and practical." With this in mind he anticipated another Washingtonian theme in his commencement address at Storer College in Harper's Ferry, the need to shift from a reparations rhetoric, based on "past servitude," and to focus on "duty and service, in the present." When Crummell lectured in 1885 on "Common Sense in Common Schooling," he addressed a theme that would be appropriated by Washington – the need for education that would make black Americans into a service-oriented class of well-paid suppliers, profitably meeting the needs of white consumers.

Washington recognized, as had Crummell, the need to rebuild the industrial machine. Both called for structural reform, recognizing the painful irony that emancipation had meant a shift from an exploitative industrial organization under slavery to an exploitative industrial disorganization in freedom. Their plan was nothing less than social engineering, to have black people assume the responsibilities of building their own industrial institutions. Washington's ambition was to reconstruct the industrial machine assigning black Americans greater control over its workings. Alas, economic behavior, unlike machine processes, is visibly more chaotic and subject only to a limited predictability. Business, as Veblen realized, is a game that constantly throws a monkey wrench into machine processes and interferes with the industrial logic of social engineers.

Washington called for black Americans to cast down their buckets "in agriculture, mechanics, in commerce, in domestic service, and in the professions."[15] His emphasis, however, was always on the practical. When he saw a black student talented in science or mathematics, he wondered why anyone would encourage that student to waste the talent on stargazing. Wouldn't it make more sense to direct such a student toward engineering or architecture? If he found a young woman with the talent to study the

---

[15] *Up From Slavery* in *Booker T. Washington Papers*, Vol. 1, p. 331.

biological sciences it would certainly make more sense to train her as a veterinarian rather than a student of dinosaur bones. If a divinity student should be blessed with rhetorical gifts and a grasp of biblical languages, it would be well to supplement those theological skills with some training in carpentry and bookkeeping, so that the aspiring minister might be prepared to lead his flock toward the material as well as the spiritual values embodied in what came to be called the Protestant ethic.

Although the terms "Protestant ethic" and "conspicuous consumption" did not occur in Washington's vocabulary, neither was beyond his notice. Washington observed feckless patterns in black spending, which bothered him to the extent that they were race specific.

> I often found sewing-machines which had been bought, or were being bought on installments, frequently at a cost of as much as sixty dollars, or showy clocks for which the occupants of the cabins had paid twelve or fourteen dollars.... [in one cabin] was an organ for which the people told me they were paying sixty dollars in monthly installments....
>
> In most cases the sewing machine was not used, the clocks were so worthless that they did not keep correct time – and if they had, in nine cases out of ten there would have been no one in the family who could have told the time of day – while the organ, of course, was rarely used for want of a person who could play upon it....
>
> In a few instances, I found that the people had gotten hold of some bright-colored cards that had been designed for advertising purposes, and were making the most use of those [as Christmas decorations].[16]

The purchasing of luxuries, such as musical instruments, suggests a remarkable degree of "consumer confidence" among the most depressed class of black Americans in the 1890s. The use of advertising cards for Christmas decorations demonstrates their exposure to the growing advertising industry. It is to be assumed that black peasants were also getting hold of Sears and Roebuck catalogues, which further stimulated their appetites for consumer goods. This could certainly not have disappointed Julius Rosenwald, the Sears and Roebuck tycoon, who eventually became a major Tuskegee benefactor.[17] If Washington's anecdotes represent typical behavior, debt and the encouragement of debt were the basis of a conspicuous consumption that was becoming prevalent among the peasantry.

Not surprisingly, Washington disapproved purchasing pianos, but his negativism on sewing machines is odd, especially since he famously

---

[16] *Up From Slavery* in *Booker T. Washington Papers*, Vol. 1, pp. 274–75, 287.
[17] Harlan, *Booker T. Washington*, Vol. 2, pp. 140–42.

encouraged use of the washing machine. One of his Tuskegee gems suggested that the only obstacle between "The Old Washerwoman" and a washing machine was ignorance of modern industrial methods.

Without industrial education, when the black woman washes a shirt, she washes with both hands, both feet, and her whole body. An individual with industrial education will use a machine that washes ten times as many shirts in a given time with almost no expenditure of physical force; steam, electricity, or water doing the work.[18]

The problem of the washerwoman was not poverty, but lack of know-how – it was her ignorance that made her position menial. Was it a contradiction that Washington should disparage investment in sewing machines but not in washing machines? Seemingly so, for Tuskegee training would seem no less applicable to clothes making than to clothes washing. The work of a seamstress, with or without a machine, requires greater training than the work of a washerwoman, to be sure, and since industrial education was supposed to teach skills and provide motivation, it might have benefited the owners of the unused sewing machines, supposedly so ubiquitous in southern cabins. Perhaps it was more practical for black people in Alabama to establish commercial laundries than garment factories, but that was not what Washington said.

Washington often repeated the slogan "credit is capital," which was true enough, but the sharecropper system was notorious for making "capital" available in the form of credit. A feature of the crop-lien system was that it provided easy credit on exploitative terms, and it was based on payment in goods rather than money. Washington knew that black people would never acquire economic power so long as they continued to exchange labor for consumer goods, but his solution was to preach the "Protestant ethic," not to attack the crop-lien system directly. And black Americans knew nothing of saving. Du Bois maintained that the failure of the Freedmen's Bank had disillusioned many of them when it came to the possibility of accumulating capital.[19]

Washington's "intuitive grasp" of the "speech and thought of triumphant commercialism" did not rely on any systematic display of economic

[18] *Black Belt Diamonds*, p. 14.
[19] The Freedmen's Bank failed as a result of an interrelated set of economic catastrophes that occurred in the early 1870s, and African Americans were not the only losers. Walter L. Fleming, *The Freedmen's Savings Bank: A Chapter in the Economic History of the Negro Race* (Chapel Hill: University of North Carolina Press, 1927); Carl R. Osthaus, *Freedman, Philanthropy and Fraud: A History of the Freedmen's Bank* (Urbana: University of Illinois Press, 1976).

theory. It was not that Washington was unconcerned with theory, but his theory was a pragmatic blend of materialism and idealism without any anxiety over which ought to come first. Washington's position, with respect to the issue of materialism versus idealism, showed an Emersonian inconsistency, which some might call "pragmatism." Emerson had hedged his bets when discussing the issue of whether mind or matter determined economic progress, and Washington was likewise theoretically equivocal.

Nonetheless, the Sunday sermons that Washington delivered at Tuskegee Chapel were unambiguously committed to the promotion of enlightened self-interest, delivered in the safe homiletics of traditional nondenominational religion. They were based on the same theme of public service and benevolent capitalism that underlay Carnegie's *The Gospel of Wealth*. His preachments, some of which were excerpted in *Black Belt Diamonds,* contained Franklinean warnings against late night entertainments and public amusements, which were directly linked to moral dangers, but, worse than that, to economic disaster.

Quite a number of our young men in the cities stay up until twelve, one, and two o'clock each night. Sometimes at the gambling table, or in some brothel or drinking saloon. As a result they go late to their work and in a short time you hear them complaining about having lost their position. They will tell you they have lost their jobs on account of race prejudice, or because their former employers are not going to hire colored help any longer. But you will find, if you learn the real circumstances, that it is much more likely they lost their jobs because they were not punctual or on account of carelessness.... There is nothing worse for a young man or a young woman than to get into the habit of thinking that he or she must spend every night on the street or in some public place.[20]

The above words would have made excellent grist for Max Weber's mill, illustrating as they do the tradition associated with Franklin of converting religious idealism into a formula for success. Weber does not find it useful to emphasize that the invisible hand that adjusts self-interest to conventional Christian morality is codified elsewhere than in Franklin, and perhaps even more significantly.

While it was clear that Washington followed the tradition of self-interested utilitarian religion, it was not at all clear whether his utilitarianism was ultimately idealistic or materialistic. Was religion the prime mover behind industrious habits and enlightened self-interest, or were industrious habits necessary to the generation of true religion? At times,

[20] Washington, *Character Building*, p. 31.

Washington's philosophy seemed to be materialistic. "It is not easy to make a good Christian of a hungry man," he once said. "I mean that just in proportion as the race gets a proper industrial foundation – gets habits of industry, thrift, economy, land homes, profitable work, in the same proportion will its moral and religious life be improved."

At times he seemed to believe that economic reform was dependent on the inculcation of a Protestant ethic, at others he seemed to be saying that the Protestant ethic must make ready the path for reform. Far from being narrow and simplistic, as Du Bois suggested, Washington revealed complexity and ambivalence in straddling the controversy of whether heads or hands were to be the ultimate determinant in the reconstruction of American labor and commerce. His thinking was more complex than Weber's because it pragmatically recognized, rather than fortuitously dismissing, the problematic of idealism versus materialism, and it was more empirical because it arose from an experimental methodology.

Washington, like most men, was both "materialist" and "idealist." As a materialist, he was an economic determinist who believed that the progress of black Americans would be best assured by establishing a solid base in the capitalist system; as an idealist, he believed that economics could be shaped by religious values. Asserting that economic success could never be achieved by a people who retained the habits of slavery, he set out to eradicate the vestiges of slave culture that he perceived in African American mass religion. He believed that exposure to Anglo-Protestant civilization was a providential by-product of the evil of slavery. Protestantism, properly controlled, could be a source of industrial values and ultimate economic strength. He justified his strategy of temporarily accepting political disfranchisement and working toward economic and industrial power in terms of the exigencies of the times. Indeed, one may ask if he could have accomplished any more by a rhetoric of militancy. Washington acknowledged, in a spirit that was both realistic and cynical, that American civilization in the late nineteenth century was hostile to the presence of black persons in politics. For this reason he insisted that the best way for black men and women to get ahead was to ignore politics for a season, and to concentrate on institutional development, starting with the nuclear family.

Furthermore, Washington's theory was more serious than Weber's. He did not simply set out to attack Marxian materialism as an abstract exercise, or with a view to establishing his importance as an intellectual. Washington's theory, in both its materialistic and its idealistic aspects, was developed with applications in mind. Ideology was to nurture mechanics, and mechanics, reciprocally, were to reinforce ideology. Students in the night school – those who arrived at Tuskegee with the most primitive needs, both cultural and financial – worked eight hours a day, then studied academic subjects in the evening. After a good night's sleep, they assembled in the chapel to hear sermons on how to accumulate property.

Up From Slavery gave Washington a place in the broader tradition of the American self-made man as the herald of homely pragmatism. He encouraged practicality in religion, as in all other things, and ridiculed the otherworldly emotionalism of untrained rural preachers. He was utterly impatient with the secular enthusiasms of the black masses, and their putative love for expensive gew-gaws and frivolous ostentation. The capitalism he advocated was not the cloying excess of the gilded age, but the rough blend of philanthropy and social Darwinism represented in Andrew Carnegie's *Gospel of Wealth*. Carnegie too was a prophet of Franklinism, and almost became a caricature of Weber's capitalist who compulsively piles up wealth merely for the sake of wealth. At the end of his life, Carnegie redeemed himself, presumably to his own satisfaction, by retiring and taking up civic and intellectual pursuits – again like Franklin.[21]

Late in life, Du Bois, who did not admire Carnegie, wrote a very puzzling short biography of Benjamin Franklin, remarkably as an attempt to reconcile the bourgeois democratic values of Franklin's "higher individualism" with his own Stalinism.[22] It is not surprising that Du Bois celebrated Franklin's commitment to the abolition of slavery and the slave trade. What is surprising is that he also celebrated in Franklin the same "Protestant ethic" that Max Weber had earlier identified with Franklin, although without reference to Weber. And this seems to me to be a missed opportunity since Weber's ambivalence on Franklin's Protestant ethic resembled Du Bois's ambivalence on Washington's. This is all the more

---

[21] Robert Heilbroner, "The Master of Steel, Andrew Carnegie," *American Heritage* (August 1960), brilliantly, but without reference to Franklin, sketches the failure of Carnegie to realize his Franklinean dream – retiring from business at thirty-five, with an income of $50,000, and "Beyond this never earn – make no effort to increase fortune, but spend the surplus each year for benevolent purposes.... Settle in Oxford and get a thorough education, making the acquaintance of literary men.... Settle in London and purchase a controlling interest in some newspaper... taking part in public affairs, especially those connected with education and improvement of the poorer classes."

[22] Du Bois, *Benjamin Franklin* (Vienna: World Council for Peace, 1956). Members said this was not a communist front organization, although communists did participate, but Marxist influences were neither repudiated nor confirmed by Du Bois at the time.

puzzling because Du Bois's treatment of Franklin neither acknowledged nor reflected Weber's observations on Franklin and the "spirit
of Capitalism." Despite his onetime intellectual association with Weber,
whose thesis had become ubiquitous in intellectual circles, Du Bois ignored him.[23]

Du Bois was justified in expressing his disagreement with Washington's
taciturnity on civil rights. Du Bois was in a position to be more vocal
and he rightly took advantage of that position, but he was wrong in accusing the Wizard of Tuskegee of uncritically endorsing every mandate of
commercialism. Tuskegee was subsidized by Sears and Roebuck magnate
Julius Rosenwald, who certainly must have understood the functions of
his catalogue as a possible spur to consumptive extravagance. Washington
actually criticized the fascination with advertising circulars that pervaded
the homes of sharecroppers. His critique was issued prior to Thorstein
Veblen's, and was hardly, as Du Bois claimed, the speech and thought of
"triumphant commercialism."

Ida B. Wells's criticisms were more appropriate, for she had witnessed
the consequences of practicing the very capitalist values that he preached.
She had been forced to tragic recognition that the problems of black
Americans did not derive from a failure to embrace commercial values.
The lynching of three black businessmen in Memphis illustrated a grim
reality. Their crime had been to establish a successful grocery store at a
convenient point in the streetcar line, exploiting a business opportunity
that white men had failed to anticipate. Their lynching was economic
terrorism inflicted on black Americans for practicing exactly the doctrines
that Booker T. Washington preached. Wells never repudiated the economic
aspect of the Bookerite formula, but she insisted that economic power
could never be separated from political realities.

Washington's advice to the white businessman and industrialist was to
trust in the potential of a reconstructed black labor force. "Cast down
your bucket," he advised them in his celebrated *Atlanta Exposition Address*,
"among the eight millions of Negroes whose habits you know, whose
fidelity and love you have tested in days when to have proved treacherous

---

[23] Du Bois based his work on "the monumental work" by Carl Van Doren, *Benjamin Franklin*
(New York: Viking, 1938), and a shorter work that he incorrectly attributed to Samuel
Morse, actually John Torrey Morse, *Benjamin Franklin* (Boston: Houghton Mifflin, 1898).
Van Doren's work remains indispensable and Morse's is seldom, if ever, referenced, but
Veblen's is excerpted, with footnotes, in the standard teaching text edited by Leo LeMay
and P. M. Zall, *Benjamin Franklin's Autobiography: An Authoritative Text, Backgrounds,
Criticism* (New York: Norton, 1986), pp. 279–88.

meant the ruin of your firesides." Craftily appealing to Anglo-Protestant ethnocentrism with references to emigrants from Southern and Eastern Europe, and exploiting xenophobic fears of those "of foreign birth and strange tongue and habits," he promised on behalf of black America a loyalty "that no foreigner can approach."

Four months later, he delivered an address, "Our New Citizen," before the Hamilton Club of Chicago. The themes were largely the same as those of Atlanta and identical to those that Crummell had articulated at Harper's Ferry a decade earlier – preparation for usefulness and service. He pointed to an "industrial village" where eight hundred young men and women were preparing themselves to be producers.

... in literature, in science, in agriculture, in dairying, in fruit-growing, in stock-raising, in brick making, in brick masonry, in woodwork, in ironwork, in tin-work, in leatherwork, in cloth, in cooking, in laundering, in printing, in household science – in the duties of Christian citizenship – preparing themselves that they may prepare thousands of others of our race that they may contribute their full quota of virtue, of thrift and intelligence to the prosperity of our beloved country.... We shall turn water into steam, into electricity, into food and raiment – and thus wind our life about yours and thus knit our civil and commercial interests into yours...

Washington's Protestant ethic was a pragmatic religion in which Christian idealism was transubstantiated into economic determinism with a promise of material salvation "of the body in this world." With its emphasis on increasing productivity and accumulating capital, Tuskegee's prescription resembled Weber's description. Unlike Weber's sociology, however, Washington's formula was not intended as an abstract theory of history; it was an instrument for social reform. But Washington's analysis shared a weakness with Weber's, for both assumed that people would prefer, under any circumstances, to acquire capital rather than debt. In reality, debt-burdened sharecroppers were the forerunners of a consumer culture where borrowing in order to spend was destined to become a standard for measuring patriotic duty.

Veblen guessed correctly that conspicuous consumption, not the Protestant ethic, was the more powerful motivator in any economic environment, and that American consumerism was typical, not exceptional. Washington disparaged what he thought of as mindless consumption, forgetting that African Americans were not particularly foolish in this respect. They were the harbingers of a twentieth-century consumer culture, and, as he said with unconscious irony, on their way "to set the world an example." Ironically, this example was not to be set in Tuskegee's industrial village, but among peasants tied to the crop-lien system, who decorated their cabins with advertising circulars, seemingly devoted to proving the functionality of Say's law – supply creates demand. More truly than he realized, but not for the reasons he anticipated, African Americans were destined to become the ideal model of "Our New Citizen."

W. E. B. DU BOIS: THE DEMOCRAT AS
AUTHORITARIAN

10

W. E. B. Du Bois on Religion and Art

Dynamic Contradictions and Multiple Consciousness

Of the five figures discussed in this book, Du Bois is the one most often subjected to a naive dialectic approach. His writings provide, in fact, an illustration of how the term "dialectics" can be inadequate for any study in the history of ideas, where multiple perspectives are always in opposition. He drafted a well-known dialectical passage applying the idea of internal contradiction to his own mentality, reducing himself to a double consciousness – "One ever feels this twoness – an American, a Negro; two souls; two thoughts; two unreconciled strivings; two warring ideals in one dark body, whose dogged strength alone keeps it from being torn asunder." It is a crime that a presumably free society should ever have driven anyone to write such lines, for they cannot do justice to the complexity of any human consciousness.

A sketch in black and white can be almost tactile, as we realize on those happy but rare occasions when we view a classic film projected on a real-world screen. There is nothing, in other words, artistically deficient about the monochromatic. Confinement to black and white can force upon the photographer the discipline of artificial restraint, just as confining the poet to the structure of a sonnet may test creativity and produce interesting surprises. But sketches in black and white must always be recognized as abstractions from reality, as shadows of the world. Pictorial art, including even the most "realistic depiction," is always by definition abstract, for it reduces a four-dimensional world to its square root. As it is in a painting, so too in literature – black and white abstractions are, at best, virtuoso displays of the author's mimetic skill, exercises in a medium that is intentionally restricted.

Du Bois's writings, taken as a whole, illustrate no mere two-dimensional dichotomy, but a series of contradictions – he was a democratic liberal who joined the Communist Party; a crusader for integration who constantly employed the rhetoric of racial romanticism; an elitist who celebrated peasant culture; an Afrocentrist who sat with Shakespeare; a civil libertarian who ended his days in the service of a Ghanaian dictatorship; and a socialist who was a sometime landlord. Du Bois's identity, like that of most African Americans, was far too complex to be subsumed under the condescending heading of "double consciousness."[1]

The *Sturm und Drang* of contradictions within his soul led naturally to his pondering religious questions and to a rhetoric from which religious themes are not easily extricated.[2] There was more to his religious concern than a Jeffersonian hypocrisy that advocated religion for the masses as a support for the existing order. His own mysticism and artistic romanticism kept him fascinated with the role of religion in human aesthetics. As Plato could not banish the poet from his republic, Du Bois could not banish religion from his world of expression, and he continually valued religious myth for what it added to artistic and intellectual expression. He approached religion sometimes, but not always, through the medium of African American tradition. Much of his sociological writing and a good bit of his creative writing mingled religious metaphor with idealistic flights of literary imagination.[3]

---

[1] It is important to respond to the growing body of secondary literature, both scholarly and interpretive, that encrusts the bones of Du Bois. August Meier completely revised our understanding of the relationship between Washington and Du Bois in his *Negro Thought in America, 1880–1915: Racial Ideologies in the Age of Booker T. Washington* (Ann Arbor: University of Michigan, 1963). Louis Harlan also enlarged our understanding of the Du Bois–Washington debate in *Booker T. Washington: The Making of a Black Leader, 1856–1901* (New York: Oxford University Press, 1972) and *Booker T. Washington: The Wizard of Tuskegee, 1901–1915* (New York: Oxford University Press, 1983). David Lewis, *W.E.B. Du Bois: Autobiography of a Race* (New York: Henry Holt, 1993), sets a new standard in the field. The critical edition by David Blight and Robert Gooding-Williams of *The Souls of Black Folk* (Boston: Bedford Books, 1997) contains much scholarly apparatus that simply cannot be ignored, particularly the notes on pp. 196–219 and the related correspondence on pp. 256–68. Shamoon Zamir, *Dark Voices: W.E.B. Du Bois and American Thought*, which is archivally based, discusses textual, biographical, and other matters of substance. Recent tendencies to overstress the "two souls" paradigm have been criticized by Adolph Reed in *W. E. B. Du Bois and American Political Thought: Fabianism and the Color Line* (New York: Oxford, 1997), Chapter 7 and elsewhere; check index.

[2] Herbert Aptheker, in his introduction to *Prayers for Dark People*, provides a more serious discussion of Du Bois's religious attitudes than does Cornel West in *The American Evasion of Philosophy* (Madison: The University of Wisconsin Press, 1989), pp. 140–41.

[3] This paper originated in commentary prepared in response to papers by Herman Beavers and Barbara Savage at the University of Pennsylvania conference "The Study of African

Du Bois's autobiographical writings, viewed in retrospect, present his life as a neat teleology in the direction of Marxist materialism, but even in his later years, he remained artistically dependent on religious mythology. Very little in his life's work can be explained in terms of linear change, although in his autobiographical writings and interviews, Du Bois showed a fondness for presenting his life as an evolutionary process.[4] In his *Autobiography* he attributed to himself a steady drift away from religion; nonetheless, his writings continued to employ religious allusions. He was not always unconvincing when he spoke of reversals in his ideology, whether dramatic or gradual. When he wrote of a mid-career departure from social scientific method and a shift to the methods of literary propaganda he was, for example, unconvincing. I once uncritically accepted Du Bois's periodization of his life, especially as he represented processes of change in his intellectual and religious development. I now admit that Du Bois contradicts himself and I am no longer certain that I can accept Du Bois's interpretation of his own evolution.[5]

Indeed, he did not accept it himself.[6] There are, inevitably, contradictions in everyone's recollections, and Du Bois, like most autobiographers, tended to view his life's progress differently at different moments. While in the *Autobiography* he discovered a telos in his life, I have come to suspect

American Problems: Papers Presented in Honor of W. E. B. Du Bois." They also reflect discussion that occurred during a luncheon meeting for presenters at the conference. The conference planners offered no rationale for scheduling these papers for the same session and it was left to the imagination of the present author to discover or invent underlying thematic unities.

[4] In the famous oral retrospective that he recorded for Folkways Records, he presents his life teleologically, but his own unpublished writings may often call the retrospective assessments into question. Anyone who has ever written biography will recognize, as Du Bois confesses, the constant reshaping of recollection. See *Autobiography*, p. 12.

[5] Du Bois periodicized his life in various ways at different stages of his career. See, for example, *Dusk of Dawn: An Essay Toward an Autobiography of a Race Concept* (New York: Harcourt Brace and World, 1940; reprinted Schocken, 1968), pp. 268–69. Du Bois retrospectively describes his shift from social scientist to propagandist in *Darkwater: Voices from Within the Veil* (New York: Harcourt Brace, 1920), p. 21. Elliot Rudwick in *W. E. B. Du Bois: A Study in Minority Group Leadership* (Philadelphia: University of Pennsylvania, 1960), p. 54, legitimately reads this statement not as the basis for rigid periodization, but as a description of growing activism. Twenty years ago I less cautiously imposed periodization on the life of Du Bois, stressing a shift from sociology to propagandistic art. See Wilson J. Moses, "The Poetics of Ethiopianism: W. E. B. Du Bois and Literary Black Nationalism," in *American Literature* (November 1975), p. 426. Arnold Rampersad seemed to agree and graciously quoted me in his *The Art and Literary Imagination of W. E. B. Du Bois* (Cambridge: Harvard, 1976). Another periodization scheme appears in *The Autobiography of W. E. B. Du Bois* (New York: International, 1968), p. 289.

[6] Du Bois wisely acknowledges the differences in the various forms of his autobiography in *Autobiography*, pp. 12–13.

that whatever evolutionary structure he later imposed, it existed mainly in retrospect. A good example of this retrospective teleology can be found in Du Bois's recollection of his youthful admiration for Bismarck, "Bismarck was my Hero." I once took this literally, but now, as I have said elsewhere, Du Bois's own writing calls the statement into question.[7] In an earlier document we find a remarkably sophisticated and prophetic statement revealing a remarkably precocious skepticism, indeed, a distaste for both Bismarck and German ideology. Skepticism should govern all interpretations of autobiography, as William McFeely and David Lewis remind us in their first-rate biographies of Frederick Douglass and Du Bois.[8]

In my studies of Du Bois, I do not see his life as a unilinear progression of transformations from one paradigm to another. I observe, rather, an intellect and an imagination that constantly set up rhetorical dichotomies. These are utilized for the purpose of heightening the everlasting contradictions of the human predicament. Du Bois's work, whether as a student of religion or as a theorist of the arts, is sometimes idealistic, sometimes materialistic, sometimes Apollonian, sometimes Dionysian, but always dialectic. In the course of a day, Du Bois – like many of us – could express himself first as an African, later as an American; first as a conservative, later as a liberal; first as an idealist, later as an economic determinist; first as a sociologist, then as a journalist; first as a Stalinist, then as a bourgeois democrat. The list is as endless as the list of interests that swept through his capacious mind.

Du Bois had more than two souls; he had many souls. The approach of rejecting his self-deprecating two-souls paradigm may assist us in answering the question that Herbert Aptheker has found so intriguing, "Was Du Bois religious?" In the "Credo," which he appended to his *Darkwater*, completed in 1919, when he was around sixty, he wrote, "I believe in God...." But in his *Autobiography*, he wants us to believe that by the

---

[7] In the manuscript of his commencement address, in the microfilm edition of the *W. E. B. Du Bois Papers*, the young Du Bois describes Bismarck as "one of the strangest personalities the world has ever seen...No lie ever stood between him and success." Bismarck had "made Germany a nation that knows not the first principle of self-government... [His life] carries with it a warning lest we sacrifice a lasting good to temporary advantage; lest we raise a nation and forget the people." Compare this to his clouded recollections in *Dusk of Dawn*. Cornel West accepts unquestioningly, as I once did, Du Bois's false memories concering his early opinions of Bismarck. I have discussed his Bismarckism elsewhere; see my *Afrotopia*.

[8] William McFeely, *Frederick Douglass* (New York: W. W. Norton, 1990), compares Douglass' "unidentical" autobiographies on pp. 7–8, 180, 181, 311, 360. David Lewis, *W.E.B. Du Bois: Biography of a Race* (New York: Henry Holt, 1993). See Lewis, op. cit. index references to *Dusk of Dawn*; cf. Du Bois, *Autobiography*, p.19.

age of thirty he was on the pathway to atheism. Which confession is to be taken literally? Scholarship can never provide us with the tools to read the heart of another human being. We cannot know if his statement in the "Credo" was intended to be taken literally or metaphorically. We are free to contemplate the possibility that he was being more honest when he examined his beliefs retrospectively, although the statement of 1919 derives some credibility from being written in the present tense. Aptheker edited Du Bois's retrospective denial of faith without comment in 1968, but took the risk of stating in 1980, "Du Bois never lost a certain sense of religiosity, of some supernatural creative force."[9]

In *Notes on the Definition of Culture*, T. S. Eliot placed religion at the center of the study of culture, making it an essential ingredient, if not the defining element, of every culture or civilization.[10] Many other literary scholars, including those like C. S. Lewis, who rejected many of Eliot's basic assumptions, also considered religion basic to the study of literate culture. But, as is well known, Lewis, one of the great Christian humanists of the twentieth century, also gave us one of the most important material-istic/economic interpretations of religious culture – a work that integrated the study of religion and economic history.[11]

Many literary scholars, whether inspired by Lewis or Eliot, or through their independent studies of religion, have insisted that there can be no culture without religion. The Catholic Church has always shared one idea with Bolsheviks and Fascists, respecting the arts. The Church is an au-thoritarian institution, identified historically with the doctrine that the arts are essentially (rather than accidentally) propagandistic in their pur-poses. The idea of an intrinsic connection between art and morality has been entertained by classicists and neoclassicists – from Plato to Horace to Sir Philip Sidney. It was accepted in the early nineteenth century by bourgeois romantics and transcendentalists, notably Percy Bysshe Shelley

---

[9] Aptheker, introduction to *Prayers for Dark People*, pp. vi–xi.

[10] T. S. Eliot, *Notes on the Definition of Culture* (1948; London: Faber and Faber, 1962), pp. 122–24 and elsewhere in the text.

[11] Lewis's most impressive demolition of Eliot was in C. S. Lewis, *A Preface to Paradise Lost* (New York: Oxford University Press, 1942). Lewis would have been uncomfortable with any description of himself as an economic determinist. Nonetheless, economics were the basis of his masterpiece, *The Allegory of Love* (London: Oxford University Press, 1936), an explanation of the "courtly love tradition" in materialistic, rather than idealistic, terms, viz., "the coming of Christianity did not result in any deepening or idealizing of the conception of love." The tradition had nothing to do with the "cult of the virgin," but resulted from the "feudalization of love." The implication is inescapable. Lewis attributed a fundamental idea of medieval literary culture to material, rather than idealistic or religious, factors. See *Allegory of Love*, pp. 2, 8–10.

and many of his contemporaries. The idea of art separated from religion or from other aspects of society and culture, of art as a self-contained and fully self-referential system, is a bizarre and marginal idea in Western civilization – and in every other civilization. *Ars gratia ars*, the freakish idea that art can be divorced from propaganda, is alien to Western civilization and must be fundamentally destructive to any culture.

Du Bois, like his sometime collaborator Max Weber, pondered the problem of the relationship of religion to social structure and values. Was religion a source of social inspiration, or simply a brand of escapism? It is the question posed by Gary T. Marx some decades later, in his essay "Religion: Opiate or Inspiration of Civil Rights Militancy?" Du Bois, like Weber, was involved in the chicken/egg controversy of whether economic ideas are generated by material circumstances or by ideological projections. The historical determinist must always assume that history creates ideas, or at least that history generates the parameters within which ideas evolve. But historical/economic determinists, like theological determinists, must always – whether Catholics or Calvinists – face an internal contradiction within their position. If, indeed, it is human will that determines history and politics, then history – whether material or divine – cannot be the absolute determinant of historical developments.[12]

Marxism, like Calvinism, is historically deterministic, albeit one system is economic and the other theological.[13] Furthermore, and ironically, among the dogmatic adherents of each system there are some "true believers" who deny being determinists.[14] Numerous authoritative readers, from Karl Popper to Bertrand Russell to Isaiah Berlin, have noted the deterministic element in Marxism with varying degrees of sneering sarcasm.[15] Indeed, Marxists, like Calvinists, are forced to reconcile the

---

[12] See Gary T. Marx, *Protest and Prejudice: A Study of Belief in the Black Community* (New York: Harper & Row, 1967), pp. 94–105. Karl Marx says in *German Ideology*, "circumstances make men just as men make circumstances." In *Theses on Feuerbach* he says, "circumstances are made by men." He also says, "Men make their own history, but they do not make it under circumstances chosen by themselves." All quotations are reprinted in Ernst Fischer, *Marx in His Own Words* (New York: Penguin, 1978), pp. 92–93. Some aspects of the ideological interaction of Du Bois and Weber are discussed in Moses, *Afrotopia: The Roots of African American Popular History* (New York: Cambridge University Press, 1998), pp. 141, 142–43, 275.

[13] Neither Calvinists nor Marxists believe that historical determinism relieves humans of the responsibility for their transgressions or of the responsibility for vigorous political activity. One need not be a "good Marxist" to accept the reality of class interests, the inevitability of class antagonisms, and the necessity of class struggle.

[14] John Milton, for example, accepted the Calvinistic doctrine of predestination, while insisting that Adam was "sufficient to have stood, yet free to fall."

[15] Karl Popper's tendentious attacks on Marxian determinism are in *The Open Society and its Enemies From Plato to Marx* (London: Routledge and Kegan Paul, 1945). For Isaiah

seeming inconsistency of arguing for the agency of human will as a historical force, despite their commitment to theories based in extra-human, and explicitly deterministic, forces.

There is an old controversy as to whether Marx himself (or Du Bois) was an economic determinist. The issue is moot. Regardless of what Marx "believed," Marxism or "scientific socialism" is a deterministic doctrine. Marx caused himself an intellectual indignity by attempting to straddle the issue during his lifetime, and the problem was of crucial significance during the Menshevik-Bolshevik clash, which lasted from the beginnings of the Russian Revolution through the 1930s and still survives in the present. Like the poor horse in Dostoevsky's *Crime and Punishment* the issue has been beaten beyond death. It was not, in fact, necessary for Du Bois to become a Marxist to become involved in the dispute over whether ideas fashioned material events or material events shaped ideas. The nature of the interaction between the two forces is omnipresent in Western intellectual life, and inflames debate among proponents of every ideology from the fundamentalism of Christianity to the biological determinism of Ayn Rand, who repugned theological determinism and held Christian teleology in contempt.

Booker T. Washington's writings addressed the issue, but Washington never could decide where he stood. Were hungry bellies the determinants of religious commitment? Or did religion offer means to solving the problem of hungry bellies? The question is tacitly and specifically addressed throughout his writings and is a matter of continuing fascination. All thinkers of any worth are concerned with attempts to reconcile contradictions. Intellectual history, the history of ideas, and the sociology of knowledge are worthwhile only insofar as they attempt to probe the ways in which various thinkers have attempted, consciously and unconsciously, to reconcile their contradictions. Washington, like his contemporaries Max Weber and Thorstein Veblen, hedged his bets when it came to the question of the primacy of ideas versus material forces. It is thus interesting to observe how Washington's ideas dovetail with, and in some cases anticipate, those of Max Weber and Thorstein Veblen.

Berlin's views on Marxian determinism, see his *Historical Inevitability* (London: Oxford University Press, 1954). See Peter Geyl's response to Berlin in Geyl, *Debates With Historians* (New York: Meridian, 1958), p. 267. Bertrand Russell irreverently attributes messianic delusions to Marx, whose theory he describes as an "eschatology," that is, an inescapable course of predictable events. See Bertrand Russell, *A History of Western Philosophy* (New York: Simon and Schuster, 1945), pp. 363–64. Alan Donagan denies that Marx was a determinist, and attributes any determinism in Marxism to Friedrich Engels in *Dictionary of the History of Ideas*, Vol. 2, p. 25.

Washington viewed African American religion pragmatically. The concepts of social gospel and progressive Christianity influenced his belief that the black church was potentially a reform institution. W. E. B. Du Bois shared this view, but the much younger E. Franklin Frazier came to believe that the black church was incurably conservative and an obstacle to reform. The question of whether the black church was an obstacle or an impetus to reform begs the question of whether "the black church" is an institutional reality or a purely conceptual invention. Is it reasonable to lump together a variety of independent Protestant denominations – not to mention various sects of Black Muslims and Black Jews – under one construct called "the black church"?

Was the black church – as has prominently been assumed – an institutional substitute for the black family?[16] A line of explicit and implicit assumptions attributed to Du Bois, and later to E. Franklin Frazier, was that in the absence of the "nuclear family," the black church provided the only institutional scaffold in the black community around which sound socioeconomic organization and political activism could be structured. Assumptions along these lines have led succeeding authors to continually seek in the "Negro Church" a function to which it was neither logically nor pragmatically suited. Did Du Bois and Frazier inadvertently close the doors to alternative structures of perception, biasing all subsequent studies of African American institutional life – especially studies of family and church functions in African American communities?

Du Bois's dismissive statements about religion in the *Autobiography* contradict the persistence of religious mythology in the poetic writings of his middle and later years. Herbert Aptheker, his literary executor, offers the following assessment, which rings true:

John Brown personified Du Bois's ideal of a religious person. . . . Personally, too, Du Bois never lost a certain sense of religiosity, of some possible creative force. In

---

[16] Du Bois described the black church as "the only social institution of the Negroes which started in the African forest and survived slavery" in "Some Efforts of American Negroes for their Own Social Betterment," (Atlanta: Atlanta University Publications, 1898), p. 4. E. Franklin Frazier dismissed African retentionism in *The Negro Church in America* (1963; reprinted New York: Schocken, 1964), pp. 1–9. Nonetheless, Du Bois and Frazier agreed on one crucial point – both were convinced that the "Negro Church" provided the fundamental basis for social cohesion in America after slavery had broken up traditional African culture and social organization. Frazier, ibid., p. 9; Du Bois, "The Function of the Negro Church," in *The Philadelphia Negro: A Social Study, Together with a special report on domestic service by Isabel Eaton* (Philadelphia: The University of Pennsylvania, 1899).

many respects, Du Bois's religious outlook in his last two or three decades might be classified as agnostic, but certainly not atheistic; this remained true even when he chose to join the Communist Party.[17]

He continued to search for a way to adapt some version of the Christian message to the material needs of black Americans. Like Alexander Crummell and Booker T. Washington, who were contemptuous of religious escapism, he was impatient with evangelical enthusiasm. While teaching at Wilberforce and living above the chapel, he had been "driven almost to distraction by the wild screams, groans, and shrieks that rise from the chapel below me."[18] Crummell had sought in his African and his American religious work to forge a tradition that might deemphasize the conversion experience as an end in itself, and he sought to inspire adherence to an economically and politically useful Christian activism. In that same tradition, Du Bois wrote in 1896:

We as American Negroes, are resolved to strive in every honorable way for the realization of the best and highest aims, for the development of strong manhood and pure womanhood, for the rearing of a race ideal in America and Africa to the glory of God and the uplifting of the Negro people.[19]

Uplift was essential, but as a modern social scientist, Du Bois must guard against his elitist predisposition and his reflexive intolerance for the mass folkways. Where Washington disparaged the frenzy of the "shout" as a distraction from the social gospel, Du Bois was constrained to voice some sympathy for this manifestation of black culture. He would not allow himself to take a position of complete hostility to the mass evangelical tradition. He was too much the *Volksgeist* theorist for this, and must follow the German cultural history tradition of viewing culture as rising from the masses; hence, black proletarian culture (because it was mass culture) must be good.[20] This *Volksgeist* perspective cannot be attributed to Marxist proletarianism. Du Bois's immersion in Germanic scholarship and cultural studies made him aware of traditions in scholarship that

---

[17] Herbert Aptheker, introduction to W. E. B. Du Bois, *Prayers for Dark People* (Amherst: University of Massachusetts Press, 1980), p. x. Also see Aptheker, *The Literary Legacy of W. E. B. Du Bois* (White Plains, NY: Kraus, 1989), p. 235, where the following statement appears: "Actually, Du Bois did not exclude from his company Christ or Marx."

[18] Elliot M. Rudwick, *W.E.B. Du Bois: Propagandist of the Negro Protest* (New York: Atheneum, 1969), p. 28, mentions Du Bois's hostility to noisy religiosity in the college chapel, but provides no source.

[19] W. E. B. Du Bois, *The Conservation of Races* (Washington, DC: Published by the Academy, 1897), p. 15.

[20] Moses, *Afrotopia*, p. 152.

derive from early German linguistic theory, from Hegel, rather than from Schleiermacher, and from the nascent traditions of Pan-Germanism, so readily applicable to, or at least adaptable to, "the souls of black folk." Du Bois found himself to be of two minds or of two souls when it came to evaluating the emotional frenzy of African American religious practices, and it is not surprising that he sought to discover, in the religion of the masses, some elements of culture that might be useful in shaping progressive social and political traditions.[21]

In the published and reasonably obtainable novels of Du Bois, *Dark Princess* and *The Quest of the Silver Fleece*, which I have treated elsewhere, Du Bois addresses some of his abiding concerns respecting black religion.[22] In his appraisal of folk culture, Du Bois was proficient in finding values consistent with his own convictions and ambivalences. That Du Bois's soul was torn between puritanical and libertine influences is a point to which I have tiresomely alluded in previous work. He adopted the practice of Crummell who was given to attributing, Victorian sexual values to the pristine barbarians of West Africa.[23] Thus, Du Bois finds in religion an essential problem that he addresses in *The Quest of the Silver Fleece*, the fact that religion can lead either to cavalier escapism or to roundhead virtue. Once again the question: Is religion an opiate or a stimulus to social militancy? Many deep thinkers have addressed both possibilities.

Du Bois's *Dark Princess* confronted "the proletarian problem" in African American leadership. How can one claim to be a representative of peasants and unskilled workers when one has so obviously striven to be initiated into the traditions of the European university, and when one ministers at the altars of Western civilization? Frederick Douglass candidly and specifically refused any obligations to serve the masses on a consistent basis at the grassroots level. Crummell showed an awareness of the problem by sometimes writing grammatical errors into his speeches. Or he sought to conform to the supposed needs of the masses by delivering sermons that emphasized Jesus's coming on clouds of glory to judge the living and the dead. Du Bois paid homage to responsible black leadership by painting a sympathetic portrait of the black clergyman in *Dark Princess*. Earlier, he had illustrated in *The Quest of the Silver Fleece* the clichés of

---

[21] Barbara Savage, op cit., notes the commitment of Du Bois, along with other black men and women, to this line of thinking.

[22] Herman Beavers treats *Dark Princess* with sensitivity and brilliance, op. cit. Also see Wilson J. Moses, *Black Messiahs and Uncle Toms*, and Wilson J. Moses, *Afrotopia*.

[23] Moses, *Afrotopia*, p. 293.

good and the clichés of evil of grassroots folk religion. The cliché, when expertly handled, is a supremely effective literary device.

In his *Dark Princess*, Du Bois made use of themes related to what Weber called – for better or for worse – the Protestant ethic, while at the same time conforming to the tradition of art as propaganda. In one of the prayers that he wrote for delivery in chapel at Atlanta University, Du Bois combined art with religion for the propagation of his faith.

God teach us to work. Herein alone do we approach our Creator when we stretch our arms with toil, and strain with eye and ear and brain to catch the thought and do the deed and create the things that make life worth living. Let us quickly learn in our youth, O Father, that in the very doing, the honest humbled determined striving, lies the realness of things, the great glory of life. Of all things there is fear and fading – beauty pales and hope disappoints; but blessed is the worker – his are the kingdoms of earth – Amen.

The closing pages of *Dark Princess* are structured around a series of letters between Matthew and the Princess. In one of these letters, Matthew announces that "Work is God." He seems to be thinking along the same lines as Friedrich Engels in *Anteil der Arbeit in der Menschwerden des Affen.* I translate the title loosely as, "Participation in Labor as the Process Whereby the Ape Becomes Human."[24]

Engels's suggestion that labor is the creator of humanity is paralleled in Matthew's "Work is God." Engels's essay presumes that in the beginning there is labor, which is the generator of all ideology. This is not necessarily a Marxist invention, the germs of the concept are detectable in the opening pages of Adam Smith's *The Wealth of Nations*, where the nature of labor determines the nature of economic and political thought. For Smith, as for Marx and Engels, the socialization of production creates the basic matrix within which modern economic and political thought is inevitably structured. Marx stood on the shoulders of Adam Smith, just as Newton stood on the shoulders of Galileo, and Marx never forgave Smith for this.

Du Bois does not specifically attribute to Engels the idea that "Work is God"; I take responsibility (or accept the blame) for that connection. But I am willing to place myself in the same camp as Bertrand Russell, who developed alternative, but convincing, reasons for asserting Marxism is a form of theological historicism. Perhaps Russell is not all wrong. Perhaps Matthew Towns is not entirely wrong. But the Princess seeks to lead

[24] Professor Beavers calls attention to the fact, and to his observation I have added my own observations on Engels.

Matthew away from this materialism, so clearly reminiscent of Engels, with the following words

And, Matthew, Work is not God – Love is God and Work is his Prophet.[25]

Whether or not Du Bois ever became an atheist we cannot know, but he certainly continued to see the practical usefulness of religion as a literary device and preserved it as a literary device even in his later poetry. Religious rhetoric, whether it is to be seen as a literal manifestation of faith or simply as a dim echo of youthful belief, appears in the following, where he lists the historic crimes of American commercialism.

Enslaved the Black and killed the Red
And armed the Rich to loot the Dead
Worshipped the whores of Hollywood
Where once the Virgin Mary stood
And lynched the Christ.[26]

I think it is wrong to view Du Bois as a person whose life revolved around the one controversy centered in "the problem of the color line" or in the problem of "the two souls" – one African, the other American. The frequently cited two-souls conflict was just one of many conflicts in the heart and mind of Du Bois; it was neither the central conflict, nor the most important. Furthermore, as Adolph Reed has intelligently argued, there is something weird, regressive, and disempowering in the current fashion of obsessing on the "double consciousness" theme in Du Bois.[27]

Several conflicts are present in the thought of Du Bois and more than two souls are at war; there is constant warfare in the thought and feeling of most persons.[28] *Du Bois was not two souled, because he was not two dimensional!* Du Bois struggled with the social meaning of religion and the moral functions of literature. These two areas of intellectual endeavor are locked together in dialectics that can heighten the level of debate, but never permanently resolve conflict. There is considerable evidence that numerous areas of conflict are of equal dynamism within the legacy of Du Bois. These observations may be seen as contributing to the view that several dynamic contradictions represent issues of more fundamental importance to Du Bois than the dialectic centered in the two-dimensional idea of black-white opposition.

[25] W. E. B. Du Bois, *Dark Princess: A Romance* (New York: Harcourt Brace, 1928), pp. 272, 273.
[26] W. E. B. Du Bois, "Ghana Calls," *Freedomways* (Winter 1962).
[27] Adolph Reed, *W.E.B. Du Bois and American Political Thought*.
[28] Moses, *Afrotopia*, p. 149.

11

Angel of Light and Darkness

Du Bois and the Meaning of Democracy

William Edward Burghardt Du Bois in his prime could be an intimidating figure with his supercilious bearing, impeccable attire, carefully trimmed goatee, *pince-nez*, Phi Beta Kappa key, silver-engraved walking stick, imported cigarettes, and taste for Rhein wines. So matter-of-factly did he refer to his "days of rollicking boyhood" in the hills of New England that he successfully distracted readers from the fact that he was born in poverty, under the shadow of scandal in a strait-laced New England town. Mary Silvina Burghardt Du Bois was a single black woman, and, at the time of his birth, already the mother of five-year-old Adelbert, the result of an affair, perhaps with a coachman named James Craig, or perhaps, as she claimed, with a first cousin. Willie, as no one except Mary Church Terrell called him in adulthood, was the issue of her tenuous marriage to the Haitian-born Alfred Du Bois, a possible bigamist who disappeared from the lives of both his wives, and from the life of Willie, before the boy was old enough to know him.[1]

No amount of writing on his early years is likely to obliterate the commonplace myth that Du Bois was a New England aristocrat, and this is unfortunate because the mythology that places him within a historical or geographical elite has led to egregious misinterpretations of his

---

[1] For an almost universal impression, see Francis L. Broderick, *W.E.B. Du Bois: Negro Leader in a Time of Crisis* (Stanford: Stanford University Press, 1959), p. 69. "Washington had the appearance of a sturdy farmer in his Sunday best; Du Bois with his well-trimmed goatee, looked like a Spanish aristocrat." Irving Howe makes much of Du Bois's aristocratic mien in "Remarkable Man, Ambiguous Legacy," *Harpers* (March 1968). Also see Marcus Garvey's hostile, but skillful exploitation of Du Bois's autobiographical mythology in *Philosophy and Opinions of Marcus Garvey*, Vol. 2 (New York: Amy Jacques Garvey, 1925), p. 314.

political philosophy. Du Bois's hostility to certain aspects of American democracy did not derive from aristocratic or upper-class bias, but from his fear of the racist majority. He was conscious of vulnerability as a member of a despised caste, and this was amplified by the typical insecurity of the self-made man. There is no reason to doubt the sincerity of his sentimental devotion to the black peasantry or of his commitment to politicizing the stable working classes, both white and black. He was no populist, however, and he viewed the working classes, both agrarian and industrial, with tragic realism, convinced by experience that "the ignorant Southerner hates the Negro, the workingman fears his competition."[2]

His tragic realism led him to compromise democratic ideals in recognition of the political shortcomings that were the heritage of the black masses. In this respect, he resembled the avowed Hamiltonian, Alexander Crummell. He also inherited the Federalist tradition of George Washington and Lincoln, which recognized that undemocratic means may be compatible with the ends of a democratic republic.[3] Perhaps Du Bois's ability to rationalize contradictions and to make compromises is what is meant by those who make frequent references to his "pragmatism." Numerous scholars have enormatized the extent of William James's influence on Du Bois.[4] "The Doctor" was loyal to his academic patrons, respected their ideas, and was willing to learn, but his intellect and his personality were well formed before he arrived at Harvard, and by the time *The Souls of Black Folk* was completed, his thinking had been deepened by experiences in Berlin and Atlanta. Furthermore, his ideology was influenced by internal traditions of the black world.

Although he sometimes characterized it as dualistic, Du Bois's perception of the world was pluralistic. There is more than one set of ideological tensions in his life and writings, and certainly evidence of more than two souls, as I have already observed, for all minds reveal numerous

---

[2] *Souls of Black Folk* (Chicago: McClurg, 1903), p. 56.

[3] George Washington signed the Jay Treaty, which was ratified by the Senate in 1795, over the objections of Jeffersonians, angered because the treaty deprived them of their inalienable right to compensation for slaves freed by the British in the Revolutionary War. Lincoln deprived slaveholders of both inalienable and Constitutional rights when he freed the slaves by dictatorial fiat, not by democratic means.

[4] Cornel West in *The American Evasion of Philosophy* (Madison: University of Wisconsin Press, 1989), Richard Cullen Rath in *Journal of American History* (September 1997). West's essay is described as a "distorted reading" by Shamoon Zamir, *Dark Voices: W. E. B. Du Bois and American Thought, 1888–1903* (Chicago: University of Chicago Press, 1995), p. 11. An informed and interesting discussion of Du Bois and pragmatism is Ross Posnock, *Color and Culture: Black Writers and the Making of the Modern Intellectual* (Cambridge, MA: Harvard University Press, 1998).

dynamic contradictions and Du Bois's internal dialectics were many. There was constant conflict between his romanticism and his realism, his idealism and his materialism, his Afrocentrism and his universalism. These observations I make in appreciation of his intellectual powers, and not in deprecation of them. The great myth makers and ideologues who purport to represent the human condition always synthesize realities out of fundamental contradictions. The greatness of thinkers may arise from efforts either to reconcile or to exacerbate these contradictions. Inevitably, however, all serious thinkers must acknowledge their contradictions and somehow reconcile them.

Du Bois's intellectual life cannot be broken down into discrete chronological segments, although – as all honest thinkers must – he formulated variable responses to intellectual challenges throughout his life. As said previously, however, his thinking did not progress along a neat teleological line.[5] At every stage of his life he debated numerous issues within his spacious mind. His approach to ideology involved a constancy of tension, as the resolution of every intellectual conflict inevitably disclosed or generated new contradictions. His contemporary Casely Hayford recognized his ambivalence with respect to black nationalism, and his lack of authority as an African voice, as have more recent scholars like John H. Bracey.[6] I would suggest that Du Bois was ambivalent on many ideological issues, as thinking persons frequently are.

Some of this ambivalence was to be found in his approaches to the varied and contradictory phenomena encompassed within the term "democracy." If democracy meant racial egalitarianism Du Bois supported the idea for obvious "pragmatic" reasons. But if democracy meant majoritarian government by the people, then the issue of whether to support it became more problematic. Majority rule does not always lead to racial equality. In fact, it may lead to racial oppression. The people may elect an Andrew Jackson to promote an agenda of enslaving Africans and murdering Indians – all in the name of democracy. Crummell's admiration for Hamilton derived in part from recognizing, as did Hamilton, that the

---

[5] In *The Autobiography of W. E. B. Du Bois* (New York: International, 1968), Du Bois saw the inconsistency of his divers retrospectives (p. 13): "One must see these varying views as contradictions to truth and not as final and complete authority." I have discussed Du Bois's periodization in Chapter 10.

[6] Casely Hayford offers gentle castigation of Du Bois in *Ethiopia Unbound* (1911; reprinted London: Frank Cass, 1969), pp. 179–82. For more on Hayford's reaction to *Souls of Black Folk*, see Moses, *Afrotopia*, Chapter 5. Bracey sees Du Bois as ambivalent in Bracey, Meier, and Rudwick, *American Black Nationalism* (Indianapolis: Bobbs Merrill, 1969), p. lvii. Compare to Richard Cullen Rath's defense of his Afrocentrism.

ambitions of a demagogue are almost invariably masked by the rhetoric of democracy.

Thus, if democracy was to be defined as political egalitarianism, Du Bois was no democrat. He consistently endorsed leadership by elites, as he made clear in such early writings as *The Philadelphia Negro* and "The Talented Tenth." He endorsed the collectivist ideal of the American Negro Academy and its racialist founder Alexander Crummell. At mid-career he expressed his elitism in terms of progressivism, or rule by enlightened public servants. At the end of his seventy-five-year public career, he voiced admiration for such authoritarian figures as Stalin and Nkrumah.[7] He finally gravitated to statist authoritarianism, represented by the Communist Party. As did the mainstream American political theory, the Communist Party defined democracy as "representative government," a concept that Du Bois found acceptable, since he believed that only elites were capable of leadership – at least, for the nonce. His idea of "representation" eventually ran afoul of bourgeois liberalism as defined by the Western capitalist democracies, for he came to believe that capitalism was incompatible with democracy.[8]

At the age of twenty-nine, in his perennially controversial essay "The Conservation of Races," Du Bois repudiated (at least rhetorically) the ideals of bourgeois liberalism, calling on black folk to embrace a destiny of racial collectivism. He questioned bourgeois liberal democracy as represented in "the individualistic philosophy of the Declaration of Independence and the laissez-faire philosophy of Adam Smith," although he apparently respected the libertarian ideals of the Bill of Rights. "The Conservation of Races," like his later writings, revealed a tension that often arises when social theorists try to draft blueprints for democracies. Du Bois wrestled constantly with the difficulty of reconciling individual liberty, majority rule, and social engineering by talented elites. He was

---

[7] Racial collectivism was the fundamental preachment of Crummell's essay "The Social Principle Among a People," an oblique attack on the individualistic philosophy (but not the personality or character) of Frederick Douglass, published in Alexander Crummell, *The Greatness of Christ and Other Sermons* (New York: Thomas Whittaker, 1882). The same antiindividualistic themes dominated his addresses before the American Negro Academy, "Civilization, The Primal Need of the Race" and "The Attitude of American Mind Toward Negro Intellect," published as *American Negro Academy Occasional Papers*, No. 3 (Washington, DC: The Academy, 1898).

[8] I have naturally consulted the *Oxford English Dictionary*, Raymond Williams, *Keywords*, Stephen Graubard's article in *Dictionary of the History of Ideas*, and *Merriam Webster* in order to verify my a priori intuition that democracy is – except in the crudest etymological sense – undefinable.

not the first African American to recognize the implications of a tyranny of the majority. His awareness of the problem was heightened with the rise of communism and fascism in Europe. Both ideologies enlisted, or claimed to enlist, mass support, and thus stifled individualism in the name of democracy.

Du Bois resembled Alexander Crummell in rejecting the rhetoric of Jeffersonian democratic egalitarianism. This was not simply a naive reaction to its hypocrisy, but a rejection of its implicit individualism. The indifference that he expressed toward the enlightenment attitudes of Adam Smith and Thomas Jefferson represented conservatism, not liberalism. Indeed, his rhapsody on the virtues of the old South demonstrated a sympathetic harmony with Jefferson's feudal agrarianism. However, like Crummell, Du Bois argued the need for planned communalism and authoritarian social structures. This "Hamiltonian" doctrine of social organization was articulated in Crummell's writings and self-evident in Du Bois's once neglected, but now too frequently cited youthful essay, "The Conservation of Races."[9]

Du Bois's early writings, including *The Souls of Black Folk*, contained very little that could be described as "democratic." The book was a defense of racial egalitarianism but did not support democracy in the sense of majority rule or one person, one vote. His ideas were essentially elitist and he was not opposed to withholding the vote from black folk until they could be brought up to an educated level of appreciation; but the same standard should be applied to the great masses of the white unwashed.[10] This having been said, Du Bois went on record in support of bourgeois democracy – many times. Thus, I recognize the current of bourgeois liberalism in his intellectual life that has been correctly identified by Saunders Redding, Rayford Logan, and Lerone Bennett. We cannot deny the existence of this liberal commitment in such essays as his brilliantly

---

[9] Anthony Appiah's sparsely footnoted "The Uncompleted Argument: Du Bois and the Illusion of Race," in H. L. Gates, ed., *"Race, Writing and Difference"* (Chicago: University of Chicago Press, 1980), condescendingly, and with apparent inadvertence, rehashes Ashley Montague's familiar argument in *Man's Most Dangerous Myth: The Fallacy of Race* (1942; Cleveland: Meridian, 1964), to uselessly challenge a biological racialism that is not Du Bois's concern in "Conservation of Races." Du Bois tacitly considers various definitions of race, but settles on a cultural-historical definition and specifically refers to race as an "invention." Tommy Lott makes this point in "Du Bois on the Invention of Race," *Philosophical Forum* (Fall, Spring, 1992–93). A similar point is made by Richard C. Rath in "Echo and Narcissus: The Pragmatism of Du Bois," *American Historical Review* (September 1997).

[10] *Souls of Black Folk*, p. 176.

precocious valedictory oration on Jefferson Davis.[11] His essays and poetic sketches from *The Crisis*, later collected in *The ABC of Color*, are markedly liberal in content and spirit. Du Bois endorsed bourgeois liberalism in his short biography of Benjamin Franklin, the man who Max Weber made paradigmatic as the embodiment of *The Protestant Ethic and the Spirit of Capitalism.*

In 1896, the year in which Du Bois took his Ph.D. in history from Harvard University, black political writing was dominated by men who had achieved prominence in the abolitionist struggle before the Civil War. Two of the leading figures from Du Bois's angle of vision were Alexander Crummell and Frederick Douglass; Booker T. Washington was in the process of seizing power at the time, and Du Bois did not immediately assert intellectual independence from Booker T. Washington until seven years later.[12] The clash, when it came, led to bitter conflicts among African Americans concerning leadership ideology. Years later, Du Bois became embroiled in an even more acerbic intellectual battle with the brilliant publicist Marcus Garvey (1887–1940). Du Bois's interactions with Crummell, Douglass, Washington, and Garvey provide a useful way of understanding his theories of democracy and his place in intellectual history.

His brief interaction with Alexander Crummell has been discussed by several authors, and some argue that Crummell's American Negro Academy offered a tacit challenge to Washington's leadership.[13] This is a correct appraisal, as far as it goes. It should not be forgotten, however, that Crummell testified before the United States Congress in favor of industrial education. Additionally, he was the author of two well-known essays which argued that industrial education was best suited to the practical needs of the black masses.[14] The cultivation of a business and industrial elite was a top priority for both Crummell and Du Bois and it did not in any way imply rejection of a literary and intellectually oriented

[11] W. E. B. Du Bois's Harvard graduation speech, 1890, is reprinted in Eric Sundquist, ed., *The Oxford W. E. B. Du Bois Reader* (New York: Oxford University Press, 1996), pp. 243–45.

[12] In his essay "Of Mr. Booker T. Washington and Others," in *Souls of Black Folk* (1903), Du Bois provided a list of putatively more assertive, and hence, presumably, more authentic black leaders.

[13] Moses, *Alexander Crummell*, pp. 258–77. John Oldfield, *Alexander Crummell (1819–1898) and the Creation of an African-American Church in Liberia* (Lewistown, NY: Edwin Mellen Press, 1990), pp. 115–32.

[14] "Common Sense in Common Schooling" was printed in Crummell's *The Greatness of Christ;* "Right Mindedness" was printed in his *Africa and America.* Also see Moses, *Alexander Crummell*, especially pp. 232–36.

"talented tenth." Similarly, Washington never denied the necessity of the liberal arts, albeit the elite he envisioned must assign a higher priority to industry and business than to classical literature and the more abstract sciences.

It should never be forgotten that even those most opposed to Washington admitted the value of his accomplishments at Tuskegee. His opponents condemned only his dictatorial policies, which existed in such ironic juxtaposition to his damnably obsequious public demeanor. Du Bois supported the puritan ethos of Tuskegee with its Prussian values of cleanliness and hard work. Du Bois had, after all, adopted for himself what he called "the Gospel of Sacrifice," and accepted as his motto the lines from the German poet Goethe, "*Entbehren sollst du, sollst entbehren*" (You must renounce; you must deny yourself).

Du Bois, although an inveterate supporter of integration, always endorsed the Washingtonian principle of separate institutional development. In a short editorial published in *Crisis* (January 1919), he published an essay remarkable for its employment of such terms as "paradox" and "dilemma," arising out of "contradictory facts." He maintained that it was "impossible to build up a logical scheme of a self-sufficing separate Negro America inside America or a Negro world with no close relations to the white world." At the same time he maintained that "if the Negro is to develop his own power and gifts, . . . then he must unite and work with Negroes and build a new and great Negro ethos." Du Bois, by the mid-1930s, found it impossible to work with the NAACP, which opposed his endorsement of African American institutional separatism.

Neither Crummell nor the American Negro Academy – and the two *were not* the same – claimed that industrial education was misguided. Crummell simply felt that all education must do more than pay lip service to the "large, majestic, and abiding things" that lift humanity above the level of brutes or automatons. The knowledge of crafts, agriculture, and modern industrialism must be combined with education in the social and historical patterns of labor, commerce, and economics in the broadest and most cosmopolitan sense. Tuskegee was committed to the liberal arts and social sciences, as evidenced by the fact that Washington offered Du Bois a position teaching there. The American Negro Academy supported industrial education, a pet project of Alexander Crummell. It was not Washington's industrial philosophy that his opponents eventually protested. It was his hegemonic power.

Implicitly, if not directly, it was the philosophy of Frederick Douglass, not that of Booker T. Washington, that Du Bois attacked in his address to the American Negro Academy. Unlike Washington, Douglass had seldom shown enthusiasm for race-based institutions, and had displayed little interest in working among the black masses.[15] He had not escaped criticism from black leaders for this attitude, and some members of the black clergy had noticed his isolation from the masses of African Americans. Douglass' religious skepticism and disdain for the religious roots of African American ethnicity were well known, but he was never an avowed atheist, or even an agnostic; he was committed to the Christian ethos of the Protestant ethic, the doctrine that God helps those who help themselves, and the pragmatic gospel of work and wealth.[16]

All black leaders of the 1890s revealed a commitment to the so-called "Protestant ethic," the bourgeois ideals of cleanliness, efficiency, hard work, and frugality. It is true that Du Bois questioned the presumably individualistic values of bourgeois capitalism associated with Adam Smith's *Wealth of Nations*, but he did not criticize middle-class consciousness or acquisitive values. In *The Philadelphia Negro*, he advocated the presumably bourgeois capitalist ideals associated with the Protestant ethic. The latter work, written in the "best foot forward tradition," offered the prescriptions of "cleanliness is next to godliness" and "work makes you free" as formulae both for personal advancement and for racial progress.

Urban populations must be converted into self-conscious classes, endowed with awareness of their economic interests as artisans, capitalists, and professional elites. The peasants of the South, while sentimentalized as a repository of "simple faith and virtue," were never viewed as the vanguard of black culture. Du Bois's ambitions revealed, as those of Marcus Garvey later would, a conflict between democracy and authoritarianism. Each man had a megalomaniac ambition to be the most important star in the black cosmos. There was, in Du Bois, a conflict between his tendency to authoritarian planning and the desire to encourage a democratic ideal. In works as youthful as "The Conservation of Races" and as late as the posthumously published *Autobiography*, we see him urging racial collectivism and questioning individualism. Throughout his life, he asserted the need to sacrifice individual aspirations to communal goals and to subordinate communal goals to racial strategies.

---

[15] Shortly after the Atlanta Exposition address, Du Bois sent a letter to Booker T. Washington, commending his "word fitly spoken." See Herbert Aptheker, ed., *The Correspondence of W. E. B. Du Bois: Selections 1877–1934*, Vol. 1, p. 39.

[16] David E. Swift, *Black Prophets of Justice: Activist Clergy Before the Civil War* (Baton Rouge: Louisiana State University Press, 1989), pp. 254–55.

Du Bois's ideal of American government was reflected in his essay on the Freedmen's Bureau in *The Souls of Black Folk*. As did many turn-of-the-century progressives, he preferred Hamiltonian to Jeffersonian theories of government, and he inherited the Whig-Republican ideology of centralized nationalism as well. He liked vigorous government, not only because it brought "democracy" to the South, but because it imposed by authoritarian means a system of bureaucratic efficiency. It employed military force to bring about egalitarian ends. This was a contradiction that Du Bois found easy to reconcile. The Old South had, after all, been an authoritarian slavocracy, beneath the facade of its egalitarian rhetoric and its disingenuous preachments about economic freedom.

But Du Bois had his own contradictions to reconcile, such as his consistently Hamiltonian predilection for authoritarian government with his sporadic Jeffersonian rhetoric of civil liberties and his reflexive preachments of government by the people.[17] Racism was an affront to individualism and a crime against the human soul. The human soul was not infallible, however; it must be guided by the educated intellect. Thus, in *The Quest of the Silver Fleece* he made clear his belief that black peasants and white workers must be educated to appreciate the relationship of their labors to international economics, specifically the global textile market. In *The Souls of Black Folk*, he asserted that mass education must include, not only the practical arts, but an appreciation for "the best that has been thought and said in the world."

First as a progressive, and then later as a Marxist, Du Bois asserted that the masses of the people could be educated up to an appreciation for Cicero as well as Marx. *Pro Archea Poeta* was as important as the theory of surplus value. Democracy could be realized only if the masses were intelligent enough to sniff the pseudo-populism of Jacksonian demagogues who confused them as to their interests and plied them with whiskey on election day. Only an educated population could be trusted with democratic politics. Majority rule would be possible only after the majority were educated. Thus, Du Bois became the sort of Marxist who believed that bourgeois liberal values would eventually arise out of authoritarian state-controlled processes. This process would open up the possibility of the "higher individualism, ... a loftier respect for the sovereign human soul."[18]

---

[17] For a study of Jefferson's political pragmatism, see Leonard W. Levy, *Jefferson and Civil Liberties: The Darker Side* (Cambridge, MA: Harvard University Press, 1963).

[18] *Souls of Black Folk*, p. 108.

Du Bois's definition of democracy extended to an ideological endorsement of women's rights, and he frequently and convincingly protested sexism and gender discrimination. But his marriage and domestic relations with his first wife, Nina Gomer, illustrated a more conservative example of post-Victorian conventions. She apparently felt no desire to compete with those women who assumed the obligations of home and family while working as schoolteachers and remaining active in community service. Du Bois would have been anxious not to repeat the irresponsible behavior of his father, who abandoned his wife and her two children. It was a matter of some importance to late-nineteenth-century African American males that their wives would not have to work outside the home, and that they maintain bourgeois lifestyles solely on the husband's income. Nina would certainly have taken pride in her ability to win and keep the loyalty of a young man morally and economically capable of supporting a black middle-class lifestyle. As Elizabeth Fox-Genovese has observed, late-nineteenth century black Americans, embarrassed by the stigma of black family disruption under slavery, "resisted to the best of their abilities the need for a married woman to work outside the home."[19]

Discussion is frequently evoked by W. E. B. Du Bois's essay "The Talented Tenth." The piece first appeared in a book made up of essays by Booker T. Washington, W. E. B. Du Bois, and six other black leaders, *The Negro Problem* (1903). "The Talented Tenth" was written in response to a specific set of historical circumstances. Politicians, educators, celebrities, and businessmen frequently attacked the idea that African Americans should attend college. White racialists of the day felt that attempting to educate black people at the college level was simply a waste of time and money. They believed that black people should not be in any college of arts and sciences. Joel Chandler Harris, in one of his Uncle Remus stories, has his fictional character say, "I can take a barrel stave and knock more sense into a young Negro's head than all the colleges between here and Michigan."

"The Talented Tenth" addresses the special obligations of the leadership class and encourages college education for the work of helping the African American masses. The basic, the central, the fundamental idea is one of service. The Talented Tenth are commanded to be servants of the servants of God, missionary-servants to the masses of African-Americans. Du Bois argued that persons who were intellectually able and willing to

---

[19] Elizabeth Fox-Genovese, *Within the Plantation Household: Black and White Women of the Old South* (Chapel Hill: The University of North Carolina Press, 1988), pp. 297–98.

work should be strongly encouraged to attain higher levels of abstract and theoretical knowledge, as well as practical knowledge, so that they would be equipped for leadership and service.

We as American Negroes, are resolved to strive in every honorable way for the realization of the best and highest aims, for the development of strong manhood and pure womanhood, for the rearing of a race ideal in America and Africa to the glory of God and the uplifting of the Negro people.[20]

Never before have work and sacrifice and service meant so much, never before were there so many workers, such wide-spread sacrifice, such world-service.

Is not this, then, a century worth living in – a day worth serving? And though toil, hard heavy toil, be the price of life, shall we not, young men and women, gladly work and sacrifice and serve.

And we serve first for the sake of serving – to develop our own powers, gain mastery of this human mankind, and come to the broadest, deepest self-realization. And then we serve for real end of service to make life no narrow, selfish thing, but to let it sweep as sweeps the morning – broad and full and free for all men and all time, that you and I and all may earn a living and earn, too, much more than that – a life worth living.

. . . but if above and beyond mere existence you seek to play well your part because it is worth playing – to do your duty because the world thirsts for your service, to perform clean, honest, thorough work, not for cheap applause but because the work needs to be done, then is all your toil and drudgery transfigured into divine service and joins the mighty lives that have swept beyond time and into the everlasting world.[21]

Du Bois's path after the 1930s is confusing and seemingly contradictory to those who do not have the stamina to trace his intellectual odyssey through voluminous publications over a period of seventy years. Du Bois, despite his left-liberal inclinations, expressed a black nationalist ideology when he called for voluntary segregation in his *Dusk of Dawn* (1940), a book in which he specifically endorsed Washington's program of economic self-help and self-separation. On the one hand, he defected from the integrationist line of the NAACP, grudgingly admitting that perhaps Booker T. Washington had correctly understood the importance of building an economic and institutional base upon which political activism might more successfully be grounded.[22]

[20] W. E. B. Du Bois, "The Conservation of Races," American Negro Academy Address, 1896.

[21] W. E. B. Du Bois, "College Bred Negroes," commencement address, Fisk University, June 1898.

[22] Documents related to Du Bois's rift with the NAACP in 1934 are reprinted in Nathan Huggins, ed., *W. E. B. Du Bois Writings* (New York: Library of America, 1986), pp. 1252–63. For extended discussion see David Levering Lewis, *W. E. B. Du Bois: The Fight for Equality and the American Century, 1919–1963* (New York: Henry Holt, 2000), pp. 335–47.

Du Bois's socioeconomic theories sporadically embraced black nationalist separatism and frequently denounced capitalism. Like Washington, he sometimes sounded like an economic determinist, and now he went a step beyond Booker T. Washington, embracing at least some aspects of Marxist economic theory. In 1962, the year before his death, he joined the Communist Party, although there is some controversy as to whether he ever became a doctrinaire Marxist, because Du Bois never seemed to supplant his Hegelian idealism with Marxist materialism. On the other hand, he did embrace a Leninist internationalism, and he became an apologist for Stalinism, attempting, as did Stalin, to reconcile Marxist internationalism with nationalist multiculturalism.[23] His framework for doing this was the Pan-African supranationalism championed by Kwame Nkrumah, president of the Republic of Ghana. Du Bois eventually migrated to Ghana, ironically retracing the steps of the followers of Chief Alfred C. Sam, whom he had once condemned. Du Bois died in Ghana in 1963, a supporter of Nkrumah's increasingly ruthless dictatorial policies.

The definition of democracy that Du Bois ultimately came to endorse was not simple Jeffersonian majoritarianism, which Hamilton and Adams loathed and Madison considered unworkable. It was, in fact, republican as opposed to democratic. Unlike Madison, however, Du Bois did not draw a line of demarcation between a democracy and a republic; he accepted the idea of representative democracy. In other words, Du Bois accepted the idea of a republican form of government in which the right to decision making was delegated to the representatives of the people rather than distributed among the people themselves. Democracy has never meant that every issue must be subjected to public referendum. In fact, American politicians, by boasting that they ignore polls, tacitly endorse Edmund Burke's position that elected officials are not obliged to represent the opinions of their constituencies. Du Bois went even further:

Democracy does not and cannot mean freedom. On the contrary it means coercion. It means submission of the individual will to the general will and it is justified in this compulsion only if the will is general and not the will of special privilege.[24]

He offered this antiindividualistic statement in a commencement address, "College Bred Negroes," at Fisk University and he had, as we have

---

[23] Du Bois's eulogy on Stalin in *The Guardian*, March 16, 1953, is reprinted in Julius Lester, ed., *The Seventh Son: The Thought and Writings of W. E. B. Du Bois* (New York: Vintage, 1971), Vol. 2, pp. 617–19. "He Knew the Common Man . . . Followed His Fate."

[24] W. E. B. Du Bois, "The Revelation of St. Orgne the Damned," commencement address, Fisk University, 1938, reprinted in *W. E. B. Du Bois Writings*, Nathan Huggins, ed., (New York: Library of America, 1986), pp. 1048–70.

seen, similarly attacked the doctrine of individualism in "The Conservation of Races." The theme of antiindividualism and the responsibility of elites to the masses was the dominant idea of "The Talented Tenth," his frequently mentioned, but seldom studied essay of 1903.

In both the theoretical sense and the pragmatic sense, Du Bois's definition was factually based and historically demonstrable. His definition reconciled the theories of Alexander Hamilton, James Madison, and Edmund Burke, who recognized that democracy can lead to tyranny of the majority and mob rule, sometimes to silly enthusiasm. His *nunc dimitis*, delivered to the All Africa Conference in Accra, was *"Entbehren sollst du, sollst entbehren,"* advising the Conference members to seek freedom in order to renounce it.[25]

In some historical instances democracy has meant surrendering freedom to the will of the *"Sieg Heil!"*– chanting majority. Neither James Madison nor Alexander Hamilton would have been surprised by the rise of Hitler as a triumph of the democratic will. A Hamiltonian, as well as a Platonist, Alexander Crummell recognized that democracy in the real world – as opposed to the world of ideals – was seldom consistent with freedom. While a true ideal of democracy exists in the mind of God, he wrote after the collapse of Reconstruction, "in the hands of man it has indeed suffered harm" and given way to the "fanaticism of blatant American democracy."[26]

Democracy is sometimes disingenuously confused with "republicanism," which is defined as "representative democracy." In practice, and semantics aside, both systems involve surrendering freedom to "representatives" selected by a fickle mob for idiotic reasons, who, in the name of the people, dictate the conduct of our lives, the nature of our liberties, and the legitimacy of our pleasures. Under Stalin and Mao, democracy meant surrendering all power to "the Party," because in a "people's republic," only "the party" can represent the will of the people. What Marx called "dictatorship of the proletariat," de Tocqueville called "tyranny of the majority," but the principle is the same. Du Bois spoke truthfully in the passage cited previously – "Democracy does not and cannot mean freedom. On the contrary it means coercion."

---

[25] *The Autobiography of W. E. B. Du Bois,* p. 404.
[26] *Africa and America,* pp. 52–53; reprinted in Moses, ed., *Destiny and Race,* p. 238.

12

Du Bois and Progressivism

The Anticapitalist as Elitist

"It is as though Nature must needs make men narrow in order to give them force," he wrote of Booker T. Washington, but it was not "Nature" that created the enduring image of Washington; it was the fine Machiavellian hand of Du Bois. In order to render his subject a more wieldy symbol, Du Bois found it convenient to exaggerate his narrowness. The doctor's brilliant surgery on Washington's image – so ingenious and so disingenuous – is comparable to the scalpel wielding that Thomas Jefferson performed on George Washington. Scrupulously antiseptic hands such as those of Jefferson and Du Bois are careful to avoid charges of intentional contamination. Each meticulously professed admiration for his respective Washington's intellectual power and insight. Jefferson did not say that the father of his country was mediocre, only that he lacked the genius of an Isaac Newton; he did not say that he lapsed into royalism, only that he might be in the company of others who were perceived as doing so.[1] Du Bois did not say that the Sage of Tuskegee was pedestrian, only that he lacked the imagination of a Socrates or the beatific vision of a St. Francis. Persons like Jefferson and Du Bois are so skillfully incisive that the results of their snipping and suturing are undetectable to the credulous. Usually those who inherit such carefully molded impressions of personalities and events have no inkling of their derivations.

[1] My obvious intent is to compare Du Bois's essay "Of Mr. Booker T. Washington and Others" to Thomas Jefferson's appraisal of George Washington in a letter to Walter Jones on January 2, 1814, reprinted in Merrill Peterson, ed., *Thomas Jefferson: Writings*, Library of America (New York: Literary Classics of the United States, 1984), p. 1317. Further discussion of Du Bois and Washington is accessible through copious index references in David Lewis, W.E.B. *Du Bois: Autobiography of a Race* (New York: Henry Holt, 1993).

The common image of Washington, which isolates him from the realm of intellectualism, was created by Du Bois. In two remarkable chapters of *The Souls of Black Folk*, Du Bois presented two contrasting examples of African American leadership. The better known, Chapter 3, "Of Mr. Booker T. Washington and Others," is remarkable for its frankness, if not its candor. The other, Chapter 12, "Of Alexander Crummell," is an exercise in evasive sentimentality. Not surprisingly, many people who have read *The Souls of Black Folk* cannot remember the chapter on Crummell. In both of these essays, Du Bois displays a lack of interest in intellectual biography that is equally apparent in his reminiscences on William James. He makes one fleeting reference to William James's work on pragmatism in his *Autobiography*, but focuses almost exclusively on the man's character, and spares not a line to express his own understanding of pragmatism or any specific influences that the thought of James may have had on him. Du Bois never published an essay comparable to Bertrand Russell's summary of James's ideas, although he was far better equipped than Russell to perform the work.[2]

Du Bois was self-consciously a social historian, and apparently rejected the school historical scholarship that centered on "Great Ideas." One almost suspects that he held the methods of intellectual history and the history of ideas in contempt.[3] It was not that he disparaged the contributions of black minds. His works respectfully allude to the intellectual legacies of Frederick Douglass, Alexander Crummell, and John Mercer Langston, but he does not discuss them. His most frustrating reference is to J. C. Price, who unfortunately did not leave behind a trove of papers or a body of publications. Du Bois offers us no help in our search for the thought and words of Price, and we suspect that he must have known much more about Crummell than he cared to reveal. He never addressed the complicated intellectual evolution of Frederick Douglass, to whom he attributed the goal of "ultimate assimilation," a contestable proposition, for Douglass' presumed advocacy of biological assimilation may be

---

[2] Russell, in *A History of Western Philosophy* (New York: Simon and Schuster, 1945), pp. 811–18, confirmed Du Bois's opinion, in *Autobiography*, pp. 127, 143, 148, that James was a nice guy.

[3] John Huizinga in *Men and Ideas* (New York: The Free Press, 1959) relates the thought of Erasmus, Abelard, and other selected individuals to what he calls "cultural history." Bertrand Russell applied methods that were not strikingly dissimilar. A. O. Lovejoy's approach to the history of ideas would hardly have been inconsistent with the Hegelianism so often imputed to Du Bois's earlier work. Alternatively, the increasing influence of Marxism might have led him to view socioeconomic forces as the determinants of ideologies, an approach associated with Karl Mannheim's sociology of knowledge.

inferred, but not precisely documented, in his writings.[4] Du Bois's omission cannot be attributed to a lack of sources, as some of these authors' published writings were readily available. More likely, the reason for Du Bois's neglect of intellectual history and history of ideas was his tendency toward materialism in his theory of social change.

Du Bois's hostility to the "thought and speech of triumphant commercialism" represented a hostility to the crudities of plutocratic philistinism, and this attitude constituted a variety of conservatism, a nostalgia for a mythical past when the planter classes were refined aristocrats, guided by a traditional sense of honor.[5] The present chapter is an attempt to reconcile conservatism with progressivism or late-nineteenth-century liberalism.[6] In Du Bois's case, this involves integrating Christian perfectionism, managerial elitism, and sentimental racialism. Du Bois struggled, as every complicated thinker must, to reconcile pragmatic as well as intellectual contradictions, such as those mentioned previously. A pragmatic contradiction, for example, between rhetoric and behavior is readily observed in the image of Du Bois, nattily attired in a three-piece suit, with trim Vandyke, Phi Beta Kappa key, and occasional *pince-nez*. His elite affectations, hostility to consumer culture, vague nostalgia for a precapitalist utopia, and evolving socialism interestingly paralleled some patterns observable in the self-presentation of Bertrand (third Earl) Russell (1872–1970).

In addition to their elitist anticapitalism, a singular point of direct intellectual similarity between Du Bois and Russell was their admiration for

---

[4] Douglass believed that the question of interracial marriage was moot because he was convinced that it was inevitable. Even without amalgamation, environmental influences would ultimately whiten the Negro. See "Claims of the Negro Ethnologically Considered" (1854), reprinted in Blassingame, et al., *The Frederick Douglass Papers*, Vol. 2 (New Haven: Yale University Press, 1982), pp. 522–23. Note particularly Douglass' remarks on the effects of climate and environment on the physiognomy of the Jewish people, white Americans, and native Africans. He implicitly advocated biogenetic assimilation, but Waldo Martin discusses his twists and turns on the subject in *The Mind of Frederick Douglass* (Chapel Hill: University of North Carolina Press, 1984), pp. 220–21.

[5] *The Souls of Black Folk* manipulates the southern "myth of the lost cause." Compare to Edward A. Pollard, *The Lost Cause* (New York, 1866), pp. 45–66, for postbellum sentimentalism reminiscent of the antebellum agrarian tradition of Jefferson, Calhoun, and Fitzhugh. A northern variation on this theme is in William Dean Howells, *The Rise of Silas Lapham*, where the protagonist reveals agrarian virtue when he resists the temptation to exploit the ignorance of other businessmen. The "old money class" is also positively portrayed, and Howells conveys faith that American virtue is not doomed to oblivion.

[6] Works stressing, correctly, Du Bois's "progressivism" include Adolph Reed, *W. E. B. Du Bois and American Political Thought: Fabianism and the Color Line* (New York: Oxford University Press, 1997); Manning Marable, *W. E. B. Du Bois: Black Radical Democrat* (Boston: Twayne, 1986); Gerald Horne, *Black and Red: Du Bois and the Afro-American Response to the Cold War* (Albany: State University of New York Press, 1986).

the thought of William James. Unlike Du Bois, however, Russell expressed something more than his hearty affection for the man. He published an extended analysis of James's thought, which Du Bois never did.[7] Du Bois said in later years that he became a "devoted follower" of James, but one wonders if this statement should be relegated to the same specious category as his "Bismarck was my hero," an indisputable case of "false memory."[8] Du Bois says his Harvard experiences "encouraged his questions" about religious orthodoxy, without mentioning James specifically. As did James, Du Bois rejected Protestant orthodoxy, but continued to view religion as a guide to morality. It is remarkable, however, how little influence one finds in Du Bois's papers from the Harvard years – even those notes and observations that deal specifically with James's lectures.

There is an apparent contradiction between the universal moralism implicit in the social gospel of American civil religion and the relativism associated with pragmatism. There is something contradictory about Du Bois's and James's persistent reiteration of their very similar social gospel in the same sort of nondenominational rhetoric that one might have heard in the Tuskegee chapel. The manipulation of religion resembles the pragmatism of Jeffersonian civil religion. The "Sage of Monticello" did not actually say that religion is necessary to government. Jefferson's notion of civil religion was based, like James's, on the idea that religious faith could exert control over public morality. Jefferson, putting it bluntly, believed in religion as a means of social control, and so did the pragmatic social gospelers.[9] James's pragmatic system of civil religion, with its social gospel instrumentalism, resembled that of Du Bois and Booker T. Washington.

---

[7] Other discussions of Du Bois's ties to James and pragmatism are mentioned in the previous chapter, including those of Richard Cullen Rath's article in *The Journal of American History* and books by David Lewis; Ross Posnock, *Color and Culture*; Adolph Reed, *W. E. B. Du Bois and American Political Thought*; Cornel West, *The American Evasion of Philosophy*; and Shamoon Zamir, *Dark Voices*.

[8] Discussed in a previous chapter and in Moses, *Afrotopia*, pp. 167–68. Microfilm edition of *The Papers of W. E. B. Du Bois* is hardly replete with references to James. The papers contain a few lecture notes, but these do not indicate any obsession with attempting to define pragmatism or, for that matter, any particular interest in determining the singularity of James's contribution to the history of philosophy.

[9] Jefferson, although famous for his quasi-constitutional preachment on the unbreachable wall of separation between chuch and state, pragmatically enlisted religion in support of governmental principles. His big stick approach to civil religion was to inspire fear in the hearts of the masses. "And can the liberties of a nation be thought secure when we have removed their only firm basis, a conviction in the minds of the people that these liberties are of the gift of God. That they are not to be violated but with his wrath." Thomas Jefferson, *Notes on the State of Virginia*, edited and with an introduction by William Peden (Chapel Hill: University of North Carolina Press, 1955), pp. 137–38.

James displayed a religious perfectionism consistent with the benevolent moral sentimentalism of an Adam Smith rather than the relativistic notions of pragmatic philosophy. The issue that is most intriguing here is not that James displayed an apparent contradiction, but the fact that he somehow found it possible to reconcile that contradiction.[10]

An essay entitled "The Moral Equivalent of War" reflects the thought and speech of the Social Gospel Movement, and in it James offered a pragmatically muscular alternative to the militaristic progressivism of Theodore Roosevelt, whose ideas he specifically rejected. As did Veblen, James recognized the "exploitive" or "atavistic" elements of the Rooseveltian genius. James's thought is not imbued with the rhetoric of commercial and industrial efficiency that pervades the thought of Andrew Carnegie, William Graham Sumner, or J. P. Morgan, nor does it include the sometimes harsh social Darwinism. There is an undeniable truth to Russell's claim that his soul was stamped with an indelible Protestantism. A social gospel mentality was a point of emotional and intellectual sympathy between James and Du Bois.[11]

Du Bois's sociology was more learned than Washington's, but did not neglect its undeniable virtue of practicality. Like Washington's, his sociology transcended the purely descriptive and was "instrumentalist" in the broad sense that it was intended to make a difference. As did Washington, Du Bois saw religion as potentially – if not always in practice – a vehicle of social reform. His progressive thought is inseparable from American Protestant perfectionism – both social and personal – which includes not only the mythology of the "city on a hill," but also the idea of ridding one's private character of weakness. Du Bois's admiration for Benjamin Franklin has already been observed, and the prayers he wrote at Atlanta reveal the same perfectionist spirit as Franklin's private program

[10] The project of the history of ideas or the sociology of knowledge or of intellectual history is to attempt to make observations concerning words on paper, recognizing that documents constantly change as they pass through time and space, and realizing that interpretations shift and change given the peculiarities of readers and the transmogrifications effected by divers circumstances.

[11] George Hutchinson makes the helpful observation that James recommended *The Souls of Black Folk* to his brother Henry as an accurate description of American life in *The Harlem Renaissance in Black and White*, pp. 36–37. Ross Posnock, *Color and Culture*, p. 18, is overly generous in attributing to Hutchinson the view that Du Bois "influenced the social turn of James's late thought." Posnock proceeds a step beyond Hutchinson, and I shall go a step farther to add that James's "The Moral Equivalent of War" is in the same spirit as Du Bois's descriptions of his youthful work among black peasants in *The Souls of Black Folk*. If this is what Posnock and Hutchinson are getting at, they are certainly on the right track.

for eliminating his personal vices. Theodore Roosevelt's program for self-improvement is well known, as is the rigorous Protestant perfectionism, directed both at self and society, that pervades the thought of Richard T. Ely, William James, and Jane Addams.

Du Bois's progressivism, like Addams's, was a secularized social gospel with roots in what Aptheker calls "Social Christianity."[12] Like Crummell, Douglass, and Washington, he showed confidence in a teleological view of history, a mystical confidence in the inevitability of progress, and a faith that scientific knowledge could reinforce the tenets of Christian humanism. The doctrines of the American Negro Academy were concretized, although unacknowledged, at Tuskegee, with its mission of engineering a new institutional order for the Negro based on reason and Prussian discipline.

Douglass' death in February 1895 left a vacuum in black national leadership, but the twenty-seven-year-old W. E. B. Du Bois was, as yet, unready to assume the position. He had yet to complete his Harvard doctoral dissertation and take his degree, which he did sixteen months later. Washington, on the other hand, was well positioned to assume Douglass' mantle, especially after he delivered his famous "Atlanta Exposition Address" on September 18, 1895. Du Bois sent him a congratulatory missive, which he seemingly forgot by the time he published *Dusk of Dawn* in 1940. At the time of the Atlanta address, Du Bois was still teaching at Wilberforce University, having declined Washington's offer of a position at Tuskegee. "It is interesting to speculate on what would have happened if I had received the offer of Tuskegee first," he later wrote.[13]

One must be wary of generalizations concerning the state of black America at the time that Du Bois entered public life. Civil and political rights were eroding, but cultural life was becoming tremendously more cosmopolitan and economic life more diversified. While black Americans witnessed the erosion of much of the tentative political progress accomplished by the Emancipation Proclamation and the three Reconstruction amendments to the Constitution during the late 1890s, their literacy rate was rapidly increasing. Furthermore, urban black communities were experiencing the emergence of a middle class, which was becoming – despite the conservative, venal, and often ridiculously self-important qualities that Booker T. Washington disparaged – more inclined toward, and capable of, protesting its segregation and disfranchisement.

---

[12] Herbert Aptheker, ed., W. E. B. Du Bois, *Prayers for Dark People* (Amherst: University of Massachusetts Press, 1980), p. viii.

[13] *Autobiography*, p. 185.

With the end of Reconstruction the nation seemed, as Du Bois observed, "a little ashamed of having bestowed so much sentiment on Negroes." By the turn of the century, it was apparent to him that black citizenship was being sacrificed to the ideal of white national unity. The birth of a nation called for unity among white Americans in the North and South. Whites were fatigued after the great internecine struggles of the Civil War and Reconstruction, and the passion for social reform was overwhelmed by the rush of the nation's response to industrialism. Some historians have described this as the period of "counterreconstruction," the "nadir" in post–Civil War race relations, and a time of "betrayal" for black Americans.

Du Bois never denied that Washington was a genius who "by singular insight... intuitively grasped the spirit of the age which was dominating the North." The problem was that he had learned his lesson too well and "so thoroughly did he learn the speech and thought of triumphant commercialism, and the ideals of material prosperity, that the picture of a lone black boy poring over a French grammar amid the weeds and dirt of a neglected home soon seemed to him the acme of absurdities." Du Bois's summary statement on Washington was, "So far as Mr. Washington preaches Thrift Patience, and Industrial Training for the masses, we must hold up his hands and strive with him.... But so far as Mr. Washington apologizes for injustice, North or South, does not rightly value the privilege and duty of voting, belittles the emasculating effects of caste distinctions, and opposes the higher training and ambition of our brighter minds, – so far as he, the South, or the Nation, does this, – we must unceasingly and firmly oppose them."

Du Bois did more than criticize the shortcomings of Tuskegee leadership in *The Souls of Black Folk*; he represented, in the character of Alexander Crummell, those traits of character that were presumably more desirable. But what was the exact essence of his admiration for Crummell? This is difficult to determine; the essay was beautiful, sentimental, poetic, but made no revelations about Du Bois's relationship with Crummell, and said nothing about his thought. The presentation of a deceased Hamiltonian as an alternative to Washington did not foreshadow the economic and social radicalism toward which Du Bois was drifting. Eventually he moved from the industrial democracy of Richard T. Ely and "Talented Tenth" elitism resembling Veblen's elite of engineers to embrace a more radical socialism, like that of Eugene V. Debs.[14]

---

[14] *Souls of Black Folk*, Chapter 12, "Of Alexander Crummell," who is contrasted to Booker T. Washington also on p. 49.

Du Bois became associated with a more progressive form of political activism fashionable in 1910 when he joined a group of seven white progressives to found the National Association for the Advancement of Colored People (NAACP). The organization favored public relations as a direct means of promoting integration, equal employment, and voting rights. The NAACP retained its dominance as the leading black civil rights organization for the greater part of the twentieth century. It became increasingly militant in its opposition to segregation as the century progressed. It obtained the services of a battery of lawyers to challenge the constitutionality of *de jure* segregation and, by mid-century, had won a series of legal battles against segregation in the military and in government-related industries. It was instrumental in bringing about the 1954 Supreme Court decision *Brown v. Board of Education*, which ruled that segregation implied inequality and was therefore unconstitutional.

In some ways, the pragmatic Washington fit the definition of a "progressive" better than the classical-humanist Du Bois.[15] As I have argued in a previous chapter, Washington's conception of sociology was pragmatic; the ideas developed descriptively by Weber and Veblen were preconceived by Washington "instrumentally," or in terms of how they might be used to "make a difference." James's pragmatism or instrumentalism defined "truth" in terms of answering the question, "What difference does it make?" This was clearly always the bottom line for Washington – without the benefit of sitting at James's feet. The Tuskegeean's "hands-on" method of educational practice anticipated that of John Dewey. He was equally willing to rely on philanthropic capitalism or a benevolent federal government, whichever worked best, and saw no reason to speak against the economic progressivism of Richard T. Ely, or Du Bois, and certainly not that of Theodore Roosevelt.

The merger of pragmatism and Christian progressivism was self-evident in the writings of the deeply religious Richard T. Ely, who shared William Graham Sumner's belief in the inevitability of industrial consolidation, but not his views on religion, which confirmed the ethics of J. P. Morgan, not of Jesus Christ. Ely's Christian socialism was rooted in the Social Gospel Movement begun by Washington Gladden. But Ely differed from Sumner on the implications of industrial consolidation, and shared with Du Bois a commitment to evolutionary (nonrevolutionary)

---

[15] Ross Posnock takes exception to such assessments insisting that Washington is a "pragmatist," only in the sense that the term is vulgarly employed. My impression is that such objections are inconsistent with the meaning of "pragmatism," at least if we define the term democratically as Cornel West would have us do.

socialism. Du Bois and Ely shared social status as college professors who had studied in Germany and come under the influence of German bureaucratic socialism. Ely insisted, as did Du Bois, that major industrial combinations should be under state ownership, or at least under very strict government regulation.[16] Du Bois summarized this position, which he shared, as follows:

I am a Socialist-of-the Path. I do not believe in the complete socialization of the means of production – the entire abolition of private property in capital – but the Path of Progress and common sense certainly leads to a far greater ownership of the public wealth for the public good than is now the case. I do not believe that government can carry on private business as well as private concerns, but I do believe that most of the human business called private is no more private than God's blue sky, and that we are approaching a time when railroads, coal mines and many factories can and ought to be run by the public for the public. This is the way, as I see it, that the path leads and I follow it gladly and hopefully.

The manifestations of progressivism in mainstream politics are sometimes at variance with the intellectual construction of the idea. For example, the progressivism associated with the American presidency represents two sets of ideas that overlap, but presents striking discordances. Theodore Roosevelt, a republican, embraced a progressivism that was consistent with the collectivist positions of the Christian socialists. That is, he believed that some trusts could be good, but that these good monopolies should be regulated in the public interest. In articulating his ideology, which was called "The New Nationalism," Roosevelt was seconded by Herbert Croly, a neo-Hamiltonian republican. Woodrow Wilson, an avowed Jeffersonian democrat, defined progressivism in terms articulated with the assistance of Louis Brandeis, who formulated an ideology of anticollectivism, which he called "The New Freedom." This involved sustaining small business and protecting it from being squeezed out or taken over by monopolies. It also avowed a commitment to protecting the rights of laborers in the workplace.

In 1912, Du Bois naturally gravitated to the industrial progressivism of Roosevelt and Croly. This is hardly surprising, if one recalls the affinity for regulatory bureaucracy he had expressed in his essay on the Freedmen's Bureau in *The Souls of Black Folk*. But to call Du Bois a "progressive"

---

[16] J. P. Morgan believed, as did Sumner, Veblen, and John D. Rockefeller, that industrial consolidation was a natural evolutionary process toward efficiency and functionality, destroying "wasteful competition." Thus, by cannibalizing inefficient small-timers, the great monopolists fulfilled what Veblen ironically called the "heroic role of the captain of industry." Cf. Du Bois, "Socialist of the Path," *Horizon* (Feb. 1907), pp. 7–8.

points up the contradictions implicit in that term. American progressivism in 1912 linked together concepts that were fundamentally in opposition. The term *progressive era* applies to two contradictory mythologies, the cult of localism and the cult of centralism. The two ideas are so clearly in opposition that one wonders how we can persist in using the same word, "progressivism," to refer to such contradictory sets of ideological goals. His commitment to industrial progressivism led him to overtures to Roosevelt, but when he was rebuffed, he joined Bishop Alexander Walters of the AME Church in giving his support to Wilson, of the decentralizing rhetoric. The exigencies of a world war would eventually compel Wilson to centralize and nationalize the economy, but never to abandon his segregationist regionalism.

But the contradictions of Du Bois's ideological shifts were even more interesting. His adaptations of German ideology involved mixing a socialistic bureaucratizing tendency with an incongruous *Volksgeist* humanism and a reverence for the folkways of peasants. He was not entirely indebted to Germany for the latter idea. His youthful experience in the South led him early to the romanticization of folk culture. Tom Lutz has addressed this tendency toward sentimental regionalism in American thought very nicely with his phrase "regionalism as a cure for the malaise of civilization."[17] Throughout his life, Du Bois appealed repeatedly to traditional cultural and esthetic ideals. He penned counterhistorical and romantic reveries on a golden age of genteel observances, when "a certain type of Negro, – the faithful, courteous slave of other days, with his incorruptible honesty," was complemented by "the old type of Southern gentleman."[18] Like Roosevelt, he questioned the fashionable bastardization of laissez-faire economics that grafted social Darwinism onto market capitalism. He rejected the individualistic biological competition model of Herbert Spencer, but implicitly accepted the collectivist Darwinian model of William Graham Sumner in which competition led to industrial consolidation.

As the major spokesman for the NAACP from 1910 to 1934, Du Bois represented the mainstream of black leadership, and yet, ironically, this

---

[17] Tom Lutz, *These Colored United States* (New Brunswick, NJ: Rutgers University Press, 1996), p. 8, is correct. I would add that Du Bois's regionalism exploits agrarian sentimentalism in ways suggestive of Ferdinand Tönnies, *Gemeinschaft und Gesselschaft* and the "culture-civilization dichotomy" in Robert E. Park, *Race and Culture* (New York: The Free Press, 1950) and Oswald Spengler, *Der Untergang Des Abendlandes*. This is interesting in connection with Richard Hofstadter's analysis of reactionary elements in populism.

[18] *Souls of Black Folk*, pp. 203–4.

"mainstream" leader was ousted from the leadership of the NAACP in 1934 because he could not bring himself to unqualified endorsement of the association's integrationist agenda. To his mind the NAACP, under the leadership of Walter White, failed to address the full implications of integration, which must ultimately imply the integration even of such basic institutions as the church and the family. Du Bois's eventual break with the NAACP was based in his belief that, for the foreseeable future, white churches and families would remain white, while black churches and families would remain black. Since Du Bois, unlike Frederick Douglass, did not view biological and institutional assimilation as the solution to America's race problems, he could not view integration as a panacea. An identifiable black population was destined to exist in America, and Du Bois believed that an identifiable institutional structure would have to be maintained.

He thus attempted to foster a distinctly African American economic tradition, which presumably would lead to the generation of politics, arts, and literature. His Germanic training had left its impression on him, and he had been influenced by the concept of *Volksgeist*, which may be translated literally as soul of the folk, or spirit of the people.[19] *Volksgeist*, an idea derived from the benevolent cultural relativism of the philosopher Herder, represents a theory that dominated much of German cultural nationalism at the time. Du Bois was to become the first American intellectual to attempt a theory of African American culture rooted in the folkways of the masses. His "scientific" paper read before the American Negro Academy in 1897, "The Conservation of Races," like most racial theory of the time, was flamboyant and mystical. Arguing for "the development of Negro genius, of Negro literature and art, of Negro spirit," he said:

Only Negroes bound and welded together, Negroes inspired by one vast ideal, can work out in its fullness the great message we have for humanity. We cannot reverse history; we are subject to the same natural laws as other races, and if the Negro is ever to be a factor in the world's history – if among the gaily colored banners that deck the broad ramparts of civilization is to hang one uncompromising black, then

[19] I have commented previously on Du Bois's involvement with German social thought, for example, in "The Evolution of Black National-Socialist Thought: A Study of W. E. B. Du Bois," in Henry J. Richards, ed., *Topics in Black Studies* (Buffalo, NY: Black Academy Press, 1971), pp. 77–99. *Afrotopia*, pp. 67, 137, 141–42, 150, 152. For a well-researched alternative argument, see Axel R. Schafer, "W. E. B. Du Bois, German Social Thought and the Racial Divide in American Progressivism, 1892–1909," *The Journal of American History* (December 2001), pp. 925–49. Also see Francis L. Broderick, "German Influence on the Scholarship of W. E. B. Du Bois," *Phylon* (December 1958), pp. 367–71.

it must be placed there by black hands, fashioned by black heads and hallowed by the travail of 200,000,000 black hearts beating in one glad song of jubilee.

For this reason, the advance guard of the Negro people – the 8,000,000 people of Negro blood in the United States of America – must soon come to realize that if they are to take their just place in the van of Pan-Africanism, then their destiny is not absorption by the white American.

Although political economy and other social sciences were important to Du Bois, the centrality of racial romanticism throughout his entire career simply cannot be denied. Du Bois's work at Atlanta University, where he was professor of economics as well as history, aimed at a long-term, systematic project to study the life and culture of African Americans in what he called "The Laboratory in Sociology at Atlanta." The Atlanta University Studies were a project aimed at gathering information and publishing a series of documents with such titles as *Morality Among Negroes in Cities*, *The Negro in Business*, *The Negro Church*, and *The Negro American Family*. These works were all based on certain assumptions about the organic relationship between economies and the cultures and societies generated by them. In *Dusk of Dawn*, he later confessed to attitudes typical of progressivism. His opening sentence contains a pensive note of self-mockery:

My vision was becoming clearer. The Negro problem was in my mind a matter of systematic investigation and intelligent understanding. The world was thinking wrong about race, because it did not know. The ultimate evil was stupidity. The cure for it was knowledge based on scientific investigation.[20]

Du Bois took a step in this direction with his dissertation, *The Suppression of the Slave Trade*, thus violating two basic tenets of Jamesean pragmatism. Methodologically it presupposed the "positivistic objectivism" that James called into question. More significantly, it was based on a moral absolutism that fundamentally contradicted the tenets of pragmatism.[21] Du Bois simply could not accept the relativistic position that his moral indictment of the slave trade could be adjusted to the situational ethics of eighteenth-century Virginia. The title of the concluding section of his dissertation promised and delivered a "Lesson for Americans," namely that the moral compromises of the Founding Fathers violated a universal and self-evident truth and "opened a highway that led straight to the Civil War." Unlike James, he based morality on *a priori* truth, but

[20] *Dusk of Dawn* (New York: Harcourt Brace and World, 1940), p. 58.
[21] Du Bois, *The Suppression of the Slave Trade* (Cambridge, MA: Harvard University Press, 1896).

although moral truth was eternal and intuitively recognizable, it could be scientifically observed, empirically demonstrated, and advanced through knowledge and reason.

It behooves the United States, therefore, in the interest both of scientific truth and of future social reform, carefully to study such chapters of her history as that of the suppression of the slave-trade. The most obvious question which this study suggests is: How far in a State can a recognized moral wrong safely be compromised?[22]

Du Bois's *The Suppression of the Slave Trade*, presented as a history dissertation, was not only a direct repudiation of philosophy as a profession, it was a conscious statement of preference for Rankean empiricism over Jamesean relativism. Du Bois's second book, *The Philadelphia Negro*, was dictated by the same empiricism in the service of moral absolutism, and was consistent with James's progressivism, but not his pragmatism. There was no situationalism in its moral preachments; indeed, all Du Bois's early work utterly rejected the relativistic assumptions of pragmatism.

Not much later, in *The Souls of Black Folk,* Du Bois displayed one of his most dynamic contradictions; he sentimentalized the agrarian myth of the old South in Chapter 5, after advancing the progressive ideals of bureaucratic government in Chapter 2, an essay on the political economy of Reconstruction. Appearing originally in the *Atlantic Monthly* of 1901, it represented the author's sympathies with German socialism and the efficient centralized bureaucracy of the Prussian welfare state. The essay has American roots as well, illustrating Du Bois's concurrence with the Hamiltonian tradition of big government that, during and after the Civil War, successfully defended the interests of northern capital in Congress by imposing military reconstruction on the South. The Whig leviathan, nurtured by Lincoln and sustained by the radical republicans, had extended the powers of the federal government, healthily undermining states' rights. Du Bois referred to the Freedman's Bureau as a "government," and viewed congressional Reconstruction as the lost opportunity for the complete reforming of the United States government as a whole, not only with respect to race relations, but in terms of centralizing health, education, and welfare. He realized, of course, that his praise for the Bureau pragmatically contradicted the sentimental mythology of localism he advanced elsewhere.

---

[22] W. E. B. Du Bois, *The Suppression of the African Slave Trade to the United States of America, 1638–1870* (1896; New York: Schocken, 1969), p. 199.

The contrasting rhetorical devices of several chapters in *The Souls of Black Folk* reveal its author's constant alternation between political science and agrarian sentimentality as he sought to address the material and emotional issues of American race relations. His ideas were developed against the background of the author's familiarity with the developing contemporary social scientific rationalism, yet filled with idiosyncratic rhapsodies on the faith and virtue, the color and harmony, of an African American *Volksgeist*. He was irrepressibly committed to the celebration of both approaches. While the content of his work never denied economic or political realism, the style was unquestionably romantic and sentimental.

I have seen a land right merry with the sun, where children sing, and rolling hills lie like passioned women wanton with harvest. And there in the King's highway sat and sits a figure veiled and bowed, by which the traveler's footsteps hasten as they go. On the tainted air broods fear. Three centuries thought has been the raising and unveiling of that bowed human heart, and now behold a century new for the duty and the deed. The problem of the Twentieth Century is the problem of the color line.[23]

Du Bois drafted his "problem of the century" clause in 1901, and circulated it for at least another two decades, although with increasing defensiveness.[24] The clause was a product of its times, drafted at the very height of American segregation and European imperialism. It was a statement made before the rise of Hitler, Stalin, Roosevelt, the New Deal, or the Second World War. It antedated the rise of Japan, the independence of India and Algiers, the revolution in China, the coming of independence to Africa, the establishment of Israel, and the Islamic revival. It predated the Civil Rights movement, the sexual revolution, and the radicalization of gender discourse. It preceded radio, television, the atomic bomb, genetic engineering, and intertribal pogroms in which Europeans have slaughtered Europeans and Africans have murdered Africans. Du Bois could hardly have anticipated these developments at the time he drafted the "problem of the century" clause, but he refused to give up the phrase, to which he defensively clung in his 1925 essay, "Worlds of Color."

Insisting that the First World War was a fight for democracy, he drafted a controversial article that he never quite lived down, "Close Ranks," which called on black Americans to put aside "special grievances," in

---

[23] *Souls of Black Folk*, p. 40.
[24] Du Bois was willing to defend that "pert and singing phrase" as late as 1925. In his essay "Worlds of Color," published originally in *Foreign Affairs* (1925) and revised for Alain Locke's celebrated volume, *The New Negro*, Du Bois still clung defensively to his "problem of the century" clause.

support of the war effort, and was roundly denounced by black leaders from more than one point on the political spectrum. The old social gospeller, Francis J. Grimké, expressed something approaching disgust, and the socialist Hubert Harrison gave him a scathing rebuke.[25] Du Bois partially redeemed himself with a hard-hitting exposure of racism in the military a year later. After the war, he resumed the struggle, calling on the soldiers to take up the fight for civil rights at home.[26]

Du Bois shored up his defenses after the Second World War. He had long expressed dismay at the seduction of African Americans by corporate capitalism and vulgar consumerism, which he viewed as forces of modern mental enslavement. In 1896, he saw African Americans as the vanguard. In his later published documents he was less convinced of their fitness for leadership. The color line was still a problem, but he began to question whether black Americans were morally fit to lead the fight against neocolonialism.[27]

Du Bois championed the struggle against segregation, of course, but as the tide of public policy began to shift in the direction of a racially integrated society, Du Bois came to believe that the quality of life for black folk in America could never be improved simply by elimination of "the color line." In fact, during the 1930s and 1940s, he asserted that segregated institutions might in some ironic ways be capable of sustaining black folk in their struggles. Needless to say, such positions were bound to evoke hostility from other NAACP activists. It was hardly characteristic of Du Bois to give much credit to his intellectual predecessors, but, once again, his thinking departed from the universalistic ideology of Frederick Douglass to encompass the race-centered doctrines of Alexander Crummell.

Crummell had spoken against the "dogma . . . that the colored people of this country should forget as soon as possible, that they are colored people," an idea that he called "disintegrating and socially destructive." Because of segregation, black people were "shut out from the cultivated

---

[25] The phrase appears in "The Present Outlook for the Dark Races of Mankind," *Church Review* (October 1900); "The Freedman's Bureau," *Atlantic Monthly* (March 1901), 354–65; "Worlds of Color," *Foreign Affairs* (April 1925), 423–44.

[26] "Close Ranks," *Crisis* (July 1918), 111. "Documents of the War," *Crisis* (June 1919), 63–87. Francis J. Grimké, "Victory for the Allies and the United States," in Carter G. Woodson, ed., *The Works of Francis J. Grimké* (Washington: Associated Publishers, 1942), Vol. 1, p. 571. Du Bois is not named, but the allusion is clear as Grimké disparages letting up on agitation. George Schuyler makes an allusion to "Close Ranks" in his novel *Black No More* (New York, 1931), c.f. Hubert Harrison in *When Africa Awakes* (New York: The Porro Press, 1920), pp. 28–29.

[27] See his "Address to the Pan African Congress," 1958, reprinted in *Autobiography*, p. 403.

social life of the superior classes," and were thus forced to depend upon themselves for higher forms of social-intellectual discourse. Du Bois had practically rewritten these sentences in his essay on "Jim Crow," published in the *Crisis* of January 1919. Like Crummell he recognized that "much of the objection to segregation and Jim Crowism was in other days the fact that compelling Negroes to associate only with Negroes meant to exclude them from contact with the best culture of the day." In his *Autobiography*, he insisted that he had always been committed to separatism at some levels, and not only when it was imposed from without.[28]

With the passage of time, conditions had changed and "culture [was] no longer the monopoly of the white, nor [was] poverty and ignorance the sole heritage of the black. Crummell had rejected "the demand that colored men should give up all distinctive effort, as colored men, in schools, churches, associations and friendly societies." Resurrecting Crummell's ideas, Du Bois said, "The real battle is a matter of study and thought; of the building of loyalties; of the long training of men; of the growth of institutions; of the inculcation of racial and national ideals."

Du Bois was inflexible in an interview conducted by Al Morgan, June 4, 1957, Channel 5, New York City. When asked whether he approved of Russia's squelching of the Hungarian revolt, in a "blood bath," he responded:

I do not know just what Russia's action was. I do know that the United States of America gave the Hungarians every reason to think that if they started a revolution that they were going to get help. . . . Now, whether the Russian intervention was an intervention that was called for by the mass of the Hungarian people or whether it was intervention that was not called for, that I do not know. I am not an expert on Hungary, although I have seen it twice.[29]

Morgan referred to newspaper reports that the Hungarian revolt was an expression of the unity of the Hungarian masses. Du Bois responded that he did not believe the reports. "When we get news of foreign countries we get the kind of news that certain persons in authority want us to have." He commented on the bias of American news sources, and reiterated his disbelief of what he was reading in the American press. Inevitably, Morgan asked Du Bois if he thought he would be allowed to express dissenting opinions freely on Russian television if he disagreed with the government position.

[28] *Autobiography*, pp. 295–301.
[29] The transcript of Du Bois's interview with Al Morgan, June 4, 1957, Channel 5, New York City, is printed in Julius Lester, *The Seventh Son: The Thought and Writings of W. E. B. Du Bois* (New York: Vintage Books, 1971), pp. 700–8.

"In some cases not and in other cases yes," Du Bois responded, adding that "recently the press in Russia has been a great deal freer." He maintained that before Stalin the people of Russian were "90 per cent illiterate, were poor, were diseased, were superstitious, you were trying to bring that people up to a state where they could form a socialist government." This discipline "included being very careful of the kind of news that you let them have, that you wanted to have. It included a great deal of curtailment of their liberty." He went on to praise the Russian system of education, saying, "Now that education has gone on, it has spread, until the people have demanded more liberties, and they are getting more liberties, and in the future as they become more intelligent and effective, they will get still more." In response to a question on freedom of the press, he responded that the Russian press was presumably "as curtailed and one-sided as the American press, but I do know that of course it is curtailed." Some years later, he offered further commentary on the Hungarian crisis.

In...Hungary I sensed the age-old strife between the Roman Catholic church and land holding aristocracy in one group; the rising bourgeoisie supported by Western enterprise and capital in another group; and the great mass of degraded peasants who, as I saw them in 1893 were distinctly below the level of American Negro serfs. I was not surprised when the pushing businessmen and artisans, calling themselves "Commons" and despising laborers and serfs, rebelled against communism in 1956. I was glad when the Soviet Union intervened and thus served notice on all reactionaries that the Russian revolution was still unwilling to yield its gains before a show of force. The Hungarian Academy made me a corresponding member.[30]

Du Bois's mistakes, like his triumphs, were gigantic, but unlike today's academic superstars, he consistently showed the courage to be a minority of one. Like his contemporaries Eugene V. Debs and Bertrand Russell, he deliberately burned some of his bridges and refused to whore for Hollywood, but it is senseless to ask how he would behave if he were alive today. The politically correct, Hollywood-imitating elite of black public intellectuals, left and right, have thoroughly "caught the thought and speech of triumphant commercialism." He would not, and should not, have disparaged the goals of many black intellectuals to acquire precious and beautiful things, but one hopes that the picture of a solitary scholar sacrificing eyesight to the microfilm reader would not have seemed to him "the acme of absurdities."

---

[30] *Autobiography*, pp. 25–26.

Du Bois was thirty-five years old when he published *The Souls of Black Folk*. He would be a different person had he been born a hundred years later, a member of the so-called "generation X."[31] There would not have been any pressure for him to attend Fisk University if he had been born in 1968; more likely he would have gone directly to Harvard. A year in Berlin might have interested him, but a German doctorate has become virtually worthless, and he would have felt it no loss to take his doctorate at Harvard on schedule in 1996. Would he have asked members of the black studies department to serve on his dissertation committee? The question is mind numbing. It is impossible to conceive of anything approximating the Du Bois phenomenon in the present era.

[31] *U.S. News and World Report*, August 8, 2001, defined "generation X" as persons born 1965–1980.

MARCUS MOZIAH GARVEY:
THE REALIST AS ROMANTIC

13

The Birth of Tragedy

Garvey's Heroic Struggles

> Cast the Bantling on the rocks,
> Suckle him with the she-wolf's teat,
> Wintered with the hawk and fox
> Power and speed be hands and feet.
>
> Emerson

Literary historians recognize a linkage in classical tradition between the epic, the tragic, and the heroic – terms that arise naturally in a discussion of Marcus Garvey. The heroic genre centers always on a struggle that may be resolved either in Achilles's epic triumph or in Hector's tragic defeat. The story of Garvey necessitates the tragic mode; it contains only the possibility of defeat. Tragedy relates the history of a noble, but flawed individual, a hero who is superior to the average person and confronted by irresistible forces. As in the above epigraph taken from Emerson's essay "Experience," tragedy combines archetypal elements; in more than one classic narrative, a bantling is exposed among the rocks, struggles against a world of lupine ferocity, then, proving himself by means of a series of invigorating struggles and a vulpine cunning, soars triumphantly to the pinnacle of fame, only to be humiliated and destroyed as Garvey was.[1]

Heroism is in no way diminished when the hero's struggles lead to the inevitable agony of defeat. Tragedy implies a deterministic universe, as in a Greek drama where the audience knows from the outset that an action is moving toward its only possible conclusion. In *Paradise Lost*,

---

[1] The hero, as they say, has a thousand faces. My reference is to the archetype manifested in the Oedipus myth and various structural analogues, in the stories of Moses, Paris of Troy, Romulus, Remus, King Arthur, and Kipling's Mowgli.

Milton's Satan dares "defy the omnipotent to Arms," an action which, according to the logic of the language, is illogically futile, but Milton borders on heresy by stubbornly placing Satan in a heroic mode, thus making his actions seem heroic. This, we are told, was not his intention, but Milton's paradox is that Satan, in his defiance of an unavoidable fate, becomes heroic according to the formal definition. The critical result is William Blake's famous remark that Milton was "of the Devil's party without knowing it." Milton's heroic failure was to leave his masterwork open to an interpretation that he would have considered blasphemous. But Milton's fate was inescapable once he chose to employ the heroic mode. So effectively did he force biblical material into the conventions of epic form that his fall into the heresy of creating an heroic Satan was inevitable.

When interpreting Marcus Garvey, one may be of the devil's party, though unaware and against one's own contradictory ideological and moral code. Garvey struggled to become a world-historical figure, and in a sense, he succeeded, but he collapsed inevitably, not because of any failure of heart, but because of his heroically irrational refusal to face an unacceptable reality. He wanted to compete with the French, British, Portuguese, and Belgian empires in Africa while simultaneously challenging American capitalism. He was a defiant megalomaniac who, in an age of empire building, sought to build a black empire to acknowledge no master but God. He refused to listen to what was obviously "common-sense," because, as he said:

Oh how disgusting life becomes when on every hand you hear people (who bear your image, who bear your resemblance) telling you that you cannot make it, that Fate is against them, that they cannot get a chance. If 400,000,000 Negroes can only get to know themselves, to know that in them is a sovereign power, is an authority that is absolute, then in the next twenty-four hours, ... we would have a new race, a nation, an empire, – resurrected, not from the will of others to see us rise, – but from our own determination to rise, irrespective of what the world thinks.[2]

IMAGES OF THE STRONG JAMAICAN MALE, 1887–1912

On his birth certificate, he was registered as Malcus Mosiah Garvey at St. Ann's Bay, Jamaica, on August 17, 1887, and he was baptized three years later as Malchus Moziah Garvey in the Methodist Church at

---

[2] Amy Jacques Garvey, ed., *Philosophy and Opinions of Marcus Garvey*, Vol. 1 (New York: Amy Jacques Garvey, 1925), p. 39.

St. Ann's Bay. Stories concerning his father, Malchus Garvey, Sr., are intriguingly contradictory. Some relate that he was a master mason and a bricklayer, but one report describes him simply as a crude "breaker of stones on the roadway." He was said to be a stern, serious, solitary man who secreted himself in his private library, which was located in a building several feet removed from the rest of his home. Reportedly, he went to work only when he could tear himself away from his books and newspapers, or when pressed by necessity. Malchus Garvey, Sr., is said to have depleted a great part of whatever assets he may have possessed in a series of lawsuits, occasioned by a dispute with a neighbor over a property line. Little is known of Malchus Garvey's wife, Sarah Jane Richards, except that she was a religious, mild-mannered woman, who, according to the recollections of one informant, contributed substantially to the financial support of the family by marketing her excellent pastries. Church records reveal that the Garveys were married on December 15, 1889, two years after the birth of their son, whom the world would come to know as Marcus Moziah Garvey.[3]

Garvey emphasized that his parents were "black Negroes," thereby stressing his genetic identity with the masses of the most oppressed classes of Jamaican society. Simplifications concerning class structure in nineteenth-century Jamaica are risky, because the social structure of any society is always complex, discontinuous, and relative to the observer. In general, whites occupied the highest status in colonial Jamaica, and dark persons of African descent occupied the lowest. At the risk of oversimplification, we may say that Africans who were of lighter complexion, calling themselves "mulatto," "brown," or "people of color," usually found it easier to achieve social status than did persons who were "black" or "Negro." Nonetheless, there was frequent intermarriage between black and lighter-skinned Jamaicans and many dark Jamaicans were able to achieve relatively high social and economic status within the black and brown world. Garvey exploited color conflicts that existed among black people in the United States and referred frequently to the "caste of color" in colonial Jamaica, but this was pure rhetorical opportunism. Scholars today reject the once-prevalent canard that Garvey imported into the American context color antagonisms that were alien to American society. Personally, he did not hate brown people; in fact, his second marriage

---

[3] Biographical details are in church records published in Robert A. Hill et al., eds., *The Marcus Garvey and Universal Negro Improvement Association Papers, Volumes 1–6* (Berkeley: The University of California Press, 1983–89), Vol. 1, pp. 124–34.

was to a brown woman, but he always spoke of himself as "black," "African," or "Negro," and vehemently rejected the terms "colored" and "people of color."[4]

Although his family was poor and his father often unemployed, Garvey memorialized his parents in terms of conventional English, middle-class, domestic ideals of manhood and womanhood. In a short autobiographical essay, "The Negro's Greatest Enemy," he portrayed his mother with stereotypical feminine virtues, as the epitome of long-suffering gentleness, "always willing to return a smile for a blow, and ever ready to bestow charity upon her enemy." He endowed his father with masculine characteristics, seeing him as "severe, firm, determined, bold, and strong." The senior Garvey was portrayed as a man "unafraid of consequences," who "took human chances in the course of life, as most bold men do." According to Garvey, he once possessed "a fortune," including the controversial parcels of real estate, but "died poor." He attributed to his father a principle that he expected every black person, but especially black men, to emulate – a "refusal to yield even to superior forces if he believed he was right."[5]

Garvey received eight years of formal education at the Church of England school in St. Ann's Bay. His playmates of both sexes were white and black, and he later claimed that, until the age of fourteen, he remained remarkably unaware of the social convention prohibiting contact between white women and black men. He described an Edenic relationship with the little white girl who lived next door, saying, "We were two innocent fools, who never dreamed of a race feeling and problem." Suddenly, she was forbidden to play with him and was packed off to school in England. Garvey tells of his increasing racial awareness when, at the age of eighteen, his white male playmates also rejected him. He realized then that he would "have to make a fight for a place in the world . . . however, I had

---

[4] On color distinctions among American blacks and Garvey's exploitation of them, see Benjamin Quarles, *The Negro in the Making of America* (New York: Collier, 1969), p. 196. Alexander Crummell expressed antimulatto sentiments to John E. Bruce. See Wilson J. Moses, ed., *Destiny and Race: Selected Writings of Alexander Crummell* (Boston: University of Massachusetts Press, 1992), pp. 85–89. William H. Ferris defends Marcus Garvey on the mulatto question in a letter to Francis J. Grimké. See Carter G. Woodson, ed., *Works of Francis J. Grimké*, Vol. 4 (Washington, DC: Associated Publishers, 1942) p. 297. A recent treatment of color and black Americans is Kathy Russell, Midge Wilson, and Ronald Hall, *Color Complex: The Politics of Skin Color Among African Americans* (Garden City, NY: Anchor Books, 1992).

[5] Garvey, "The Negro's Greatest Enemy," p. 124. Garvey says more of his father on pp. 310–11.

not much difficulty in finding and holding a place for myself, for I was aggressive."[6]

In his early teens, Garvey was apprenticed to another serious West Indian man, Alfred Ernest Burrowes, "printer, book binder, and stationer" at St. Ann's Bay, who eventually assigned him the management of a branch office in Port Maria, Jamaica. A product of the emerging "information age," Garvey took advantage of the printed matter that was accessible in Burrowes's office, and constantly eavesdropped on the conversations of the older men who hung around discussing their opinions of the wide world beyond St. Ann's Bay. His early obsession with journalism and publicity led to his later demonstrated genius at staging media events – his brilliance at using every opportunity for gaining publicity. Historians know little about Burrowes other than what Garvey reports of him. He claimed Burrows as his godfather and said he "taught me many things" before Garvey was twelve, making a strong impression on the boy whose father was so stern, distant, and ultimately disappointing. Burrowes belonged to a small class of literate Jamaicans of humble means. What sorts of things he printed is not known. It is reported that Burrowes "had many books, and the 'wise heads' of the town would drop in, especially on market days, to swap news and discuss happenings." Garvey portrayed Burrowes as a moral and intellectual leader and claimed the legacy of this "highly educated and alert man," who "in the affairs of business and the world...had no peer." In constructing memories around the fancied images of his father, "a man of brilliant intellect and dashing courage," and his godfather, the "apprentice master" who infused him, by the age of fourteen, with "intelligence and experience to manage men," Garvey displays a singular quality among the figures studied in this volume. Indeed, he is almost unique among black authors of his period in paying tribute to senior black males as embodiments of "strong and forceful character," or models of how to be "manly."[7]

Garvey's biographers have made the reasonable assumption that Burrowes awakened Garvey's interest in journalism and that his work for Burrowes not only taught him the technical aspects of the printer's trade, but introduced him to the techniques of putting ideas into words. This is

[6] Garvey, "The Negro's Greatest Enemy," in *Philosophy and Opinions*, Vol. 2, p. 125. Cf. W. E. B. Du Bois's autobiographical description of a similar incident in *The Souls of Black Folk* (Chicago: McClurg, 1903), p. 2.

[7] *Marcus Garvey Papers*, Vol. 1, pp. 35–38. Amy Jacques Garvey says Burrowes was his godfather in *Garvey and Garveyism*, p. 4.

evident from the fact that when Garvey moved to the Jamaican capital of Kingston he was already an able compositor and an accomplished writer. Burrowes later reported that Garvey, while working for him, had become qualified for a career "in the field of journalism." In his later teens Garvey came under the influence of the black publisher Dr. J. Robert Love, who as publisher of the militantly nationalistic *Jamaica Advocate* encouraged his interest in journalism. The training under Burrowes and the influence of Love served him well in later years when he established his enormously successful newspaper, *Negro World*, which was the main outlet for his ideas and, perhaps, the best-edited black newspaper of its day.

The details of Garvey's young adult life are fragmentary. We know that he was politically active, intellectually adventurous, and eager to see the world. He tells us he participated in the labor movement in Kingston, Jamaica, between 1906 and 1910, when he left Jamaica for Central America. In "The Negro's Greatest Enemy," he made cryptic remarks about getting "mixed up in public life," but there is scant record of his public affairs during this period, and historians have discovered few references to Garvey's activities. He became active in the National Club of Jamaica, an organization dedicated to agitation for Jamaican self-government, and began to develop a reputation as a public speaker. His intellectual vigor and curiosity led him to travels in the West Indies and in South and Central America, where he discovered that conditions were no different than in Jamaica. Wherever he went, white people ruled and black people were subordinate. After unsuccessful attempts to start newspapers in Costa Rica and Panama, he returned to Jamaica and was employed for several months in the Government Printing Office.[8]

Around 1910, Garvey became friends with W. A. Domingo, a young political activist. Domingo later claimed that he introduced Garvey to Edward W. Blyden's *Christianity, Islam, and the Negro Race*, which was published in 1887 but was still an influential work on Pan-Africanism.[9] Blyden advocated the goal of political independence for Africa, although he counseled gradual change rather than armed revolution. Blyden, like Garvey, was a West Indian by birth, but left his St. Thomas birthplace in

---

[8] *The Marcus Garvey Papers*, Vol. 1, pp. 20–23.
[9] For Wilfred Adolphus (W. A.) Domingo's influences on Garvey, see *Garvey Papers*, Vol. 1, pp. 527–30. On Blyden see Hollis R. Lynch, *Edward Wilmot Blyden: Pan-Negro Patriot, 1832–1912* (London: Oxford University Press, 1964), and Thomas W. Livingston, *Education and Race: A Biography of Edward Wilmot Blyden* (San Francisco: Glendessary Press, 1975). Blyden wrote prolifically. His best-known work was *Christianity, Islam, and the Negro Race* (London, 1887).

1850 at the age of eighteen. After a brief sojourn in the United States, he migrated to Liberia, where he interacted closely, for a time, with Alexander Crummell, and shared with him a hostility to the mulatto elite who dominated Liberian politics. Garvey, like Blyden, insisted at all times on being called "black," "African," or "Negro," rather than colored, which to dark West Indians of the time was a matter of principle.[10] Like Blyden, he asserted that black people had been the creators of civilization and that the Egyptians, the first civilized people, "had black-skins and frizzled hair." Blyden spent the greater part of his adult life in Liberia, with occasional speaking tours of the United States. His writings encouraged worldwide unity among all African peoples, whether in Europe, Africa, or the New World, toward the goal of racial advancement.[11] As a speaker, Blyden was something of a living legend among the masses of black Southerners.[12] Historians believe that Garvey's conception of black nationalism was strongly influenced by his exposure to Blyden's "Afrocentric" ideology.

THE LONDON YEARS, 1912–1914

As were many intelligent and ambitious young people from the far reaches of the British Empire, Garvey was drawn to London by a desire to see the capital of the English-speaking world. He spent a little over two years in the metropolis from April 1912 to June 17, 1914. During that time, he matriculated informally in Birkbeck College, an institution for working people that was later incorporated into the University of London. He became acquainted with Duse Mohamed Ali, an Egyptian-Sudanese nationalist, Pan-Africanist, and publisher of a newspaper called *The African Times and Orient Review* (*ATOR*), which supported African and Asian movements for independence from colonial rule.[13] The complete range of Garvey's contributions to *ATOR* is unclear, but his reading habits, editing

---

[10] *Philosophy and Opinions*, Vol. 2, pp. 127, 128.

[11] See Blyden, *Christianity, Islam, and the Negro Race*, p. 154. Also see Blyden's *From West Africa to Palestine* (Freetown, Sierra Leone: T. J. Sawyerr, 1873), reprinted in Hollis Lynch, ed., *Black Spokesman* (New York: Humanities Press, 1971), pp. 152–53.

[12] Edwin S. Redkey, *Black Exodus: Black Nationalist and Back to Africa Movements, 1890–1910* (New Haven, CT: Yale University Press, 1969), pp. 47–58.

[13] *The Marcus Garvey Papers*, Vol. 1, pp. 519–21, identify him as Duse Mohamed Ali, but also comments on the various forms of his name. He is identified as Mohamed Ali, Duse, in the index to J. Ayodele Langley, *Pan-Africanism and Nationalism in West Africa, 1900–1940: A Study in Ideology and Social Classes* (Oxford: Clarendon Press, 1973). His name is given as Duse Mohamed on the facsimile title page of his partially plagiarized book, *In the Land of the Pharaohs: A Short History of Egypt* (London: Frank Cass, 1968).

experience, and assertive intellect impressed the cosmopolitan editor Ali, who in the 1920s became a contributing editor to Garvey's newspaper, *Negro World*.[14]

In October 1913, Ali published Garvey's essay, "The British West Indies in the Mirror of Civilization." The article revealed the author's liveliness of style, his ability to manipulate facts and figures, and his tendency to see the world in terms of race. It also revealed Garvey's black chauvinist sentiments as he revealed his uneasiness with "the hybrid or colored element," and his impatience with the "parochial feelings" that had prevented the federation and independence of Great Britain's West Indian possessions. Nonetheless, he prophesied that there would "soon be a turning point in the history of the West Indies," and that their inhabitants would some day "found an Empire on which the sun shall shine as ceaselessly as it shines on the Empire of the North to-day."[15]

Some of Garvey's later American contacts were anticipated in this early association with Duse Mohamed Ali, who, because of his wide-ranging international interests, was able to enhance Garvey's knowledge of conditions among black people in the United States. For example, in the winter of 1913, *ATOR* featured an article on the American Negro Academy, a black power cultural organization founded by Alexander Crummell some years earlier. Possibly, Garvey was already aware of the Academy because of his admiration for J. Robert Love, editor of the Jamaica *Advocate* and an associate of Crummell, who had printed a glowing report on the Academy at the time of its founding. Ali was one of several non-Americans who were elected corresponding members of the Academy. Edward Wilmot Blyden was another. Ali encouraged Garvey's interest in Blyden and wrote a letter in support of Garvey's application for a reader's ticket to the British Museum, where he went to study the works of Blyden.

---

[14] Marcus Garvey, *The Philosophy and Opinions of Marcus Garvey*, Vol. 2, Amy Jacques Garvey, ed., with a new introduction by Robert A. Hill (New York: Atheneum, 1992), p. 72. The editors of *The Marcus Garvey Papers* say that Duse Mohamed Ali employed Garvey as "a messenger and handyman." Their source is presumably his obituary in *The Comet* 8:16 (August 17, 1940). Duse Mohamed Ali later played down his relationship to Garvey, describing him as "a messenger in his office, [whose] conduct was unsatisfactory...discharged after about three months." See Robert A. Hill, "The First England Years and After," in John Henrik Clarke, ed., *Marcus Garvey and the Vision of Africa* (New York: Vintage, 1974), p. 39.

[15] Marcus Garvey, "The British West Indies in the Mirror of Civilization," in *The Marcus Garvey Papers*, Vol. 1, p. 31. Garvey was obviously alluding to the well-known slogan "The sun never sets on the British Empire." See *Bartlett's Quotations* for some of its various forms.

Two members of the Academy who later became Garveyites were the Crummell protégés, William H. Ferris and John E. Bruce.[16]

QUESTIONING THE BOOKER T. EPIPHANY

As did every other person with leadership ambitions in the black world, Garvey knew of the criticisms launched against the "Wizard of Tuskegee." Thus, he later maintained that while his ideal included the program of Booker T. Washington, it went "much farther." The problems of the era "must be solved not by the industrial leader only, but by the political and military leaders as well."[17] Nonetheless, Garvey frequently invoked the name of Washington and, in "The Negro's Greatest Enemy," even gave the impression that reading Washington's autobiography was the turning point in his life.

I read *Up from Slavery* by Booker T. Washington, and then my doom – if I may so call it – of being a race leader dawned upon me in London after I had traveled through almost half of Europe.

I asked, 'Where is the black man's Government?' 'Where is his King and his kingdom?' 'Where is his President, his country, and his ambassador, his army, his navy, his men of big affairs?' I could not find them, and then I declared, 'I will help to make them.'[18]

Garvey's references to *Up From Slavery* are invoked today by African Americans who correctly recognize that the Universal Negro Improvement Association (UNIA) program was consistent with the self-help philosophy of African American conservative groups.[19] Connections between Washington's policies and Garvey's program should not be overstated, however. Historians cannot judge with precision exactly when Garvey first read Washington or what aspects of Washington's philosophy would have inspired him to become a Pan-Africanist. Garvey wrote the passage

[16] Alfred A. Moss, Jr., *The American Negro Academy: Voice of the Talented Tenth* (Baton Rouge: Louisiana State University Press, 1981), pp. 47, 129; John W. Cromwell, "American Negro Academy," *African Times and Orient Review* 2 (November–December, 1913), 243–44. In 1921, Bruce proposed that Garvey be invited to address the twenty-fifth annual meeting of the ANA, but the Executive Committee issued no invitation. See Moss, *American Negro Academy*, pp. 276–77.

[17] *Philosophy and Opinions*, Vol. 1, p. 56.

[18] Garvey, "The Negro's Greatest Enemy," Vol. 2, p. 126.

[19] Harold Cruse follows after E. Franklin Frazier in recognizing the Washington-Garvey connection in *The Crisis of the Negro Intellectual* (New York: Morrow, 1967). Raymond L. Hall also notes this connection in *Black Separatism in the United States* (Hanover, NH: Dartmouth College and the University Press of New England, 1978), p. 242.

while he was in prison in 1923, and published it in *Current History*, a magazine read mostly by whites. By invoking the name of Washington, he may have intended to associate himself in the minds of white readers with a leader who was perceived by whites as trustworthy, responsible, and conservative. Nonetheless, Garvey's references to Washington, spoken and written, were so frequent and consistent that one may rightly assume that his admiration for the organizational abilities and the self-help philosophy of Washington was abiding and sincere.[20]

RETURN TO JAMAICA AND ORGANIZATION OF THE UNIA, 1914–1916

In July 1914, after returning to Jamaica, Garvey held the first official meetings of the Universal Negro Improvement Association and African Communities League.[21] The overlapping organizations are collectively referred to simply as the UNIA and the purpose of the dual title was apparently to emphasize dual and complementary functions. He intended to universally uplift all people of the African Diaspora, politically, economically, and culturally. He also would guarantee their universal respect by establishing modern nationalism, economic enterprise, and military might on the African continent. Neither the movement nor its institutional expression was ever able to function independently of Garvey's powerful personality. During the first two years of its existence, the UNIA established the characteristic pattern of its most successful activity – organizing large public meetings where inspirational speakers attracted enthusiastic crowds.

In the words of Amy Jacques Garvey, his second wife, Garvey was "unable to get the masses to unite and cooperate for their own good." During "many months of hardship and disappointment" in Jamaica, Garvey reflected on stories he had heard of the superior economic opportunities enjoyed by black people in the United States. He brooded particularly on the success of Booker T. Washington in winning the support of white philanthropists for his Normal and Industrial Institute at Tuskegee, Alabama. He began to correspond with Washington and planned a visit to the United States. At this point in his career, Garvey apparently did not envision a

---

[20] Reference to several volumes of *The Marcus Garvey Papers* will reveal the continuing importance of Booker T. Washington throughout Garvey's career.

[21] Amy Jacques says in *Garvey and Garveyism*, p. 8., that Garvey established the UNIA before going to England. *The Garvey Papers* chronology dates the first UNIA meeting as July 20, 1914. An early UNIA manifesto and application for membership gives a founding date of August 1, 1914. See *Marcus Garvey Papers*, Vol. 1, p. 117.

prolonged stay in the United States and aspired only to found a trade school in Jamaica, similar to Tuskegee. In a series of letters to Washington, Garvey described a planned lecture tour of the United States and requested Washington's assistance. Washington's responses to Garvey's overtures were hospitable but noncommittal.

Garvey expressed to Washington his hostile feelings toward persons of mixed racial background. "The prejudice in these [Caribbean] countries is far different from that of America," he wrote. "Here we have to face the prejudice of the hypocritical white men who nevertheless are our friends as also to fight down the prejudice of our race in shade colour."[22] Garvey's distrust of lighter-skinned people cannot, however, be explained away by the hackneyed reference to his Jamaican background. Antimulatto attitudes were a home-grown African American tradition as evidenced in the correspondence between Alexander Crummell and John E. Bruce, later an editor for Garvey's *Negro World*.[23] Furthermore, many Jamaican immigrants of Garvey's generation seem to have come to the United States without manifesting any antimulatto prejudice. Garvey apparently overlooked the fact that Booker T. Washington was a mulatto in appearance, and would have been identified as such in many parts of the Caribbean.

It seems unlikely that the theatrical Garvey could have achieved a working relationship with the circumspect Tuskegeean, and in any case, they never met. Washington would not have openly endorsed Garvey's confrontational approach – the military uniforms. Or would he? Students did, after all, wear military uniforms at Tuskegee, but certainly this was intended only to symbolize their submission to the discipline and their readiness to march in step with America's industrial needs.

Washington passed away on November 14, 1915, several months before Garvey left for the United States. In the meantime, Garvey had sent a letter to W. E. B. Du Bois, who had spent a two-week vacation in Jamaica without encountering him. He also exchanged letters with Robert Russa Moton, Washington's successor at Tuskegee, and Emmet Scott, who had been Washington's private secretary. Garvey never achieved any meaningful working relationship with Moton but he maintained cordial relations with Scott. As later events indicated, Garvey was willing to work with

---

[22] *Marcus Garvey Papers*, Vol. 1, p. 67.
[23] Alexander Crummell to John E. Bruce, in Wilson J. Moses, ed., *Destiny and Race: Selected Writings of Alexnder Crummell* (Boston: University of Massachusetts Press, 1992), pp. 85–89. William H. Ferris defends Marcus Garvey on the mulatto question in a letter to Francis J. Grimké. See Carter G. Woodson, ed., *Works of Francis J. Grimké*, Vol. 4 (Washington, DC: Associated Publishers), p. 297.

any credible black American leader, so long as he could be the dominant party.[24]

There was conflict between Du Bois and Garvey, not surprisingly, for both had high ambitions to be the foremost ambassador of Pan-Africanism to the Negroes of the world. Du Bois was happy enough to see Garvey depart the United States after his conviction of using the mails to defraud. Although there were serious disagreements between Du Bois and Garvey on matters of real substance, there was much overlap between their ideological pronouncements. Both were devout Afrocentrists who claimed a glorious past for the African peoples. In Du Bois's words, Egyptian civilization was African civilization "flourishing on the Nile but never separated from the great lakes of inner Africa." For Garvey Egyptians were black people, separated from the rest of Africa by an essentially racist and Eurocentric anthropology.

EARLY ACTIVITIES IN THE UNITED STATES, 1916–1919

When Garvey arrived in New York on March 24, 1916, he discovered a city that was only beginning to attain its reputation as a "black metropolis." Black New Yorkers were not typical of the African American population of the United States, which was largely rural, Southern, and engaged in agricultural pursuits. Many black farmers were engaged in cotton production under a system known as sharecropping. Farmers were advanced loans in order to finance planting of their crops and were required to share the crop with the persons who had advanced the capital. The usual result of this system was that the farmers fell deeper into debt with the passing of every year. White supremacy, enforced by violence, was the culture of the South, and black Americans lived in constant fear of lynching. During 1915, economic factors provoked a migration to the northern cities. Farm labor wages fell to seventy-five cents per day and an insect known as the boll weevil ravaged the cotton crop. In 1916, severe flooding in Mississippi devastated the prospects of many poor farmers.

The beginning of World War I brought many changes to the black American population. Disruption of European society led to a decline in European migration and cut off the supply of European immigrant labor. In the search for industrial workers, northern industry began to

---

[24] Garvey to R. R. Moton, February 20, 1916; Emmet Scott to Marcus Garvey, March 2, 1916; Marcus Garvey to Emmet Scott, June 9, 1916; Marcus Garvey to R. R. Moton, June 1, 1917; R. R. Moton to Marcus Garvey, June 6, 1917. All letters in *Marcus Garvey Papers*, Vol. 1.

recruit black labor from the South. During 1916 the number of African Americans migrating out of the South amounted to 350,000, according to Department of Labor estimates. In 1917, the Chicago *Defender*, a newspaper operated by Robert S. Abbott (later a Garvey detractor) began to encourage African Americans to migrate northward. The resettlement of black Americans in metropolitan areas obviously affected the nature of black American culture.

In the cities, Garvey discovered a diverse population including West Indian immigrants, transplanted peasants from the South, a small class of skilled workers, a few small capitalists, and a clergy with political ambitions. At first he seemed clumsy and ill at ease speaking before American audiences, but within a year he was on the way to creating the most ambitious mass movement among African Americans prior to the Civil Rights Movement of the 1950s. The urban communities had already demonstrated that they could support a labor movement, a network of women's clubs, a newspaper industry, and a wide variety of fraternal institutions. Garvey's ability to exploit the crowd emotions present in African American communities gave him enduring popularity and lasting influence superior to anything he had known in Jamaica.

After coming to the United States, Garvey, who had been struggling in obscurity, was catapulted within the space of a single year into the leadership of an impressive organization. The dynamic young Jamaican instinctively grasped and exploited the powerful emotional impetus toward racial solidarity and ethnic nationalism among black Americans. He understood the anger and resentment that black Americans felt toward white people, and he understood that many of the African American masses were cynical about the prospects of racial integration. They knew that integrationist leaders like W. E. B. Du Bois were not fully accepted as equals by the white liberal community. Garvey exploited the anger and cynicism of the black masses, who saw him as offering a realistic assessment of white American racism. Garvey did not believe that America had a multicultural future. This placed him in conflict with the civil rights leadership and the NAACP, whose goal was to attain the political rights of African American citizens and who attempted to encourage optimism with respect to a multicultural future.

Garvey recognized that African Americans had maintained a black nationalist tradition in the United States. He knew that many of the intellectuals viewed themselves within the old American Negro Academy tradition of a "nation within a nation." Masses and intellectuals alike felt an emotional sympathy with West Indians and Africans that they did not feel with white Americans. Many black Americans maintained an unforgiving attitude toward white people and denied any desire to blend into the American population at large. The black nationalist tradition to which Garvey was drawn had always been more concerned with internal organization and the struggle to maintain cultural institutions. While resentful of white violence and oppression, they did not oppose racial separatism as such. Garvey tapped the reservoirs of Pan-African and black national consciousness that he discovered among stable working people, aspiring entrepreneurs, religious leaders, and educated "race men," many of them a generation older than himself.[25]

The extreme racial orientation of Garvey's program was hardly surprising within the American environment of the war years. In a more open society Garvey might possibly have utilized his skills as a publicist along some less racially oriented line of activity, but during the decade he spent in the United States (1916–27) race was the dominating and inescapable factor in determining the African American role in society. Black people had few rights that white people felt bound to respect. Garvey appealed to African Americans in terms of the concrete reality of American racism rather than the abstract reality of American citizenship. He defined the "Aims and Objects of the Movement for the Solution of the Negro Problem" in the preamble to the constitution of the UNIA.

To establish a Universal Confraternity among the race; to promote the spirit of pride and love; to reclaim the fallen; to administer to and assist the needy; to assist in civilizing the backward tribes of Africa; to assist in the development of Independent Negro Nations and Communities; to establish a central nation for the race; to establish Commissaries or Agencies in the principal countries and cities of the world for the representation of all Negroes; to promote a conscientious Spiritual worship among the native tribes of Africa; to establish Universities, Colleges, Academies and Schools for the racial education and culture of the people; to work for better conditions among Negroes everywhere.[26]

Garvey's shifting strategies toward achieving his goals sometimes led him into apparent contradictions. Although he was a great advocate of capitalism, Garvey seemed, in 1916–17, to have an affinity to black socialists. Socialists preached that economics, not race, was the source of

---

[25] The historian E. U. Essien-Udom has described "race men" as persons "who were above all concerned with reconstructing the economic, moral, and cultural life of their people." E. U. Essien-Udom, *Black Nationalism: A Search for an Identity in America* (Chicago: University of Chicago Press, 1962), p. 2. Also see Khalil Mahmud, "Introduction" to Duse Mohamed, *In the Land of the Pharaohs*, p. xxxii.

[26] Garvey, "Aims and Objects of the Movement for the Solution of Negro Problem," Vol. 2, p. 38.

African American difficulties and were hostile to black nationalism. They argued that African Americans could achieve justice only by working with like-minded whites for the abolition of private property and for the establishment of state control over all aspects of the economy. Many of Garvey's followers were extreme black nationalists, who thought of cooperation with whites as silly and futile. Other associates, like W. A. Domingo, endorsed the universal moralism and the humanitarian appeal of socialism, and eventually abandoned Garveyism. In due course, many erstwhile friends denounced Garvey as an opportunist whose separatism was an irresponsible accommodation to white racism and segregation.

In 1916, however, Garvey seemed to be in league, not only with Domingo, but with such black socialists as Asa Philip Randolph and Chandler Owen.[27] For a brief period, the UNIA and the socialists seemed to have complementary goals, simply because both groups were black and militant, but the alliance was short lived. Garvey always remained committed to the idea of black business and he seems never to have seriously entertained socialist ideas. In 1916, Randolph provided Garvey with an opportunity to address a Harlem crowd, sharing his soapbox at the corner of Lennox Avenue and 125th Street. Garvey opportunistically exploited the occasion to push his own personality and gain publicity for himself.[28] In 1917, Randolph and Chandler Owen founded *The Messenger* and soon turned their magazine against Garvey, realizing that he was not only opposed to socialism, but willing to cooperate with white segregationists.

After his initial appearances before New York crowds, Garvey embarked on a year-long speaking tour that took him throughout the United States. No one knows at what point Garvey decided to remain in the United States, but by May 1917, he had decided that there were many interesting things to do in America, and he postponed, indefinitely, his original goal of returning to Jamaica to found a trade school. He returned to New York, based his movement in that city, and founded the main United States chapter of the UNIA. The following month he registered with the Selective Service as a resident alien, giving his profession as "journalist." Thus situated, Garvey began to demonstrate his ability to generate large audiences and sizable contributions on the basis of his messianic appeal. Few of his speeches from this period are extant, but his address on July 8, 1917, delivered in the wake of a race riot in East

---

[27] Jervis Anderson, *A. Philip Randolph: A Biographical Portrait* (New York: Harcourt Brace Jovanovich, 1973).
[28] Tony Martin, *Race First*, p. 316.

St. Louis, Illinois, reveals his appeal to the seething resentments of African Americans.

> The East St. Louis Riot or rather massacre of Monday 2nd, will go down in history as one of the bloodiest outrages against mankind for which any class of people could be held guilty. (hear! hear.) This is no time for fine words, but a time to lift one's voice against the savagery of a people who claim to be the dispensers of democracy. (cheers) I do not know what special meaning the people who slaughtered the Negroes of East St. Louis have for democracy of which they are the custodians, but I do know that it has no literal meaning for me as used and applied by these same lawless people (hear! hear!). America, that has been ringing the bells of the world proclaiming to the nations and the peoples thereof that she has democracy to give to all and sundry, America that has denounced Germany for the deportations of the Belgians into Germany, America that has arraigned Turkey at the bar of public opinion and public justice against the massacres of the Armenians, has herself no satisfaction to give to 12,000,000 of her own citizens except the satisfaction of a farcical inquiry that will end where it begun, over the brutal murder of men women and children for no other reason than that they are black people seeking an industrial chance in a country that they have laboured for three hundred years to make great. (cheers)[29]

Garvey filed a certificate of incorporation for the UNIA under the laws of the state of New York on July 2, 1918, stating the organization's purposes simply as the promotion and practice "of Benevolence . . . protection . . . and social intercourse of its members, . . . and their mental and physical culture and developments, and to extend a friendly and constructive hand to the Negroes of the United States." The African Communities League, incorporated on July 31, had a far more ambitious list of goals, including the establishment of commercial and manufacturing enterprises, the promotion of international trade, the purchase and management of real estate, and the disposition of patents and trademarks.

The UNIA was a diffuse and complicated organization, which, although it was always tied to Garvey's personality, did achieve a semblance of free-standing institutional life for the first ten years of its existence. Such a statement may seem paradoxical since the organization fell into decline as soon as Garvey's influence in the United States came to an end. Nonetheless, it must be recognized that in its heyday, the UNIA represented a successful black agency of protest and propaganda. In this regard, the UNIA's functions were not dissimilar to those of the NAACP.

---

[29] *Conspiracy of the East St. Louis Race Riots Speech by Marcus Garvey Delivered at Lafayette Hall, New York, Sunday, July 8th, 1917* (Washington, DC: Moorland-Spingarn Research Library, Howard University). Reprinted in *Marcus Garvey Papers*, Vol. 1, pp. 212–20.

It protested against racial injustice and was committed to promoting the rights of African Americans.

There was at least one important difference, however. The NAACP, at its inception, was an organization of whites, and only gradually did a few black persons come to play roles of increasing importance. The UNIA was founded by black people and from the first was under the control of black people. The UNIA was unable to maintain its protest functions after 1922, when Garvey began to repudiate his radicalism and to seek alliances with white reactionaries such as the Ku Klux Klan and the Anglo-Saxon Clubs of America. In its early days, however, as some historians have observed, the UNIA was more closely associated with racial protest.[30]

As a spur to business enterprise, however, the lasting accomplishments of the UNIA are more difficult to identify. The UNIA was fantastically successful in raising large amounts of capital, but squandered capital even more fantastically. During a period when such American corporate institutions as General Motors and Du Pont Chemical were developing increasingly sophisticated managerial techniques, the UNIA was tragically inept. Nonetheless, the UNIA achieved some victories. It sponsored a variety of small- and medium-sized businesses, including a steam laundry, a chain of grocery stores, and, of course, the ill-fated Black Star Line, of which more will be said hereafter.

A MOVEMENT AT ITS PEAK

Stern ranks of black men and women marched in military uniform through the streets of New York, Chicago, and other American cities, under a banner of red, black, and green, dramatizing their dedication to the "racial uplift" and the "redemption of Africa." But what did these clichés represent, and why were these uniformed people really marching? Garvey's most extravagant proposition was to transport his legions of racial nationalists back to "the land of our Fathers," but did they all intend to go "back to Africa?" Was it Garvey's intention to take them back? If Garveyism was, as it has been called, "the first and only real mass movement among Negroes in the history of the United States," what exactly did his movement represent? "Africa for the Africans" was the rallying cry and that was not a new slogan; it was a traditional expression of the belief that the redemption of all black people everywhere was dependent on

[30] Cronon, *Black Moses, The Story of Marcus Garvey and the Universal Negro Improvement Association* (Madison: University of Wisconsin Press, 1995), p. 188; Wm. Z. Foster, *The Negro People*, (New York, 1954), 447–49.

the redemption of Africa. His Universal Negro Improvement Association founded a steamship company, the ill-fated Black Star Line, but Garvey denied it was his purpose to have everyone clamber on board. "We do not need all the Negroes in Africa," he said in a speech at Madison Square Garden in 1924. "Some are no good here, and naturally will be no good there." What was needed was a cadre of dedicated "American and West Indian Negroes" who would "build up Africa in the interests of our race." The main purpose of the Black Star Line would be to develop commercial ties with Africa, although even in this rational and legitimate undertaking, it ultimately failed.[31]

Historians have estimated the UNIA peak membership between 30,000 and 80,000, although Garvey, with characteristic extravagance, asserted that the number of his supporters extended into the millions. In the absence of any concrete evidence, it is difficult to believe that all were serious about returning to Africa. There were many who simply stood on the sidelines and cheered in sympathy with the militancy that Garveyism symbolized, but fewer who purchased stock in his business enterprises. Any understanding of the appeal of Garveyism must center on those programs that did not involve mass repatriation, or the assumption that large numbers of Africans were ready to leave the United States.[32]

The undeniable popularity of Garvey's movement stemmed not entirely from its romantic racial chauvinism and Pan-African rhetoric; it grew out of its appeal to commercial values and attitudes of self-help and independence that have always been strong among black Americans. The UNIA represented a yearning for economic self-sufficiency and political self-determination and a larger goal of economic improvement for black people throughout the world. Garveyism elicited an emotional response among African Americans of all classes with words such as the following:

At this time millions of Negroes are idle and unemployed in different parts of this Western Hemisphere. There seems to be absolutely no hope on this side of the Atlantic. The best advice I can give, therefore, is that all who can afford it should give the necessary support to the Black Star Line Steamship Corp. and the

---

[31] Garvey, *Philosophy and Opinions*, Vol. 1, p. 70.
[32] John Hope Franklin offered this remarkable appraisal of Garvey's significance in *From Slavery to Freedom: A History of Negro Americans*, third edition (New York: Vintage, 1967), p. 492. In the seventh edition (New York: McGraw-Hill, 1994), coauthored with Alfred A. Moss, Jr., the modified statement reads, "the first mass movement among African Americans." Garvey's declaration of purpose is in *Philosophy and Opinions*, Vol. 1, p. 70; his statement on "the no-good Negro" in Vol. 2, p. 122. For estimate of UNIA numbers, see Edmund David Cronon, *Black Moses*, pp. 204–7.

Universal Negro Improvement Association, and enable these two organizations to lay plans and carry through the program for the ultimate redemption of our suffering race. Let us concentrate on the building up of West Africa. Let us put our energy, our money, our brains, our all behind the Universal Negro Improvement Association and thus help one great universal movement to succeed in the program of the Negro's economic freedom.[33]

Garveyism publicized the movement called "Pan-Africanism," a term fraught with contradictions. Sometimes it refers purely to a call for unity among black or African peoples, wherever they might reside. At other times it refers to the goal of uniting the entire African continent under one government, to be controlled by Africans. Garvey believed that all African peoples suffered to some degree from the effects of slavery, colonialism, and racial prejudice. His goal of liberating Africa from European colonialism was thus related to the objective of commanding universal respect for all African peoples. Pan-Africanists assumed that once Africa became associated in the common mind with "Armies, navies, and men of big affairs" (his words), Africans would no longer be denied legal rights or be subjected to violence. More important, they would no longer be ridiculed, humiliated, or treated, with pity and contempt. Garvey's goal was to command respect for Africans everywhere by identifying them with a geographical center of military and economic power. In 1920, at an emotional meeting in Madison Square Garden, 25,000 people met to elect him "provisional president of Africa." Many people viewed this as mere posturing, but it symbolized the UNIA goal of liberating the continent and uniting it under one government.[34] In principle, this goal was understood and endorsed by most African Americans, West Indians, continental Africans, and Africans living in Europe.

Garveyism offered an economic expression of "Afrocentrism," which had up to his time been a purely abstract intellectual phenomenon. The term was not used until Du Bois invented it in 1962, but it existed as a cultural movement focused on Africa as the center of black history and cultural identity, and provided a psychological balm for the embattled egos of African peoples.[35] Garveyism offered a view of African history that would bolster the self-confidence of African people everywhere. Garvey celebrated, and more importantly, turned to profit, a monumental African

[33] *Negro World*, February 19, 1921.
[34] Judith Stein, *The World of Marcus Garvey: Race and Class in Modern Society* (Baton Rouge: Louisiana State University Press, 1986), p. 86.
[35] For origins of term "Afrocentrism" and history of concept, see Moses, *Afrotopia*, pp. 1–2.

history, focusing on the histories of Egypt and Ethiopia, and sought to create a sense of a mighty African past.

When the great white race of today had no civilization of its own, when white men lived in caves and were counted as savages, this race of ours boasted of a wonderful civilization on the Banks of the Nile. . . .
    This race of ours gave civilization, gave art, gave science, gave literature to the world. But it has been the way with all races and nations. The one race stands out prominently in the one century or in the one age; and in another century or age it passes off the stage of action, and another race takes its place. The Negro once occupied a high position in the world, scientifically, artistically and commercially, but in the balancing of the great scale of evolution, we lost our place and some one, other than ourselves occupies the stand we once held.

Garveyism also made profitable business out of the black messianic tradition. Since the late eighteenth century, there had been a tradition of messianic black nationalism among African Americans in the North.[36] Essentially, African American messianism asserted that God was on the side of the black race, and that African Americans were a chosen people who had a special destiny.[37] Messianism frequently centers on the idea of a day of deliverance that will usher in a messianic era known as the "millennium," the thousand-year reign of righteousness.[38] Contemporaries often described Garvey as a black messiah who had come to redeem his people, or as Black Moses who was destined to lead African Americans out of the "house of bondage." Garveyism incited an almost religious enthusiasm among its adherents. Roy Ottley, a leading black journalist, recalled in later years the color, the excitement, and the contagious messianic appeal of Garveyism at its peak.

Noisy meetings at Liberty Hall were climaxed by a magnificent parade in which more than fifty thousand Garveyites marched through Harlem. His Excellency, Marcus Garvey, Provisional President of Africa, led the demonstration bedecked in a dazzling uniform of purple, green, and black, with gold braid and a thrilling hat with white plumes, "as long as the leaves of Guinea grass." He rode in a big, high-mounted black Packard automobile and graciously, but with restraint

---

[36] *Webster's Ninth New Collegiate Dictionary* defines "messianic" as "marked by idealism and an aggressive crusading spirit." Discussions of Garvey in connection with black nationalism and messianism are in Wilson Jeremiah Moses, *The Golden Age of Black Nationalism* (New York: Oxford University Press, 1988) and *Black Messiahs and Uncle Toms*, 2nd ed. (University Park, PA: Penn State Press, 1993).

[37] Wilson J. Moses, *Black Messiahs and Uncle Toms*; Gayraud S. Wilmore, *Black Religion and Black Radicalism: An Examination of the Black Experience in Religion* (Garden City, NY: Doubleday, 1973).

[38] Ernest Tuveson, "Millenarianism," in Philip P. Wiener, ed., *Dictionary of the History of Ideas* (New York: Charles Scribners, 1973), pp. 223–25.

becoming a sovereign, acknowledged the ovations of the crowds that lined the sidewalks. Behind him rode his Grace, Archbishop McGuire, in silk robes of state, blessing the populace. Then the Black Nobility and Knight Commanders of the Distinguished Order of the Nile followed, the hierarchy of the state, properly attired in regalia drawn from a gold palette. Arrayed in gorgeous uniforms of black and green, trimmed with much gold braid, came the smartly strutting African Legion; and in white, the stretcher-bearing Black Cross nurses.[39]

Garvey represented something more than the staging of racial fantasies, and it would be an egregious error to attribute his charisma primarily to pageantry and costumes. Many African Americans were attracted to Garvey less for his showmanship than because of his commitment to black economic power. For the black working people who bought five-dollar shares in the Black Star Line, the enterprise represented, not a desire to escape from America, but the basis of a financial and industrial empire, which would command universal respect. According to government estimates, Garvey's Black Star Line had between 30,000 and 40,000 stockholders, and it has never been suggested that any of them were white.[40] Overwhelmingly, the stockholders were people who worked in low-paying or menial occupations, although middle-class blacks were also represented. African Americans chose to invest in the Black Star Line, although they had the option of investing in other sorts of black businesses, such as newspapers, real estate agencies, and insurance companies. Black Star Line investors were seemingly attracted by the opportunity to become involved in an enterprise that represented, not only black capitalism, but an attitude of assertiveness and militancy in defiance of white power.

At the risk of oversimplification, we may explain the appeal of Marcus Garvey and the UNIA in terms of the desire of African Americans for "Black Power." Garveyism sought to achieve military power, economic leverage, and political unity for the entire continent of Africa as a means of improving the condition of Africans in the Western hemisphere. Garveyism and the UNIA represented the desire of West Indians and African Americans to determine their own status from a position of power, rather than relying on the condescending charity of outsiders.

[39] Ottley's description is based on the UNIA parade of 1920 and seems to be a composite narrative rather then a description of an actual event, but it catches the flavor of events as they were reported in the press. See J. A. Rogers, "Marcus Garvey: Provisional President of Africa and Messiah," in *World's Great Men of Color*, Vol. 2 (New York: Collier, 1947), pp. 415–31, for another description. Estimates of the size of the annual UNIA parades vary greatly.

[40] A discussion of problems associated with estimating Garvey membership is to be found in Edmund David Cronon, *Black Moses*, pp. 204–7.

As head of an international information and advertising agency, Marcus Garvey was not a failure. He successfully marketed the dream of a "New Negro" with potential as a factor in the world of commerce, politics, and military affairs. Garvey's dream of a black-controlled, African-Atlantic economy disintegrated after his imprisonment in 1925 on charges of using the mails to defraud. In the minds of many historians, his ill-starred career represents little more than a case study of incompetence, megalomania, and delusions of grandeur. His tragic attempts to create an African business empire were romantically conceived and doomed to failure. But while Garveyism failed in its most grandiose undertaking, the Black Star Steamship Line, he prospered in the most visible. His newspaper, *Negro World*, proved that Marcus Garvey was a skillful journalist, an information specialist, a publicity genius, and a brilliant stager of media events.[41]

If the Black Star Line was the UNIA's most spectacular failure, the weekly newspaper *Negro World* was its most striking success. Garvey launched his weekly newspaper on August 17, 1918, after he had been in the United States for two years and five months and had already achieved a remarkable degree of popularity with the masses. When it came to running a newspaper, Garvey decidedly knew what he was doing. He arrived in the United States an experienced journalist, for although he had never worked as a newspaper reporter, he had served a long apprenticeship in the more technical areas related to newspaper work. In Jamaica, he had been exposed to the business aspects of journalism before trying his skills as an independent publisher. He was an accomplished compositor in a time and place when the trade implied a solid knowledge of grammar, as well as the ability to proofread for style and content. In addition, Garvey had an aptitude that was even more important for a journalist. He was a born publicist. He knew his market and he understood those aspects of the black world that transcended national boundaries. He knew how to appeal to the Afrocentric and Pan-African feelings of readers in the United States, the West Indies, Central America, and Africa. It was no idle boast when Garvey claimed that his newspaper was known throughout the world.

At its peak, *Negro World* boasted a regular circulation of 50,000.[42] It certainly reached a much wider audience than that, for it must be

---

[41] For many years I have been indebted to Professor Wilfred D. Samuels for the insight on the singular success of Garvey's newspaper at a seminar at the University of Iowa during the early 1970s.

[42] E. David Cronon, ed., *Marcus Garvey* (Englewood Cliffs, NJ: Prentice Hall, 1971), p. 5. Scholars have shown little interest in challenging this figure.

remembered that even the illiterate portion of the black population had exposure to newspapers. In black communities at that time, newspapers were commonly read aloud in workplaces, beauty salons, barber shops, and Sunday schools. Thus, many people who could not read were nonetheless exposed to Garvey's editorials. Garvey showed excellent business sense, as well as intellectual integrity, by making certain that *Negro World* included on its staff a number of experienced writers including William H. Ferris, T. Thomas Fortune, John E. Bruce, Duse Mohamed Ali, and J. A. Rogers. All of these writers were popular with black audiences, particularly because of their frequent columns on the history of Africa and the black world.

Soon after its founding, the editorship of *Negro World* was assumed by William H. Ferris, a man of considerable ability, whose career was a classic example of the cruel frustration that was the lot of educated black people in segregated America. An eccentric, but well-educated man, Ferris had been educated at Yale and Harvard Universities and held master's degrees from both institutions. He was the author of a two-volume work entitled *The African Abroad*, and before coming to *Negro World*, he had previously edited *The Champion* in Chicago. Among the editorial staff and occasional contributors to *Negro World* was Duse Mohamed Ali, erstwhile publisher of *African Times and Orient Review*, with whom Garvey had worked while in England. A contributing editor was John E. Bruce, who had published or edited a number of periodicals since the 1870s. The literary editor was the self-educated, but erudite, J. A. Rogers, whose works on Pan-African history continue to attract a large following among African American readers.

The presence of the fair-skinned, sandy-haired Fortune at the helm of *Negro World* from 1923 till his death in 1928 was ample evidence that the newspaper's occasional antimulatto diatribes were rhetorical flourish, and not to be given undue weight. Fortune, like Garvey, had been an admirer of Booker T. Washington, but he had been more vocal than Washington in his opposition to segregation and racial violence. The editorship of *Negro World* offered Fortune the best of both worlds. He was able to voice his militant opposition to white supremacy, while at the same time advancing the goal of black separatism and self-help.

Inept though he was as the manager of a steamship corporation, Garvey was a brilliant advertising genius, and he centralized his appeals to "black nationalism" in his newspaper. As the nineteenth century drew to a close, there were still only three independent black nation–states on earth. Haiti, the island nation in the Caribbean, had been independent since 1804. Liberia, in West Africa, had declared itself an independent republic in

1847 but lacked power in any real economic or military sense. Ethiopia, an ancient monarchy in East Africa governed by a venal royal family, was preindustrial, a vestige of the Middle Ages. All three of these nations were economically powerless and industrially backward. As for the rest of Africa, it had been carved up at the Congress of Berlin in 1885 and divided into colonies by European nations.

Although the obstacles were daunting, the idea of creating a powerful African republic was extremely attractive to many African Americans who had been made to feel that the United States was not their country. The United States was a "white man's country" in the minds of most Americans – black and white. Black Americans were treated with open contempt in public places, denied employment in any but menial occupations, allowed to hold almost no political offices, and subjected to the constant threat of violence.

Marcus Garvey understood the carnival quality of the American political tradition and shrewdly exploited it, but there was more to the appeal of Garveyism than pageantry, costumes, and black nationalist hyperbole. Politics in the United States has always had circuslike extravagance, and its appeal has not been confined to black Americans, who were, in any event, attracted to Garvey not only because of his showmanship or even his promises of black economic power. Certainly there was more to his appeal than a naive escapism or a simple back-to-Africa fantasy. Garvey sympathizers, whether Black Star Line investors, uniformed marchers, or cheerers on the sidelines, understood that the movement represented an assertive modernity. Garvey's speeches and editorials did more than conjure up sentimental images of the ancient African past; they addressed contemporary issues of politics and economics, globalization, and imperialism. By utilizing the communications opportunities provided by the telephone, the Atlantic cable, and the print media, Garveyism instinctively exploited the science of mass psychology and the manipulation of mass images in the emerging "information age." Garvey was essentially a propagandist, an inspired stager of media events, whose career in America coincided with that of a very similar media genius, Edie Bernays, a nephew of Sigmund Freud.

Working for the U.S. Committee on Public Information during the first World War, Bernays discovered "possibilities of regimenting the public mind," which he soon applied to the developing art of public relations. There was a sinister side to this rising science of wish fabrication. Ironically, Bernays, the son of Jewish immigrants, became a profound influence on Hitler's propaganda minister, Joseph Goebbels. The culture historian William Leach calls Bernays an "architect of 'pseudoevents,' a finagler of the truth [who] staged happenings, carrying packaged information for immediate public consumption."[43]

Like Bernays, Garvey was a seller of dreams, and like Bernays, Garvey stood at the nexus of public relations and militarism.

We were the first Fascists. We had disciplined men, women and children in training for the liberation of Africa. The black masses saw that in this extreme nationalism lay their only hope and readily adopted it. Mussolini copied fascism from me but the Negro reactionaries sabotaged it. (J. A. Rogers, *World's Great Men of Color* [1947; repr. New York: Collier, 1972], p. 420.)

The militaristic aspect of Garveyism was politically continuous with the black nationalism of the nineteenth century and culturally continuous with the mainstream commercialism of twentieth-century America. The ideological continuity between Garveyism and Bookerism should be neither understated nor overstated. Garvey both clarified and falsified a distinction when he said:

Things have changed wonderfully since Washington came on the scene. His vision was industrial opportunity for the Negro, but the Sage of Tuskegee has passed off the stage of life and left behind a new problem – a problem that must be solved, not by the industrial leader only, but by the political and military leader. (*Philosophy and Opinions*, Vol. 1, p. 56.)

But Garvey was not the first to realize the usefulness of a black military program; he merely refashioned the images of those uniformed Tuskegee students, poised attentively at drafting tables in regimented classrooms.

Militarism was not simply an afterthought, but an essential ingredient of Garveyism, which fostered an image of black men and women marching in precision step toward a glorious destiny. He was a brilliant showman, in his "uniform loaded with tassels and gold braid that rivaled that of a British monarch."[44] He harnessed the martial *Zeitgeist* of the times, creating an African Legion, resplendent in black and red uniforms, and a corps of Black Cross nurses. Garvey's colorful parades in the streets of New York provided black folk with images of broad appeal to the "New Negro." Whereas the "Old Negro" was putatively lethargic, dreamy, and sensual, the New Negro would be crisp, efficient, and decisive.

---

[43] William Leach, *Land of Desire: Merchants, Power and the Rise of a New American Culture* (New York: Vintage Books, 1993), pp. 319–22.

[44] J. A. Rogers, *World's Great Men of Color*, p. 419.

14

Becoming History

Garvey and the Genius of His Age

> The Lords of life, the lords of life, –
> I saw them pass,
> In their own guise
> Like and unlike,
> Portly and grim...
>
> Emerson

REPRESENTATIVE GENIUS, DETERMINISM, AND DOOM

Words, as we know, may sometimes gain or sometimes lose powers with the passage of time. The word "genius" is an example, or the word "portly," as used above. When Benjamin Brawley wrote *The Negro Genius* (1937), he meant something more generous than what is implied by its more confined meaning of superior artistic or intellectual ability. He was thinking of its older usage, which is related to "genus" and denotes the distinguishing characteristics of a racial or ethnic group. It was common to speak of the genius of a nation or the genius of an age, which connoted the commonalities of a group, not necessarily the superiority of an individual. Emerson was able to employ both meanings of the word "genius" in "Self Reliance" (1841) and a third in "Experience" (1844).[1] A good writer seeks to exploit a word's multiple meanings, which may disappear in the vulgate, which sometimes reduces a word to a single colloquial meaning.

---

[1] He uses the term in a third way in "Experience," where it refers to the idea of a guardian spirit, related to the word genii, or genie, which has its Arabic cognate in "Jinni," sometimes transliterated as "Djinn."

Likewise, the word "portly," in the Emerson quotation above, has been reduced to the insipid, one-dimensional meaning of "fat." In the Renaissance poetry of Edmund Spenser, "portly" suggests a perhaps excessive dignity. It is related to "comportment," implying gravity to the point of hubris, or the pride that "goeth before the fall." If Du Bois had referred to Marcus Garvey as "portly," rather than "fat," he would not only have spared himself an indignity, he would have shown an appreciation for the tragic implications and ultimate destiny of Garvey's "military tinsel and braggadocio."[2] Du Bois saw Garvey as a threat, and with good reason took him seriously, for he recognized in him more than a rival. Garvey was, in a purer sense than Du Bois, a "world-historical figure."

In the creative interplay of contradictions in Emerson's idea of "Self-Reliance" and in his *Representative Men*, he splendidly presages the "portly" figure of Marcus Garvey. Emerson asserts that it is by "self-reliance" that an individual becomes great, but the "great man" also sacrifices individuality to become "representative," merged with an aggregate. It is, says Emerson, by "confiding themselves childlike to the genius of their age" that men have become "Great." We may recognize how tidily Emerson reconciles the contradiction, while retaining our appreciation of the paradox. The world-historical figure, like the Nietzschean protagonist of Theodore Dreiser's novel *The Titan*, is at once the product of deterministic economic and biological forces and at the same time a powerful self-satisfying expression of individual will. It is in the merger of individual will with world spirit that an individual like Garvey confides himself to the genius of his age and realizes "my doom – if I may so call it – of being a race leader."[3]

CONTRADICTIONS OF THE AFRICAN COLONIZATION MOVEMENT

The internal contradictions of the African Colonization Movement and the conflicts between the American Colonization Society and innumerable other colonization schemes in the nineteenth century have been observed by John Hope Franklin, John Henrik Clarke, E. U. Essien-Udom, Edwin

---

[2] Du Bois described Garvey as "A little, fat, black man, ugly but with intelligent eyes and big head," and sneers at Garvey's "uniform of the gayest Victorian type" in "Back to Africa," *Century Illustrated Magazine* (February 1923), 539. Garvey took umbrage at being called ugly and black, but not fat, in "W. E. Burghardt Du Bois – A Hater of Dark People," *Philosophy and Opinions* 310. Du Bois refers to "military tinsel and braggadocio" in "Credo," prologue to *Darkwater*, in 1920, at the peak of Garvey's career.

[3] *Philosophy and Opinions*, Vol. 2, p. 126.

S. Redkey, and Floyd Miller. All of the foregoing are agreed that the back-to-Africa movement held many meanings and that its participants were inspired by numerous motives. Nonetheless, one continually encounters interpretations of the colonization and emigration movements based on credulous readings of the Society's constitutional charge, or on uncritical assessments of William Lloyd Garrison's and David Walker's passionately moral diatribes. Thomas Jefferson, who advocated colonization, but significantly never joined the American Colonization Society, was cynical from the start. Henry Clay, one of the Society's founders, was a gradual abolitionist who aimed to use the Society to undermine slavery – in violation of its charter.

Abraham Lincoln was even more foxy and vague, for while he nominally supported colonization, he behaved as if he were unaware of the Society's existence. The pretensions of the American Colonization Society ought to be assessed by present-day historians at least as skeptically as they were by Alexis de Tocqueville. If a nineteenth-century French visitor could see the pragmatic contradictions between rhetoric and reality, Abraham Lincoln could hardly have missed them. The American Colonization Society along with other colonization and emigration groups, was a network of local agencies, with numerous contradictory ideologies, and was driven, as John Hope Franklin correctly observes, by conflicting goals – sometimes racist, as in the case of Andrew Jackson, sometimes humanitarian, as in the case of Harriet Beecher Stowe.

Summarized briefly, the American movement to establish a black nation in Africa predated Garveyism by more than a century. African Americans who supported both the British and the American side were settled in Sierra Leone after the American Revolution. A few hundred were settled in Liberia throughout the nineteenth century. There was support for the movement among African American writers and intellectuals of widely divergent ideological positions during the 1850s and even throughout the Civil War and thereafter. With some significant exceptions, black leaders abandoned Liberian emigration during Reconstruction, but there was some talk of an African exodus during the late nineteenth century and actual resettlements. There was an "African return" at the beginning of the First World War, under the leadership of Orishatukeh Faduma, from Barbados, and Alfred C. Sam, a native of the Gold Coast. Garvey was known to become highly agitated and indignantly noncommunicative when comparisons were made between his movement and that of Alfred C. Sam.

THE TRAGEDY OF THE BLACK STAR LINE

The Black Star Line, the UNIA's steamship company, was incorporated in 1919 and commenced selling stocks at five dollars per share.[4] Many African Americans who supported the Black Star Line did so simply because they desired the opportunity to invest in some grand black enterprise. The UNIA presented numerous additional opportunities to likeminded persons. Real estate was the most obvious option at a period when numerous black entrepreneurs were investing in Harlem residences, and at least one prominent Black Star Line investor became wealthy by independently speculating in real estate. But the Black Star Line offered something more than a business venture; it offered an opportunity to assert an Afrocentric conception of black independence and to promote a symbol of militant Pan-African self-consciousness.

Unfortunately, the Black Star Line made a series of disastrous investments that eventually led to Garvey's being prosecuted for fraud. The vessels that were purchased turned out to be dilapidated or downright unseaworthy. The *Yarmouth*, renamed *Frederick Douglass*, was purchased on September 17, 1919, at the advice of Captain Joshua Cockburn, a West Indian, who received a $1,600 fee from the brokerage firm that made the sale. The *Yarmouth* was a small, rather unimpressive cargo ship that had been used to transport cargoes of cotton during the war, but its maiden voyage attracted much attention in Harlem and seemed, initially, to give substance to Garvey's entrepreneurial ambitions. With Cockburn as its captain, however, the *Yarmouth*'s fortunes went from bad to worse. It made a voyage to Cuba, carrying a cargo of whiskey, during which it ran aground off the Bahamas while Cockburn reportedly slept.[5] After losing several weeks making repairs, the *Yarmouth* finally arrived in Cuba, but the expedition had cost the company far more than it had produced. Later, Cockburn ran the *Yarmouth* aground for a second time off Boston. Eventually on December 3, 1921, the ship was sold at public auction to defray debts against the Black Star Line.[6]

The ancient *Shadyside* was a picturesque little vessel with paddle wheels at its sides. It was purchased in April 1920 for use as an excursion boat.

---

[4] *Marcus Garvey Papers*, Vol. 1, p. 454.
[5] Cockburn complained to Garvey of the drunkenness, insubordination, and incomptency of the ship's chief engineer in Cockburn to Garvey, December 2, 1919, and December 5, 1919, in *Marcus Garvey Papers*, Vol. 2, pp. 157–62.
[6] *Marcus Garvey Papers*, Vol. 4, p. lii.

It made a few voyages up and down the Hudson during the UNIA conventions, but sank while docked in the winter of 1920–21. The *Kanawha*, rechristened *Antonio Maceo* and purchased in April 1920, was abandoned in Cuba in the fall of 1921. A fourth ship, the *Goethals*, rechristened *Booker T. Washington* and purchased on January 10, 1925, was sold at public auction on March 29, 1926.[7] The Black Star Line negotiated for a fifth ship, the *Orion*, which was to be rechristened the *Phyllis Wheatley*, but the sale was never completed. Garvey's failures in the shipping business were predictable. He knew nothing of such ventures and was taken advantage of by bad advisors. When he undertook a business that he understood, that is, journalism, Garvey was a splendid success.[8]

The Black Star fantasy appealed to internationalist and Afrocentric sentiments that had been present among black Americans since the early nineteenth century. It was the fulfillment of Paul Cuffe and James Forten's long-deferred dream of black control over transportation, not only to and from Africa but connecting all corners of the black world. Strangely, although Garvey reclaimed the vigorous rhetoric of nineteenth-century Pan-Africanists and invoked the intellectual heritage of Blyden and Crummell in his speeches and writings, it is significant that he paid greater tribute to the self-effacing Booker T. Washington, who would never have associated himself with his theatrical schemes.[9] Nonetheless, and not surprisingly, some of Washington's disciples were inspired by Garvey's grand designs. For all their impracticality, his schemes were symbolic manifestations of that same spirit of capitalism that Washington had represented, but with the added ingredient of independence from white economic power.

---

[7] *Marcus Garvey Papers*, Vol. 4, pp. 337, 476, and Vol. 6, p. lxiv. E. David Cronon, *Black Moses: The Story of Marcus Garvey and the Universal Negro Improvement Association* (Madison: The University of Wisconsin Press, 1996), pp. 85, 91–92; Cronon, *Black Moses*, pp. 92–99.

[8] I am grateful to Wilfred D. Samuels for this insight. It also seems likely that Garvey's employment of such experienced senior journalists as John E. Bruce and T. Thomas Fortune benefited *Negro World*.

[9] Tony Martin notes that Garvey commended Blyden to his readers in an early pamphlet, where he quoted extensively from Blyden's book, *Christianity, Islam, and the Negro Race* (1887). See Tony Martin, *Race First: The Ideological and Organizational Struggles of Marcus Garvey and the Universal Negro Improvement Association* (Dover, MA: The Majority Press, 1976), p. 82; and Marcus Garvey, *A Talk With Afro-West Indians* (New York: African Communities League, ca. 1915), p. 3. George Alexander McGuire, *The Universal Negro Catechism* (n.p., 1921), paid tribute to Crummell. There is also some possibly that Garvey's newspaper editorial "Character, Character, Character," in *The Black Man* (September–October 1936), p. 6, may have been inspired by Crummell's tract "Character, The Great Thing" (1898).

While Garvey acknowledged intellectual indebtedness to Booker T. Washington and expressed hostility toward Du Bois, one must be cautious in appraising his statements concerning his intellectual heritage. Garvey's dreams resembled the romantic racialism of Du Bois, whom he came later to oppose, but who, like Garvey, was a Pan-Africanist, given to rhapsodic pleas for intellectual and cultural independence. Garvey knew that both Washington and Du Bois had called for self-help and the development of a leadership elite. Du Bois was, of course, more vociferous in his opposition to racial discrimination than was Washington, thus Garvey in 1916 would have endorsed the following well-known statement by Du Bois, along with its masculinist rhetoric:

Mr. Washington apologizes for injustice, North or South, does not rightly value the privilege and the duty of voting, belittles the emasculating effects of caste distinctions, and opposes the higher training and ambition of our brighter minds, – so far as he, the South, or the Nation, does this, we must unceasingly and firmly oppose him.[10]

Garvey, at the time of his arrival in the United States, favored political agitation for full inclusion in American life. Later he endorsed the more compromising aspects of the Bookerite program that Du Bois had attacked.

MILITARY TINSEL AND THE CONTRADICTIONS OF CHRISTIANITY

With the end of the First World War, African peoples on both sides of the Atlantic focused their attention on the Paris Peace Conference, especially as its work affected Germany's former colonies in Africa. Numerous black American leaders, including W. E. B. Du Bois, attempted to represent the interests of Africans and African Americans. Militant individuals such as William Monroe Trotter, Ida B. Wells, and Hubert Harrison, and even moderates like Madam C. J. Walker, attempted with varying degrees of success to make their opinions known to the victorious powers meeting in Paris. Du Bois convened the first of his Pan-African Congresses in 1919. Garvey viewed the congress with disdain and made plans for his own series of international meetings, which he convened in New York during the early 1920s.[11]

---

[10] W. E. B. Du Bois, *The Souls of Black Folk: Essays and Sketches* (Chicago: McClurg, 1903), p. 59.

[11] Attempts by black Americans to influence the proceedings in Paris have been discussed by Stephen R. Fox in *The Guardian of Boston: William Monroe Trotter* (New York: Altheneum,

It was at these conventions that Garvey staged his pageantry and parades, his gala receptions and his gaudy ceremonies. Garveyism recognized the high-cultural aspirations of the stable black working class, their desire to build "more stately mansions." Rare recordings of Garvey's voice illustrate one of the ironies of traditional black nationalism. He does not employ the slangy dialect of the blues man, nor the prissy affectations of the social climber. His dramatic monotone is more reminiscent of the Shakespearean stage than the storefront sermon, and his Jamaican accent is not extreme. Garvey's voice, for all its passion, could be somber and laden with portent. He understood the desire of the stable working class and the aspiring middle class for symbols of dignity and stability. Garvey illustrated the essential paradox of classical black nationalism, the fact that it combined political separatism with cultural assimilation. For while Garvey opposed biological amalgamation, he advocated the emulation of those traits that had given white folk their power. He believed that Europe had become great by following the laws of nature, and he advocated that black folk do the same. The races existed in a state of fierce competition with one another. It was the will of God.

God is a bold Sovereign – A Warrior Lord. The God we worship and adore is a God of War as well as a God of Peace. He does not allow anything to interfere with His power and authority....

I believe with Napoleon. When some one asked him "On what side is God?" he replied. "God is on the side of the strongest battalion." Napoleon was right. He had a true concept of God. God is really on the side of the strongest peoples because God made all men equal and He never gave superior power to any one class or group of people over another, and any one who can get the advantage over another is pleasing God, because that is the servant who has taken care of God's command in exercising authority over the world.[12]

In connection with Garvey's appeal to a "Warrior God," a word is in order on the religious aspects of Garveyism. The movement aligned itself with black nationalist religious groups in Harlem and elsewhere. J. Arnold Ford, leader of Harlem's community of Black Jews and head of Beth B'nai Abraham congregation, served as UNIA musical director and was presumably among the six hundred Black Jews who marched as a special contingent in the 1922 parade.[13] Many Garveyites were attracted to the Moorish Science Temple, a group of fez-wearing Black Muslims

---

1970), pp. 221–35. For descriptions of the major International Conventions of the UNIA, held in New York in 1920, 1921, 1922, and 1924, see the *Marcus Garvey Papers* for appropriate years.

[12] *Philosophy and Opinions*, Vol. 1, pp. 43–44.

[13] Theodore Vincent, *Black Power and the Garvey Movement* (Berkeley, CA: Ramparts Press, 1971), pp. 97, 123, 134–35, 152, 159, 222, 251. William R. Scott, *Going to the Promised*

headed by Noble Drew Ali. After the death of Ali and the deportation of Garvey, many of the followers of both men became active in the Nation of Islam, led by Elijah Muhammad, who admired Garvey.[14]

Garvey's main religious connections were Christian, however, and it was Alexander McGuire, organizer of the African Orthodox Church, who served as the UNIA Chaplain General. Garvey's preference for McGuire was short-lived, and as historian Randall K. Burkett has shown, the UNIA attracted the support of numerous Protestant churchmen whose roles in the movement were at least as important as that of McGuire. Burkett highlights the political consciousness and progressive activism of these churchmen, and, observing the importance of religious myth and ritual in Garveyite organizational life, argues that Garveyism may properly be understood as a highly political "civil religion."[15] The UNIA, like the black churches, promoted self-esteem, moral consciousness, and ritual exaltation of leadership. In terms of pomp and circumstance, only the Anglican and the Roman Catholic churches could have rivaled Garveyism, but these churches were hopelessly dominated by whites, and the latter asked that its clergy practice celibacy. The Universal Negro Improvement Association gave its adherents a formal ritual and ceremonial grandeur that were unavailable at any price from traditional black denominations.

CONTRADICTIONS OF HARLEM RENAISSANCE STYLES

Conflicting images of African American culture were manifest in the emergent societies of the urban North during and after the First World War. Garvey's heroic view of African American culture sometimes found itself in contention with the cultural manifestation refered to as the "Jazz Age" or "Harlem Renaissance."[16] As African Americans migrated to urban centers, such as New York's Harlem, they brought blues culture with them. During the 1920s, American culture, white and black, was influenced by the lively tempo of jazz music and the liberated sexual ethos

---

Land: Afro-American Immigrants in Ethiopia, 1930–1935 (Atlanta, GA: IBW Press, 1975), pp. 5–6.

[14] See Claude Andrew Clegg, III, *An Original Man* (New York: St Martin's Press, 1997).

[15] Randall K. Burkett, *Garveyism as a Religious Movement: The Institutionalization of a Black Civil Religion* (Metuchen, NJ: Scarecrow Press, 1978); Randall K. Burkett, *Black Redemption: Churchmen Speak for the Garvey Movement* (Philadelphia, PA: Temple University Press, 1978); and Alice Felt Tyler, *Freedom's Ferment* (St. Paul: University of Minnesota, 1944).

[16] See Tony Martin, *Literary Garveyism: Garvey, Black Arts and the Harlem Renaissance* (Dover, MA: The Majority Press, 1983); Tony Martin, *African Fundamentalism: A Literary and Cultural Anthology of Garvey's Harlem Renaissance* (Dover, MA: The Majority Press, 1983).

associated with the new music. The Harlem Renaissance produced a new group of African American writers who celebrated the new urban culture along with its folk roots in the South. Classic expressions of Harlem Renaissance themes dominated the novel *Home to Harlem* by the Jamaican novelist Claude McKay.

'I ain't got a cent to my name,' mused Jake, 'but ahm as happy as a prince, all the same. Yes I Is.'

He loitered down Lennox Avenue. He shoved his hand in his pocket – pulled out the fifty-dollar note. A piece of paper was pinned to it on which was scrawled in pencil:

'Just a little gift from a baby girl to a honey boy!'

The appearance of such literary themes evoked Garvey's hostility, and, in fact, Garvey's entire program might be interpreted as an attack on the identification of exotic sexuality with African American literary culture. There is no reason to suspect Garvey of hypocrisy on this point. While he was not puritanical, he was personally honest and lived a clean, frugal life, disdaining the use of intoxicating spirits and tobacco, and avoiding the cabaret.[17] The opposition of Garvey to certain aspects of "Jazz Age" culture was based on his belief that white intellectuals encouraged the exotic qualities of African American culture in order to degrade black folk. Thus, in *Negro World* (September 29, 1928) he lambasted *Home to Harlem*.

Our race, within recent years has developed a new group of writers who have been prostituting their intelligence, under the direction of the white man, to bring out and show up the worst traits of our people. Several of these writers are American and West Indian Negroes. They have been writing books, novels and poems under the advice of white publishers to portray to the world the looseness, laxity and immorality that are peculiar to our group for the purposes of these publishers circulating the libel against us among the white peoples of the world, to further hold us up to ridicule and contempt and universal prejudice.

The white people have these Negroes write [this] kind of stuff . . . so that the Negro can still be regarded as a monkey or some imbecile creature.

Garvey wrote passionately on the need to establish positive images and to celebrate a pantheon of black heroes, and yet he neglected opportunities to associate himself with a preexisting black nationalist tradition in the United States. When it came to naming his steamships, for example, he did not name them for Martin R. Delany, Alexander Crummell, or John Russwurm, as would have been appropriate. Remarkably, the first

---

[17] Amy Jacques Garvey, *Garvey and Garveyism*, p. 70.

steamship he acquired was rechristened the *Frederick Douglass*, after the nineteenth century's bitterest foe of black nationalism and back-to-Africa movements.

As the quintessential "race man," Garvey was the polar opposite of Frederick Douglass; his separatist policies were a radical repudiation of everything Douglass had stood for.[18] Douglass asserted that "every pretension we set up in favor of race pride is giving the enemy a stick to break our own heads."[19] His program was based on an appeal to universal morality and human rights. He believed that success must depend almost entirely on individual efforts, and was known for the remarkable statement, "our union is our weakness."[20] Douglass usually opposed independent black political organization; indeed, he believed that the ultimate solution to racial problems in America was complete assimilation and amalgamation of the black population, both biologically and culturally. It is, therefore, unlikely that the decision to name a steamship after Douglass represented any ideological sympathy with the sainted abolitionist; it simply illustrated Garvey's ability to exploit the hero-worshipping tendencies of black Americans. Garvey shared Douglass' respect for the abstract concepts of universal justice and human rights, but unlike Douglass, Garvey opposed interracial marriage and was an unapologetic advocate of black self-determination. He made it clear that he believed that no nation or race could expect to enjoy human rights simply by appealing to the power of morality.

EXODUS SCHIZOPHRENIA: BEING PHARAOH AND MOSES

As noted above, Garvey was influenced by Edward Wilmot Blyden and Duse Mohamed, cosmopolitan Pan-Africanists of an older generation, who brought with them traditions of African vindication informed by biblical and classical exegesis. When he founded *Negro World*, Garvey

---

[18] Also see Khalil Mahmud, "Introduction" to Duse Mohamed, *In the Land of the Pharaohs: A Short History of Egypt* (London: Frank Cass, 1968), p. xxxii.

[19] Frederick Douglass, *The Nation's Problem*, an address delivered in Washington, DC, on April 16, 1889. Reprinted in John W. Blassingame and John R. McKivigan, eds., *The Frederick Douglass Papers*, Series 1, Vol. 5, pp. 412, 415.

[20] *The Frederick Douglass Papers*, Series 1, Vol. 5, p. 414. "They [antecedent unidentified] say that in union there is strength; that united we stand and divided we fall. My position is the reverse of all this 'I hold that our union is in weakness.'" Howard Brotz, *Negro Social and Political Thought, 1850–1920* (New York: Basic Books, 1966), pp. 318–19, prints a version of the text that reads "our unity is our weakness," which makes more sense in the context of the paragraphs from which it is taken.

drew on the experience of senior journalists William H. Ferris, John E. Bruce, and T. Thomas Fortune. All of them accepted doctrines of Afrocentrism, the idea that Africa should be at the center of every black person's understanding of world history and culture. They were committed to redeeming knowledge that had been withheld by conspirators of the slave power. It is important to note that in the cases of Bruce and Fortune, both had been born under slavery. The idea that whites had withheld knowledge from blacks was by no means an academic question in their views.[21]

Afrocentrism involved vindicating the humanity of the black race by glorifying the African past, establishing the idea of a black contribution to world history, and establishing the idea that Egyptian civilization was a part of African history because the earliest dynasties were essentially bound to the civilizations of the upper Nile and inner Africa. Afrocentric assertions are sometimes fundamentally reasonable; at other points they may be imaginative inventions of the most creative ilk. These traditions were not new with the Garveyites. African Americans gave evidence as early as the 1820s of a willingness to identify with Egyptians. A contradiction arose, however, as it is well known that in slavery times black religious traditions viewed life in America as analogous to the bondage of Israel "away down in Egypt's Land." How could they "tell ol' Pharaoh to let my people go," if they were in fact descendants of the house of Egypt? It is in the nature of all mythologies, not only those of African Americans, to yoke together contradictory mythologies, for myths must accommodate the diverse spiritual goals of complex aggregations of people – not to mention reconciling the paradoxes within individual psyches.[22]

---

[21] For short biographies of *Negro World* editors mentioned, consult Robert A. Hill, ed., *Garvey Papers*, Ferris, Vol. 1, p. 76, n. 3, Fortune, Vol. 5, p. 285, n. 2, Bruce, Vol. 1, p. 200, n. 2.

[22] Literature that discusses the self-image of African Americans in relation to religious themes is voluminous. For some examples see Benjamin Mays, *The Negro's God as Reflected in His Literature* (New York: Chapman and Grimes, 1938); Miles Mark Fisher, *Negro Slave Songs in the United States* (New York: The American Historical Association, 1953); Leonard Sweet, *Black Images of America, 1784–1870* (New York: Norton, 1976); Gayraud Wilmore, *Black Religion and Black Radicalism: An Examination of the Black Experience in Religion* (Garden City, NY: Doubleday, 1973); David E. Swift, *Black Prophets of Justice* (Baton Rouge: Louisiana State University Press, 1989); Theosophus H. Smith, *Conjuring Culture: Biblical Formations of Black America* (New York: Oxford, 1994); George Frederickson, *Black Liberation: A Comparative History of Black Ideologies in the United States and South Africa* (New York: Oxford University Press, 1995). The uses of myth as a means of achieving a unity of opposites is discussed in Moses, *Black Messiahs and Uncle Toms* (University Park, PA: The Penn State Press, 1982), illustrated in

Garvey made use of the "Afrocentric" tradition, which for over a century had emphasized the mythic connections between the Egyptians, the Ethiopians, and the other races of Africa. Like his arch rival Du Bois, he conjured up images of the pyramids, the Sphinx, and a majestic Ethiopian presence. Like latter-day Afrocentrists, Garvey and Du Bois repudiated the association of African American life with the profane exoticism of popular culture. Both opposed the "proletarian-bohemian" manifestations of the Jazz Age and what Sterling Brown called "primitivism grafted on decadence" that was associated with the cultural movement called the "Harlem Renaissance." They were hostile to the image of black Americans that associated them with easy sexuality or the fast life of the cabaret. They preferred to think of black culture in terms of a noble and majestic Ethiopia, destined to see the restoration of her glory. But neither deigned to admit that on this point at least, they were in agreement.[23]

Garvey and Du Bois both published poetry expressing their hostility to theories of the Aryan origins of civilization.[24] In "The Riddle of the Sphinx," Du Bois conferred "honorary Negro" or mulatto status on virtually every ancient race:

Who raised the fools to their glory
But black men of Egypt and Ind?
Ethiopia's sons of the evening,
Chaldeans and Yellow Chinese
The Hebrew children of Morning
And Mongrels of Rome and Greece?

the symbol of the Blessed Virgin, who embodies the contradictory values of motherhood and virginity. It might also be said that the original Moses/Exodus myth also reconciles the opposition between Egyptian and Hebraic myths. See Sigmund Freud, *Moses and Monotheism* (1939). The Holy Family's flight into Egypt is another blending of Christian, Hebraic, and Egyptocentric historiographies.

[23] Kevin Gaines made me aware of Sterling Brown's "The New Negro in Literature," in a publication of The Graduate School, Howard University, *The New Negro Thirty Years Afterward: Papers Contributed to the Sixteenth Annual Spring Conference of the Division of the Social Sciences* (Washington, DC: The Howard University Press, 1955). Some insight into the responses of Du Bois and Garvey to Harlem Renaissance culture can be gained from a reading of their reviews of *Home to Harlem* and *Nigger Heaven*, discussed in Wilson J. Moses, "The Lost World of the New Negro," in *Black American Literature Forum* 21. 1–2 (Spring–Summer 1987), especially pp. 73–75. Reprinted in Wilson J. Moses, *The Wings of Ethiopia* (Ames: Iowa State University Press, 1990).

[24] Garvey's *The Tragedy of White Injustice* was published as a pamphlet by Amy Jacques Garvey in 1927. It has been republished in *The Poetical Works of Marcus Garvey*, ed. Tony Martin (Dover, MA: The Majority Press, 1983). Du Bois's "The Riddle of the Sphinx" has more than one version and a complicated publishing history. See Moses, *Afrotopia*, p. 277, n. 77, and Herbert Aptheker, ed., *Creative Writings by W. E. B. Du Bois*.

Garvey's verse was even more pointed:

> Out of cold old Europe these white men came
> From caves, dens and holes, without any fame
> Eating their dead's flesh and drinking their blood
> Relics of the Mediterranean Flood.

Garvey was convinced that whenever a black population contributed to world civilization they were robbed of their history by being reclassified as white. A case in point was the statement attributed to the French government and to American anthropologists that Moroccan and Algerian troops employed in the invasion of Germany were not "Negroes." He interpreted this to mean that "whenever a black man accomplishes anything of importance, he is no longer a Negro," and therefore, by definition, "A Negro [was] a person of dark complexion or race, who has not accomplished anything and to whom others are not obligated for any useful service." The prejudice against black folk was not on account of our color, but our condition. White folk seemed to redefine black people variously as Negroes, mulattos, or whites, depending on the occasion or as it suited their convenience.

What was true of the race was true of the individual. Garvey sarcastically noted that whenever a black person accomplished anything, he or she seemed to be immediately reclassified as white or "colored," as opposed to Negro. In South Africa, for example, the white ruling class seemed determined to drive a wedge between the Bantu population and the so-called "Cape coloreds." Garvey would have none of this. He was prepared to "agree with the American white man, that one drop of Negro blood makes a man a Negro." Garvey noted, as did other racial vindicationists of his generation, that once one accepted this definition of "blackness," the Pharaohs of ancient Egypt ironically became black.[25] As would the Afrocentrists of a later day, he enjoyed the sardonic humor of hoisting racist history on the petard of racist anthropology.

CIVILIZATIONISM AND ANTICIVILIZATIONISM

Garvey believed that Europe's ability to establish imperial power and industrial might was no accident. France and England had been able to

---

[25] J. A. Rogers makes his ironic contributions to the definition of race in *Sex and Race: Negro-Caucasian Mixing in All Ages and All Lands*, three vols. (New York: H. M. Rogers, 1942–67), and *Nature Knows No Color Line: Research into the Negro Ancestry of the White Race*, 3rd ed. (New York: H. M. Rogers, 1952).

establish their imperial dominions over darker peoples because they were better organized, more technically proficient, and more highly cultured than their colonial subjects. The solution to the problems of the black world was not protest, but discipline and competition, and the cultivation of a higher racial ideal. Garvey believed that African peoples had no one but themselves to blame if they failed to throw off the shackles of Western imperialism. They would never accomplish this, however, so long as they persisted in "the looseness, laxity, and immorality that are peculiar to our group."[26]

On the other hand, Garvey was by no means uncritical of Europe. He identified himself with the critique of postwar Western civilization that one observes in the writings of Oswald Spengler, T. S. Eliot, Ernest Hemingway, and countless others.[27] He made the observation that the human race is "discontented with the civilization of today," at least six years before Freud's *Das Unbehagen in der Kultur* was translated as *Civilization and its Discontents*.[28] He warned that "If the Negro is not careful he will drink in all the poison of modern civilization and die from the effects of it."[29] A typical representative of "classical" black nationalism, he reconciled opposites, linking cultural assimilationism to political separatism, and traditionalism to modernism. In the ungainly metaphor of an anonymous and legendary undergraduate, he stood "with one foot planted firmly in the past, while with the other he hailed the dawn of a new day."

Garvey was caught up in a paradox that many leaders encounter in the process of establishing reform institutions. Much of the appeal of the UNIA was based in its appropriation of the rhetoric of "evolution and human progress," but institutional development implies cultural continuity and the maintenance of tradition.[30] A leader like Garvey must convince his audience that he is future oriented and that he has caught the tide of history. On the other hand, a great deal of his task is related to

[26] *Negro World*, September 29, 1928.

[27] Oswald Spenger, *The Decline of the West*, translated by Charles Francis Atkinson (New York: Knopf, 1926). Cf. Du Bois, "What is Civilization: Africa's Answer," *Forum*, February 1925. Reprinted in Weinberg, *Du Bois: A Reader*, p. 374.

[28] This phrase was utilized by Garvey, *Philosophy and Opinions*, Vol. 1, p. 31, six years before Sigmund Freud published *Das Unbehagen in der Kultur*, translated in 1930 as *Civilization and its Discontents*, although Freud's suggestion for the English translation was *Man's Discomfort in Civilization*. See James Streachy's introduction to *Civilization and its Discontents* (New York: W. W. Norton, 1961), pp. 3–4.

[29] Marcus Garvey, "Present Day Civilization," *Philosophy and Opinions*, Vol. 1, p. 31; *Philosophy and Opinions*, Vol. 2, pp. 119–20.

[30] Marcus Garvey, "Evolution and the Result," *Philosophy and Opinions*, Vol. 1, pp. 19–21.

the maintenance of an authoritative value system. Thus, a great deal of Garvey's "revolutionary" rhetoric centered around the invocation of values that were supposedly universal and timeless. Garvey, like most leaders of prophetic or messianic movements, offered a mix of conservative and progressive values. His movement necessitated an appeal to revolutionary conceptions of black manhood and black womanhood. At the same time, he instinctively recognized that black empowerment in the early twentieth century must be linked to the manipulation of symbols of power. Garvey believed that British middle-class ideals of warrior manhood and domestic womanhood were the key to a strong race ideal, and he thus attempted to encourage traditional gender roles.

Garvey's concept of manly honor was fundamental to his political philosophy. Within his view, white supremacists were only acting out the natural principle of survival embodied in the social Darwinist slogan "root hog or die," and there were elements of social Darwinism in the Garvey movement.[31] Those black folk who allowed themselves to be dominated by whites were morally culpable, unless they practiced the manly art of self-defense and measured arms with them in the struggle for survival. His concept of racial struggle was based on a nineteenth-century view of manhood in which a man had no one but himself to blame if he allowed himself to be beaten or bested. This became evident when he commented on the 1936 defeat of the African American boxer Joe Louis by the German Max Schmelling and the 1936 military defeat of the Ethiopian emperor Haile Selassie by Italian dictator Mussolini.[32]

Garvey was a product of the late-nineteenth-century manhood code, with its preachments of the "strenuous life" and exhortations to "self-reliance." Not surprisingly, he insisted that dependence "upon the progress and achievements of others for a consideration in sympathy, justice and rights is like a dependence upon a broken stick, resting upon which will eventually consign you to the ground."[33] Racial self-reliance was a rational goal albeit difficult of achievement. Garvey pointed to the disposition of many African Americans "to depend upon the other races for a kindly and sympathetic consideration of their needs, without making

---

[31] For social Darwinism in the Garvey movement, see Kevin Gaines, *Uplifting the Race*, pp. 100–104. William Graham Sumner had a strong influence on Yale-educated William H. Ferris, editor of Garvey's *Negro World*. See William H. Ferris, *The African Abroad or His Evolution Under Caucasian Milieu*, two vols. (New Haven, CT: Tuttle, Morehouse & Taylor, 1993), pp. 522–24. For influences on other black intellectuals, see Mia Bay, *The Black Image in the White Mind* (New York: Oxford, 2000), pp. 190–95.

[32] *The Black Man* (March–April 1937), 8–9, and (July 1938), 1.

[33] *Philosophy and Opinions*, p. 23.

the effort to do for themselves, [as] the race's standing disgrace by which we have been judged and through which we have created the strongest prejudice against ourselves." If this sounded like blaming the victim, it should be noted that the accusation of victim blaming was one charge never leveled at Garvey by his rivals. The term had not yet become a standard cliché of African American politics. Then, too, there was one difference between the self-reliance advocated by Garveyism and that advocated by black "conservatives" of a later period. Garvey's program called consistently for internal organization and independent institutions. These are the essential ingredients that separate the self-help program of black nationalism from the victim-blaming preachments of so-called black conservatism in the late twentieth century.

WOMEN IN THE GARVEY MOVEMENT

Garvey chose to place himself in the ranks of classical black nationalists of the nineteenth century who were surprisingly receptive to black women. Alexander Crummell had stood firm on two basic issues: opposition to oppression of women in traditional African tribal rites, and insistence on the importance of higher education for women. Garveyism advocated a broad range of political and economic roles for women in the UNIA, but the language of Garveyism, while progressive in the rhetoric of its times, cannot be reconciled to late-twentieth-century American feminism. The historian Nell Painter has correctly identified a masculinist strain in black nationalism, and that strain was present in Garveyism, but it is important to note that numerous black women supported the movement and made important contributions to it.[34] The UNIA, more than any black nationalist organization, provided a sphere in which black women were accepted into positions of leadership. It is clear, however, that Garveyism never questioned the idea of male dominance. The Constitution and Book of Laws of the UNIA and ACL provided that each local division should have both a "Male President" and a "Lady President." The Male President was, of course, the real leader of the division. The Lady President was to be in control of "all those departments of the organization over which she may be able to exercise better control than the Male President," but all her reports were to be "submitted to the Male President for presentation to the general membership."[35]

[34] Tony Martin, *Race First*, p. 35.
[35] *Garvey Papers*, Vol. 1, p. 269.

Ida B. Wells, a strong-minded, independent woman, was quick to criticize Garvey, but more for his generally imperious attitude than for his specific positions on women's issues. Wells first met Garvey when he passed through Chicago shortly after his arrival in the United States and her husband brought him home to dinner. She subsequently followed his career with measured enthusiasm. The UNIA elected Wells a delegate to the Paris Peace Conference after the war, but she was prevented from attending, mainly by financial constraints. In her posthumously published *Autobiography*, Wells claims she attempted to persuade Garvey to defer the matter of launching his Black Star Line because she felt it was "a more complicated program than he had helpers to carry out."[36]

Garvey's personal relationships with women provide significant insight into his character and personality. Historian Judith Stein has noted, accurately enough, that he was "drawn to strong women, who could do things for him."[37] A more positive reading might be that he appreciated assertive women, and sought their company, because he admired strength and intelligence. This may be interpreted as a demonstration of his own strong self-esteem. The first Mrs. Garvey, Amy Ashwood, was headstrong and not easily intimidated. Her relationship to her husband after her arrival in the United States was contentious and short. She was certainly a woman of ability and, after their divorce, she went on to become a successful businesswoman, author, and actress.[38] His second wife, Amy Jacques, was likewise able and intelligent. As Garvey's private secretary and office manager she was known for her "uncompromising efficiency."[39] Amy Jacques became the chief apologist for Garvey after his imprisonment, editing the two volumes of his speeches on which this volume is based. In 1963, she published her lively and insightful *Garvey and Garveyism*, which remains an important source for the details of his life.

MARCUS GARVEY AND HIS ENEMIES

As the UNIA demonstrated its ability to attract public attention and to win the financial support of many African Americans, the organization

---

[36] Ida B. Wells-Barnett, *The Autobiography of Ida B. Wells*, Alfreda M. Duster, ed. (Chicago: University of Chicago Press, 1970), pp. 380–82. Wells's inability to attend the conference was apparently not for purely financial reasons. Like most other black persons who wanted to go to Paris, she was faced with obstruction by the governments of the victorious powers.

[37] Judith Stein, *The World of Marcus Garvey*, p. 151.

[38] Note on Amy Ashwood in *Garvey Papers*, Vol. 1, p. 74, n. 2.

[39] Note on Amy Jacques in *Garvey Papers*, Vol. 2.

came under increasing scrutiny from local, state, and federal authorities. Various agencies began to initiate the series of legal actions that ultimately broke the movement. There was also dissatisfaction within the movement, as became apparent in 1919, when George Tyler, a disillusioned investor, attempted to assassinate Garvey in the offices of the UNIA, shooting him four times. Tyler was taken into custody and the state attorney general, Edwin P. Kilroe, claimed that Tyler would make damaging revelations concerning Garvey's business practices. But when Tyler died mysteriously while in police custody, rumors spread and considerable credibility was given to Garvey's claims that the UNIA was the victim of a plot by Kilroe himself. Many black Americans, then as now, had a reflexive distrust of police and government agencies and automatically believed Garvey's claim that Tyler had announced that he had been sent by Kilroe and was killed because he was in a position to implicate the attorney general.[40]

Garvey's clashes with the legal authorities and his rising popularity brought him into conflict with powerful rivals. The most notable of these was W. E. B. Du Bois, whose favor he had once courted. Shortly after his arrival in the United States, the UNIA leader presented himself at the offices of the *Crisis*, but Du Bois did not encourage his overtures. On April 25, 1916, Garvey wrote to Du Bois asking him to "take the chair" at what he termed his "first public lecture" in the United States. Du Bois had a member of his staff write to "express his regret at not being able to be on hand on account of his being out of town." Du Bois never welcomed Garvey's presence in New York, mainly because of the monumental egotism of both parties. Du Bois was uncomfortable with the flamboyant program of the UNIA and repeatedly found excuses to ignore Garvey's invitations to UNIA activities. The hostilities between the two men are illustrated in Garvey's article "W. E. B. Du Bois – A Hater of Dark People." Du Bois wrote several articles on Garvey in which he accused him first of flamboyance, but later of outright criminal activity. Norton Thomas, an associate editor of *Negro World*, attributed the hostilities to jealousy, and composed an adaptation of Shakespeare's *Julius Caesar*, in which he substituted the names of well-known Harlemites, including Du Bois, Garvey, and NAACP field secretary James Weldon Johnson, for those of Brutus, Caesar, and Cassius.[41] Garvey attributed the opposition of Du Bois to a worldwide mulatto conspiracy for which the NAACP provided the leadership and voice.

---

[40] Cronon, *Black Moses*, pp. 44–45. Garvey, *Philosophy and Opinions*, Vol. 2, p. 130.
[41] In *Negro World* (May 10, 1924), reprinted in Tony Martin, *Race First*, pp. 303–4.

One of Garvey's bitterest clashes was with Robert S. Abbott, publisher and editor of the *Chicago Defender*, and this clearly had nothing to do with skin color. Abbott was a man of unadulterated African ancestry – stocky, tough-talking, and contentious with piercing eyes and a derby hat. Abbott gained Garvey's permanent enmity when he questioned the sincerity of Garvey's commitment to black people and hired a black private detective agency to investigate the Black Star Line in hopes they might turn up anything that could be used against the UNIA. Convinced that Garvey was a fraud, Abbott published attacks in his newspaper comparing the Black Star Line to Alfred C. Sam's ill-fated endeavor. Abbott's allegations concerning Garvey's honesty resulted in Garvey's being arrested and fined in Chicago. Garvey successfully sued for libel, although the court awarded Garvey only a token amount. Nonetheless, Garvey experienced some satisfaction from the judgment, and claimed that the court had implicitly recognized a distinction between his movement and the Sam fiasco.[42] Abbott later joined with other black leaders in urging the U.S. Attorney General to press the case against Garvey for using the mails to defraud.[43]

On January 12, 1922, in response to increasing negative press concerning the fiscal irresponsibility of the Black Star Line, Garvey was arrested, and in late February 1922, he was indicted, along with three other officials of the line, on twelve counts of using the mails to defraud. That same month Garvey announced that the Black Star Line had suspended its activities. With constant demands coming from the black press for some evidence of a viable shipping corporation, the Black Star Line announced its intention to purchase the vessel called the *Orion* from the United States Shipping Board, and *Negro World* began to carry advertisements for this vessel, which was to be renamed the *Phyllis Wheatley*. Transactions for purchase of the ship were never completed, however, due to numerous complex legal and financial difficulties. Anthony Rudolph Silverstone, the white agent who negotiated the purchase for the Black Star Line, appropriated almost a third of the deposit money to cover his "expenses." Under pressure from the Federal Bureau of Investigation, the United States Shipping Board demanded a bond of $450,000, three times the purchase

---

[42] Edmund David Cronon, *Black Moses: The Story of Marcus Garvey and the Universal Negro Improvement Association* (Madison: University of Wisconsin Press, 1955), pp. 75–76.

[43] Cronon, *Black Moses*, pp. 107–12. Tony Martin, *Race First*, pp. 326–27; Judith Stein, *The World of Marcus Garvey*, pp. 165–70. The document "Why I Have Not Spoken in Chicago Since 1919" offers Garvey's version of the conflict with Abbott. See Stein, *The World of Marcus Garvey*, p. 79; Martin, *Race First*, pp. 316, 324, 327; and Cronon, *Black Moses*, pp. 75–76.

price, before releasing the vessel to the Black Star Line. Garvey now found himself in the position of being accused by the government of fraud, while that same government was actively preventing him from delivering on his promises.[44]

As the ranks of his enemies increased, Garvey searched for allies in unlikely places. He followed a strategy employed by Booker T. Washington of appealing to white conservatives under the dubious theory that in all things purely social the races could be as separate as the fingers of the hand. He went much farther than Washington, however, in completely denying any interest in integration and claiming that all those who supported integration were really in favor of interracial marriage. Garvey's anti-mulatto and anti-Jewish statements had a bizarre relationship. American racists had concocted a weird conspiracy theory according to which Jews and mulattos controlled the NAACP for the purpose of fostering interracial marriage. When critics drew comparisons between the UNIA and the Klan, Garvey accepted the comparison. Then, to the horror of many supporters, he actually explored making an alliance with that organization.

In June 1922, during a trip to Atlanta, Garvey responded to an invitation to a meeting with Edward Young Clarke, acting Imperial Wizard of the Klan. Garvey later justified the two-hour meeting by saying, "I was speaking to a man who was brutally a white man, and I was speaking to him as a man who was brutally a Negro." The meeting was a serious tactical error that provided his rivals with powerful ammunition.[45] Garvey's willingness to cooperate with the Klan, and growing public dissatisfaction with the UNIA's finances, as well as personal rivalry, led to the defection of Reverend J. W. H. Eason, a former official of the UNIA. Eason revealed UNIA financial statements to W. E. B. Du Bois, who published them in the *Crisis*, and on January 1, 1923, Eason was shot in the back in New Orleans and killed.[46] While it was widely assumed that the murder was a political assassination carried out by Garveyites, the charges were never proven in a court of law. The controversies surrounding Garvey had become very ugly and he was beset by enemies on all sides calling for his deportation and accusing him of financial mismanagement.

In the meantime, Garvey's erstwhile friend A. Philip Randolph initiated his own campaign against him. The socialist spokesman sincerely

[44] Cronon, *Black Moses*, pp. 95–101.
[45] William Z. Foster, *The Negro People in American History* (New York: International, 1954).
[46] *Crisis* (May 1924), 27(7). On Eason, see Judith Stein, *The World of Marcus Garvey*, pp. 172–76.

believed that Garvey was a tool of white racists and was willing to abdicate the claims of black Americans for full citizenship rights in the United States. His magazine *The Messenger* (July 1922) carried an editorial bearing the headline, "MARCUS GARVEY! The Black Imperial Wizard Becomes Messenger Boy of the White Ku Klux Kleagle." A few days earlier, Marcus Garvey had spoken in New Orleans and the press had reported him as saying,

> This is a white man's country. He found it, he conquered it, and we can't blame him if he wants to keep it. I am not vexed with the white man of the South for Jim Crowing me because I am black.
>
> I never built any street cars or railroads. The white man built them for his own convenience. And if I don't want to ride where he's willing to let me ride then I'd better walk.[47]

If any white person or any mainstream black leader had made such a statement, he would have been hissed and booed from the platform, but Garvey had sufficient credibility with the black masses to voice even this extreme separatism and get away with it. Sympathetic hearers accepted his statement as black nationalism, rather than Uncle Tomism, and he lost no credibility with the true believers among his followers. Garvey was not the first or the last black nationalist to blame African Americans for their lack of power. His words presaged the rhetoric of Elijah Muhammad, Malcolm X, and Louis Farrakhan, and other black nationalists' mockery of the integration movement. Garvey well understood the traditional emotions associated with grassroots black nationalism. He knew that many of his followers hated white people and truly believed that black folk could "go it alone." They thrived on Garvey's dream of a black empire with "armies, navies and men of big affairs," and considered integration in America a ridiculous impossibility.

A. Philip Randolph, fully committed to attaining all the rights to which he was entitled as a United States citizen, was appalled by Garvey's capitulation to segregation and began to work in earnest to have the Jamaican firebrand deported. For the next two months, Garveyites exchanged broadsides with the socialists who occupied an office in the same building with the UNIA. Then, on Tuesday, September 5, 1922, at around 2:30 in the afternoon, Randolph received a package marked "from a friend." His suspicions aroused by a whitish powder leaking from it,

---

[47] *The Messenger* (July 1922), p. 437, derived this passage from the *New Orleans Times Picayune* (June 24, 1922). See Stein, *The World of Marcus Garvey*, p. 155. According to popular folklore, W. E. B. Du Bois refused to ride the streetcar during his years in Atlanta.

Randolph called the police, who doused the package in water. "To the utter amazement and horror of everyone, upon opening the package a human hand was found." No one ever claimed or identified the hand, which appeared to have once been the property of a white man.[48] The accompanying note was signed K.K.K. and threatened Randolph if he did not join the "nigger improvement association," which Randolph interpreted to mean the UNIA. "Obviously," he wrote, "the Klan has come to the rescue of its Negro leader, Marcus Garvey, as is indicated in the letter of warning."

Randolph dedicated increasing amounts of space in *The Messenger* to attacks on Garvey, culminating in a "Garvey Must Go" campaign. An organization called "The Friends of Negro Freedom" was formed, which organized numerous protest meetings against the UNIA during its convention of August 1923. In January 1923, a "Committee of Eight," made up of Randolph and other enemies of Garvey, sent a letter to the Attorney General of the United States protesting the fact that a year had passed since Garvey's indictment without any trial. The imperious Du Bois declined to join the Committee of Eight, but continued his independent attacks. Finally, the trial got under way on May 18, 1923, in U.S. District Court, the Honorable Julian William Mack presiding. Four days earlier, Garvey had addressed a petition to the court in which he submitted his honest belief that the judge should disqualify himself. Garvey asserted that Julian Mack was a member of the NAACP, and that the NAACP, "actuated by cruel and sinister motives," was out to destroy him. Historians have been unable to find any documentary evidence that Mack was ever an official member of the NAACP, or that he participated in activities of the association.[49]

The thrust of the government's case was that Garvey and his codefendants had intentionally misled the public by using the U.S. mail to market stocks in a corporation that they knew to be on the verge of bankruptcy. In the view of many historians, the government never proved anything of the sort. Garvey, the victim of his own personality, decided to plead his own case and dismissed his able attorney, Cornelius McDougald, an African American. Historians seem agreed that Garvey prejudiced the jury against himself by engaging in courtroom theatrics. In subsequent descriptions of the Black Star Line's collapse, Garvey referred to his erstwhile broker, Anthony Silverstone, as "Silverstone, the Jew." He

[48] Judith Stein, p. 166.
[49] *Marcus Garvey Papers*, Vol. 5, p. 301, n.3.

also referred to Judge Mack as "the eminent Jewish Jurist."[50] Garvey's anti-Jewish references were neither so constant nor so vitriolic as his diatribes against the international mulatto conspiracy, but Jewish people were, understandably, less inclined than mulattos to overlook his abuses.

Garvey was convicted of mail fraud on June 21, 1923, and entered New York City's Tombs Prison, but was released on bail on September 10, pending appeal. During the ensuing two years, he appealed his case and was unrelenting in his attempts to advance the business of the UNIA and the Black Star Line. In November, he traveled south to address the faculty and students of the Tuskegee Institute, where he said much in praise of its founder, Booker T. Washington. Early the following year he addressed the faculty and students of Howard University in Washington, D.C. Given the dictatorial power of the presidents at these two institutions, it is unlikely that Garvey could have been invited to speak at either without the consent of the administrations. These appearances amounted to something of a publicity coup and illustrated the fact that Garvey had not fallen into disgrace as a result of his conviction.

OVERTURES TO THE LIBERIAN GOVERNMENT:
CONTRADICTIONS OF A SETTLER STATE

While Garvey was appealing his case during 1923 and 1924, the UNIA was attempting to concretize its plans for an African business venture focusing on Liberia, the West African republic founded by African Americans. As noted above, Liberia was one of only two independent black states on the continent, and the only one with anything resembling a republican form of government. Since its founding, Liberia's population, politics, and culture had developed a complex social structure. In addition to former slaves from the United States, the population included the descendants of West Indian settlers. The population also included many descendants of "recaptives," Africans taken from illegal slave ships and dropped off in the coastal capital of Monrovia by naval officers attempting to suppress the slave trade. Because some of the repatriates, in addition to those who came from the Americas, were from Africa, the entire repatriate population eventually came to be known disparagingly as "Congoes." By 1923, the country was divided into two groups – the ruling class of Congoes, who were identified with Monrovia, and the so-called "Country" peoples, who were identified with indigenous, traditional ethnic

[50] *Philosophy and Opinions*, pp. 199, 218.

groups. The UNIA's attempts at establishing a Liberian base would obviously be forced to build bridges with the Congo elite.

The economy of Liberia was severely underdeveloped, but the growth of the American auto industry had led to an increased interest in the nation as a rubber producer. American business focused on Liberia as a source of rubber, and the Liberian government was eager to cooperate with the American rubber industry as a source of revenue. The interest of the UNIA in establishing African independence was therefore in conflict with powerful American industrial interests. The Liberian government eventually found the Garvey movement an embarrassment with all its talk of Africa for the Africans and the establishment of a new black elite. Although Garveyism never offered a serious challenge to the Liberian ruling class, it clearly offered a potential threat.

The UNIA's attempt to establish an economic base in Liberia began in 1920 when Garvey sent a delegation to Liberia. The Liberian president, Edmund Barclay, promised to set aside lands for development by the UNIA, which began selling stock in a Liberian Development Corporation. Unfortunately, most of the 750,000 dollars that were raised never arrived in Liberia, disappearing without a trace after the mysterious fashion of so much UNIA capital, and no progress was made toward the development of any enterprise on the continent. In the meantime, the Liberian government was becoming increasingly skittish about the publicity being generated. Garveyism presented a threat to the existing order and seemed an undependable source of the capital that Liberia needed for its development. Under pressure from France and Great Britain, the Liberian government finally announced that the UNIA would not be allowed to land in Liberia, and when the delegation arrived, they were promptly deported.

The hostility of British authorities was motivated, as historian J. Ayodele Langley has documented, by the perception that Garveyism must, of necessity, "create a spirit of unrest in Africa."[51] The British were doing everything to stave off nationalistic movements in their African colonies. The French government also felt that Garveyism would be disruptive of their interests. Professor Langley has shown that England and France took action against persons suspected of being Garvey sympathizers.[52] The reason for American hostility was partially the result of diplomatic pressure from the colonial powers, primarily France and Germany.

[51] Langley, *Pan Africanism and Nationalism*, p. 97, quotes a manuscript in the Public Record Office (London), C.O. 583/118/34197: Nigeria Confidential 'C' 9 July 1923: "Marcus Garvey–Proposed Visit to West Africa."

[52] Langley, *Pan Africanism and Nationalism*, pp. 89–98.

There is circumstantial, but inconclusive, evidence that Firestone Rubber Corporation's ambitions in Liberia may have contributed to the hostility of the United States government toward the UNIA in Liberia.[53] A subsequent deal with Firestone Rubber Company included a ninety-nine year lease of the lands that had been promised to the UNIA. Within a decade, the rubber industry in Liberia had become an international scandal, as reports of Firestone's complicity and that of the government in the use of slave labor became known.[54]

In appraising the character of Marcus Garvey, one should neither overlook his defects nor fail to understand his importance. Garveyism had set a legitimate goal in its attempt to create a black power structure, so that African peoples would be able to negotiate with the rest of the world from a position of strength. If he accomplished nothing more, Marcus Garvey revealed the ability of African Americans to combine capital, organize politically, create jobs, provide a forum for writers and intellectuals, and sustain institutions independent of white philanthropy. Garvey's thinking was complex, and pragmatic, as he modified strategies to suit changing situations. Students who desire a simple definitive explanation of the aims of Garveyism, or any other mass movement, for that matter, will be rushing into areas where serious scholars are reluctant to tread. Although it may be tempting to sum up Garvey's aims with cliché-ridden language about "race pride" or "self-help," the employment of such terminology raises far more questions than it answers.

The action of the United States government in charging Garvey with using the mails to defraud was fundamentally hypocritical. The ostensible basis of the government's case was the failure of the Black Star Line, but the true reason for the persecution of Garvey had more to do with a profound dislike, on the part of the United States government, for any signs of black militancy and for any threat, on the part of the colonial powers, to African imperialism. Legal harassment in the form of investigations and suits brought against the UNIA were motivated primarily by the anti-Negro hatreds that were given free rein in American domestic

[53] Garvey was convinced that Firestone Rubber Corporation was involved in thwarting UNIA plans, a reasonable enough assumption, and there is some circumstantial evidence to support this view. See Tony Martin, *Race First*, pp. 136–37. Judith Stein was unable to discover any direct evidence that Firestone perceived the UNIA as a threat. See Judith Stein, *The World of Marcus Garvey*, pp. 213–14.

[54] See Raymond Leslie Buell, *The Native Problem in Africa*, 2 vols. (New York: Macmillan, 1928). U.S. Department of State, Vol. 1. *Report on Slavery in Liberia* (1931). I. K. Sundiata, *Black Scandal: Americans and the Liberian Labor Crisis, 1929–1936* (Philadelphia, PA: Institute for the Study of Human Issues, 1980).

policy of the time. The U.S. government during the 1920s stood squarely behind the states' rights doctrines and antiblack sentiments of the American South. But while Garvey's enemies were real enough, one cannot discount the fact that Garvey's egotism and overly optimistic ambitions, both political and economic, were the source of much of the opposition he encountered among black people themselves. He did not possess sufficient expertise to operate a modern steamship company, and the time was, regrettably, not ripe for the creation of a United States of Africa.

IMPRISONMENT, DEPORTATION, FINAL YEARS

The story of Garvey's trial and conviction has been recounted elsewhere.[55] It is universally acknowledged that the charges were far removed from the spurious technicality of his commercial offense. As Judith Stein has correctly observed, "his prosecutors were driven by the political goal of deporting the leading black alien agitator in the United States.... [T]he Justice Department fastened on the crime of mail fraud, accidentally and after a long search for a deportable offense." To this I would add a stress on the point that Garvey had committed the addtional offenses of being articulate, sophisticated, and black. When lawyers are unable to secure convictions on honest grounds, they resort invariably to technical or procedural charges.[56] He was convicted; his appeal was unsuccessful; he was sentenced to the federal prison in Atlanta; and he was incarcerated on February 8, 1825. Six days later he published a stirring and frequently cited editorial in *Negro World*:

If death has power, then count on me in death to be the real Marcus Garvey I would like to be. If I may come in an earthquake, or a cyclone, or plague, or pestilence, or as God would have me, then be assured that I shall never desert you and make your enemies triumph over you.

If I die in Atlanta my work shall then only begin, but I shall live, in the physical or spiritual to see the day of Africa's glory. When I am dead wrap the mantle of the Red Black and Green around me, for in the new life I shall rise with God's grace and blessing to lead the millions up the heights of triumph with the colors that you well know. Look for me in the whirlwind or the Storm.[57]

---

[55] See Garvey, *Philosophy and Opinions of Marcus Garvey*, Vol. 2, part 2; Martin, *Race First*, Chapter 9; Stein, *The World of Marcus Garvey*, Chapter 10.

[56] In many cases these are convictions for trumped-up charges for crimes that are, by their very nature, spurious, for example, perjury, conspiracy, or obstruction of justice. Convictions on these charges are often obtained on the basis of testimony from informants who have been threatened with lengthy prison sentences, or even death, unless they agree to bear false witness.

[57] *Negro World* (February 14, 1925).

Garvey endorsed an anthology of his writings, *Philosophy and Opinions*, edited by Amy Jacques Garvey, from his jail cell in Atlanta. He watched helplessly as the Black Star Line lost yet another vessel, the *General G. W. Goethals*, rechristened the *Booker T. Washington*. In 1927, President Calvin Coolidge commuted Garvey's sentence and the UNIA leader was deported to Jamaica, where he founded a new journal called *The Black Man*. In August 1929, the UNIA held a Sixth International Convention in Kingston, Jamaica, which was spectacularly well attended. The Jamaican UNIA had survived its founder's imprisonment and deportation in America, as well as the efforts by black American leadership to discredit him. But Garvey was unsuccessful in gaining a position in Jamaican politics, and a rift had begun to develop between the American and the Jamaican movements. The Seventh UNIA International held in Kingston in 1934 was poorly attended, and Garvey moved to England. He attempted to maintain his North American connections by holding meetings in Toronto in 1936, 1937, and 1938.

From 1935 to 1939 Garvey continued to edit *The Black Man*, this time as a London-based monthly. As had his mentor, Duse Mohamed Ali, he expressed opinions on affairs throughout the black world, commenting with glee on the ousting of W. E. B. Du Bois from the NAACP. Ironically, Du Bois's policies had become too nationalistic, and too Pan-Africanistic, for his white liberal supporters. Garvey berated Joe Louis for his loss to Max Schmelling in 1936, and Haile Selassie for his defeat by Mussolini that same year. He noted with dismay the rise of Father Divine's Peace Mission Movement in the United States, a movement that seemed to play to the irrational, apolitical elements in black American consciousness, but which attracted not a few of Garvey's former followers. He was apparently unimpressed by the rise of Rastafarianism, a movement that came to hail him as a hero. Given his opinions on Haile Selassie and Jamaican cults, we can be certain that he would have viewed the movement with contempt. Denied access to the African American population, Garvey continued to decline in influence and never regained his full spectacular power.[58]

Garvey died in London in 1940, impoverished and embittered, but still attempting to revitalize his shredded organization. Alas, the dream of unifying all the African peoples of the world under a single administrative organization was hopelessly unrealistic. The reasons for the failure of

---

[58] There have been numerous sentimental attempts on the part of Rastafarians to link their movement to Garveyism. See Leonard E. Barrett, *The Rastafarians: The Dreadlocks of Jamaica* (London: Heinemann, 1977).

the UNIA, aside from the grandiosity of its schemes, were the organized opposition of the United States and the European colonial powers. The organization also suffered from a lack of technical and financial expertise among the UNIA membership. Ida B. Wells sometime admirer of the movement, provided an epitaph that was both critical and sensitive.

> Undoubtedly Mr. Garvey made an impression on this country as no Negro before him had ever done. He was able to solidify the masses of our people and endow them with racial consciousness and racial solidarity. Had Garvey had the support that his wonderful movement deserved, had he not become drunk with power too soon, there is no telling what the result would have been. . . .
>
> Perhaps if Mr. Garvey had listened to my advice he need not have undergone the humiliation which afterward became his. Perhaps all that was necessary in order to broaden and deepen his own outlook on life. It may be that even though he has been banished to Jamaica the seed planted here will yet spring up and bring forth fruit which will mean the deliverance of the black race – that cause that was so dear to his heart.[59]

No less assertive than Garvey and no more apologetic, Ida B. Wells saw in him a kindred spirit, and portrayed him as the classic hero, complete with tragic flaw. Speaking a decade before his death, she recognized in his personality something larger than life, taking his "look for me in the whirlwind" as more than bombast. Was this "black tempest in the distance" a world-historical figure? That question and its answer, both of which demand an Emersonian disposition, must be the "everlasting yea" that follows in the concluding chapter of this work.[60]

---

[59] Ida B. Wells-Barnett, *The Autobiography of Ida B. Wells* (Chicago: University of Chicago Press, 1970), pp. 381–82. She dictated these words to her son's secretary around 1930, according to her daughter, Alfreda M. Duster, editor of the *Autobiography*, p. xxx.

[60] "Black tempest in the distance" and "everlasting yea" from Thomas Carlyle, *Sartor Resartus*. Carlyle, an oft-mentioned influence on Emerson, also penned fulminations on "The Nigger Question" and "Heroes and Hero Worship." As Arnold Rampersad and David Lewis have observed, Du Bois was influenced early by Carlyle, whom he mentions in at least one youthful effusion, *Fisk Herald* (March 1888), pp. 8–9. Du Bois must have recalled *Sartor Resartus* as Garvey, in archducal raiment, came within his ken.

CONCLUSION: RESCUING HEROES FROM THEIR ADMIRERS

15

Rescuing Heroes from Their Admirers

Heroic Proportions Imply Brobdingnagian Blemishes

Three criteria were applied in selecting the historical figures included in this volume. First, their intellectual activity and influence must have been observable between 1885 and 1923, the dates of the Douglass-Crummell confrontation at Harper's Ferry and the Du Bois-Garvey conflict in Harlem, although in all cases the conflicts implicitly extend beyond those years. Second, there had to be mutual antagonism between them and their contemporaries, and the results of these antagonisms must have been observable and persistent into the years when this book was being drafted. Third, every author considered must have left behind a body of writings, and these writings had to illustrate the presence of internal conflicts within their own ideologies and manifest the thought processes whereby they rationalized or attempted to reconcile them.

The five personalities that dominate these pages illustrate the dynamic and generative powers of contradiction and the energizing effects of struggle in all serious thought, but particularly African American thought during the so-called "progressive era." The friction generated by the personality and ideology conflicts chronicled in these pages have led to the popular conceptions of these figures as saints, villains, or charlatans, conceptions that most college teachers discover in the remarks of their students. This is not surprising, since all were activists who sought to seize the fire of power through turbulent struggles in both the African American arena and in the larger arena of world history.[1] The intellectual struggles and

---

[1] Kevin Gaines, *Uplift Ideology: Black Leadership, Politics, and Culture in the Twentieth Century* (Chapel Hill: University of North Carolina Press, 1996) explores conflicts and ironies in the ideology of uplift.

conflicts of these figures constitute the material that pervades these pages. The conflict between the rhetoric of individual morality and the rhetoric of collective reform is present throughout, and it is one of the dynamic tensions with which this book is concerned.

Each of these five figures has been lionized, as well as villainized, and I have, therefore, found it necessary to defend each from his friends as well as from his detractors. In Frederick Douglass' presence, even the usually objective Allison Davis, a distinguished professor of psychology, becomes a hero-worshipper, and his book *Leadership, Love and Aggression* contains a chapter entitled "Douglass, the Lion." Douglass-worshippers seldom discuss, or even recognize, their subject's contradictions, which were recognized by such contemporaries as Alexander Crummell and John Mercer Langston – strong-minded persons in their own right. Several present-day authors, including Waldo Martin, Mary Helen Washington, and William McFeely have spoken to Douglass' inconsistencies with commendable rigor. The willingness of past and present critics to engage Douglass' ideas adds to, rather than detracts from, a full appreciation of his very real genius and courage. It is not necessary to endorse a critique to recognize the merits of that critique, but the reasoning of the various critiques must be understood in order to appreciate Douglass' responses to them. The process of understanding his positions leads, likewise, to an appreciation of Douglass' opponents, including those who were ethnocentric, black nationalist, integrationist, or assimilationist.

Booker T. Washington has a surfeit of admirers, today as in his lifetime, but few of those who engage in debate over his character or his programs have bothered to read *Up From Slavery*. Even fewer have perused the fourteen volumes of his published papers or the studies of his career produced by Emma Lou Thornbrough, August Meier, and Louis Harlan. Most of the clichés that are constantly recycled by Bookerite conservatives – or by anti-Bookerite liberals – reveal scant knowledge of the Tuskegeean's philosophy. Both camps invoke his name for the purpose of "presentizing" history and recklessly employ a caricature to buttress a present-day agenda. Washington was a man of the "progressive era." He was totally immeresed in its rhetoric, as Du Bois correctly observed. Thus, I have discussed him as a progressive liberal in terms of both his means and his ends. At the same time, I have not ignored the conservative demeanor of this man, whose confrontational words or actions might overtly challenge the customs of the segregated South.

Washington refused to waste time explaining the obvious to the disingenuously obtuse, but he demonstrated an unusual capacity for reflection and an unobtrusive ability for ideological abstraction. In independently inventing the economic theories later invented and more systematically developed by Weber and Veblen, he showed himself to be a pragmatist in the Deweyan sense of developing educational theory out of praxis, and in the Jamesean sense of establishing truth in answer to the question "what difference does it make?" If I have made unsustainable claims for Washington, there is nothing of hero worship in my stance. My objections to him are strong, and in conformity with those of Ida B. Wells, but I cannot accept Du Bois's idea that he was narrow or lacking in intellectual creativity.[2] Only by examining Washington's contradictions have I been able to recognize the depth of his insight and the originality of his thinking. Du Bois portrayed him as a credulous follower of the "triumphant commercialism" of his time, a proposition I have questioned. Washington was no mere simplistic moralizer, platitudinous sycophant, or narrow pedestrian. In my analysis, which stresses internal contradiction, he becomes a thinker.

In the African American pantheon, Du Bois is no less revered than Frederick Douglass. In fact, he is entitled, in the minds of many, to a complete apotheosis. Of this we were reminded when David Lewis's monumental biography of Du Bois came under attack from Sterling Stuckey, who took exception to Lewis's less reverent tone. But Du Bois was hardly a saint in his own time. His well-publicized confrontation with Booker T. Washington at the turn of the twentieth century was bitter but gentlemanly, withal. His clash with Marcus Garvey in the 1920s was crude and bombastic, indicating the roughness beneath the refined vocal inflections and sophisticated prose in which the antagonists usually expressed themselves.

Du Bois was greater than his myth. His life and its meaning should not be reduced to fit the requirements of national fetes, nor should they be rendered harmless to satisfy the publishers of children's books. If Du Bois is to be mythologized, it should be remembered that the best-known heroes of traditional mythology invariably commit acts of Herculean folly, suffer Promethean humiliations, or make Faustian bargains. The hero's quest is always a struggle with himself, and his existential joy exists in defining himself in terms of a quest that often may seem Quixotic. Ralph Ellison, with sardonic humor, described this quest as the pursuit of "that promise which, like the horizon, recedes ever brightly and distantly beyond the hopeful traveler."[3]

---

[2] *Souls of Black Folk*, p. 43.
[3] Ralph Ellison, *Invisible Man* (1952; reprinted New York: Vintage, 1992), p. 191. It is inconceivable to me that Ellison was unaware of the fact that Du Bois concluded *The*

Whether angelic or satanic, Du Bois's epic embodies one of the titanic struggles of the twentieth century. I have endlessly reiterated the point that "struggle" must be more than a synonym for incompetent floundering or failure to meet a challenge. The historical Du Bois would have difficulty understanding a universe in which victory must be constant and effortless in order to be convincing. He gave evidence of a belief that struggle is its own reward in his often-cited, but seldom read essay, "The Talented Tenth." These are not the words of a person who defined struggle as ineffectual floundering.

We serve first for the sake of serving – to develop our own powers, gain mastery of this human mankind, and come to the broadest, deepest self-realization.[4]

There is, indeed, a connection between Du Bois and James, in this sense of duty, in this search for "moral equivalent of war," of a holy war of toil and sacrifice toward the millennium of the "Social Gospel" that will transform drudgery into divine service. Not every philosopher or intellectual historian has viewed James in connection with Christian progressivism, religious perfectionism, or the Social Gospel, as Du Bois apparently did. Despite his reputed atheism, he was in the tradition advanced by Martin Luther King, Jr., who tied the struggle for racial equality to American traditions of mission, destiny, and redemptionism that anticipate "the end of history" and rejoice at the coming of "The Kingdom of God in America." American civil religion, especially in its Christian-socialist form, is a social gospel of perfectionism that presumes change to be progressive, inevitable, and divinely inspired. Americans have always believed that evil can be eliminated from the universe, and the doctrine has been rediscovered, not invented, in the portentous rhetoric of the second President Bush, who seems, like Captain Ahab, driven to banish terror from the face of this earth.

The hope of a millennial society, to be achieved through some permutation of a social gospel, or industrial democracy, or reform Social Darwinism, is central to the ideology of Du Bois.[5] Friedrich Engels's evolutionary

---

Souls of Black Folk by quoting the music and verse from a traditional spiritual, "Let us Cheer the Weary Traveller." The concluding words of his last chapter are, "And the traveller girds himself, and sets his face toward the Morning, and goes his way."

4 Du Bois, "The Talented Tenth," in Booker T. Washington et al., *The Negro Problem* (New York: James Pott & Co., 1903), pp. 33–75.

5 Mia Bay and Kevin Gaines have observed that African American thinkers may profitably be discussed within the context of social Darwinism. Gaines's *Uplifting the Race* contains several index entries to social Darwinism. Also see Mia Bay, *The White Image in the Black Mind*, pp. 190–95.

theory assigned an essential role to labor in evolutionary struggle, for it was the material factor of intelligent labor that transformed the ape into a human being. Du Bois seems to have accepted this fundamental principle of Marxist anthropology. Nonetheless, he was always too much the transcendental theist to be a good Marxist, and thus he wrote, not only of the pragmatic and material benefits of labor, but of the holiness of work.

There is no God but Love, and Work is his prophet – help us to realize this truth, O Father, which Thou so often in word and deed has taught us. Let the knowledge temper our ambitions and our judgments. We would not be great, but busy – not pious but sympathetic – not merely reverent, but filled with the glory of our Life-Work. God is Love and Work is His Revelation. Amen.[6]

Marcus Garvey has, in some ways, been the easiest of my subjects to approach, and in other ways the most difficult. Easy because his contradictions are so obvious that a child could see them. These have made him an easy target for the unimaginative reductionism of Mary Lefkowitz and Tunde Adeleke. But I have found Garvey difficult, complicated, and interesting, because he struggled, as did Crummell and Du Bois, to reconcile the apparent contradiction between Afrocentrism and Eurocentrism – a point that cannot be overstated. His legions of supporters have often been aware of his cosmopolitanism, and this is precisely what has attracted them to him, although Garveyites have often been caricatured as ethnocentric provincialists. The contradiction implicit in Garveyism's goal of African uplift through emulation of Europe was not some unique manifestation of ignorance that could be attributed to his Jamaican origins. Garvey's African civilization movement, like Du Bois's Pan-Africanism, had roots in the eighteenth century and is easily placed in a tradition of mutual influences between African, Afro-European, and black New World thinkers. Thanks to the work of Robert A. Hill and his publication of the *Marcus Garvey Papers*, there are few historians today who would dismiss Garveyism as naive back-to-Africa movement.

Garveyism was about the circulation of information, the shaping of opinion, and the manipulation of images. Its goal was to challange Europe's emotional subordination of Africa, and to counter mass feelings of humiliation and defeat in the face of omnipresent white supremacy. But Garveyites were not mere racialists; *Negro World*, despite its bombast and its unquestionable ethnocentrism, often displayed surprisingly cosmopolitan content. The ever-present contradiction between Garvey's

---

[6] Du Bois, *Prayers for Dark People*.

racial orientation and his Eurocentric style of self-presentation represents his awareness of the necessity to assimilate the values of industrial capitalism and his respect for traditions of English literacy. There was more to his ideology than a condescending black neocolonialism or sentimental escapism.

Garvey was never able to marshal his "armies, his navies, his men of big affairs," and if that is what is required of a "world-historical personality," he does not pass the test. But Garvey's significance was in his understanding that a movement for Africa's material and spiritual redemption could not mindlessly ignore the achievements of European civilization. Thus, his Pan-Africanism, like that of Crummell, Blyden, and Du Bois, was consistent with the nationalism of such African intellectuals as Crowther, Horton, and Hayford. Numerous historians of Africa cited throughout this study have shown that the attempts of New World Africans to merge the Eurocentric and the Afrocentric were in accord with continental Pan-Africanism and African nationalism.

As I have said elsewhere, "classical" black nationalism has often merged cultural assimilation with political and geographical separatism.[7] Garvey embraced the political goal of African independence, but he was never ethnocentric to the extent of abandoning European literary and intellectual traditions. The contradiction between nationalism and cosmopolitanism in Garvey's thought is a contradiction that can be seen in the thought of other historical individuals whose importance is less frequently contested. The same conflict between provincialism and world citizenship is evident in Thomas Jefferson and, even more strikingly, in his ideological successor, Woodrow Wilson. Those who plunder history in search of heroes in alabaster or ebony do their heroes a disservice, for they fail to understand that the greatest reverence we can show for anyone's thought is to pay it the homage of a critical response.

---

[7] Moses, *The Golden Age of Black Nationalism*, Chapter 1, "Political Nationalism and Cultural Assimilation," argued the point as early as 1978. The perfect example of this Eurocentric-Afrocentric type is William H. Ferris (1874–1941), an editor of *Negro World*, discussed in my *Afrotopia*. Also see Kevin Gaines's excellent chapter on Ferris in *Uplift Ideology*, pp. 100–27. J. A. Rogers (1883–1965), another editor of *Negro World* and author of *Nature Knows No Color Line: Researches in the Negro Ancestry of the White Race* (New York: Helga M. Rogers, 1952), also reconciles Afrocentrism and Eurocentrism. The literary pages of *Negro World* belie any accusation of narrow ethnocentrism or parochialism, demonstrating, on the contrary, attempts to reconcile Afrocentrism with Eurocentrism, for example, Norton Thomas's 1924 parody on *Julius Caesar*, reprinted in Tony Martin, *African Fundamentalism: A Literary and Cultural Anthology of Garvey's Harlem Renaissance* (Dover, MA: The Majority Press, 1991), pp. 242–44. Also see Duse Mohamed Ali on Shakespeare in Martin, *African Fundamentalism*, pp. 256–57 and 264–65.

I conclude with Alexander Crummell, who has always had fewer admirers than the other subjects of these studies. Nonetheless, he represents some of the most fascinating contradictions in African American thought in any era. What Du Bois said of him one hundred years ago remains true, "His name to-day, in this broad land means little." Self-styled black nationalists are most dismissive of him, although he devoted the prime of his life to nation building in Africa and his later years to the development of African American institutions. Crummell was a blend of Eurocentric and Afrocentric values – an admirer of classical and English literary traditions – a champion of West African nationalism. If primeval Britons had profited so effectively from the Roman contacts, why should not Africa steal culture from the English? He praised the ancient Hebrews, Greeks, and Romans as "cosmopolitan thieves," celebrating the trait of imitativeness that had made the Mediterranean a crucible of civilization. Christianity was less alien to Africa than was Islam, in his view. Indeed Christianity had been in Africa much longer, and had been shaped by Cyprian of Carthage and Augustine of Hippo. And which language was more alien to the Mende or the Temne people – English or Swahili? They were equally alien. A few hours before his death Crummell rejoiced in the fall of Khartoum, saying, "Thank God. That marks the downfall of slavery in Central Africa." To be sure, there was a grand contradiction between his Anglophilism and his final struggle to stimulate a distinctive African American culture, one that would not be limited to elite individuals but would serve the entire ethnic group. Crummell recognized the contradictions of his positions; he had found them inescapable since early childhood.[8]

I suspect that Alexander Crummell was right when he said that "both angels and men are created for the unending, the everlasting ventures and anxieties of their spirits in the deep things of God." Reality proceeds out of contradictions, and African Americans are as imaginative as everyone else when it comes to contradictory thinking – no less and no more. My search for conflicts and contradictions in African American thought has not been a process of negation, but an attempt to postpone consensus and to maintain the tension of struggle, which must always accompany every triumph of the human spirit.

---

[8] Crummell's position on "cosmopolitan thieves" is in his sermon "The Destined Superiority of the Negro," reprinted in Wilson J. Moses, *Destiny and Race: Sermons and Addresses by Alexander Crummell* (University of Massachusetts Press, 1992), p. 202. His final days and final words are discussed in Moses, *Alexander Crummell*, pp. 272–73. For challenges of early childhood, see *Destiny and Race*, p. 48.

Index

**DO NOT REMOVE !
**PUT IN TECH UPON
RETURN!

∞∞∞∞∞∞∞∞∞∞∞∞∞

NORTH BABYLON
PUBLIC LIBRARY
Circulation Department
Tel: (631) 669-4020

This item had the following
damage at checkout:

✓___ Water damage
____ Stained or soiled pages
____ Writing on pages
____ Crayon/Scribble in book
____ Underlining/Highlighting
____ Ripped or Loose pages
____ Spine/Binding broken
____ Cover Damage
____ Broken CD/DVD case
____ Booklet missing
____ Other:

Date: 3/15/19 Initial: SP